Women Poets of Spain,

1860–1990

Women Poets of Spain, 1860–1990

❧

Toward a Gynocentric Vision

John C. Wilcox

UNIVERSITY OF ILLINOIS PRESS

URBANA AND CHICAGO

Publication
of this book was supported in part by a grant
from the Program for Cultural Cooperation between Spain's
Ministry of Culture and United States' Universities.

1   2   3   4   5   C   P   5   4   3   2   1
This book is printed on acid-free paper.
Library of Congress Cataloging-in-Publication Data
Wilcox, John C. (John Chapman), 1943–
Women poets of Spain, 1860–1990 : toward a gynocentric
vision / John C. Wilcox.
p.   cm.
Includes bibliographical references and index.
ISBN 0-252-02260-2 (cloth : alk. paper). —
ISBN 0-252-06559-X (pbk. : alk. paper)
1. Spanish poetry—Women authors—History and
criticism. 2. Spanish poetry—19th century—History
and criticism. 3. Spanish literature—20th century—
History and criticism. 4. Women in literature.
5. Sex role in literature.
I. Title.
PQ6055.W55   1997
861.009'9287—dc20   96-9948
CIP

To

the memory of Inez Wilcox

née Chapman

$(1912–90)$

Contents

Acknowledgments

In the late 1970s, female graduate students asked me why I did not include any women poets in my seminars on twentieth-century Spanish poetry: they made me realize the extent of my own ignorance and I thank them for nudging me into a new area of research. As I was interested at the time in studying contemporary poetry, I asked the young Spanish poet and critic Ignacio Prat for help in the fall of 1981, and it was he who sent me a copy of Ana Rossetti's *Los devaneos de Erato* (Erato's flirtations), on which I cut my (gynopoetic) teeth—at a 1981 MLA session in New York. Ignacio Prat died tragically at that time, but my debt of gratitude to him is undying. It was not until December of 1985 that I had time to pursue this line of research. I was in Madrid and saw in a shop window Ramón Buenaventura's *Las diosas blancas* (White goddesses). I made my way to Librería Hiperión, the publisher, and was lucky to meet Buenaventura and solicit his advice, which he gave willingly. He directed me to the Biblioteca Nacional, where my exploratory research was conducted.

For some years I worked only on the new women poets of post-Franco Spain. In my attempts to read these poets and to devise a critical approach adequate to their vision, I had the help and encouragement of Sharon Keefe Ugalde, to whom I owe a very special thanks. Her infuence on my work is such that I no longer recognize it—owing to my anxiety to continue to write! She and others—in particular, Biruté Ciplijauskaité—encouraged me to present papers and write articles on Spain's women poets of the 1980s. I thank them for pushing me to keep up the work. I also thank the owner and staff of Hiperión for all the attentive help they paid to my requests, without which chapters 7 and 8 could not have been written.

After I had drafted many of my ideas on contemporary poets—which became the last two chapters of the present book—I began looking back. I turned first to Angela Figuera, and I wish to thank several colleagues for the help they gave as I studied her: Roberta Quance, Ellen Engelson Marson, Martha LaFollette Miller, Linda Gould Levine, and Andrew Debicki. For urging me to consider Francisca Aguirre, and providing me with photocopies of unavailable books, I thank Mario Paoletti, of Toledo, Spain. For encouraging me to explore women poets of the Generation of 1927, I thank Martha LaFollette Miller. I want also to thank Margo Persin for her sustained collegial support and sound advice. Over the last seven years, Biruté Ciplijauskaité has provided me and my work with much needed encouragement and extremely helpful criticism. This book benefited immensely from her unstinting advice, her critical acumen, and her sound recommendations during its revision: I owe her a very special debt of gratitude.

Moreover, I received initial stimulus and inspiration by teaching a seminar in the late 1980s on Spain's women novelists. I am indebted to studies by Biruté Ciplijauskaité, Elizabeth Ordóñez, Janet Pérez, Nancy Miller, and Susan Kirkpatrick in this area (as well as others which I acknowledge at the appropriate time).

I wish to thank International Programs of the University of Illinois at Urbana-Champaign for awarding me a grant of $500 to purchase contemporary texts, the Research Board of the university for a grant to photocopy numerous texts borrowed through interlibrary loan, and the Interlibrary Loan office of the university library for attending to my frequent requests. I am indebted to Humanities Released Time, of the College of Liberal Arts and Sciences, University of Illinois at Urbana-Champaign, for releasing me from teaching one course during spring 1992. I wish to thank Larry R. Faulkner, then dean of the College of Liberal Arts and Sciences, now provost and vice-chancellor for academic affairs, who provided me with a research assistant—John Paul Spicer—for fall 1992: I am indebted to both of them. I also thank the Research Board of the University of Illinois at Urbana-Champaign for providing me with a research assistant—Jim Hammerstrand—for summer 1994 for the revision of this manuscript. I also wish to thank the University of Illinois Press, and in particular Ann Lowry, senior editor, for the evaluations they acquired for the manuscript I originally submitted in 1993; those evaluations helped turn that draft into a sounder and I trust better book. To Pat Hollahan, my copyeditor at the press, I offer sincere thanks for her attention and my gratitude for her sharp insights.

Thanks also to my Friday night "Embassy" friends—they know who they are—who kept me sane during my interim headship: decisions and chores that more than belabored the gestation of this book.

My most recent debt of gratitude is to my colleagues, Pilar Ocaña and Matt Ray (UC-Davis), in the Barcelona office of the Year Abroad Program of the Universities of California and Illinois, for the help and support they provided as this book went through its final revisions (and for the way they humored me on those mornings when I had worked late into the night).

Ernesto Carratalá, professor emeritus of the Central University of Barcelona and instructor for the California-Illinois Program, gave me on numerous occasions pertinent advice on my translations and clarified obscurities of Spanish syntax and lexicon. I am indebted to him for his learned help—and very grateful to him for his support and friendship.

Special thanks to my wife, Julie, who provided the total support that only she can, who suffered stoically through it all, and who during 1994–96, while I was resident in Barcelona, did a great deal of bibliographical work for me in the University of Illinois library. Special thanks also to our dog, Rusty, for pawing me until I arose from the shackles of my desk so that he could take me on good long walks! Without the help and encouragement of all of the above friends, this book would never have been written.

Much earlier versions of chapters 2, 4, 6, and 7 have already appeared in print. I wish to thank the following for granting me permission to quote from them. Editorial Orígenes for "Visión y revisión en algunas poetas contemporáneas: Amparo Amorós, Blanca Andréu, Luisa Castro y Almudena Guzmán"; Greenwood Press for "Angela Figuera Aymerich"; Promociones y Publicaciones Universitarias, Universidad de Barcelona, for "Clara Janés: hacia su poemario de los años ochenta"; *Revista Canadiense de Estudios Hispánicos* for "Ana Rossetti—y sus cuatro musas poéticas"; *Siglo XX/20th Century* for "Blanca Andréu: A 'poeta maldita' of the 1980s" and "Ernestina de Champourcín and Concha Méndez: Their Rescision from the *Generation of 27*"; *Studies in Twentieth Century Literature* for "A Reconsideration of Two Spanish Women Poets: Angela Figuera and Francisca Aguirre"; Tulane University Press/"La Chispa" for "Observaciones sobre el *Devocionario* de Ana Rossetti"; *Zurgai: Revista de Poesía* (Bilbao, Spain) for "El feminisimo en las *Obras completas* de Angela Figuera: algunas observaciones preliminares"; Arturo del Vilar and Los Libros de Fausto for "Impresiones juanramonianas en los primeros libros de poesía de Angela Figuera Aymerich"; and *Revista de estudios hispánicos* for "María Victoria Atencia: '*serenissima—ma non troppo.*'"

Preface

My principal concern in these essays is critical: to question andro-centric reading habits and to demonstrate what gynopoetic strategies might uncover. However, the overall stucture of the book is histori-cal. I chose a major poet from the latter part of the nineteenth century in Spain, Rosalía de Castro, and subjected her poems to a gynopoetic reading practice. For each principal school of the twentieth century in Spain, I selected poets whose work I find significant; I asked myself why these poets were ignored and what their gynocentric visions contribute to Spanish poetry. My two concerns — critical and historical — are those of feminist scholarship which, write Greene and Kahn, "undertakes the dual task of deconstructing predominantly male cultural paradigms and reconstructing a female perspective and experience in an effort to change the tradition that has silenced" women ("Feminist Scholar-ship" 1).[1] I believe, with Furman, that "by retrieving works written by women and by giving these works the kind of visibility and authority hitherto accorded to men's literary production," I can contribute to the establishment of "the corpus of a female literary tradition" in Spain ("Politics of Language" 63).

In "Toward a Feminist Poetics" Elaine Showalter emphasizes the need to recuperate women's literature. She declares: "Before we can even begin to ask how the literature of women would be different and special, we need to reconstruct its past, to rediscover the scores of women novelists, poets, and dramatists whose work has been obscured by time, and to establish the continuity of the female tradition from decade to decade" (137). It is not my intention to reconstruct the entire past of women's poetry in Spain, but I have attempted to indicate some of its contours. Hence, this book is a series of essays on the work of women poets that focuses not on what is traditional and normal (i.e., male) in their poems but on what is gynocentric. The book focuses on texts that refer directly or indirectly to experiences that the poets intuit as central to their selves; it then interprets those experiences from a feminist perspective. While I sympathize with Octavio Paz, who believes that to classify poets along gender lines is to judge racehorses by the color of their eyes, I believe that to analyze and thereby foreground the gynopoetic forms and content of poetry written by women is a valid strategy.[2] It draws attention to the extensive corpus of—largely ignored—poetry they have produced, and it allows one to trace and describe that work's special features.

Because I—a male reader—throughout this book allege that discourses are "feminine," "feminist," and "female" I should state at the outset that my use of these epithets is not political. My deployment of the adjectives "female," feminine," and "feminist" is a heuristic device to explore "sexual/textual differences" (Stanton, "Autogynography" 16). It is not my intention to rank or categorize based on degrees of feminism. By using these terms, I am attempting to describe how a series of poetic texts written by women impress me as developing a tradition that is different from the male-generated poetic discourses which conditioned my expectations as a reader of Spanish poetry. In effect, this means that I tend to foreground thoughts and imagery that I personally have not encountered in the poetry written by men. The styles and visions I confront in this book have been inspired by the agonic relationship into which a woman writer is cast by the patriarchal, phallogocentric culture into which she is thrown. It is against that ethos that she struggles in order to find her own voice.

I should also add, because of the rigid—but rhetorical—dichotomy I employ between gynocentric and androcentric styles, that I am not proposing that female writers are different in essence from their male counterparts. As a postmodern reader, I focus on linguistic texts which I see as constituted by social, cultural, literary, and historical dynamics; it is those dynamics I am studying in the following pages. "Female" and "male" as used here are not biological categories, they are discursive constructs constituted by, and constituting themselves in, struggle with the dynamics of living, experiencing, writing, and reading. As Domna Stanton has written: "there are social and cultural, but not sexual, differences between female and male inscriptions of the self" (*Female* x). Hence, when I do refer to biological realities (e.g., breasts, vagina, pregnancy, child-rearing) my interest focuses on the symbolic and affective meanings such realities acquired for the poet under discussion.

My working hypothesis has been that this body of poetry would be different in some ways from the poetry that had "educated" me. I hold this view because critics of the novel have discovered, for example, that the female *bildungsroman* does not manifest the linear model of steady progress of its male counterpart; hence, my "strategic supposition" has been that I would encounter an analogous asymmetry in poetry.[3] Most of the poets I study in the following pages would have little or no sympathy for the rhetorical dichotomy I deploy between "androcentric" and "gynocentric" visions. For example, in a recent interview Ernestina de Champourcin explained that she "writes guided by a poetic tradition" that is valid for every time and place and that "must have been born with the first poet" (*El Ciervo* 21).[4] Carmen Conde, however, believes that the woman poet can bring "unknown worlds" to poetry, that she "is obliged to give of what she as a woman knows inside out," and that women write "from their female essences, out of their entrails" (Cabello, "Carmen Conde" 30).[5] Concha Zardoya, who enjoys the poetry of "libertarian delights" of Fanny Rubio, may well have some intellectual sympathy for my undertaking. Gloria Fuertes, as the reader knows or will discover, would certainly enjoy my working hypothesis; but Angela Figuera, Amparo Amorós, and Blanca Andréu would reject it.[6] Clara Janés and Ana Rossetti, in their interviews with Sharon Ugalde, imply that they might be somewhat sympthetic to such an undertaking. Then there are others—interviewed by Ugalde—who assert that a woman's experience and preoccupations are different from a man's, and that women articulate their visions in a rhetorically different manner (Rubio Monge, J. Castro, Luca). Although I do not study their work here, I confess that my sympathies lie with them—women poets of the postmodern, virtual reality in which we live, move, and lose our being. My sympathies lie with them because of what I uncovered as my research progressed: refreshing visions which literary history in Spain has devalued; a long tradition my formal education implied I should ignore.

Such a project would not have been undertaken if it were not for the flowering of poetry by women in Spain that occurred after the death in 1975 of the Spanish dictator Francisco Franco. Nor would it have been undertaken without the reeducation feminist critics and theorizers have offered readers (of both sexes) over the last twenty years. Sympa-

thetic readers—and I include myself, a male reader, in this category—
are now able to appreciate some of the "distinctive features"[7] of female
discourse, features to which we—as "modern" readers of poetry—had
been blind. Much insight is now at hand, but because so much has
been written—at this belated stage in the game—by and about feminist
critics and criticism, it is almost impossible to adequately acknowledge
one's intellectual debts. However, such readings have re-formed and
reeducated my reading practice; in the introduction, I try to acknowledge those influences in a discussion of gynopoetics.

My introduction also offers a brief conspectus of Spanish poetry
written by women prior to 1860—that is, before Rosalía de Castro published her first volume of poems. My intent here is to provide an, albeit
cursory, historical frame for these essays and to indicate that poetry
written by women in Spain is not just a modern phenomenon, as this
book might otherwise imply, but has its roots in a largely ignored tradition that reaches back to the very beginnings of poetry in the Peninsula.
The introduction also discusses the preoccupations Spain's poets share
with women poets of the rest of the world from Enheduanna (born
ca. 2300 B.C.) to the present.

Chapter 1 reevaluates the poetry of Rosalía de Castro (1837–85), the
one "Modern" Spanish woman poet who has not been ignored. My
focus is on the feminist infrastructure of Rosalía's poetry. For *Cantares gallegos* (Galician songs), I study what is protogynocentric in her
vision: the social, political, psychological, and esthetic marginalization
she experienced while writing her first book, the female personae she
included in this collection, and her search for matrilineal roots. My
reading of *Follas novas* (New leaves) and *En las orillas del Sar* (On the
banks of the Sar) contrasts the negative and positive images of womanhood and woman poet which abound in these books. I also study the
gynocentric imagery and the subversion of the androcentric worldview
which lie at the heart of her mature poetry.

Chapter 2 focuses on two of the marginalized and ignored women
poets of the male-dominated Spanish Generation of 1927—Ernestina
de Champourcin (b. 1905) and Concha Méndez (1898–1986)—both of
whom were praised by their male peers but afterwards fell into oblivion.
I analyze the female personae inscribed in their work; their articulation
of female desire; their gynocentric metaphors; their nontranscendental
vision; their subversion of an androcentric worldview; their confronta-
tion with a female's aging; their religious impulse; and their concern for

mothering. Méndez's poetry in particular has all the strong features—such as subversion of patriarchal values, revision of male myths, gynocentric metaphors—we find in the women poets of the post-Franco era.

Chapters 3 through 5 study representative women poets of the Franco era (1939–75). Chapter 3 is devoted to the work of Carmen Conde (1907–96) and Concha Zardoya (b. 1914). Both poets are concerned with mothering, and with marginalization; they offer a critique of patriarchal culture, and each selects gynocentric metaphors to articulate that vision. Conde expresses female desire and Zardoya develops a nontranscendental view of life. Chapter 4 is devoted to Angela Figuera (1902–84) whose perception of motherhood is considerably different from her precursors'; she develops a gynocentric and exoskeletal poetics that subverts patriarchal standards; her gynocentric vision also articulates female desire, despair of talent, and anger. Chapter 5 studies the irreverent and ironical vision of Gloria Fuertes (b. 1918): her perception of the woman poet, her symbiotic poetics, and her rebuttals of her male precursors; her development of self-reliance and the inscription of her own life and body; as well as her subversion and demystification of the male and his values.

Chapters 6 and 7 study certain women poets of the post-Franco era (1975 to the present). Chapter 6 is devoted to the work of three representative poets who were born before mid-century: Francisca Aguirre (b. 1930), María Victoria Atencia (b. 1931), and Clara Janés (b. 1940). I study Aguirre's sense of masochistic self-destruction, her corrosive demystification of male myths, her subversion of male esthetics, and her gynocentric metaphors; for Atencia, I discuss her inner spaces, her sense of a female self, her gynocentric style, her concern for mothering, and her revision of androcentric values; for Janés, I focus on her desire, her appreciation of life's small pleasures, her female poetics, and her inscription of a female self. Chapter 7 studies three representative poets from the 1980s: Amparo Amorós,[8] Ana Rossetti (b. 1950), and Blanca Andréu (b. 1959). For Amorós, I study her female poetics, her articulation of female myths, her concern for the female self, and her subversion of male stereotypes; for Rossetti, I focus on her subversive use of feminist desire and her exploration of the female self; for Andréu, I discuss her inscription of the female self, her belief that inspiration stems from self-sacrifice, and her revision of literary and cultural myths.

In my conclusion, I compare the preoccupations that emerge and reemerge, appear and/or disappear, during the 130 years under discussion. This is a field ripe for investigation, and I urge students to sharpen whatever "insight" my "blindness" might have brought to this largely unstudied terrain. In addition, I urge them to pay heed to the numerous poets I could not include here, some of whose names I do mention. For the 1980s, for example, I study only those poets who attracted attention in both Spain and the United States. There are many other exciting poets—whose originality is only now, in the 1990s, becoming clear—such as the lesbian Andrea Luca and the revisionary mythmaker Juana Castro, whose gynocritical visions require serious study; I leave it to others to do just that.

Finally, I have translated into English all titles, lines of verse, and stanzas quoted in the chapters. I did so in order that the English reader may easily follow the line of thought. In the endnotes, I have translated quotations which I deem necessary to the argument of the book. Titles are usually not translated in endnotes, in particular when I am merely indicating that a feature discussed in the chapter can also be found in those additional poems. The translations are my own. I strove to offer an adequate simulacrum of the original. When faced with a lexical choice, I opted for a translation that suggests the gynopoetic thrust of the text. Also, when the possibility of hinting at the rhythm and interior rhyme of the original line of verse suggested itself, I went for it. Hence, my translations are not faithful dogs to their original masters. No language can be faithful to another; nor even to itself.

Notes

1. They also defined "the two major foci of feminist scholarship" as "deconstructing dominant male patterns of thought and social practice and reconstructing female experience previously hidden or overlooked" (Greene and Kahn, "Feminist Scholarship" 6).

2. Cited by María Victoria Atencia in her *Conversaciones* (Conversations) with Ugalde.

3. On this, see Gardiner ("Mind Mother" 126–27). The phrase "strategic presupposition" is Gayatri Spivak's. Let me add that Ciplijauskaité's and Ordóñez's work on Spain's women novelists influenced my position.

4. For Champourcin's antifeminist remarks, see Ascunce Arrieta ("Ernestina de Champourcin" 22–23). Of Méndez, Valender writes: "nunca se consideraba feminista" ("never considered herself a feminist" ["Introducción" 34]).

5. Cabello is referring to an early interview with Conde in *Cuadernos de literatura* 1 (1947): 110.

6. For Zardoya, see chap. 2, p. 139; for Figuera, chap. 4, n. 1. For Amorós and Andréu, see Ugalde's *Conversaciones*.

7. This term comes from linguistics. A distinctive feature is one that enables a contrast to be made between linguistic units (e.g., voicing in phonology). See Crystal, *Encyclopedic* 107.

8. The year of Amorós's birth is never given (see chap. 7, n. 1).

Women Poets of Spain,

1860–1990

Introduction

Before analyzing the poetry written by significant women in Spain between 1860 and 1990, I want first to explain the gynopoetics—female and feminist discursive strategies—I refer to in my reading of the poetic corpus written by women in "Modern" Spain, second to comment on the work of their precursors, and third to discuss the poetry of women from other national literatures.[1]

Gynopoetics

Despite the historical tradition for women's poetry which I will sketch below, the texts that Spanish literature has canonized are those written by men. Male texts present a polarized view of woman as either an angel (Fray Luis de León's "la perfecta casada" ["the perfect married woman"] and Juan Ramón Jiménez's "la mujer desnuda" ["the naked woman"]) or a monster (Fernando de Rojas's "Celestina" and Fernando Arrabal's "Lis"). Such texts reflect—and perpetuate—a distorted image of woman; they refract their own androcentric and patriarchal vision of what a woman is. This book is written as a critique of such a fractured perspective.

Moreover, poetry written by women is assessed in histories of literature and elsewhere by male standards: it is judged by tastes that were formed by the reading of poetry written by males. Hence, poetry by women is almost totally ignored or at best condemned for failing to satisfy the expectations of such an exclusively masculine worldview. Spain is not alone in this cover-up for, as feminist critics remind us, "feminist psychic spaces [have been] repressed throughout 2,000 years of Western history" (Jardine, "Opaque Texts" 112).[2] Moreover, in their "Ceremonies of the Alphabet," Gilbert and Gubar observe that "the development of writing made possible . . . the widespread pronouncement [and] long-term perception of power" which inevitably associated "the alphabet with the ineradicable lineaments of a history that has always silenced and excluded women" (23). This book is written in the belief that a critique of the blinkered vision fostered by such injustice is in order.

Given such historically entrenched perspectives, I am convinced that traditional reading practices could not do justice to the originality of the poetry written by women in Modern Spain. To compensate for masculine bias, and to avail myself of a critical apparatus that is more adequate to the texts under study, I apply and develop in the following essays the gynopoetic insights attained by feminist critics of poetry during the last twenty years. I now introduce these insights in order to explain my understanding of gynopoetics.

Taken as a whole, my study of women poets of Modern Spain reflects the evolution Elaine Showalter uncovers in her study of British women novelists. She writes: "First, there is a prolonged phase of *imitation* of the prevailing modes of the dominant tradition, and *internalization* of its standards of art and its views on social roles. Second, there is a phase of *protest* against these standards and values, and *advocacy* of minority rights and values, including a demand for autonomy. Finally, there is a phase of *self-discovery*, a turning inward freed from some of the dependency of opposition, a search for identity" (*Literature* 13). Showalter calls her three phases—of imitation, protest, and self-discovery—feminine, feminist, and female respectively; and I endeavor throughout these essays to adhere to her distinctions. I shall demonstrate that Rosalía de Castro thought of herself as *imitating*— what she perceived to be—the superior male talent of Antonio de Trueba, but that in fact she generates feminist texts in which she subconsciously foregrounds a gynocentric vision and style. For the 1920s, when women poets had *internalized* the dominant esthetic posture of the time, I focus on characteristics of their poetry which a traditional (androcentric) reading would not elucidate, such as protest against confining norms and the articulation of a female self. My readings of the poetry of the women of the Franco era uncover the *protest*, the anger, the negative views on the condition of women, and they discuss aspects of the poetry in which *advocacy* is implicit and female self-discovery is apparent. For poets of the post-Franco era, I focus on the female *self-discovery* and self-determination to be encountered in their work.

Imitation, protest, advocacy, and self-discovery are aspects of a gynocritics that feminist scholars have developed over the last few decades. Just as the New Critics generated an interpretative code that provided us with the model to explain the originality of the poem as verbal artifact, feminist scholars have created for today a critical discourse that is better equipped than earlier and alternative models to describe the special vision and style that can be inscribed in female-authored texts.[3]

Earlier in the twentieth century, Virginia Woolf had pointed to this possibility, as Showalter notes when she cites Woolf's opinion that "women's literature held the promise of a 'precious speciality,' a distinctly female vision" (*New Feminist* 137). Showalter herself has written that "the most consistent assumption of feminist reading has been the belief that women's special experience would assume and determine distinctive forms in art" (*New Feminist* 135). Ostriker states this more directly when she claims that "writers necessarily articulate gendered experience just as they necessarily articulate the spirit of a nationality, an age, a language" (*Stealing* 9). A similar point has been made by several other critics. Nancy Miller argues persuasively that it most certainly does matter that a woman authored a text, and she quotes Catharine Stimpson, who says: "A male writer may speak of, for, to and from the feminine. He cannot speak, except fictively, of, for, to and from the female. This inability hardly has the dignity of a tragic fact, but it does have the grittiness of simple fact" (*Subject* 72; quoting Stimpson, "Ad/d Feminam" 179). In the following essays, I try to describe the "grit" that differentiates the "gynocentric" and "gynocritical" visions of Spanish women poets from the established, androcentric norms; I do so in the hope that their difference might be recovered from what Nancy Miller has called "the indifference of the aesthetic universal" (*Subject* 97).

Writing in more global terms in her 1979 essay "Toward a Feminist Poetics," Showalter argues that "the program of gynocritics is to construct a female framework for the analysis of women's literature, to develop new models based on the study of female experience, rather than to adapt male models and theories." To achieve this goal, she explains, gynocritics draws on "feminist research in history, anthropology, psychology, and sociology, all of which have developed hypotheses of a female subculture including not only the ascribed status, and the internalized constructs of femininity, but also the occupations, interactions, and consciousness of women" (131).

Hence, with respect to the interpretation of poetry, the point is that as reading habits have been constructed by male critics working on predominantly male texts, readers will fail to understand the poetic artifacts created by women. Jardine has written: "Feminism, while infinite in its variations, is finally rooted in the belief that women's truth-in-experience-and-reality is and always has been different from men's and that it as well as its artifacts and productions have consequently been devalued and always already delegitimized in patriarchal culture" (*Gynesis* 147). I agree with Jardine that the "artifacts and productions" of women can be different from those of men, and my goal in the following essays is to point out differences in the articulation of a male and a female poet's vision and inscription of the self. Hence, if I were here to deploy my "normal" reading practices, I would run the risk of overlooking the originality of significant parts of this work, or I would condemn its difference for not meeting "normal" (male) expectations of what constitutes a "good" poem. As an empathetic reader, I aim to analyze and account for that difference and this means gendering my reading practice. Abel observes that "gender has not been assimilated as a pertinent category" into the analysis of the novel ("Introduction" 5); nor has it been assimilated into the appreciation of poetry.

My gynopoetic insights for the reading of women's poetry have been gained from interpretations North American and English feminist critics make of various women poets. In reading their work, I have discovered a host of distinctive features which, it seems to me, characterize female as opposed to male poetic texts; those features have re-formed and reshaped my reading practice: they have provided me with a gendered reading strategy; they have prescribed for my andromyopic eyes gynocentric bifocals.

Gynocentric Vision

I use the term "gynocentric" to indicate distinctive features—distinct also from the hegemonic norm—of a feminine, feminist, and female vision. In Spain's poets I encountered a negative and a positive gynocentric vision. The negative vision is one of the woman as marginalized creature; the positive vision manifests a woman's autonomy and quest for self-determination. The polarities of this gynocentric vision have been studied by numerous critics of women's poetry and culture.

Gilbert and Gubar described the most distinctive features of the negative gynocentric vision in 1979 in their analysis of such metaphors as the angel/monster polarity, the anxiety of authority, the confined woman, and the aesthetics of renunciation.[4] The "angelic" woman stays at home and provides a refuge from the world for her man; she denies herself personal fulfillment and exudes "eternal feminine" virtues (*Madwoman* 23).[5] On the other hand, the monster-woman, who may possess the enchantments of sensuality, is often a supernatural being (a witch) or a deformed creature (a hag). Women quickly learn that if they attempt to define themselves, they will be typecast as monsters. However, this may be a mask a woman will need to don in order to become creative.

The "anxiety of authority" from which a woman writer may suffer stems from the fact that established and entrenched literary authority has been devised by men, "to tell male stories about a male world"; if women appropriate this tradition, they become "diseased and infected by the sentences of patriarchy" (Gilbert and Gubar, *Madwoman* 67, 71). The guilt and anxiety experienced by women who employ patriarchal plots and genres is manifested in obsessive imagery of confinement (claustrophobia, agorophobia) and entrapment (the attic). Such images indicate that the woman writer feels—"captured, fettered, trapped, even buried alive" (83–86). Gilbert and Gubar urge women writers to overcome their anxiety of authority by rejecting patriarchal prescriptions and "deal[ing] with central female experiences from a specifically female perspective" (72).

A woman's anxiety may also be manifested in an "aesthetics of renunciation." Because women have in the past been constrained by culture to be self-effacing as opposed to self-assertive, to be humble and unassuming as opposed to conceited and opinionated, the poetry they wrote is informed by a style of renunciation. They repressed their personal ambitions and resigned themselves to poetic isolation and obscurity (Gilbert and Gubar, *Madwoman* 575). Emily Dickinson asks: "I'm Nobody! Who are you?" Walt Whitman retorts: "I am large, I contain multitudes." In 1982, Cheryl Walker studied the "aesthetics of renunciation" in greater depth. Walker's symbol for the thwarted and disillusioned condition of the woman artist is Philomel, the nightingale.[6] Philomel's texts reveal a "suffering sensibility" and a sense of "powerlessness"; her "sanctuary poems" and "free-bird" poems are palimpsests of her hurt and violated self, as well as of her aspirations which, though excited, are forever repressed.

A further distinctive feature of the gynocentric vision is anger, which Gardiner sees as an aspect of "the psychology of oppression" that can be observed in "a woman writer's mind" ("Mind Mother" 121). Ostriker believes that the textual expression of anger by women is a strategic maneuver that counteracts male rationality and power (*Stealing* 161). Anger is an attack on culture's systemic phallocentrism, and women need to embrace it despite the horrendous self-division it entails. The maenads provide the model for this course of action. The name derives from a Greek word meaning "to be mad," and the maenads went wild in their worship of Dionysus, "tore apart their sacrificial victim and devoured him during their orgies" (Barbara Walker, *Woman's Encyclopedia* 564). To accept anger as a tenet of poetry is to run counter to one of the prescriptions of modern poetics, in which the poet is instructed—by a Yeats or an Eliot—to separate the self that suffers from the mind that creates (pace Juhasz, *Naked and Fiery Forms* 138–42).

Many of the women studied in this book—the exceptions are those who began publishing after the death of Francisco Franco in 1975—express their marginalized condition in one form or another, and manifest some of the distinctive features of a negative gynocentric vision that I have just outlined. However, all of the women I study manifest to a greater or lesser degree the distinctive features of a positive gynocentric vision, of autonomy and self-determination. Such features signify the inscription of a feminized self in poetic texts; they are strategic maneuvers engaged in by self-actualizing and self-determining poets who are intent on establishing their autonomy and securing their independence from the male-dominated poetic canon. The positive gynocentric vision manifests a poet's resolve "to construct herself as an independent female will directed toward self-involvement" (La Belle, *Herself Beheld* 69).

Self-revelation is one distinctive feature of the positive gynocentric vision. Juhasz argues that female poetry reveals the self whereas male poetry conceals it; that the male shields the self behind an impersonal mask or persona (pace T. S. Eliot), whereas the female aims at more direct revelation of personal experience (identifying the mind that creates with the woman who suffers). Juhasz also argues that whereas male poets will generalize because they see themselves as belonging to a larger tradition, "that of being a poet whose life and consciousness is in some sense and to some degree meant to typify the consciousness of [their] age" (*Naked and Fiery Forms* 58), women see themselves as inhabiting a more particular, personal, and private realm; they write poems that deal specifically with the experience of women, texts that are "shaped by the fact of their womanhood" (57).[7]

A second distinctive feature of a positive gynocentric vision is the conscious quest for poetic identity. Ostriker has argued that Bloom's model for poetic individuation—a Freudian jungle warfare—does not apply to women. Instead she posits a version of the Demeter/Kore myth as symbolic of the way women poets cease to be "Nobody" and become "Somebody." By describing women poets as daughters who descend "to Hades, step by step, to retrieve and revive a mother" (*Stealing* 16), she shifts the goal of the quest away from the male ideal of totality of knowledge and toward identity through recuperation and connectedness.

The notion that the woman writer descends into a cave to retrieve the lost self is fundamental to feminist thought. Traditionally the cave has been a place into which the male artist/seer withdraws in order to confect an image (in Platonic terms) of Truth and Beauty that no longer obtains on this earth. Or, the male hero descends into cave-like darkness (e.g., the belly of the whale) where he wrestles (e.g., with dragons) and reappears only when he has found the light—which illuminates *man*kind's darkness. Feminist critics of poetry argue that such a cave is tantamount to a prison for a woman artist because there is no totality of knowledge down there which she can recover. French feminists have argued that women should reconceptualize the cave as their uterus, a locus of *jouissance* and *jouiscience*.[8] For Cixous, "the voice is the uterus" and she redefines Plato's cave "as a uterine symbol."[9] For North Americans, the cave the woman enters is "the cave of her own mind"— or as Adrienne Rich puts it, "the cratered night of female memory"— where she finds "scattered leaves" of her power and of "the tradition that might have generated that power," and where she attempts to connect the scattered fragments—"revitalize the darkness, retrieve what has been lost, regenerate, reconceive, give birth" to the new land of the future (Gilbert and Gubar, *Madwoman* 98-99).[10]

A third distinctive feature of a positive gynocentric vision is a woman's preference for intimacy over isolation, interpersonal engagement over separateness. Chodorow has found that women are socialized "to be empathetic and nurturant," and that the "feminine sense of self remains connected to others in the world" (quoted by Gardiner in "Mind Mother" 134). Juhasz found that female poetry displays "engagement, involvement, commitment," that it "tends to get involved with concrete feelings, things, and people," and that it entertains and develops "relationship, communication, and identification as poetic devices" (*Naked and Fiery Forms* 140-41). Abel has explained that "recent feminist psychoanalytical theorists . . . have revised the traditional, hierarchical account of psychosexual differences." She adds that whereas in "Freudian orthodoxy . . . the female is simply a defective male," feminist theories "construct a picture of femininity as alternative, not inferior, to masculinity"; they do this "by shifting focus from Oedipal to pre-Oedipal experience and by highlighting interpersonal relation- ships rather than anatomy" ("Introduction" 9-10).[11] The pre-Oedipal is "that pre-history of women . . . almost impossible to revivify"; it is a state of "unboundedness, relatedness, plurality, fluidity, tenderness, and nurturance" (Stanton, "Difference" 164-65, 176). Also, Ostriker insists that "the imperative of intimacy" and touch has become a motif in women's poetry where "mutuality, continuity, connection, identifica- tion" are encountered (*Stealing* 165, 70ff.).[12] Closely related to this is the fact that French feminists have foregrounded "the role of the mother in mother-daughter relationships" (Jones, "Inscribing Femininity" 100) and have argued that a return to the mother constitutes liberation.[13] Hence, some women poets now embrace their emotions, explore their sexuality, reconnect with their mothers, and reflect on their maternal instincts. They may also be found to challenge the fixed boundaries of self and other and to offer images of integration (often androgynous).

The above characteristics—self-revelation, descent into the cave of the mind, intimacy, interpersonal relationships, and connectedness— are distinctive features of the positive gynocentric visions of many of the poets studied in this book. To chart their emergence and develop- ment in Spain from 1860 is to witness the inscription of a feminized discourse and to question the hegemonic norm of what constitutes a good or great poem.

Gynocritical Vision

In addition to gynocentric visions of the marginalized and the eman- cipated selves, "gynocritical" visions are inscribed in the texts of all of the poets studied here. I limit the expression "gynocritical" to indicate strategic ways in which Spain's women poets critique, demystify, sub- vert, and revise the androcentric structure of their culture and textu- alize alternate views. Gynocritical visions subvert androcentric values (e.g., of culture's stress on autonomy over connectedness); they are a revision and demystification of the legends and myths of Western civili- zation, in which women are backgrounded and female values displaced; and they are subversions and demystifications of the poetic idealism reified in male precursor texts.

Sharon Keefe Ugalde's distinction—which I translate—between

"subversion" and "revision" is crucial in the analysis of a gynocritical vision: "Subversion is a destructive tactic intended to disarm the verbal symbolization that has existed historically and which has subjugated a woman; revision, on the other hand, allows a woman to construct her own identity with precision and texture, to transform and to make her own the cumulative richness of the literary language" (*Conversaciones* 12). Elsewhere, Ugalde includes "embracement" as another strategy. She writes that "embracement . . . reflects the predicament of a poet living roles imposed by male domination, but sensing the presence of a silenced, imprisoned self." She adds that subversion is a "destructive force . . . aimed at dismantling patriarchally defined reality," whereas "revision permits women to move beyond protest to the inscription of a true female self" ("Feminization" 167 and 173).

The Judeo-Christian God of Western culture is constantly subverted and revised in women's poetry. The "death" of God, which as Ostriker noted (*Stealing* 46) haunts all Moderns, is less important for women poets who desire to disassociate spirituality from theology (*Stealing* 168) and to return to a pre-Christian religious object of a fertile and nourishing Mother (*Stealing* 161). In her study of those religions, Marija Gimbutas writes of a time when a woman's reproductive powers were considered to be sacred and were worshiped as a life-giving force. She speaks of a Great Goddess who was self-generating and whose basic functions were "Giver of Life, Wielder of Death, and, not less importantly, Regeneratrix"; she adds that this goddess was "the single source of all life" and "took her energy from the springs and wells, from the sun, moon, and moist earth" (*Language of the Goddess* xix). However, contemporary studies of these epochs are much more cautious. They specify that female-centered civilizations flourished in the Neolithic age (6500 B.C. to 3500 B.C.) and persisted into the Eneolithic age (3600 B.C. to 2200 B.C.). Moreover, they studiously avoid such terms as "Great Mother," "matriarchal," or "Great Goddess" and write instead of matrifocal, matrilineal, and goddess-worshiping societies (see Kessler, "Matriarchy"). Miriam Robbins Dexter, for example, observes that such goddesses were revered for their powers over both life and death and that "the female principle was worshiped for its fertile, life-giving properties." In addition, she clarifies Gimbutas's metaphor of the "Goddess of Regeneration" as follows: "In her life-giving aspect, the 'Goddess of Regeneration' was creatrix, bestowing fertility upon the womb and fruitfulness upon the earth. In her death-giving aspect, she became queen of the underworld, withdrawing the same life which she had created, and she held responsibility for the wintry barrenness of the Earth" (*Whence the Goddesses* 4–5).[14]

A second distinctive feature of gynocritical writing is its revision of the patriarchal myths of Western culture, its rewriting of the mythologies of classical civilization, and its reconceptualization of the myths of today (as Barthes defined them in his essays). With respect to the past, Ostriker states that for women poets "historic and mythic heroines will provide a means of self-exploration, self-projection, self defense" (*Stealing* 22). Woman has been typecast as Other and must convert that Other into Subject. To do so, she needs to dismantle literary conventions, but such dismantling entails a complete reevaluation of the social, political, and philosphical tenets of Western civilization. Jardine goes much further than this in her discussion of Derrida. She argues that a true feminist author would not accept "a simple inversion of the hierarchy" but would require "the very transformation of the notion of hierarchy itself" (*Gynesis* 195). Indeed, lesbian poets, according to Liz Yorke, have this as their ideal.[15] They desire a "vast cultural change," she writes, "not only of the phallogocentric symbolic, but also of social, religious, political, sexual and psychical structures in the real world" (*Impertinent Voices* 3).

Hence, the subversion of phallogocentric ideals and phallocratic structures is a feature of women's poetry. In opposition to the pragmatic, ego-bound, goal-oriented male mind and psyche, women foster "unity" through "mutual balance." They demystify the myths of patriarchy, and they subvert the male poetic canon.

Nontranscendentalism is a third distinctive feature I have found in the poets studied here: in their cultivation of a minimalist vision of life, in their down-to-earth celebrations of living, in their delight in life's simple pleasures, in their joy of the here-and-now. This is not a feature I personally have encountered in feminist criticism but it is implicit in the thoughts of several writers. In her discussion of Erica Jong in *Herself Beheld* (169–70), La Belle notes how Yeats's "Byzantine Saint" was "transported into the immutable of art." She adds, "the woman's 'problem' here is defined as an inability to deploy a transcendentalizing semiotic to overcome mere physicality." Although posed here as a problem, the opposition between male transcendence and female nontranscendence is fruitful. We have just noted how Judeo-Christian dogma—the transcendent signifier par excellence—excluded women from its domain. But such exclusion is not limited to theology. In her study of Rosalía de Castro, Stevens observes that women are excluded from the "transcendent processes of culture" (Stevens, *Rosalía de Castro* 33). Greene and Kahn discuss Sherry Ortner's focus on women's more rooted experience, when they observe that "Ortner holds that women tend to experience things, feelings and people as concrete rather than abstract, subjectively and interpersonally rather than objectively" ("Feminist Scholarship" 9). Indeed, for nineteenth-century America, Carroll Smith-Rosenberg documented "a 'female sphere' of intense intimacy and interdependence that was estranged from the male public sphere" (quoted by Gardiner in "Mind Mother" 136). To this can be added the voice of the French feminists, which Jones explains thus: "Irigaray's book *Speculum de l'autre femme* (1974) is an analysis of the suppression of the feminine from Platonic idealism through Hegel to Freud and Lévi-Strauss: woman has been defined as irrational, the Other (a negativity to be transcended), an imperfect man (a man without a penis), an object of exchange among men." Jones also observes that Cixous maintains that "women have a pre-conceptual, non-appropriative openness to people and to objects, to the other within and outside them" ("Inscribing Femininity" 84, 89). Although women have been excluded from a transcendentalizing semiotic, or perhaps because of that very fact, they have developed a form of immanent transcendence.

The unsung heroine of this philosophy is Hestia (a goddess of hearth and home [Rabuzzi, *Sacred* 38]). Rabuzzi, who has championed a form of nontranscendentalism, has explained that "women must cope with quotidian experience in which no miraculous intervention can occur" (20); she adds that their salvation consists not in "divinization and flight from the body but [in] humanization and reconciliation with the earth" (26; quoting Ruether, *Liberation Theology* 125). Moreover, she shows that within the profane and ordinary reality of their lives women encounter the sacred; they find that their deity is immanent within the universe (58). It is that indwelling spirit that is a distinctive feature of a nontranscendental vision of life, a vision that spiritualizes the earth and feminizes the sky. This alternate and gynocritical vision is found in some of the poets studied below.

It is true that male poets occasionally express such pleasures of quotidian reality—Neruda's *Odas elementales* (Elemental odes), Jorge Guillén's "Beato Sillón" (Blessed armchair), Gabriel Celaya's "Momentos felices" and "placeres cotidianos" (Happy moments; "daily pleasures"). However, at such "happy moments" they are championing—by foregrounding the "quotidian pleasures" of life—an antitranscendental philosophy of life; they are tilting at Christian dogma and arguing that fullness is in the here and now, not in the thereafter. Male poets are part and parcel of the transcendentalizing idealism of the West—whether they like it or not—in which mind and spirit are valorized over body; in which you become yourself by standing outside yourself (La Belle, *Herself Beheld* 50, 172). When males voice a contrary philosophy, they are merely being irreverent inside their own church; they are distancing themselves from a metaphysics with which they disagree, but—more significantly—one that does not exclude them. Women have always been excluded from that metaphysics for being too material, too involved with the body. The different vision they offer is one of nontranscendence, in which spirit is immanent in matter, in which the feminine earth is in touch with celestial heaven.

A concern for the Great Mother, the subversion and revision of cultural and literary myths, and nontranscendentalism are features of the gynocritical vision I encounter in Spain's women poets. They manifest a resolve to inscribe the female self as distinct from the "analytic rationality" (Gilbert and Gubar, "Ceremonies" 40) of the male ego and culture.

Gynocentric Style

One of the more contentious issues in gynopoetics is whether or not one can describe a gynocentric style. However, as Gardiner observed: "If women have more flexible, less rigid ego boundaries than men, define themselves through relationships, especially intense and ambivalent mother-daughter bonds; experience difficulties with autonomy, independence and heterosexuality; and feel morally responsible to a human network rather than to an abstract code of rights, then their writing should reflect these qualities" ("Mind Mother" 135).[16]

At the level of image and metaphor, there is some agreement on the fact that images of entrapment do reappear in female-authored texts (Gilbert and Gubar, *Madwoman;* Cheryl Walker, *Nightingale's Burden*). For many women poets, the sea is a secure, even gratifying place (Ostriker, *Stealing* 109–10); in French, the homophony "mère/mer" encourages this association. I have found metaphors based on menstrual blood, weaving, and the mirror to be additional recurrent images. There are many others, and I have indexed them at the end of this book. Such imagery is one aspect of a gynocentric style, one distinctive feature of its expressive arsenal. I have deliberately commented on what I consider to be a gynocentric lexicon—nouns, verbs, and adjectives that tend to occur in female as opposed to male-authored texts—because I see it as challenging our perception of what constitutes a period style. Other features of a gynocentric style include the text as palimpsest, the exoskeletal form, writing-with-the-body, and nonlinearity.

Within an androcentric culture a woman writer may generate a palimpsestic text. To conform to patriarchal norms, a woman may feel constrained to create texts that reflect images of what women are supposed to be (i.e., angels). However, ingenious women writers who desire to shatter the distorted and fragmented image they see of themselves in patriarchal texts will conceal within their texts less socially acceptable levels of meaning. Palimpsestic texts are those "whose surface designs conceal or obscure deeper, less accessible (and less socially acceptable) levels of meaning" (Gilbert and Gubar, *Madwoman* 73). Over such texts, the woman poet exercises a cunning and crafty power by embedding in them hidden significance, subversions of patriarchal literary taste and judgment—just as Medusa's beauty attracted men while her serpent hair turned them to stone.

Women also generate "exoskeletal" texts: a "stylistically hard, cold, rigid, and rational rather than soft, warm, pliable, and sensitive" style of expression (Ostriker, *Stealing* 88). Moreover, Ostriker says, "the woman poet who adopts an impermeable tone is less in danger of being dismissed as sentimental or overemotional by critics" (88). And the selection of a hard object (stone, metal) can signify a woman poet's fragmented being—one that is unable to unify itself.

A conscious attempt to "write with the body" is a characteristic of certain poets. In practice, this style would have to become the opposite of the exoskeletalism noted above, as it would evoke "fluidity, softness, movement, life," which are "antithetical to masculine solidity, hardness, rigidity, and death."[17] French feminists in particular are committed to reconceptualizing a woman's relationship to her body, and to foregrounding female corporality. The intention of such thinkers is to undermine Freudian psychoanalysis in which a woman's body is defined as a void or nonentity (for "lacking" a penis). French theorists stress that women should enjoy their bodies, that they should get in touch with them: they emphasize the pleasure ("jouissance") that women can find in the female body, and they urge that a woman writer "write with her body." On a more pragmatic level, there is an increased reference to body parts in recent women's poetry, probably as a reaction to the shackles decorum placed on the mention of women's private parts. This represents a move toward synthesis with nature and with each other and away from the alienation and transcendence of the body which is typical of (male) Western philosophies.

Finally, several theorists hold that a nonlinear style is a distinctive feature of women's discourse. Showalter, writing of the female esthetic, notes that women have "experimented with efforts to inscribe a female idiom in critical discourse and to define a feminist critical stylistics based on women's consciousness" ("Feminism and Literature" 187). Some theorists, she adds, argue for "a 'discursive, conjunctive' style instead of the complex, subordinating, linear style of 'classification and distinction.'" Cixous believes that if a woman writes she will tap the unconscious which is where "the repressed" — by which she means woman — "manage[s] to survive" ("Laugh" 250). In the same essay, she says: "I shall speak about women's writing, about *what it will do*. Woman must write herself: she must write about women and bring women to writing, from which they have been driven away as violently as from their bodies — for the same reasons, by the same law, with the same fatal goal. Woman must put herself into the text — as into the world and into history — by her own movement" (245).[18] Cixous and Irigaray, who have related women's writing to a woman's sexuality and body, employ "such techniques as gaps, breaks, questions, metaphors of excess, double or multiple voices, broken syntax, repetitive or cumulative rather than linear structure, and open endings" (Showalter, "Feminism and Literature" 187–88). Metaphors of water (the sea) and air are foregrounded in this style (Moi, *Sexual/Textual Politics* 128). Biruté Ciplijauskaité, who analyzed this style in Rosalía de Castro, concludes — and I translate: "Hence, one can see Rosalía as one of the first representatives of what is proposed today as 'écriture feminine,' the most salient characteristics of which are: lack of rigid structure or lineal development; circularity; repetition; abolition of the boundary between the real and the fantastic; preponderance of the irregular and the fragmentary; importance of intervals of silence" ("Cárcel estrecha" 324). I shall be referring frequently to some of these features, in particular to the exoskeletal style and to images of the sea and water, throughout these essays.

A "gynocentric style" is one of three aspects of the gynopoetics I shall be applying in the following pages, the two others being "gynocentric" and "gynocritical" visions of art, life, and culture. The terms "gynocentric" and "gynocritical" are gendered reading strategies consciously deployed to differentiate the poetry under study from the canonical norm. By deploying this tripartite description I hope to achieve a better understanding of the ignored originality of Spain's women poets.

Women Poets in Spain prior to 1860

Women began to compose lyrics on the Iberian Peninsula perhaps as early as the ninth century, but their authority and originality have been overlooked. Not only has their work received comparatively little critical attention, it has been degendered by attribution to the anonymous male of the writing species. Nevertheless, the poets who concern me in this book do have their female precursors—mothers and sisters whose texts can be read as initiating a poetic discourse in Spanish poetry that explores the concerns of a writing subject who is also female. It is the historical tradition initiated and developed by these poets that I would like to describe now, albeit succinctly and summarily.

The earliest lyrics in "Spanish" are the *jarchas* or *k(h)arjas*, which are the "concluding couplets" to the Arabic *muwassaha* of the eleventh through thirteenth centuries.[19] Rubiera Mata ("Introducción" 7–29) has offered convincing reasons why some of the extant *jarchas* could well have been written by women. She links them to the European *frauen-lieder*, explaining that they are a lyric in which "a woman expresses her amorous desire, her own desire with reference to her body which is not disguised by a masculine perspective, and proclaims it to her lover, herself and everyone else" (20). Here is one example of a *jarcha:*

Tanto amar, tanto amar,
amigo, tanto amar.
Enfermaron mis ojos alegres
y duelen tan mal.
   (Barnstone, *Spanish Poetry* 47)

(So much loving, so much loving, / friend, so much loving. / My happy eyes grew frail / and ache so much.)

Rubiera Mata (*Poesía femenina* 39–72) documents several categories of female *jarchas:* requests for love (often explicit); complaints about the rough treatment the woman received while making love; confidential requests to another woman; lamentations for the lover's absence; dawn songs; and erotic "lullabies" (in which the lover cradles her beloved like a baby).

Sometimes the female desire expressed is erotic: an anonymous *jar-cha*, "No te amaré," presents a female speaker who is enticing her lover into a rare erotic posture:

> No te amaré
> si no es con la condición
> que unas mis ajorcas
> con mis arracadas.[20]

(I shall not make love with you / unless you first / fasten my bracelets / to my earrings.)

As we shall note, Clara Janés chose quite recently to revise this particular *jarcha*. Despite the assertivenes of the above lines, *jarchas* are rarely gynocritical, that is, rarely does the female speaker criticize the male order of things. But the following is an exception:

> ¡Por Dios! me desahogué gritando,
> me ha roto mi pecho
> me ha herido mis labios
> y me ha deshecho el collar!
>   (Rubiera Mata, *Poesía femenina* 49)[21]

(For Christ's sake! I screamed aloud, / you've worn out my breasts, / hurt my lips, / and broken my necklace!)

Rubiera Mata maintains that women wrote *jarchas* such as these, although their *author*ity has been obliterated. The fact remains that lyrics in which a female speaking subject described her condition existed in early medieval Spain, as did those in which a young woman addressed her "love-song" of lament to another woman ("cantigas de amigo"). Hence, some of the earliest poetry in Spanish inscribes a female presence, it is gynocentric: it focuses on and expresses a woman's preoccupations and desires. This book will describe some of the traces of that tradition on which later poets have drawn. Rosalía de Castro, for example, employs the *alborada* ("dawn song"), the "cantiga de amigo," and the *romance* ("ballad") in novel ways.[22]

In the fourteenth and fifteenth centuries, gynocentric preoccupations are articulated in major forms of poetic expression—*serranillas* (shepherdess songs), *cantigas de amigo* (love songs), and *romances* (ballads).[23] Although established scholarship assigns these lyrics to the—albeit anonymous—male of the species, recent scholarship has found that women composed some of them. Rubiera Mata (*Poesía feme-*

nina 75–163) provides examples of the poetry of twenty hispano-arabic women poets from the eighth through the fourteenth centuries, and Pérez Priego brings together the work of thirteen women poets of the fifteenth century, the first dating from 1403, a "cantiga de despedida" (farewell song) by Doña Mayor Arias. He also provides examples of love poems, religious verse, and occasional witty pieces, all written by noble women for jousts and courtly celebrations (Pérez Priego, *Poesía femenina* 7–26, 43–93).[24]

However, the only poet with an individual style during the fifteenth century, as Pérez Priego observes, is Florencia Pinar. Indeed, she and Luisa Sigea in the sixteenth century are considered to be the two principal women poets of medieval Spain. Florencia Pinar, several of whose love poems ("Songs") are extant, wrote during the reign of "los Reyes Católicos" (the Catholic kings) Isabel of Castille and Ferdinand of Aragon (i.e., during the last thirty years of the fifteenth century and the first decade of the sixteenth).[25] In one of her songs she describes love as a cancerous worm:

> Ell amor ha tales mañas
> que quien no se guarda dellas,
> *si se l'entra en las entrañas,*
> *no puede salir sin ellas.*
>
> Ell amor es un gusano,
> bien mirada su figura:
> es un cáncer de natura
> que come todo lo sano.
> Por sus burlas, por sus sañas,
> dél se dan tales querrellas
> *que si entra en las entrañas,*
> *no puede salir sin ellas.*
>   (Pérez Priego, *Poesía feminina* 83)

> (Love has such wiles / that if you do not watch them, / *they get inside you,* / *and you can't live without them.* / Love's a worm, / if judged aright: / nature's cancer / that feeds on health. / With its tricks, and with its fury, / it picks so many fights / *that if it gets inside you,* / *you'll be unable to live without them.*)

Snow argues that in her poems Pinar is enslaved by love, and he clearly establishes Pinar's originality for her time. He concludes: "it is surely a keen talent which can subvert the standard conventions—while using them—to create poems which so deftly suggest a sexuality at odds with the idealized relationships those conventions were asked to portray" ("Spanish Love Poet" 327). Deyermond points to her use of concrete imagery in contrast to the abstract imagery of the *Cancioneros* (song books). He analyzes what amounts to subversion in her use of the partridge symbol and describes the "strongly sexual . . . tone" of her "animal imagery." He concludes that such imagery enables Pinar "to say about herself indirectly but very clearly things which the conventions of the time prevented her from saying explicitly" ("Spain's First Women Writers" 45–50). Deyermond is describing what has since been called a "palimpsestic text." As we shall see, Clara Janés reworked the partridge symbol, and several twentieth-century poets avail themselves of concrete imagery.

The other principal medieval woman poet, Luisa Sigea (1530?–60), was recognized "throughout Europe" for her talents (Flores and Flores, *Defiant Muse* xvi).[26] Her work is characterized by pessimism, but beneath that (exoskeletal) shell of Baroque "desengaño" (disillusionment) a gynocritical impulse is to be detected:

> fortuna contra mi enristró la lanza
> y el medio me fuyó para estorbarme
> el poder llegar yo al fin que espero,
> y así me hace seguir lo que no quiero.
> (Janés, *Primeras poetisas* 38–39)

(Lord Luck raised his lance against me, / depriving me of ways / and means to realize my desires, / and hence he forces me to live against my will.)

The frustrations of being female in a patriarchal culture possibly inspired this bitterness. We shall be observing such disillusionment in many of the women studied here.

The Renaissance and Baroque epochs—the Spanish "Siglo de oro" (Golden age)—treated women more fairly than the medieval age; it depicted them as "strong, heroic, and virtuous" (Flores and Flores, *Defiant Muse* xvi). Clara Janés's *Las primeras poetisas* (The first poetesses) anthologized around thirty-five women poets for this epoch, of whom two stand out—Santa Teresa de Jesús (1515–82) and María de Zayas y Sotomayor (1590–1660).[27]

The few poems attributed to St. Teresa are religious in nature; the most famous begins:

Vivo sin vivir en mí,
y tan alta vida espero,
que muero porque no muero.
        (Blecua, *Poesía* 1:121)

(I live without ever being alive, / and while awaiting a much higher
life, / I die because I do not die.)

Gloria Fuertes chose to subvert these lines, and few women studied in
this book embrace the Judeo-Christian, patriarchal God.

María de Zayas, by contrast, is a feminist. The prefaces to her *Nove-
las amorosas exemplares* (Exemplary love novels) are a manifesto on
women's rights.[28] In one poem she selects Narcissus as the emblem of a
cold, unloving male:

Claras fuentecillas,
pues murmuráis,
murmurad a Narciso
que no sabe amar.

. . . .

Murmurad que llama
cielos otros ojos,
más por darme enojos
que porque los ama,
que mi ardiente llama
paga con desdén,
y quererle bien
con quererme mal;
murmurad a Narciso
que no sabe amar.
(Janés, *Primeras poetisas* 119–20)

(Limpid little founts, / since you murmur, / insinuate that Narcissus /
knows not how to love. / . . . / Mutter that he calls / heavenly other
eyes than mine, / not because he loves them / but just to make me
mad, / that he treats with disdain / my burning flame, / and repays my
good / love with bad; / criticize Narcissus / for he knows not how
to love.)[29]

Many of the women studied in this book have written on the coldness of
the male ego, including Gloria Fuertes and most recently Ana Rossetti.

In the eighteenth century there are as yet few recognized women
poets. Jiménez Faro (*Panorama* 55–59) includes five, of whom Margarita

Hickey (1757–93) seems to stand out. Her poems are "acerbos retratos del sexo opuesto" (bitter portraits of the opposite sex [57]). Hickey believed that women could surpass men in the arts and sciences:

Que el verdadero sabio, donde quiera
Que la verdad y la razón encuentre,
Allí sabe tomarla, y la aprovecha
Sin nimio detenerse en quién la ofrece.
Porque ignorar no puede, si es que sabe,
Que el alma, como espíritu, carece
De sexo, y por su puro ser y esencia,
De sus defectos consiguientemente.

(Jiménez Faro, *Panorama* 57)

(For the true sage, wherever / he encounters truth and reason, / knows how to use and profit from them, / without fussing over who brought them his way. / For he cannot be ignorant of the fact, if he's a real sage, / that the soul, as spirit, is / sexless and, as pure being and essence, / also lacks the defects that go with sex.)

We shall have occasion to comment on many such "bitter portraits" during the course of this study.

The nineteenth century in Spain has many more women poets, but Rosalía de Castro's principal Peninsular precursor is Carolina Coronado (1820–1911), whose poetry Kirkpatrick has analyzed in depth.

Carolina Coronado acquired a reputation for writing amorous, sensual, and mystical verse. In "El amor de los amores" (The love of my life) she claims:

En la sierra de rocas erizada,
del valle entre los árboles y flores,
en la ribera sola y apartada
he esperado al amor de mis amores.

(Jiménez Faro, *Panorama* 67)

(On the jagged and rocky mount, / in the valley of flowers and trees, / along the river bank alone and set apart, / *I have waited for the love of my life.*)

Despite the conventional nature of much of her work, a handful of poems reveal a frustrated woman artist and nascent feminist.[30] In "El marido verdugo" (Hangman husband) she condemns society for concealing what today we call wife-beating:

Que a veces sobre el seno transparente
cárdenas huellas de sus dedos halla;
que a veces brotan de su blanca frente
sangre las venas que su esposo estalla.

(Coronado, *Poesías* 107)

(For at times on her transparent breast / she finds his fingers' purple marks; / for at times the veins her husband crushed spurt / blood on her white brow.)

In her 1845 ballad "La poetisa en un pueblo" (The poetess in a village), the guests at a wedding heap scorn and abuse on a woman who claims to be a poet, "—Jesús, qué mujer tan rara. /—Tiene los ojos de loca" (Good Lord, what a weird woman. She has the eyes of a madwoman). The same guests believe that this woman cannot have written her poems by herself:

Esos versos los compone
otra cualquiera persona,
y ella luego, por lucirse,
sin duda los apropia.

(Coronado, *Poesías* 107)[31]

(Those verses could have been composed / by anyone at all, / and then she, to show off, / undoubtedly claims them as her own.)

In her 1846 ballad "Libertad" (Freedom) she condemns the fact that "liberty" exists for men, not for women:

¡*Libertad!* ¿qué nos importa?
¿qué ganamos, qué tendremos?
¿un encierro por tribuna
y una aguja por *derecho?*
¡Libertad! ¿de qué nos vale
si son los tiranos nuestros
no el yugo de los monarcas,

. . . .

Pero, os digo, compañeras,
que la ley es sola de ellos,
que las hembras no se cuentan
ni hay Nación para este sexo,
el yugo de nuestro sexo?

(Coronado, *Poesías* 390)

(*Freedom!* What does it matter to us? / What do we gain? What will we get out of it? / A dais as our prison / and a needle by *decree?* / Freedom! What use is it to us / if it's a tyrant to us / not a yoke for the monarchs? / . . . / And I tell you, girls: / the law's for them alone; / women do not count; / and there is no Nation for this sex, / the yoke of our sex.)

Kirkpatrick's reading of Coronado is trenchant. She explains that, despite some important exceptions,[32] in her early poems (1843) Coronado conforms to the "cultural stereotype of the *ángel del hogar*" (angel of hearth and home [*Románticas* 212]). In her later work (1845 and 1852) she is more autonomous, for she explicitly characterizes "women's experience as one of suffering and repression" (231). For example, "A Lidia" (To Lydia) states that woman is a slave; "Ultimo canto" (Final song) suggests that woman is an insect who ultimately suffocates in a bell jar. "Cantad hermosas" (Sing my beauties—a phrase Angela Figuera will use in the 1950s) stresses the necessity for "self-expression even against social oppression" (274). Kirkpatrick concludes that Coronado "incorporated in one form or another in the poetic self [she] created . . . emotions that the ideology of the *ángel del hogar* rejected as unnatural and inappropriate in women," such as "ambition, aggressive self-affirmation, awareness of injustice, adventurousness, scorn, anger" (242). The latter are also some of the features of Coronado's daughters-in-poetry, as we shall see.

Carolina Coronado was in fact married to a North American diplomat, but the true Spanish-American influence on Spain's women poets had its origins in the work of a Mexican nun, Sor Juana Inés de la Cruz (1648?–95), and a Cuban who lived her life in Spain, Gertrudis Gómez de Avellaneda (b. Cuba, 1814–d. Madrid, 1873).

Sor Juana Inés de la Cruz was the most important woman poet of the Spanish Renaissance and Baroque. Her 1693 "Respuesta a Sor Filotea" (Reply to Sister Filotea) defends a woman's right to knowledge and "is a major document in the struggle for women's intellectual independence" (Flores and Flores, *Defiant Muse* xvii). In a famous poem "Hombres necios que acusáis" (Stupid men who accuse), she censures men for condemning in women the very desires they hope to provoke:

Hombres necios que acusáis
A la mujer, sin razón,
Sin ver que sois la ocasión
De lo mismo que culpáis:

. . . .
Combatís su resistencia,
Y luego, con gravedad,
Decís que fué liviandad
Lo que hizo su diligencia.

. . . .
¿O cuál es más de culpar,
Aunque cualquiera mal haga:
La que peca por la paga,
O el que paga por pecar?
(*Lírica* 371)[33]

(Stupid men, who accuse / women for no good reason, / without seeing that you are the cause / of the very thing you blame. / . . . / You combat their resistance, / and then, with gravity, / say that what your diligence provoked / was lechery in her. / . . . / Who's more to blame, / given that anyone can do evil: / she who sins for the payoff, / or he who pays to sin?)

We shall be observing numerous poems in which a woman takes delight in pointing out the inconsistencies of the male of the species.

Gertrudis Gómez de Avellaneda followed her own desires and instincts, living intensely and utterly unconventionally. Jiménez Faro (*Panorama* 74) observes that "this vehement woman will pay a high price for breaking out of the female mold, for breaking with *encorseted* sense of modesty of the epoch." In "Amor y orgullo" (Love and pride) Avellaneda describes herself as:

altanera, con orgullo vano,
cual águila real a vil gusano
contemplaba a los hombres.
(Jiménez Faro, *Panorama* 369–70)

(haughty, with vain pride, / she contemplated men / as does the royal eagle the vile worm.)

Kirkpatrick has shown how Avellaneda strove to establish the "authority of the female lyrical subject," thereby "opening to a woman the same structure of subjectivity" that Romanticism postulated for an implicit male self (*Románticas* 187). Then, in her analysis of Avellaneda's nature symbols, Kirkpatrick demonstrates how the valiant struggle to establish the feminized self is a failure, for the self that emerges is split and undermined (205). Rage becomes her antidote to feminine weakness (200), and "erotic passion leads to radical self-alienation . . . a loss of autonomous direction" (200-201). "Such a self," Kirkpatrick adds, "has little in common with Espronceda's poetically created self, which, though embittered and suffering, is never estranged from its striving, directed desire" (200-201).[34]

As we have been noting, a gynocentric vision slowly evolved in Spain between the 1400s and the 1850s. In the following chapters, we shall note the struggles of subsequent poets to create a distinctive poetic self for themselves. We shall note the fact that most of these poets are acutely aware of injustice, as was Carolina Coronado, and we shall document the scorn and anger, as well as ambition, self-affirmation, and adventurousness, to which Kirkpatrick (242) referred. And by the conclusion of these essays, I believe that we shall see that in the 1980s the historical condition for women poets did indeed improve.

Women Poets in National Literatures

As I focus in this book on the poets of one national literature, I might leave the impression that the contours of the gynocentric visions I describe are anomalous and unrelated to the poetic insights and vital concerns of women in other national literatures. To guard against that potentially false impression, and to attempt to situate Spanish poets within the tradition of women's poetry, I want to conclude this intro-duction with a brief discussion of the preoccupations Spain's poets share with their precursors and contemporaries from around the world.

Since the dawn of poetry, a negative gynocentric vision—of margin-alization through various forms of oppression and subjugation, prin-cipally phallocentric—has been articulated in poetic texts authored by women. Long before the birth of Christ, women in the Orient documented the wretched condition of womankind. The Chinese poet Chu Shu-chen (ca. 1200) describes her complete marginalization thus: "Freezing, / Alone in the dark, I am / Going mad, counting my sor-rows" (Barnstone and Barnstone, Book of Women Poets 143). Such com-plaints are not limited to China. An undatable poem in Pali, by Suman-gala's Mother, describes the relief experienced by the speaker when she was finally freed from the state of bondage in which her "brutal hus-band" kept her (Barnstone and Barnstone, Book of Women Poets 71).[35] In the eighteenth century, English and American poets began to elabo-rate on the subjugation of womankind. For example, the English poet Felicia Hemans (1793-1835), in her "Indian Woman's Death-Song," describes the plight of a woman who is "driven to despair by her husband's desertion of her for another wife" (Cora Kaplan, *Salt* 62). Emily Dickinson (1830-86) succinctly alludes to a woman's marginalization in these lines: "It would have starved a Gnat—/ To live so small as I—" (Cora Kaplan, *Salt* 154).[36] As we shall see, Spanish poets from Rosalía de Castro in the nineteenth century to Francisca Aguirre in the 1970s manifest analogous concerns.

Esthetic marginalization, which I shall discuss in relation to Rosalía de Castro's sense of inferiority toward Anonio de Trueba, was articulated by the English poets Anne Bradstreet (1612?-72) and Anne Finch, countess of Winchelsea (1661-1720). In "The Prologue" Bradstreet writes of "My foolish, broken blemished Muse" and notes ironically that her "mean pen" should avoid matters of serious import (Cora Kaplan, *Salt* 29). In "The Introduction" Finch writes: "Alas! A woman that attempts the pen, / Such an intruder on the rights of men, / Such a presumptuous Creature is esteem'd, / The fault can by no vertue be redeem'd" and continues: "Whilst the dull mannage, of a servile house / Is held by some, our outmost art, and use" (Cora Kaplan, *Salt* 62). Only in the late twentieth century did women poets cease to experience such subordination.

Women poets who attempted to discover themselves and define themselves as self-autonomous beings have left in their texts the predominantly negative trace of that experience. In "Because We Suspected" the Japanese poet Lady Ise (875?-938?) describes how women who realized their sexual desires were condemned by society (Barnstone and Barnstone, *Book of Women Poets* 164). Much later, in "Reaping," the American poet Amy Lowell (1874-1925) describes the loveless marriage of a farmer's wife whose first and only child died; she makes love with a mutual friend and informs her husband of her infidelity the night before she prepares to leave his house to atone for her self-realization (Cora Kaplan, *Salt* 207-10). More recently, the Puerto Rican Julia de Burgos (1914-53) dramatically presents the horrendous self-division of a creative woman who learns to be submissive to survive in the phallocentric culture that surrounds her ("To Julia de Burgos" [Barnstone and Barnstone, *Book of Women Poets* 271-72]). Her precursor, the Argentine Alfonsina Storni (1892-1938) actually committed suicide. The official explanation given for this is her cancer, but there can be little doubt that her attempts to define herself in opposition to patriarchal norms contributed to the solution she chose (Barnstone and Barnstone, *Book of Women Poets* 285). True self-realization—autonomy, liberation, and self-discovery despite surrounding oppression—is really only a feature of late twentieth-century poetry.[37]

Anger has also been expressed by women poets throughout the centuries. In the sixteenth century, the French poet Louise Labé writes in her Sonnet 23: "I am outraged with anger and I rave" (Barnstone and Barnstone, *Book of Women Poets* 216). In the nineteenth, in "A Curse for a Nation," Elizabeth Barrett Browning (1806-61) asserts that "A curse from the depths of womanhood / Is very salt, and bitter, and good" (Cora Kaplan, *Salt* 116).[38] In the twentieth century, the El Salvadoran Claribel Alegría articulates, for example in "Small Country," "powerful statements of third world anger" (Barnstone and Barnstone, *Book of Women Poets* 277, 279-81).

A discourse on widowhood emerges in a "Widow's Lament" of the Chinese *Book of Songs* (7th century B.C.) (Barnstone and Barnstone, *Book of Women Poets* 111); it reemerges in the French poet Christine de Pisan (1363-1430), and much later in Anna Akhmatova (1889-1966).[39] More recently, the American Ruth Stone (b. 1915), in "Years Later," describes a widow's vivid memories of her husband (Barnstone and Barnstone, *Book of Women Poets* 503-4). The poetry of such women recalls the discourse on widowhood that entered modern Spanish poetry with Carmen Conde.

A reflection on the aging process appears in Sappho (7th-6th century B.C.): "But age wrinkles my skin already, / my hair has become whiter than it was black, once, / my knees won't carry / to dance like young fawns" (*Sappho* 26). The English poet Christina Rossetti (1830-94) alludes to a woman who is dried up and apart from the world ("From Sunset to Star Rise" [Cora Kaplan, *Salt* 138]). More recently, the American Louise Bogan (1897-1970) in "The Crows" writes of "The woman who has grown old / And knows desire must die" (Cora Kaplan, *Salt* 275).[40] In this study of the poets of Spain, we shall encounter analogous reflections on aging, widowhood, anger, marginalization, and thwarted attempts at self-realization.

A more positive gynocentric vision—the articulation of female desire, sensuality, and sexual passion—is another of the strands in the tradition of women's poetry. Women poets of the Far East expressed the pain of their love in a manner that is similar to the Spanish early medieval "cantigas de amigo." In China, Ch'in Chia's wife (1st century B.C.) agonizes over the pain of being separated from her husband, who had been sent to the capital ("Ch'in Chia's Wife's Reply" [Barnstone and Barnstone, *Book of Women Poets* 113-14]). Moreover, the Chinese Chao

Li-hua (Ming dynasty, 1368–1644) has a "Farewell" song comparable to the early Spanish "cantiga de despedida" (Barnstone and Barnstone, *Book of Women Poets* 147).[41]

Other women manifested their desire in a spontaneous and direct manner. Allusive references to the female body appear in Sappho, who describes the loss of virginity thus: "As a hyacinth in the mountains that men shepherding / tread underfoot, and to the ground its flower, all purple" (*Sappho* 13). Sappho's delicacy of expression recalls an earlier poem by the Chinese Tzu Yeh (3d–6th century), who had written: "My tiresome petticoat keeps on flapping about; / If it opens a little, I shall blame the spring wind" (Barnstone and Barnstone, *Book of Women Poets* 121).[42]

Despite the fact that many women have expressed the pain of longing, the agony of unfulfilled desire, and the frustrations of rejection,[43] the articulation of sexual pleasure itself is a constant of women's poetry. The "Anonymous Hieroglyphic Texts" (ca. 1500 B.C.) of Egypt are love poems and in one of the "Pleasant Songs" a woman, who finds her lover fishing, concludes: "I offer him the magic of my thighs / He is caught in the spell." In another of these anonymous texts "The pomegranate speaks" to a woman and claims: "My leaves are like your teeth / My fruit like your breasts. I, the most beautiful of fruits" (Barnstone and Barnstone, *Book of Women Poets* 14 and 20–24 respectively). In India, Vidya (ca. 659) and Vallana (between 900 and 1100) provide—in Sanskrit—a frank expression of female awakening. The former writes: "After my darling put his hand on the knot / of my dress, / I swear I remember nothing" (Barnstone and Barnstone, *Book of Women Poets* 62, 64). Later, the expression of sexual desire and fulfillment becomes more forceful. The Chinese Huang O (1498–1569) has a poem in which she writes: "You held my lotus blossom / In your lips and played with the / Pistil" (Barnstone and Barnstone, *Book of Women Poets* 149). Most recently, the Portuguese "Three Marías"—María Isabel Barreno (b. 1939), María Teresa Horta (b. 1937), and María Velho da Costa (b. 1939)—in, for example, "Conversation between the Chevalier de Chamilly and Mariana Alcorofado in the Manner of a Song of Regret" and "Saddle and Cell"—employ explicit sexual lexicon and imagery to jolt their patriarchal culture into the reality of the late twentieth century (Barnstone and Barnstone, *Book of Women Poets* 296–99). The discourse on female desire therefore has a long tradition that dates from before the birth of Christ.[44]

A woman's experiences as mother—mothering, mother-child bonds, pregnancy—have also been confronted throughout the history of women's poetry. The "Mother's Song" of an anonymous Japanese poet (ca. 733) expresses a mother's love and care for her son (Barnstone and Barnstone, *Book of Women Poets* 158). In "In reference to her Children, 23 June 1656," Anne Bradstreet selects the metaphor of the bird and her nest to explore her own feelings of motherhood, as would Rosalía de Castro two centuries later in "Sin nido." In her "Requiem 1935-1940," Anna Akhmatova reveals that a mother's love for her son can be extended via maternal feelings into care and empathy for downtrodden humanity (Barnstone and Barnstone, *Book of Women Poets* 377-84).[45] As we shall see, the Spanish poets Carmen Conde, Angela Figuera, and Concha Zardoya reveal in their work the same empathy and anger for the powerless and underprivileged.

The bonds between mothers and daughters appear in the poetry of Sappho, who writes: "Like a child to her mother I have flown to you" (*Sappho* 19); in point of fact "Sappho had a daughter, whom she named Kleïs after her mother" (Powell in *Sappho* 33). Later, the Japanese poet Lady Otomo of Sakanone (ca. 8th century) also expresses her love for her daughter (Barnstone and Barnstone, *Book of Women Poets* 159-60). Closer to our time, Felica Hemans in "The Memorial Pillar" deals with mother-daughter love (Cora Kaplan, *Salt* 97-98).[46]

With respect to the experience of pregnancy—which several Spanish poets will confront—although the anonymous *Carmina Burana* (ca. 1200) includes a ballad (in medieval Latin) "similar to other pregnancy songs found in Middle English and other European languages" (Barnstone and Barnstone, *Book of Women Poets* 61), a serious reflection on pregnancy enters poetry only in the twentieth century with the Italian poet Edith Bruck (b. 1932), the German Hilde Domin (b. 1912), and the American Sandra McPherson (b. 1943).[47]

The self-sustaining sorority—of deep affection and communal love —which women have generated among themselves and for themselves was textualized in the seventeenth century by the English poet Katherine Philips (1631-64) when she writes, in "To My Excellent Lucasia, on Our Friendship": "But never had Orinda found / A soul till she found thine" (Cora Kaplan, *Salt* 44). In her famous "Goblin Market," Christina Rossetti initiates a reflection on the bonds developed by blood sisters (Cora Kaplan, *Salt* 127-38). Alfonsina Storni takes this up in "My Sister," and the Chilean Gabriela Mistral (1889-1957), in "Sister," develops it to reveal the community of sisters that women create for and among themselves (Barnstone and Barnstone, *Book of Women Poets* 285–86, 291).[48]

In "The Petition for an Absolute Retreat," Anne Finch writes what reads like an early statement on nontranscendent goals. She asks "indulgent fate" to give her before she dies "A sweet, but absolute retreat" (Cora Kaplan, *Salt* 65). This is a seventeenth-century affirmation of sanctuary as *locus amoenus* in which the transient cares of the world play no part and in which a life of sensual pleasures, friendship, mutual love, is lived to the full and to the exclusion of transcendent obligations. The twenty-second of Barrett Browning's "Sonnets from the Portuguese" reads: "Let us stay / Rather on earth, Belovèd" (Cora Kaplan, *Salt* 115).[49] Several Spanish poets, as we shall see, articulate similar ideals.

A gynocritical vision—critique of the male of the species, of his values and myths—is part and parcel of the tradition of women's poetry. Some poets foreground the male as predator on the female of the species. In "An Old-World Thicket," Christina Rossetti alludes to such instincts thus: "But underneath the grass there gnaws a worm" (Cora Kaplan, *Salt* 141)—a metaphor Rosalía de Castro will eventually employ in "Los tristes, 4." Other poets focus on the male's penchant for making war. In preference to this, Sappho, in whose work there is an "explicit rejection of . . . militarist . . . values" (Powell in *Sappho* 35) writes: "I'd rather see her lovely step, / her sparkling glance and her face than gaze on / all the troops in Lydia in their chariots and / glittering armor" (*Sappho* 28). The American Edna St. Vincent Millay (1892–1950)—who wrote "Say That We Saw Spain Die" (Cora Kaplan, *Salt* 252–53)—is more direct; like Angela Figuera, she condemns men for the wars they wage ("Apostrophe to Man" [Cora Kaplan, *Salt* 248]).

A critique of androcentric self-interest is found as early as the old traditional songs of Morocco, the "Ancient Songs of the Women of Fez" (Barnstone and Barnstone, *Book of Women Poets* 100–102). The male's inconstancy and inconsistency, his devious and deceptive ways, also appear very early in the history of poetry. For example, the Chinese Cho Wen-chün (179?–117 B.C.) reflects on male inconsistency in "You're telling me / Your thoughts are double" (Barnstone and Barnstone, *Book of Women Poets* 112).[50] In Western poetry, this critique emerges later. Forthright condemnation is found in H.D. (1886–1961), who in "Callypso Speaks" asserts that "man is clumsy and evil / a devil" and concludes that "man is a brute and a fool" (Cora Kaplan, *Salt* 227, 229). Likewise, Stevie Smith (1902–71) in "Major Macroo" bluntly declares: "Such men as these, such selfish cruel men / Hurting what most they love what most loves them" (Cora Kaplan, *Salt* 285). A more trenchant critique of androcentric values and phallocratic power is encountered in the contemporary North American poets Marge Piercy (b. 1936) and May Swenson (1913-89).[51]

Male coldness, which we noted earlier in María de Zayas, is a constant theme. Louise Labé satirizes a perfectly cold lover (Sonnet 16 in Barnstone and Barnstone, *Book of Women Poets* 213); the Japanese Yosano Akiko (1878-1942), in "You Never Touch," critiques the male's indifference and coldness toward the woman he loves (Barnstone and Barnstone, *Book of Women Poets* 174).[52] Women have also mocked the penis and the phallus. The English poet Aphra Behn (1640-89) satirizes male impotence ("The Disappointment" [Cora Kaplan, *Salt* 51-55]). In this century, the Japanese Shiraishi Kazuko (b. 1931) provides her friend on her birthday with a wonderful satire on the "Phallus" and its symbolic baggage, which begins "God exists" (Barnstone and Barnstone, *Book of Women Poets* 177-79). Such women, as we shall see, are Ana Rossetti's true precursors.

Other poets, akin to their twentieth-century Spanish sisters as we shall observe, have chosen to demystify God. The twentieth-century Swiss poet Claude Maillard has a "Christmas Mass for a Little Atheist Jesus," and the German Else Lasker-Schüller (1869-1945) "expresses . . . religious themes in an allegorical, often childlike manner." The Mexican Rosario Castellanos (1925-74) does not merely demystify the male deity in her "Three Poems," she totally undermines him (Barnstone and Barnstone, *Book of Women Poets* 228, 316, 269-70 respectively).

The undermining and subversion of gender stereotyping is found in the Chinese poet Wu Tsao (19th century), who describes lesbian passion (Barnstone and Barnstone, *Book of Women Poets* 151-53). In addition, the Americans Enda St. Vincent Millay and Dorothy Parker (1893-1967) fought against confining norms of conduct. The former "wrote not only about love but about lust, about woman's right to stalk and choose as well as adore and suffer" (Cora Kaplan, *Salt* 243). The latter bitterly and ironically critiqued the "society in which women are conditioned to find security in love rather than work" (Cora Kaplan, *Salt* 268) and her "Unfortunate Coincidence" (Cora Kaplan, *Salt* 269) is a delightful subversion of stereotypical love. In fact, Parker's vision and style bring Gloria Fuertes to mind.

The inscription of the female figure first occurs in the work of Enheduanna (born ca. 2300 B.C.). As she is the the earliest woman poet and her poems deal with a goddess-worshiping culture (Barnstone and Barnstone, *Book of Women Poets* 1–8), it may be argued that she inscribed what was subsequently obliterated and had to be reinscribed by her daughters-in-poetry. Anne Bradstreet concludes her poem "In Honour of That High and Mighty Princess Queen Elizabeth of Happy Memory" with this challenge: "Now say, have women worth? Or have they none?" (Cora Kaplan, *Salt* 34). Such reinscriptions of gynocentric myth are developed in the twentieth century: the Swiss poet Monique Laederach (b. 1938) published in 1970 a book of poems called *Penelope* (Barnstone and Barnstone, *Book of Women Poets* 227), using a myth the Spanish poet Francisca Aguirre revises in *Ithaca* (1972). Moreover, in "Lamentations," the American Louise Gluck (1943–) reappropriates the myth of creation (Barnstone and Barnstone, *Book of Women Poets* 558–60), but not on the scale of Carmen Conde in her 1947 *Mujer sin Edén* (Woman without Eden).[53]

In the above remarks I hope to have demonstrated several affinities in the gynocentric and gynocritical visions of poets from around the world, from Enheduanna to the present. It was not my intention to suggest that the women who will concern me in the following chapters were aware of these similarities, although I would be surprised if some of them were not. However, I did want to suggest a much broader context—a submerged tradition—for the poetic visions I now proceed to analyze.

Notes

1. Palau de Nemes has argued for considering Rosalía as an early Modern poet ("Visión" 337–39). I agree and will use the term "Modern"— following Juan Ramón Jiménez (*El modernismo*), Federico de Onís (*Antología*), Ricardo Gullón (*Direcciones*), Ivan Schulman ("Reflexiones"), and most recently Debicki (*Spanish Poetry*)—to designate an epoch in culture/literature extending from the 1870s to the Second World War. This is consonant with European and Anglo-American critical usage, but not necessarily with the restricted acceptation the term may have for some Hispanists, for whom "el modernismo" can mean fin-de-siècle literature.

2. Jardine, from whom I take this phrase, is discussing Kristeva's concept of "vréel."

3. In this respect, see Kaplan's "Varieties of Feminist Criticism" (esp. 39).

4. Parts 1 ("Toward a Feminist Poetics") and 6 ("Strength in Agony: Nineteenth-Century Poetry by Women") of Gilbert and Gubar's *Madwoman* are most relevant for the study of poetry.

5. See also Foster, who quotes Barbara Welter to explain a related image of feminine virtue: "The 'Cult of True Womanhood,' as the nineteenth-century ideal of femininity has been called, promoted the virtues of 'piety, purity, submissiveness and domesticity,' and made the home and the private-sphere woman's natural habitat" ("Neither Auction Block" 128).

6. Philomel was raped by her sister's husband the king, who had Philomel's tongue cut out in order to be certain of her silence. Philomel represents a woman's burden, the dark and sometimes secret truth she has to bear. She is mute and banished from power. If she is to pass her knowledge on to other women, she needs to develop ingenuity; if she is to overcome, she must circumvent the state of exile in which she is forced to live, and she must compensate for the mutilated condition in which she was left.

7. And, adds Juhasz, when they generalize, they write bad poems. Juhasz's dramatic if contentious polarity, between the passionate revelation of the particular self and its impersonal concealment, is a helpful reading tool, and her emphasis on a woman's private realm and on the interpersonality of female experience is shared by others. However, while her insight into self-revelation applies to some late twentieth-century women poets, it does not work for nineteenth-century women writers. For further critique of Juhasz, see Minogue (*Problems* 181–82, 184–87, 196–99).

8. Marks and Courtivron explain that "jouissance" combines "the verb *jouir* ('to enjoy, to experience sexual pleasure') and the substantive *jouissance* ('sexual pleasure, bliss, rapture')." According to them, "women's *jouissance* carries with it the notion of fluidity, diffusion, duration. It is a kind of potlatch in the world of orgasms, a giving, expending, dispensing of pleasure without concern about ends or closure. One can easily see how the same imagery could be used to describe women's writing" ("Introduction III" 36–37 n. 8).

9. See Domna Stanton's "Difference on Trial" (167, 170).

10. In "Literary Paternity," Sandra Gilbert interprets Mary Shelley's cave journey in *The Last Man* thus: "the cave is a female space . . . a space inhabited not by fettered prisoners (as the famous cave in Plato's *Republic* was) but by a free female hierophant, the lost Sibyl, a prophetess who inscribed her 'divine intuitions' on tender leaves and fragments of delicate bark" (495).

11. Nancy Chodorow's theories of mothering and Carol Gilligan's theories on woman's development are crucial to understanding this gender difference. The former's thesis is that the "feminine sense of self remains connected to others in the world" (*Reproduction* 169). The latter, in *In a Different Voice*, observes that "the qualities deemed necessary for adult-

hood—the capacity for autonomous thinking, clear decision-making, and responsible action—are those associated with masculinity and considered undesirable as attributes of the feminine self. The stereotypes suggest a splitting of love and work that relegates the expressive capacities to women while placing instrumental abilities in the masculine domain. Yet looked at from a different perspective, these stereotypes reflect a conception of adulthood that is itself out of balance, favoring the separateness of the individual self over the connection to others, and leaning more toward an autonomous life of work than toward the interdependence of love and care" (17). Gardiner's "Mind Mother" provides a lucid discussion of this psychological difference. Of Gilligan, she writes that "the ethic of responsibility, nurturance and interdependence . . . [is] quite unlike the male ethic of autonomous individual entitlement" (124). Sara Ruddick, another researcher in this area, Gardiner observes, "defines a cognitive style of 'maternal thinking'—holistic, open-ended, and field dependent—and a concomitant ethic of 'preservative love'" (124). She also notes that Erik Erikson described "girls as defending 'inner spaces' made of blocks, while boys buil[t] tall towers and knocke[d] them down again" (131). She adds that Dorothy Dinnerstein, Nancy Chodorow, and Adrienne Rich "imply that women are nicer than men," and that "empathy, responsibility and interdependence seem preferable to defensive aggression, destructive rage against women and nature, and a compulsion for control" (134–35).

12. In her research for "Autogynography," Domna Stanton observed the "binary opposition . . . that associated the female with personal and intimate concerns, the male with professional achievements." She questions that opposition as a "function of changing conventions" (11). She also notes that feminist critics "defined the personal . . . as primary emphasis on the relation of self to others" (12). She questions these dichotomies, and I agree with her salutary interrogation of them—even though I use them as a rhetorical *convention* in my analysis.

13. "Kristeva sees maternity as a conceptual challenge to phallogocentrism: gestation and nurturance break down the oppositions between self and other, subject and object, inside and outside" (Jones, "Inscribing Femininity" 86). Stanton writes that the "valorization of the maternal marks a decisive break with the existentialism of *The Second Sex*, wherein de Beauvoir rejected maternity as a solution to the problem of female transcendence (*le pour-soi*). By contrast, Cixous considers feminist denunciations of the patriarchal trap of maternity a perpetuation of the taboo of the pregnant woman, and a new form of repression, the denial of the 'passionate,' 'delicious' experiences of women's bodies" ("Difference" 160).

14. Although Gimbutas's rhetoric is challenged, she has no rival for the poetry of her descriptions. In her conclusion, Gimbutas writes that "the goddesses were mainly life creators, not Venuses or beauties, and most

definitely not wives of male gods" (*Language of the Goddess* 316). And to summarize the culture in which "Old Europeans" lived, she describes it as an "earth-centered, life-reverencing worldview" which Freud would have "denigrated" as "primitive fantasies" (321). She also observes: "The Goddess in all her manifestations was a symbol of the unity of all life in Nature. Her power was in water and stone, in tomb and cave, in animals and birds, snakes and fish, hills, trees, and flowers. Hence the holistic and mytho-poeic perception of the sacredness and mystery of all there is on Earth. . . . This culture took keen delight in the natural wonders of *this* world. Its people did not produce lethal weapons or build forts in inaccessible places, as their successors did. . . . Instead they built magnificent tomb-shrines and temples, comfortable houses in moderately-sized villages, and created superb pottery and sculptures." Gimbutas also stresses in conclusion that with the advent of Christianity, the "philosophical rejection of this world" was spread. "A prejudice against this worldliness developed and with it the rejection of the Goddess and all she stood for" (321).

15. The prominent lesbian poet of Spain is Andrea Luca. Her impact was not felt during the 1980s, which is the arbitrary but necessary closure for my present study.

16. In the same volume, Sydney Kaplan quotes Cheri Register, who has written: "If women's work is organized differently from men's, if the day is structured differently, if space is inhabited differently, if styles of verbal communication are different, then it follows that women will have a different sense of beauty and pleasure. Whether this shows up in literature depends on the extent to which women's literary forms are derived from a female culture, rather than determined by literary tradition and critical response" ("Varieties" 52; quoting Register, "Review Essay" 272).

17. These words, taken out of context, are Stanton's (in "Difference" 170), where she also explains that "the rigid hardness" or "the solid that the penis represents [for French feminists] is contrasted to an intrauterine, amniotically fluid sexuality" (169).

18. Cixous wants woman to speak the "marvelous text of her self"; she claims that "By writing her self, woman will return to the body which has been more than confiscated from her, which has been turned into the uncanny stranger on display. . . . To write . . . will give her back her goods, her pleasures, her organs, her immense bodily territories which have been kept under seal; it will tear her away from the superegoized structure in which she has always occupied the place reserved for the guilty (guilty of everything, guilty at every turn: for having desires, for not having any; for being frigid, for being 'too hot'; for not being both at once; for being too motherly, and not enough; for having children and for not having any; for nursing and for not nursing)" ("Laugh" 250).

19. The *muwassahas* had their origin in the Arabic and Hebrew cultures.

Arab tribes invaded the Iberian Peninsula in 711 and remained there until their expulsion—with the Jews—in 1492. Despite the fact that the Arabs conquered the Peninsula, in many areas they coexisted peacefully during these centuries with the Christian and Jewish inhabitants of the land. The *muwassahas* were composed by classical Arabic and Hebrew poets of Al-Andalus (the southern half of Spain) as early as the ninth century. They were written in Arabic and required for their closure that the final couplet, called a *jarcha*, be composed in the "vulgar" tongue (i.e., proto-Spanish). In his influential introduction to the anthology of traditional Spanish poetry, José Manuel Blecua notes that Menéndez Pidal described them as "songs sung by a young girl who is in love and who takes her mother into her confidence" (Introduction to Alonso and Blecua, *Antología* 44; quoting Menéndez Pidal, "Cantos románicos andalusíes" 230) In his definitive study, Samuel Stern considers that the *jarcha* is a song of lamentation. He writes that "the *karja* is represented . . . as a separate unit distinct from the poem itself" (*Hispano-Arabic* 35); that "the majority of *karjas* are . . . represented as spoken not by the poet himself but by someone else," and that "the commonest practice is to introduce as speakers love-lorn girls, who complain of the absence of their lovers (whether the plaint is about their lovers, as in erotic *muwassahas*, or whether the poet's patron is depicted as a lover)" (36); and that they are "usually written in vulgar Arabic or in Spanish" (56).

20. Barnstone's translation is much more suggestive: "I will make love / with you, / but only if you hold me / so my earrings / touch the jewelry / on my ankles" (*Book of Women Poets* 246). For the original, see García Gómez (*Jarchas romances* 426-27, no. 18). The poem alludes to a coital posture (Rubiera Mata, *Poesía femenina* 44 n. 1). García Gómez first documented that this refers to a "postura erótica" found in the classical *muwassaha* (148-49).

21. See also Barnstone, *Spanish* (53) and compare García Gómez (*Jarchas romances* 154-55, no. 10.5 ["Una vez que verla pude a solas"]).

22. *Cantigas de amigo* are "anonymous songs" of the early medieval age, which chroniclers began collecting in "Cancioneros" (song books) in the fifteenth century. It is not known if women authored these poems; however, there are the Galician-Portuguese "cantigas de amigo," which Angel and Kate Flores note are "plaintive and sad" as well as "suffused . . . with the delicate sensibilities of women abandoned, betrayed, and lonely" (*Defiant Muse* xv-xvi): "Malferida iba la garza / enamorada: / solo va y gritos daba. / Donde la garza hace su nido, / ribericas de aquel río, / solo va y gritos daba" (Badly wounded went / the love-sick heron: / alone it goes and shrieked aloud. Where the heron makes its nest, / on that river's tiny banks, / alone it goes and shrieked aloud [Alonso and Blecua, *Antología* 58]). From the perspective of the present study, the more intriguing "cantigas" are those in which a young girl protests that she is being forced to

be a nun: "No quiero ser monja, no, / que niña namoradica so. / Dejadme con mi placer, / con mi placer y alegría, / dejadme con mi porfía, / que niña malpenadica so" (I don't want to be a nun, no, / for a love-sick girl am I. / Leave me with my pleasure, / with my pleasure and my joy, / leave me with my tenacity, / for sadly awry am I [Alonso and Blecua, *Antología* 26]). *Romances anónimos* (anonymous ballads) "were part of the oral tradition of the Iberian Peninsular at least as early as the twelfth century" (Barnstone, *Spanish* 190). Menéndez Pidal (*Flor nueva* 10) states that the oldest known *romance* dates from the fourteenth century. These *romances*, which were not collected until the sixteenth century (1547 though 1600), are androcentric in the sense their main focus is to extol the feats of warriors and kings. It is not known if women wrote any of these ballads, nevertheless, within them women are given voice and their concerns and desires expressed. On a traditional level, the voice of a shepherdess courted by the king's son is heard in "Morenica me llama" (My name's Morenica [Barnstone, *Spanish* 191]). However, some ballads are less conservative: In "Fonte frida" (Cold fount [Alonso, *Poesía* 528–29]) a female voice ("la tortolica" [little turtle dove]) scornfully rejects the overtures of a treacherous and philandering male ("el ruiseñor" [nightingale]); this poem "dignifies widowhood and the negation of [female] pleasure" (Rubio, "A la busca," 70). The king of France's daughter, in "Romance de la hija del rey de Francia" (Alonso, *Poesía* 526) is so astute that she keeps a lecherous male at bay by advising him that she has leprosy and is therefore contagious. An even more astute woman is the protagonist of "La doncella guerrera" (The girl warrior [Barnstone, *Spanish* 196–97]), a ballad that describes how a girl disguises herself as a soldier and fights for her king. The comments of Flores and Flores on this ballad are most illuminating: "In medieval times . . . men were constantly at war. Taking up arms was considered noble, and war the highest good, the vindication of men's honor. It distinguished them from women, who were excluded from military pursuits and thus inescapably inferior. A man with daughters and no sons to send to battle felt disgraced. A popular ballad of this period, 'The Girl Warrior,' tells of a man with seven daughters, one of whom redeems his honor by donning battle gear and proving her valor on the battlefield. The poem is feminist in bespeaking the unfairness of women's exclusion from the 'honor' of military service when women were demonstrably as honorable as men" (*Defiant Muse* xiii–xiv). In hindsight, the poem itself may "bespeak feminism," but the "niña guerrera" in herself is not a feminist because she has been modeled on that abhorrent masculine paradigm of the Spanish code of honor. Few women are as self-determining as Blanca Flor, in "Marquillos" (Alonso, *Poesía* 524), who decapitates Marquillos for his treachery. Other ballads address the denial of sexual satisfaction to women. "La amiga de Bernal Francés" (Bernal Francés' woman friend [Alonso, *Poesía* 534–35]) voices the desires of a woman who wants to commit adultery. And in "Una gentil dama y un rústico pastor" (A gentle lady and a rustic shepherd [Alonso 527]), the lady offers herself to an unappreciative shepherd: "Vete con Dios, pastorcillo, / no te sabes entender, / hermosuras de mi cuerpo / yo te las hiciera ver: / delgadica en la cintura / blanca soy como el papel, / la color tengo mezclada / como rosa en el rosal, / el cuello tengo de garza, / los ojos de un esparver, / las teticas agudicas, / que el brial quieren romper; / pues lo tengo encubierto / maravilla es de lo ver" (Get on your way, wimp of a shepherd, / for you don't know what life's about, / the beauties of my body / I'd reveal to you: / slim in the waist, / I'm white as paper, / with a complexion as finely blended / as a rose on its bush, / I have the neck of a heron / and the eyes of a hawk, / my nipples so firm and pointed / that they want to burst out of my sari; / as I have it covered up, / it's a marvel to be seen). Hence, it can be shown that Spanish ballads and songs of the early medieval epoch — even though it is decreed that these poems were composed by men — gave voice to some of the desires and preoccupations of a female speaking subject.

23. *Serranillas* were written by male poets during the fourteenth and fifteenth centuries; they are ballads of short stanzas in which a male boasts of his serendipitous encounters with a "serrana": a beautiful, sometimes lascivious "shepherdess" or highland girl. In the main, these are poems of male wish fulfillment in which a woman's desire — alleged desire — is foregrounded. At the hand of the satirical Juan Ruiz, Arcipreste de Hita (1283?–1350?), a *serrana* herself takes the initiative and entices a noble traveler into her cottage to tumble ("luchar") with her ("Cántica de Serrana" [959; Barnstone, *Spanish* 123]).

24. In medieval courts there were numerous noble or upper-class women who were literate. Moreover, Pérez Priego offers a corpus of anonymous poetry whose speaker is a woman. These poems — like the female *jarchas* — complain about the absence of a lover, lament the lover's disappearance, express delight at meeting at dawn and sadness at parting as the cock crows. There are also texts spoken by an abused woman, by one who finds pleasure with her husband, by one whose marriage is a failure, and by a girl who refuses to become a nun (*Poesía femenina* 26–33, 95–132).

25. Snow's study of Pinar is a model of scholarship; of her poems, which he translates into idiomatic English and explicates in depth, he gives "three which are universally attributed to her" ("Spanish Love Poet" 322). Deyermond also attributes three poems to her; Pérez Priego, seven. Flores and Flores offer shrewd insights into her feminism (*Defiant Muse* xxiii–xxiv).

26. Carolina Coronado wrote a novel about Luisa Sigea (see Valis, "Introducción" 27–29).

27. See Janés, *Primeras poetisas*. Biruté Ciplijauskaité has informed me

that in the 1920s and 1930s, José Antonio Maravall was planning an anthology, and Jorge Guillén was preparing a list, of women poets of the sixteenth and seventeenth centuries, and that this project was more comprehensive that what Clara Janés offers. I discuss Sor Juana and Avellaneda later in this section.

28. For example, María de Zayas wrote: "If in childhood they gave [women] books and masters instead of lacemaking and embroidery, we would be just as well prepared as men for professorships and positions of state" (Flores and Flores, *Defiant Muse* xvii).

29. The Spanish verb "murmurar" means both to "murmur" and "murmur about"—to whisper and to slander.

30. See Valis, "Introducción" 24.

31. For a detailed critique, see Valis, "Introducción" 13–15. On the marginalized condition of the woman poet, see also "Cantad, hermosas" (Coronado, *Poesías* 506–11), and "La flor del agua"—"Tú, poetisa, flor del lago, / por amante, por cantora / has venido en mala hora / con tu amor y tu cantar: / que en el siglo extraño y vago, / a quien vida y arpa debes, / donde quiera que la lleves / puede el alma naufragar" (The water flower— You, poetess, flower of the lake, / with your love and singing, / you were born at a bad time / for loving and for singing: / for in this strange and vague century, / to which you owe your life and harp, / your soul can drown, / no matter where you lead it) (514–18).

32. For example, Coronado's flower poems (Kirkpatrick, *Románticas* 216–18), "El marido verdugo" (224), "Rosa bianca" (228), and "Cantos" where she expresses "the erotic passion forbidden to the middle-class nineteenth-century woman" (229).

33. Moreover in her "Villancico a Catarina" (Carol for Catarina), Sor Juana immortalizes a woman who shows herself to be wiser than men: "De una Mujer se convencen / todos los Sabios de Egipto, / para prueba de que el sexo / no es esencia en lo entendido. / ¡Víctor, víctor!" (A Woman convinces / all Egypt's Sages / with her proof that sex / is not of the essence where true knowledge is concerned. / Hurray! Hurrah!) (Flores and Flores, *Defiant Muse* 73).

34. For example, two of Avellaneda's symbols for the consecution of female desire are the moth that flies to the flames and the dry leaf blown by the wind. Her "jilguero" (finch) becomes the allegorical figure for the female lyrical subject: imprisoned and silenced (Kirkpatrick, *Románticas* 197) and "remaining in a position of captivity and exile to the feminine condition" (198).

35. See also Hsi-chün's (ca. 105 B.C.) "Lament," Ts'ai Yen's (162?–239?) "From 18 Verses Sung to a Tartar Whistle," and a traditional Amharic song from Ethiopia; for the brutality of a mother-in-law, see the *Haufi*—traditional women's songs of Algeria—where a speaker exclaims: "Be happy for

me, girls, / My mother-in-law is dead!" (Barnstone and Barnstone, *Book of Women Poets* 113, 118-20, 106, and 102 respectively).

36. See also Louise Bogan's "Evening in the Sanatorium" (Cora Kaplan, *Salt* 279).

37. See for example the contemporary American poet Ntozake Shange in *For Colored Girls Who Have Considered Suicide When the Rainbow Is Enuf* (Barnstone and Barnstone, *Book of Women Poets* 569-71).

38. For anger, see also the Japanese Ryojin Hisho (1179?) (Barnstone and Barnstone, *Book of Women Poets* 172). In "A Song for the Ragged Schools of London," Barrett Browning prefigures Angela Figuera's anger when she "curses" the fact that there are "Healthy children . . . Fierce and ravenous, staring . . . At the brown loaves of the baker" (Cora Kaplan, *Salt* 119).

39. For Christine de Pisan and Akhmatova see Barnstone and Barnstone, *Book of Women Poets* 203, 374, and 376.

40. On aging, see also the Japanese Lady Ise's "On Seeing the Field Being Singed" (Barnstone and Barnstone, *Book of Women Poets* 165), and "Thirty-Eight" by the English poet Charlotte Smith (1749-1806) (Cora Kaplan, *Salt* 82-83). Akhmatova's "Alone" (in which the old poet looks at her face in the mirror) and the Swedish Sonja Akesson's (1926-77) "Autobiography" also deal with aging (Barnstone and Barnstone, *Book of Women Poets* 384-85 and 362-66).

41. For the expression of traditional longing, see also the Japanese poets Empress Iwa no Hime (?-347), Princess Oku (661-701), and a Court Lady (?-671), as well as the Chinese Hsüeh T'ao (768-831), Yü Hsüan-chi (ca. 843-68), and Li Ch'ing-chao (1084?-ca. 1151) (Barnstone and Barnstone, *Book of Women Poets* 123-24, 129-30, and 138-39 respectively).

42. For desire, see also Sulpicia (1st century), Kshetrayya (17th century), and Mira Bai (1498-1573) (Barnstone and Barnstone, *Book of Women Poets* 57-59, 79-80, and 72-78 respectively).

43. For unfulfilled desire, see also the Chinese *Book of Songs* ("A Very Handsome Gentleman"); for the frustrations of rejection, see Sila (between 700 and 1050), who laments that her husband ("the same man / who first pierced me") has lost interest in her, and Louise Labé's Sonnets 8 and 19 (Barnstone and Barnstone, *Book of Women Poets* 110-11, 63, 209, and 214 respectively).

44. See also the anonymous Chinese courtesan (ca. 11th-12th centuries) (Barnstone and Barnstone, *Book of Women Poets* 142), and Aphra Behn, who expresses her desire in a manner that prefigures Angela Figuera's "Cañaveral" ("The Willing Mistriss" [Cora Kaplan, *Salt* 55]). For contemporary expression of desire, see the French poet Marguerite Burnat-Provins (1872-1952) and the American Anne Sexton's (1928-74) "That Day" (Barnstone and Barnstone, *Book of Women Poets* 218, 531-32).

45. In fact, Barrett Browning reveals such empathy in her denounce-

ment of slavery in "The Runaway Slave at Pilgrim's Point" (Cora Kaplan, *Salt* 108–14), as does the Canadian Anne Hébert (b. 1916) in "The Offended" (Barnstone and Barnstone, *Book of Women Poets* 233–34).

46. The hatred, or ambivalent feelings, that daughters have for their mothers—analogous to Sylvia Plath's "The Disquieting Muses"—is a twentieth-century phenomenon (but is not one I have noted in Spanish poetry). See "Mother" by the Japanese Nagase Kriyoko (b. 1906); "Mothers, Daughters" by the American Shirley Kaufman (b. 1923); "Child Beater" by the contemporary American poet Ai (b. 1947) (Barnstone and Barnstone, *Book of Women Poets* 175, 517–18, 532–33, 562–63 respectively).

47. See Bruck's "Birth," Domin's "Birthdays," and McPherson's "Pregnancy" (Barnstone and Barnstone, *Book of Women Poets* 311–12, 325–26, 556–57).

48. See also Amy Lowell's "The Sisters," which is a long meditation on her precursors—Sappho, Barrett Browning, Dickinson (Cora Kaplan, *Salt* 210–13).

49. See also "To Any M.F.H.," by the English poet Vita Sackville-West (1892–1962), where she writes "Sanctuary should exist on earth" (Cora Kaplan, *Salt* 259). Other poets poeticize the everyday. Marianne Moore (1887–1972), like Gloria Fuertes, builds "a poem around a prose quotation" (Cora Kaplan *Salt* 235), and Anne Hébert employs "Bread is born" as her metaphor for how a poem comes to life (Barnstone and Barnstone, *Book of Women Poets* 216.)

50. Several anonymous Chinese poets (ca. 206 B.C. to A.D. 220) and Yüeh-fu shih (1st century) also confronted male inconstancy (Barnstone and Barnstone, *Book of Women Poets* 115–17). See also the Japanese poet Ono no Komachi's (834–80) "Doesn't he realize," and, in classical Tamil, Kaccipettu Nannakaiyar (between the 1st and 3d centuries) (Barnstone and Barnstone, *Book of Women Poets* 161–62 and 65–66 respectively).

51. See Piercy's "Song of the Fucked Duck" and Swenson's "Women" (Barnstone and Barnstone, *Book of Women Poets* 541–43 and 507 respectively).

52. See also Sackville-West's "The Aquarium, San Francisco" (Cora Kaplan, *Salt* 263), and the Rumanian Veronica Porumbacu's (1921–77) "Like Gulliver" (Barnstone and Barnstone, *Book of Women Poets* 350).

53. See also Akhmatova's "Lot's Wife" (Barnstone and Barnstone, *Book of Women Poets* 373–74).

Part 1 : 1863–84

1

Rosalía de Castro

Unlike her sisters, Rosalía de Castro has established a secure reputation in Peninsular literature, but such was not the case during her lifetime (1837–85), when she fluctuated between being a "Nobody" (Emily Dickinson's word) and a "santiña" (dear little saint).[1] Few have noted her "monstrous" qualities, to use Gilbert and Gubar's metaphor for a committed woman artist whose subconscious mind is intent on self-determination; but it is the "monstrous" as opposed to "angelic" persona that interests today's students of poetry. Rosalía's "monster" persona can be glimpsed if her poems are read as texts that were generated by a writing subject who was also female. By foregrounding the monster within Rosalía, I believe that more of her poetic originality and influence on poets of this century can be appreciated.

With one or two notable exceptions, the major criticism of Rosalía's work focuses not on female or feminist impulses but on those characteristics her poems share with all poetry: themes, style, symbols, regionalism, personal angst, religious doubt.[2] These studies are empathetic and exhaustive in their careful treatment of the important characteristics of Rosalía's poems, but they focus on features that could be found in any Modern poet, most of whom are males — those very males who established the canonical standards by which poetry by women is traditionally judged. The fact that Rosalía was a woman, though not ignored,[3] is not foregrounded, a perspective that was altered in the early 1980s when Matilde Albert Robatto carefully studied the condition of woman during Rosalía's time as well as the view the poet presents in her prose and poetry of the Galician woman's predicament.[4] Then in 1986, several critics began to focus on Rosalía's female and feminist characteristics[5] and to unearth a feminized infrastructure to her poetry; that is, such studies began to allow postmodern readers to see that on one level Rosalía's work is a covert exploration of experiences that were central to her as a woman. A reader today can therefore make a legitimate attempt to find that on one level Rosalía's poetry was dealing "with central female experiences from a specifically female perspective."[6] Or, to follow Ostriker (*Stealing* 7) but to adapt her words: postmodern readers of Rosalía's poetry should begin to argue that an increasing proportion of her work is explicitly female in the sense that Rosalía chose to explore experiences central to her sex and to find a form and a style appropriate to the exploration of such experiences.

Rosalía de Castro published three principal books of poetry over a period of twenty years:[7] *Cantares gallegos* (Galician songs) appeared in 1863, in Galician; *Follas novas* (New leaves) in 1880, also in Galician; and *En las orillas del Sar* (On the banks of the Sar) in 1884, in Castilian.[8] In general, her first book is known for its regionalistic joie de vivre, while her second and third books are singled out for their resignation, sadness, and homesickness (*saudade*). Although I agree in general with this poetic trajectory,[9] I think it diminishes her work by making us see it through andromyopic eyes.[10] Hence, in the following remarks I shall focus on Rosalía's marginalization (i.e., "Nobody" status) and foreground her "monstrous"—as opposed to "angelic"—qualities. I study her anger and her negative vision of womanhood, as well as the gynocentric style and vision she selects to undermine patriarchal norms.

Rosalía's marginalization was threefold: political, social, and esthetic. Catherine Davies, the first to research Rosalía's marginalization, has demonstrated that Rosalía and her husband, Manuel de Murguía, as Galician regionalists, identified themselves with liberal and progressive policies which provoked the hostility of the conservative Castilian centralists. The latter's antiregionalist campaign of prolonged hostility, Davies says, "discouraged Rosalía during her lifetime and belittled the reputation of her work after her death in July 1885" ("Rosalía" 610). Davies documents the intense anti-Rosalía campaign initiated by the prestigious novelist Emilia Pardo Bazán.[11] In her fascinating study, Davies concludes: "it was by means of their savage attack on a pluralist society and an autonomous Galicia that Rosalía's enemies, the Church, the oligarchy, and their cultural cliques, managed to keep her out of the main current of Spanish literature for so long" ("Rosalía" 619).[12] This politically based marginalization lasted until around 1912, when, as Davies notes, both Unamuno and Azorín "wrote warmly of Rosalía"

(618).[13] Much later, in 1953, Juan Ramón Jiménez acknowledged Rosalía's originality in his lectures on Modernism.[14]

In addition to political marginalization, Rosalía, like all women artists of the nineteenth century, had to deal with pressures of a social —and psychological—nature that dissuaded her from being a writer. Some women writers of the time dealt with this by using their initials rather than their full names; others opted to publish under a male pseudonym.[15] Rosalía de Castro contemplated the latter, as a brief excursus on the extrinsic history of the *Cantares* (1863) will testify.

It was Manuel Murguía, if we are to believe him, who pressured his wife into completing the *Cantares* as well as into writing additional poems and a prologue required for their publication. For a while, Rosalía refused to oblige; she even went to the extreme of telling her husband that it would be better if the poems appeared under his own name.[16] It is quite possible to gloss over these *rapports de fait* as indications of Rosalía's modest nature. However, recent feminist criticism (Gilbert and Gubar, *Madwoman* 554–58) has clearly demonstrated that patriarchal culture conditioned the nineteenth-century woman artist to believe that she possessed neither the talent nor even the humanity to be a creative artist. The woman poet learned quickly that she was "Nobody" as far as "Poetry" with a capital "P" was concerned, and she acted accordingly.

Such an attitude is apparent in Rosalía's concluding poem to the *Cantares*,[17] where she apologizes for what she perceives as her lack of poetic finesse:

1   *Yo cantar, cantar, canté,*
    aunque mi gracia era poca,
    que nunca (y de ello me pesa)
    fui yo una niña graciosa.

5   Canté como mal sabía,
    con mil vueltas enredosas,
    como hacen los que no saben
    directamente una cosa.
    Pero después, con cuidado,
10 y un poco más alto ahora,
    fui soltando mis cantigas
    como a quien nada le importan.
    Mas en verdad bien quisiera,

que fuesen más melodiosas.
15 Yo bien quisiera que en ellas
bailasen sol y palomas,
con la luz las blandas aguas,
mansos aires con las rosas.
Que en ellas claras se viesen
20 espumas de verdes ondas,
del cielo blancas estrellas,
de tierra plantas hermosas,
nieblas de color sombrío
que las montañas arropan,
25 los gritos del triste búho,
y aún las campanas que doblan,
la primavera que ríe,
y las aves voladoras.
Canta que te canta, mientras
30 el corazón triste llora.
Esto y aún más, bien quisiera
decir con lengua graciosa:
mas donde gracia me falta
el sentimiento me sobra:
35 aunque éste tampoco basta
para explicar ciertas cosas;
por fuera a veces se canta,
mientras por dentro se llora.
No me expliqué cual quisiera
40 que soy de palabras corta;
si gracia al cantar no tengo,
el amor patrio me ahoga.
Yo cantar, cantar, canté,
aunque mi gracia era poca.
45 ¡Mas qué he de hacer, desdichada,
si no nací más graciosa!
        (*Cantares*, trans. Barja, 298, 300) [18]

(*As for me, I sing and sing, I sang, / even though I had little grace, / for I never was a graceful girl / (which distresses me). / I sang, poor singer that I am, / but with hundreds of intricate trills, / like those who've never known / a thing by heart. / But later, with care, / and now a little higher, / I chirped out my songs, / as if it were all the same to me. / But in truth, I wished / they'd been more melodious. / I really wanted the*

sun / to dance in them with the doves, / the light with the smooth
waters, / the gentle breezes with the roses. / I wanted in their clarity to
manifest / the green waves' spray / the sky's white stars, / the earth's
lovely plants, / the somber mists / that cover the mountains, / the sad
owl's cries, / and even the bells that toll, / the Spring that laughs, / and
the birds that fly. / You go on singing, while / your sad heart weeps. /
All this and more I really wanted / to express in gracious speech: / but
what I lack in grace, / I make up for in feeling: / but nor is that
enough / to explain certain things; / from the outside at times it seems
that one's singing, / when inside one's weeping. / I couldn't say what I
wanted to / because I'm poor with words; / if I'm graceless when I
sing, / it's because I choke on love for my native land. / *As for me, I sing
and sing, / I sang, even though I had little grace.* / But, woe is me, what
more could I do / if I wasn't born more graceful.)

This is a *romance* ("ballad") but unlike a traditional *romance* that
presents a coherent vision of an aspect of reality, this poem's vision is
bifurcated:[19] there is an imaginative response to the wonders of nature
(ll. 15-30) which is framed by the speaker's protestations of her inferior
talent (ll. 1-14, 31-46). Because of this dichotomy, the poem becomes
an intriguing text: is it its frame (lack of talent), or that which it frames
(nature)?

The text's frame is certainly an exercise in self-deprecation and, in
retrospect, a clear manifestation of the inferiority complex from which
Rosalía suffered at the beginning of her poetic career. Despite the fact
that she has just given her readers thirty-four original poems, the *Cantares gallegos*, in her concluding piece Rosalía chooses to apologize for
the lack of "gracia" (charm and wit [ll. 2, 33, 41, 44]) she perceives in
all those songs; she even attributes this to the fact that she herself has
never been a "graciosa" (charming woman [ll. 4, 32, 46]).[20] The words
"gracia" and "graciosa" signify "grace" or "charm," but also something
or someone "amusing," "witty," "entertaining."

Is Rosalía begging for her readers' indulgence? Is she saying: this
poem is written by a woman, therefore you should not expect linguistic
grace and mental wit (e.g., ll. 5, 6, 14, 40), and to compensate for my
gauche talents, I offer you my own honest and straightforward feelings
(l. 34)—which, of course, tradition allows women poets to display—
and my deep-felt love for the region of the country where I was born
(l. 42)?

It may well be that Rosalía is playing the modesty game. However,
she may also be protesting too much, thereby subconsciously offering

a critique of the lack of grace and wit to be found in poetry written by males at that time. Poullain notes that Murguía claimed that Rosalía published the *Cantares* in Galician because she was so disgusted by the poor use of the Galician language she found in the 1861 *Album de la caridad* (Charity album) (*Rosalía Castro* 51 and n. 67).[21] We can therefore assume that in part Rosalía was conscious of the superiority of her own talents.[22] Indeed, today's readers who carefully consider the four stanzas that constitute the body of "Yo cantar, cantar" (As for me, I sing and sing [ll. 15-30]) must disagree with the speaker of the poem and conclude that the poet displays both grace and intelligence in the way she represents that ideal world of natural beauty (which she also describes in similar terms but in prose in her prologue [*Obras* 1:67-71]). Rosalía's metaphors (ll. 16, 24) are audacious, her use of bird imagery (ll. 16, 25, 28) apposite, as is her exploitation of chiaroscuro (ll. 17, 21, 23), sound symbolism (ll. 25-26), synaesthesia (ll. 17-18), and the elements (earth, air, water). She writes what we are accustomed to think of as a "modern" poem.

Hence, for today's readers this poem (and all the *Cantares*) is more than just a paean to Galicia from one who was overwhelmed by an intense love for her native region ("amor patrio" [l. 42]). Its double vision can be read on another level as a schizophrenic response to an androcentric culture. It is a text that manifests a psychological split between a voice that claims that it has little talent and a poet who demonstrates no few poetic gifts. This double-voiced text is Rosalía's response to the patriarchal culture of her time, her way of coping with the restrictions placed on women poets in the nineteenth century, when women were conditioned to believe that it was unnatural for them to be poets. What better way of demonstrating real talent than by framing a nature poem with a reflection on one's limitations as a woman poet, by turning one's reputed physical and linguistic drawbacks into an intriguing verbal artifact?

I have been arguing that Rosalía was marginalized as a poet by both the political and social prejudices that prevailed in the latter part of the nineteenth century. There is also a third factor in Rosalía de Castro's marginalization: an esthetic self-marginalization, which derived from the fact that as a fledgling poet she tried to imitate a male model to whom she compared her own talents unfavorably.

In her prologue to the *Cantares*, Rosalía affirms that the inspiration for her poems came from *El libro de los cantares* (The book of songs) by the Galician writer don Antonio de Trueba y de la Quintana

(1819-89). Trueba's was a very popular collection of fifty-four poems (*romances* [ballads] and *coplas* [folksongs]) which first appeared in 1851. As Kulp-Hill observes in her remarks on Rosalía's debt to and striking difference from Trueba, *El libro de los cantares* "had eight editions in twenty years" (*Manner and Mood* 34-35) In addition, Poullain (*Rosalía Castro* 56) reminds us that, in his prologue to Ferrán's *La soledad* (Solitude), Bécquer himself praised Trueba highly as a model for "intimist" poetry. However, Varela (*Poesía* 152) sums up the reaction of today's readers to *El libro de los cantares* when he asserts that in comparison to Rosalía, Trueba's verse appears "pale, insipid, trite" ("pálido, soso, simplón"). More recently, Feal Deibe ("Sobre el feminismo" 313 and n. 13) found little human value in Trueba's poems. Indeed, today these fifty-four poems will strike a reader as commonplace, sentimental, jingoistic. They now read as a well-versified collection of facile tales, ridden with clichés and superficial thoughts. Let me justify these assertions and, by implication, suggest the originality and talent of Rosalía de Castro.

Trueba is both traditional and conservative in his religious views and his political outlook. He presents the perfect mother as one who indoctrinates her children in the religion of the country (no. 10). He praises the queen (Isabel II) not only because she is good but also because she is a woman and a mother (no. 1); he lauds the birth of the princess (no. 32); he glorifies the history of the motherland (no. 27), and he intones the greatness of Spain's newly formed Civil Guard:

1 Un grito de regocijo
 resonó en mi dulce patria
 y á la voz de Isabel, fué
 la Guardia civil creada,
5 y al verla el pueblo español
 cantó lleno de esperanza:
 —*¡Viva la Guardia civil*
 porque es la gloria de España!
     (*Libro* 226)

(A cry of joy / rang out in my dear homeland / for the Civil Guard, created / by [Queen] Isabel's voice, / and when they beheld it, the Spanish people / sang out with hope: / *Long live the Civil Guard / for it's the glory of Spain!*)

Likewise, Trueba's vision of womankind is conservative and traditional: a blend of simplistic stereotypes and patriarchal attitudes. In his prologue he refers to "blue-eyed virgins who hold pride of place in my nugatory portraits" ("las vírgenes de ojos azules que ocupan el primer término en mis desaliñados cuadros" [x]), and then asks: "but where is there more purity and feeling than in children and mothers?" ("pero ¿dónde hay mas [sic] pureza y sentimiento que en los niños y las madres?" [xii]). In his *cantares*, we find such descriptions as these: "To my eyes, woman / is a weak plant / threatened / by eternal hurricanes, / and hence I endeavour / to be her valiant aide / in this world" ("La mujer á mis ojos / es débil planta / de eternos huracanes / amenazada, / y así procuro / su generoso apoyo / ser en el mundo" [no. 10, 38]); or, "girls are flowers / whom even the wind can depetal" ("las niñas son flores / que hasta las deshoja el viento" [no. 16, 51)]. A later poem, "The Glories of Womanhood" ("Glorias de la mujer" [no. 41]), has a refrain—"I say that you have neither the soul / nor the heart of a woman" ("digo que no tienes alma / ni corazón de mujer")—which may well have impressed Rosalía.[23] "Glorias de la mujer" represents the state of motherhood as one of sublime delight and one to which every girl should aspire.[24] In addition to a patriarchal attitude toward the woman, Trueba's poems pretend that a woman's fulfillment consists in finding a loving man (no. 35), and they consistently present women from the male point of view as objects for sensual pleasure (nos. 5, 6, 7, 11, 13, 46):

1   ¡Salada, qué hermosa eres!
      ¡Salada, por ti me muero!
      Tienes una cinturita
      que se abarca con dos dedos,
5   tu mano y tu pié parecen
      de una niña en lo pequeños.
                    (*Libro* 151)

(Darling, how cute you are! / Darling, I die for you! / Your waist's so slender / it's just a few inches wide; / so tiny are your hands and feet, / they look like a child's.)

And finally, if women speak in these poems, it is because they have been seduced (no. 2) or because they are mad (no. 28).

As Trueba expresses so many platitudinous views, it is difficult today to understand why Rosalía thought him so fine a poet.[25] Nevertheless, in the prologue she wrote for the *Cantares*, she lauds the sophistication of "don Antonio," "Antón, el de los *Cantares*," while introducing herself as "a person of poor talent" ("un pobre ingenio" [trans. Barja 14]), "with little ability, and schooled in no other place than our poor villages" ("débil de fuerzas, y no habiendo aprendido en otra escuela que la de nuestros pobres aldeanos" [trans. Barja 16]):

Mis fuerzas en verdad quedaron muy por debajo de lo que alcanzaran mis deseos, y por eso, comprendiendo cuánto podría hacer en esto un gran poeta, aún más me dolió mi propia insuficiencia. *El libro de los cantares,* de D. Antonio Trueba, que me inspirara y me diera aliento para llevar a cabo este trabajo, pasa por mi mente como un remordimiento, y casi asoman las lágrimas a mis ojos al pensar cómo se levantaría Galicia hasta el lugar que le corresponde si un poeta como Antón el de los *"Cantares"* fuese el destinado a dar a conocer sus bellezas y sus costumbres. Mas mi patria infeliz, tan desventurada en esto como en lo demás, tiene que contentarse con unas páginas frías e insulsas, que apenas serían dignas de acercarse de lejos a las puertas del Parnaso si no fuera por el noble sentimiento que las creó. ¡Que esto mismo me sirva de disculpa ante quienes justamente critiquen mis faltas, pues pienso que el que se esfuerza por desvanecer los errores que manchan y ofenden injustamente a su patria es acreedor de alguna indulgencia![26]

(My talent was not up to my desire, and hence, realizing just how much a great poet could achieve, I was all the more pained by my own inadequacy. *The Book of Songs,* of don Antonio Trueba, which had inspired me and given me the courage to carry out this work, passes through my mind like a regret, and tears almost come to my eyes when I think how Galicia would be elevated to its due place if a poet like Antón, he of the *Songs,* had been the one destined to make known her beauties and her customs. But my unfortunate native land, as luckless in this as in all else, must be satisfied with a few dull, cold pages that would be most unworthy of approaching the gates of Parnassus from afar, if it were not for the noble feeling that created them. May this itself excuse me before those who justly criticize my faults, for I think that he who struggles to dispel the fallacies that unjustly stain and offend his native land is entitled to some indulgence!)

In her first book of poems, Rosalía sees herself as singing of the beauty and the customs of Galicia, and she feels inferior to the task. Why, when in comparison her poetry is far superior to Trueba's? I suggest that one of the reasons Rosalía fixates on the alleged paucity of her own talent is that she sets out to imitate a model for poetry supplied to her by a man; she sees herself as trying to do what a man has already done (i.e., versify the beauty and customs of a particular region). Rosalía even claims that she made every effort to "make known how some of our poetic customs still retain some primitive and *patriarchal* freshness" ("dar a conocer cómo algunas de nuestras poéticas costumbres todavía conservan cierta frescura *patriarcal* y primitiva" [*Cantares*, trans. Barja 16, italics mine]).

In imitating a male model, Rosalía is trying to succeed at doing what males do, which is to "tell male stories about a male world" (Gilbert and Gubar, *Madwoman* 67). Rosalía is suffering from an "anxiety of authority," which means that she is attempting to imitate a patriarchal literary model, one invented and historically developed by men; the more she employs that model, the more anxious she feels about her lack of talent, the more "diseased and infected by the sentences of patriarchy" she becomes (Gilbert and Gubar, *Madwoman* 71).

Rosalía de Castro's marginalization is therefore a complex web of social, political, and esthetic factors. Some of these—the social and political—she would have been conscious of, while others (psychological and esthetic) she could combat only subconsciously given her time and place.[27] This subconscious combat constitutes her "monstrous" side and gives her work its feminist infrastructure.

I turn now to the poems themselves, to argue that in many texts Rosalía struggles with the "monster" within, with a woman's experiences from a feminist and female perspective—something traditional criticism has ignored. In her *Cantares*, Rosalía is subconsciously subverting the patriarchal order and covertly undermining the androcentric worldview. This struggle is manifested in the fact that she foregrounds numerous and diverse female personae, and that she herself is engaged in a search for her own matrilineal roots. In doing this, she finds her own voice, one that can express her experience—an experience conditioned by the fact that she is a woman.

Is it not monstrous—beyond the bounds of expectation of that time —that the speaker of most of Rosalía's *Cantares* is a woman, and that the dominant experience treated in this book is female, not male? Just how remarkable this is becomes apparent when one notes that fifty-two of the fifty-five poems in Trueba's *El libro de los cantares* are spoken by males and deal with a man's experience from a male perspective.[28] In most of Rosalía's poems, by contrast, the speaker is a woman and most of her *Cantares* do not just deal with a woman's experience but also treat it from a woman's perspective.[29] Stevens, the first to investigate this feature of Rosalía's poetry,[30] concludes her study with the following assertion: "If I were to name one source with which Castro had the most intimate contact and the least ambivalence, it would be the women of rural Galicia whose lives and voices came closer than any others to expressing Castro's own predicament. Although Castro undoubtedly learned about women's emancipation from literate Spanish and European sources, the peasant women of Galicia provided her with the invaluable proof of women's artistic and spiritual achievement against all odds" (*Rosalía* 122).

In the *Cantares* there are women who sing (nos. 1, 32) and women who sin (nos. 3, 12); there are independent women (no. 4), rebellious women (no. 7), unfaithful (no. 10) and faithful women (nos. 26, 30); there are old women who dialogue with young women (nos. 3, 5); simple peasant women (no. 31) and mountain women (no. 18); there are ethereal women (no. 14),[31] seductive women (no. 24), and seduced women (nos. 2, 13, 30); there are love-struck and confused women (nos. 9, 27) and lovelorn and angry women (nos. 13, 28); there are religious women (nos. 11, 33, 37) and superstitious women (no. 16); there are snooty (Castilian) women (no. 23); silly, loquacious women (nos. 13, 27, 29); there are women who suffer from infertility (no. 20) and those who suffer from a profound longing for their native region ("saudade," nos. 17, 18, 19). All of these poems present an image of woman that is diverse, complex, and fascinating—especially in contrast with Trueba's.

But the *Cantares* do not just "present" an image of woman, female personae present themselves by articulating their desires, disappointments, and predicaments; they exchange advice and reveal the untextualized community women have always had; they criticize hypocritical women (no. 21) and the male world. For example, the female speaker of "Un arrogante gaitero" ("An Arrogant Bagpiper" [no. 8]) takes a critical look at the arrogant bagpiper and at the stupid girls he seduces in every village:

1   Ellas loquinas, bailaban,
     y a donde estaba corrían,
     ciegas..., ciegas, no veían
     las zarzas que las cercaban;
5   cual mariposas, buscaban
     a luz para irse a quemar,
       (trans. Barja 86, *Obras* 1:109)

(Silly girls, they'd dance, / and run to where he was, / blind. . . , blind, and not see / the brambles that encircled them; / like moths, they'd search out / the light to burn themselves up.)

In this poem, a woman finds fault with women. In others, a woman displays her strength of character, as for example in the poem that begins:

—Cantan los gallos al día,
yérguete, mi bien, y parte.
—¿Cómo partir, queridiña,
como partir y dejarte?
(trans. Barja 48, *Obras* 1:88)

(—The cocks are crowing in the day, / rise up, my darling, and take
your leave. /—How can I take my leave, beloved, / how can I depart
and leave you?)

This poem—like the *alboradas* ("dawn songs")—is a dialogue between
young lovers who have spent the night together and must part at day-
break. This is a frequent topos in all types of literature, but with Rosalía there is a twist. Carballo Calero notes: "Unlike what happens in the
famous scene in Shakespeare's *Romeo and Juliet*, Rosalía, like the song
she glosses, presents the man as loathe to leave" ("A diferencia de lo que
ocurre en la famosa escena de *Romeo y Julieta*, de Shakespeare, Rosalía,
como el cantar que glosa, hace al hombre representante de la actitud de
resistencia a la separación" [Castro, *Cantares*, ed. Carballo Calero 56
n. 2]). Unlike Carballo Calero, who focuses his comment on the male's
resistance in this poem, I would say that, consciously or not, Rosalía
presents a girl who takes the initiative, who pushes the boy out of bed
and makes him leave. Rosalía subconsciously undermines—or fails to
subscribe to—the androcentric worldview of traditional literature, in
which the boy (male) is resolute, decisive, quick to leave after taking his
pleasure, while the girl (female) is weak, resists his leaving, and clings
desperately to the boy.

Traditional criticism has not foregrounded the predominance of
female speakers and of a woman's experience as distinctive features of
the *Cantares*. It has not done so, I suggest, because (following Rosalía
herself) it sees the book as a depiction of Galician life. However, it is
evident that, while imitating poems about men, Rosalía in fact writes
poems about women. In subconsciously working through her "anxiety
of authority," Rosalía finds her own voice, and this leads her to deal
"with central female experiences from a specifically female perspective" (Gilbert and Gubar, *Madwoman* 72).

Cantares also reveals that the poet is involved in a quest for her
matrilineal heritage. Gilbert and Gubar interpret nineteenth-century
women's interest in idyllic settings as a "pained yearning for a lost, visionary continent," which in turn signifies "their yearnings for motherly
or sisterly precursors" (*Madwoman* 100). As the poem "Yo cantar, can-

tar" (As for me, I sing and sing) frames an idyllic, natural setting with expressions of female inadequacy, I want to pursue this line of investigation in another (but earlier) poem from *Cantares.* "Cómo llovía, suaviño" (How gently it rained) is an unusually long discursive poem in which Rosalía's struggle to find a style and an original voice is manifested. The poem begins:

> Cómo llovía, suaviño,
> cómo, suaviño, llovía;
> cómo llovía, suaviño
> día y noche por Laíño,
> por Lestrove, noche y día.
> (trans. Barja 270, *Obras* 1:215)[32]

> (How it rained, so gently, / how, ever so gently, it rained; / how it rained, so gently, / day and night on Laíño, / on Lestrove, night and day.)

In this poem, Rosalía musically descends into the depths of her own mind where she follows her thoughts poetically:[33] she muses on the regenerative effects of the rain on the earth, meditates on her recently deceased mother (d. 1862), and reflects on the decaying condition of the mansion and estate ("Casa grande") where she and her mother grew up.[34] This extremely long poem ostensibly deals with Galicia: how the fine rain refreshes the countryside, the sailboats hearten the rivers, and how the old estates lie fallow (because these days there are no decent men ["venerable cabaleiro"] to care for them and for the poor who depended on them for survival).

However, and more importantly, Rosalía's thoughts lead her back in every instance to her mother—to what Sandra Gilbert called "the powerful womb of the matriarchal muse" ("Literary Paternity" 494)— so that the poem evolves into a meditative communion with a kindred female spirit who has been lost and whom the speaker tries to recuperate. The poem's first nine stanzas describe the rain from its first appearance until it dissolves into vapor, and the tenth stanza shifts gears thus:

> 1   Así imagino a la triste
>   sombra de mi madre, errando
>   en la esfera donde existe;
>   que a ir al cielo se resiste,
> 5   por los que quiso aguardando.
>   (trans. Barja 272, *Obras* 1:216)

(That's how I imagine / my mother's sad shade, as she wanders / in the sphere where she exists, / reluctant to go to heaven, / while she waits for those she loved.)

As she thinks of her mother's spirit, Rosalía is led to recall their shared experiences of tender and affectionate memories—"ternuras," "memorias cariñosas"—one of which are the songs "cantigas" her mother sang—those very "cantares" she alluded to in the apologetic concluding poem of her *Cantares*.[35] Later she recalls the ringing of the bells and writes:

Aquéllas, sí, que animadas
me llamaban mansamente
en las mañanas dcradas,
con las cantigas amadas
de mi madre, juntamente.
(trans. Barja 278, *Obras* 1:219)

(Yes, those merry bells, / they softly called me / together with my mother's dear songs, / on golden morns.)

In this free association of childhood memories, Rosalía subconsciously connects the "cantares" she is now writing with her mother's "cantigas"—a step she did not take in the final poem of her *Cantares*.[36] She is dreaming "of an archaic language that predates the patronymics of culture . . . gaining strength through fantasies of either an original or an originary linguistic matrilineage, a 'grandmatology' that [is] implicitly set against the patrilineal linguistics of the grammatology that has historically subordinated [women] and their ancestresses" (Gilbert and Gubar, "Ceremonies" 25).

Moreover, as she searches through the past to give meaning to the present, the woman poet in Rosalía settles on a strong precursor, her mother (who loved the "cantigas" she learned as a child). The poem then moves on to meditate on the huge, abandoned house ("casa grande") where her mother was born. However, the text evolves in such an ambiguous way as to imply that the abandoned house is also her mother ("amazona malherida" [badly wounded amazon]),[37] abandoned by Rosalía's father, and maybe even the speaker herself, "abandoned" by her mother who had just died. Hence, although this poem ostensibly treats the parlous state of Galicia, on a very different level it constitutes—as Adrienne Rich might say—a dive into the wreck of the self, from which the woman poet emerges clinging to central bits and pieces of submerged and lost experience.

Ostriker describes such a process when she offers a version of the Demeter/Kore myth as a model for the way women poets cease to be "Nobody" and become "Somebody"—they "retrieve and revive" their mutilated mother. She writes: "Rather than Oedipus and Laius at the crossroads, the model among women writers, critics as well as poets, is Demeter and Kore: except that it is the daughter who descends to Hades, step by step, to retrieve and revive a mother who has been raped, or perhaps seduced, by a powerful male god. For as the mother returns to earth, the daughter expects to blossom" (*Stealing* 16). Ostriker's focus on identity through recuperation and connectedness illuminates what Rosalía achieved in her *Cantares:* her own mother had been seduced by a powerful male (a priest) and had been ostracized by society because of the shame. By incorporating her mother's memory into literature, by textualizing a small piece of the untextualized culture women have always had (e.g., "cantigas"), Rosalía the daughter "blossoms": she retrieves and revives the mother, returns her to earth, and she makes society subsequently see her worth.

Also, Ostriker's focus on identity through recuperation and connectedness suggests that Rosalía subconsciously connected submerged pieces of her female experience, bits and pieces that are dispersed, that have hardly yet found their way into the written culture of (male) hegemonic texts. In this poem, Rosalía enters the "cave of the mind"; she begins to connect the scattered fragments—"revitalize the darkness, retrieve what has been lost, regenerate, reconceive, give birth" (Gilbert and Gubar, *Madwoman* 99), as demonstrated in "Yo cantar, cantar, canté" and "Cómo llovía suaviño."

Despite my rhetorical claims, *Cantares* is not the work of an acknowledged feminist but of a woman who sees herself as conforming to—if constrained by—cultural norms. However, the contradictions in its poetic vision manifest the writer's unconscious thoughts and hint at a feminist infrastructure that underlies the entire work. This feminist vision constitutes one of the woofs or warps of the *Cantares*—one of the subtexts or codes that constitute its total discourse. If such a subtext is read today with the benefit of the novel insights of gynopoetics, Rosalía's latent feminism can be glimpsed.

Cantares, I argue, manifests a split vision: a poet who thinks negatively of her talent writes original poems that reconnect her with her matrilineal roots. A comparable polarity between negative vision and positive achievement characterizes Rosalía's subsequent work, *Follas novas* (1880) and *En las orillas del Sar* (1884), which offer a host of material for a feminist rereading of her work. In these books of poetry, Rosalía is criticizing the condition of nineteenth-century womanhood by presenting us—at times angrily—with negative views on womanhood, marriage, motherhood, and on the condition of the female poet. However, she also rebels creatively against these conditions by initiating an inscription of a strong female self; by selecting gynocentric imagery and metaphors to develop a female vision and subvert androcratic norms.

The poems of *Follas* and *Orillas del Sar* reveal how women are abused by a patriarchal culture.[38] The poet foregrounds negative perspectives on the roles phallocracy assigns a woman. Such negative imagery is inspired by a frustrated and suppressed feminist impulse; for today's readers it manifests the latent feminist infrastructure of these texts. Hence, Rosalía's mature work displays a subconscious desire to demystify the *ángel del hogar* condition which nineteenth-century culture represented as a woman's predilection.

One of the dominant metaphors for the condition of woman in *Follas* is abandonment. Women are abandoned by their husbands and their sons—through betrayal, drowning, emigration, disappearance, death. As Rosalía puts it, women are "viudas de vivos y muertos / que nadie consolará" (widows of living men / widows of dead men whom no one will console [trans. Barja 278]).[39] Traditional criticism would silence the feminist voice of these poems by shifting the focus of interpretation to the effects of emigration on Galicia. However, both the sociopolitical and the feminist voices should be heard.

A particularly poignant description of this abandonment is given by a woman whose husband has been lost:

1   Sola he tejido mi tela
     sola sembré mi nabal,
     sola voy por leña al monte,
     sola la quemo en el lar.
5   Ni en la fuente ni en el prado,
     aunque me mate el afán,
     él no vendrá a levantarme,
     él ya no me tumbará.
       (trans. Barja 292, *Obras* 1:488)

(Alone I've woven my cloth, / alone I'll plant my swede patch, / alone I
fetch firewood from the mount, / alone I burn it in the hearth. /
Neither at the fount nor in the meadow, / though I die of desire, / will
he come to raise me up, / no more will he come to lay me down.)

The emotional and physical yearning expressed by the female speaker
in the last lines above (ll. 5-8) give the poem an underlying feminist
perspective, for the simple reason that society—especially of the last
century and in Spain—traditionally forbids the widow from ever ful-
filling such deep desires for human closeness. ("Tumbar" is a colloqui-
alism for "to copulate.")

The speaker of the above poem has been abandoned only in so far
as her husband has died. However, there are several poems in which
women curse the frustrated lives they are forced to lead because the
men to whom they sacrificed themselves disappeared and left them for
others. Rosalía refers to the abuse women take for remaining faithful to men who have long abandoned them for others.[40] She refers to
women who remain enthralled by men who have long since lost interest in them.[41] Moreover, one female speaker implies that her deceitful
treatment was comparable to the sale of a piece of meat in the market
("¡Como venden la carne en el mercado / a ti su falsedad!" [trans. Barja
296, *Obras* 1:491])—which leads her to blame herself: "—¡Malhaya tu
constancia, pobre loca, / malhaya tu lealtad!" (damn your loyalty, poor
madwoman, / and damn your fidelity too [trans. Barja 296]). It should
come as no surprise that as a result of such abandonment and betrayal,
women in *Follas* think frequently about suicide and attempt it, especially by drowning.[42]

However, as she develops as a poet, Rosalía's style becomes more and
more allusive and suggestive, less dramatic and politically direct, and
hence the negative perspective on womankind is figuratively inscribed
—rather than overtly foregrounded—by means of subtly understated
symbols.[43] For example, "marchitas hojas" (withered leaves) come to
symbolize a woman's loss of innocence, her victimization by the flood-
waters of life, "el río desbordóse / arrastrando en sus aguas a las víctimas" (the river burst its banks / and dragged its victims in its flood-
waters [*Obras* 1:582]). In "Los tristes, IV" (The sad ones), rape is
implied meiotically:

Cuando en la planta con afán cuidada
la fresca yema de un capullo asoma,

lentamente arrastrándose entre el césped,
la asalta el caracol y la devora.
(Obras 1:589)[44]

(When the fresh shoot from a bud appears / on the fervently cared-for
plant, / the snail, dragging itself through the grass, / attacks and
devours it.)

The delicacy and innocence of "la fresca yema de un capullo" (l. 2) is
comparable to the "Cerrado capullo de pálidas tintas" (closed bud of
pale hues [Obras 1:623]), a poem that concludes by symbolizing a girl's
loss of her virginity. In addition, the Blakean "Viéndome perseguido
por la alondra" (Seeing myself pursued by the lark), in which a small insect with golden wings ("diminuto insecto de alas de oro") takes refuge
inside the calyx of a rose ("refugio hallé en el cáliz de una rosa") only
to be caught in a gale, concludes:

Y rodamos los dos en fango envueltos,
para ya nunca levantarse ella,
y yo para llorar eternamente
mi amor primero y mi ilusión postrera.
(Obras 1:691)

(And both of us rolled around covered in mud, / she never to rise
again, / and I to weep eternally / for my first love and my last dream.)

The rose that never rose again (l. 2) signifies a woman's loss of self
to that "diminutive insect" that is male—a palimpsestic subversion of
phallic drive. Moreover, women and children are symbolized as "tórto-
las" (turtledoves) and "palomas" (doves), whereas men and mankind are
predatory foxes, kites, eagles—"zorro, milano, águila"—or unsociable
tawny owls or frogs ("cárabo, rana").[45]

Another feature of Follas and Orillas del Sar is that they present a
negative perspective on marriage. Love, romance, marriage, all end
under the shadow of disillusionment and deceit, "la sombra de aquel
negro / desengaño sin cura" in the following poem:

Llévame a aquella fuente cristalina
  donde juntos bebiéramos
las purísimas aguas que apagaban
la sed de amor, la llama del deseo.
Llévame de la mano como antaño...
  Mas no, que tengo miedo

de ver en sus cristales
la sombra de aquel negro
desengaño sin cura, inconsolable,
que entre ambos puso el tiempo.
(trans. Barja 78, Obras 1:329)

(Take me to that limpid spring / where together we could drink / the
purest waters, those that slaked / love's thirst, desire's flame. / Take me
by the hand as of old... / But no, for I'm afraid / to find reflected
there / the shadow of that / inconsolable and incurable, black
disillusion, / which time cast between the two of us.)

Clearly, the female speaker is lamenting the utter frustration of her life,
a life she cannot change because, as another poem states, "matrimonio
dogal es" (marriage is a halter [trans. Barja 198; *Obras* 1:423]); by implication, the woman who succumbs to it must be an ass. In addition, a
female speaker condemns marriage utterly: after dying, she chooses to
wander the earth as a haunted spirit rather than run the risk of settling
where her dead husband might be (in Heaven or Hell).[46]

A third feature of *Follas* and *Orillas del Sar* is that they present
motherhood in an unflattering light. It keeps a woman chained to her
house,[47] and it keeps a mother in bondage to her young and to a life
of travail, as the following subtle poem implies in the symbol of the
"paloma":

SIN NIDO

1   Por montes y campiñas,
caminos y esplanadas,
va una paloma sola,
sola de rama en rama.

5   Aún las crías la siguen,
sedientas y cansadas,
sin que encuentre alimento
para darles, ¡cuitada!
Trae manchadas las plumas,

10   que un tiempo fueron blancas,
marchitas y rastreras
y abatidas las alas.
¡Pobre paloma, antaño
tan querida y tan blanca!

15   ¿Dónde se fue tu brillo?
      Tu amor, ¿por dónde anda?
      (trans. Barja 136, *Obras* 1:379)

("Without a Nest": Through woodland and open fields, / along roads
and esplanades, / a [female] dove alone, / hops alone from branch to
branch. / Her tired and thirsty young / still follow her, / even though
she finds no food / to give them, poor wretch! / Her feathers, / which
once were white, / are stained; / faded and trailing / and fallen, her
wings. / Poor dove, / so beloved and white of yore! / What happened
to your brilliant glow? / And your love, where's he strutting now?)

The harried state of the "paloma" (ll. 5-8) is indicative of motherhood.
Those once white feathers, now bloodied and beaten (ll. 9-12, 14-15),
are a metaphor for the woman's condition; the violence of the image indicates Rosalía's feminist impulse. If the gory detail and the violence of
the imagery are not taken into account, this poem might well be taken
as a cameo for a pathetic and fortuitous event in nature.

The "faded and trailing and fallen wings" of the above poem (l. 12)
might allude to the damaging effect of marriage and motherhood on a
woman poet's inspiration. Whether this is so or not, in her mature work
Rosalía presents the condition of the woman artist as inferior and besieged. In several poems of *Follas*, the speaker presents herself as hunted
and marginalized, and even implies that any woman who attempts self-
realization is doomed to failure.[48] The woman artist is withdrawn from
the world, she views life from her hiding hole ("yo en mi escondrijo"),
or from the inside of a deep wood.[49] In Gilbert and Gubar's terms,
Rosalía is seated at her attic window watching the world in which she
cannot participate:

Desde aquí veo un camino
que no sé dónde va;

· · · · · ·

quisiera poderte andar.

· · · · · · ·

Mas tú vas yendo, vas yendo,

· · · · · · · · ·

yo sigo clavada en donde
arraigo tiene mi mal.
(trans. Barja 310, *Obras* 1:506)

(From here I see a road / that goes I know not where / . . . / I would like to walk you / . . . / But you keep going, keep going, / . . . / Me, I am stuck to where / my disease has taken hold.)

Related to the "attic window" metaphor is Rosalía's intermittent assertion that she dwells in the depths and prefers the shadows. She exclaims:

¡Aire!, que el aire me falta.
¿Qué ves en el pozo oscuro?
    (trans. Barja 40, *Obras* 1:289)

(Air! I need air. / What do you see in the dark well?)

Falling to where there is a lack of light and air is a recurrent metaphor: "Tan bajo caí, tan bajo / que luz no me llega ya" and "ya que aquí no encuentre / aire, luz, tierra ni sol" (So far down I fell, so far / that light could not reach me; given that here I may not find / air, light, earth or sun).[50] Rosalía's preference throughout is "to wander and drift in the shadows" ("quiero errante vagar en las tinieblas" [*Obras* 1:581]); or to remain "en el dintel oscuro de mi pobre morada" (at the dark lintel of my poor dwelling [*Obras* 1:718]). As Rosalía matures as a poet, she is drawn more and more to the "aesthetics of renunciation" (whereas a late twentieth-century poet might well reconceive such a space as the darkness of the womb from which she can emerge anew).

In *Follas*, the speaker characterizes her ideas as "locas" ("mad"); later, they are mad because no one knows what will become of them in the future. However, they continue to be the poet's most intimate companions.[51] Madness, after Gilbert and Gubar, is a metaphor and must be read as a sign of the deep anxiety felt by a woman poet in the nineteenth century. Rosalía develops this metaphor in her oft-anthologized poem—discussed later—"Dicen que no hablan las plantas" (It's said plants don't speak) from *Orillas del Sar*.

The woman poet in *Orillas del Sar* is hounded by detractors and, hurt by praise that has turned to scorn, she shrinks further and further inside her "cárcel estrecha y sombría" (dark and narrow prison), inside her "asilo" and "antro" (shelter and cavern), or into a corner where she hides.[52] In "Cenicientas las aguas" (Ashen the waters), she begins to observe all from her (attic) window or "desde mis ventanas" (*Obras* 1:563):

Yo, desde mi ventana
que azotan los airados elementos,

regocijada y pensativa escucho
el discorde concierto
simpático a mi alma...
(*Obras* 1:616)[53]

(From my window / lashed by the wild elements, / I listen cheerfully
and pensively / to the discordant concert / so congenial to my soul)

The poet senses that her tastes are not of the mainstream ("Blanca
senda; camino olvidado" [White path; forgotten road (*Obras* 1:621)]),
that her poems are simple daisies ("En mi pequeño huerto / brilla la
sonrosada margarita" [In my little orchard / the rosy daisy glows (*Obras*
1:650)]),[54] and that her talent is "Como la peña oculta por el musgo
de algún arroyo" (like the rock that's hidden by the moss of a stream
[*Obras* 1:727]). The following poem in an unpretentious gesture pulls
together much of this symbolism and meaning:

Cuido una planta bella
que ama y busca la sombra,
como la busca el alma
huérfana, triste, enamorada y sola,
y allí donde jamás la luz del día
llega sino a través de las umbrosas
ramas de un mirto y los cristales turbios
de una ventana angosta,
ella vive tan fresca y perfumada,
y se torna más bella y más frondosa,
y languidece y se marchita y muere
cuando un rayo de sol besa sus hojas.
(*Obras* 1:657)

(I look after a beautiful plant / that loves and searches out the shade, /
as does the orphaned, / sad, lovesick and lonely soul, / and there where
daylight only shines / through a shady myrtle's boughs and a wide
window's / misted panes, / it lives as fresh and fragrant as can be, / and
becomes more leafy and more beautiful, / and languishes and withers
and dies / when a sun's ray kisses its leaves.)

Such images of shrinking, drying up, entrapment, isolation, and confinement may well reflect—as traditional criticism would argue—the
spiritual and psychological disposition of the poet or the illness that was
wasting her. However, if we follow Gilbert and Gubar, they also indicate
the increasing discomfort Rosalía felt the more she tried to combine

her schizophrenic roles of "angel-mother-wife" and "monster-woman-poet." In a famous poem Rosalía characterized herself as "la loca" (the madwoman):

Dicen que no hablan las plantas, ni las fuentes, ni los pájaros,
ni el onda con sus rumores, ni con su brillo los astros.
Lo dicen; pero no es cierto, pues siempre, cuando yo paso,
de mí murmuran y exclaman:
                    Ahí va la loca, soñando
con la eterna primavera de la vida y de los campos
                                        (*Obras* 1:668)

(It's said that neither plants, nor founts, nor birds can speak, / nor with their mumble the waves of light, nor with their splendour the stars. / So it's said; but it's not true, for always when I pass by, / they gossip about me and shout out: There goes that mad woman again, dreaming / about the eternal spring in life and fields.)

Certainly, this "loca" is a poet-dreamer preoccupied with her own imminent death, but she is also a harried mother, a marginalized woman, a vilified artist, and a poet who is driven mad by listening to her own inner poetic voices. The "loca" in the above poem is the woman artist in the nineteenth century who is driven "mad"—divided from herself—by the pressure she senses from the androcentric values of a patriarchal culture.

The hiding hole, the cavern, the shelter, the window, the shadowy depths—attic and sanctuary—do give us a more complete metaphorical picture of the condition of the woman artist who struggled to compete and was repulsed. Traditional criticism would react by claiming that such poems indicate Rosalía's inherent spiritual and psychological disposition. However, they also indicate Rosalía's belief that all is hopeless for the woman poet. In one poem she suddenly exclaims that "Ya se acabó la edad de las Corinas" (The age of the Corinnas is over and done with [*Follas*, trans. Barja 182, *Obras* 1:411]). (Corinna was the woman poet who instructed Pindar and gained a victory over him at the public games at Thebes.) That women poets have no comparable influence in the nineteenth century is what Rosalía de Castro implies in her own subtle, intellectual, and inoffensive manner.

A further negative perspective on the condition of the woman poet is indicated by the speaker's loss of confidence and self-worth. *Cantares* ends with an apology from the poet for her inferior poems, and *Follas* begins where *Cantares* left off. In the first poem, Rosalía apologizes for not writing traditional women's verse:

De aquellas que cantan palomas y flores
se dice que tienen alma de mujer.
Yo que no las canto, ¡ay, Virgen Santísima!,
¿de qué la tendré?
(trans. Barja 28, Obras 1:277)

(About those who sing of doves and flowers, / it's said they have a woman's soul. / Oh, Most Holy Virgin, and I who do not sing about either / what can I have?)

Such a self-questioning response is no doubt a reaction to the criticism Rosalía's work provoked. Indeed, the speaker of a later poem is a critic of Rosalía's poetry who expresses contempt for the distasteful type of verse Rosalía writes ("hechos . . . para leerse a soplamocos" [written . . . to be read under duress] in "Haces versos...?" [Do you write verse? (trans. Barja 204, *Obras* 1:430)]). Clearly, the woman poet is reacting to the negative response her verse has received: she has not produced what is expected of women poets and is therefore receiving public opprobrium.

A final negative perspective on the condition of the woman poet is her anxiety of authority. In the second poem of *Follas*, Rosalía recognizes an anxiety of authority (in the sense that the precursors to whom she turns instigate mimicry rather than inspire originality from her). She confesses that she writes things others have already thought: "Bien sé que nunca hay nada / nuevo bajo este cielo" (I know full well that there's never / anything new under the sun [trans. Barja 28, *Obras* 1:278]). Rosalía was reacting in part to the fact that her readers heard only Bécquer or Trueba in her poems, while failing to see what was truly Rosalía.[55]

However, with "¡Silencio!"—"Con torpe mano y palpitante el seno" (Quiet!—With clumsy hand and throbbing heart [trans. Barja 46, *Obras* 1:297), the manner in which she presents the Promethean battle she engages in with her muse to create her poems leaves her readers in no doubt of her originality and conviction.[56] She describes herself, while in the actual process of writing, as insecure about what she is doing, but notice, in the following lines, that no eagle or vulture eats out her bowels; it is as though she is giving birth to her own poems:

mojo en mi propia sangre dura pluma,
rompo mi vena hinchada,
y escribo..., escribo..., ¿para qué?
    (trans. Barja 46, *Obras* 1:297)

(I dip a stiff pen in my own blood, / I lance my swollen vein, / and I
write..., I write..., for what?)

The woman poet fertilizes herself by stabbing the "dura pluma" into her
own flesh, slashing her swollen vein, and making the verse flow.[57] The
woman poet must give birth to herself because, especially in the nineteenth century, there were few female precursors who could mother or
sister her along. When she questions the past, she finds male figures
(e.g., Mephistopheles [see *Obras* 654 and 686]) who are a hindrance
rather than a stimulus to her inspiration.

There is implicit in the criticism leveled against Rosalía an assumption that women should not write profound, metaphysical poems; they
should not be inquiring into the nature of existence but should merely
paint scenes in nature. For this reason, perhaps, in "A la sombra te
sientas de las desnudas rocas" (You sit in the shade of the bare rocks),
Rosalía later advises a "niña" ("young girl") that

encierra el alma humana tan profundos misterios,
que cuando a nuestros ojos un velo los oculta,
es temeraria empresa descorrer este velo:
no pienses, pues, bien mío, no pienses en qué pienso.
    (*Obras* 1:655-56)

(the human soul keeps such profound mysteries cooped up, / that
when a veil hides them from our eyes, / it's a risky business to draw
this veil back: / so don't think, my dear, don't think about what
I think.)

But the "niña" does just that, and she dies from the anguish ("la pena")
it brings her. The implication is that women who are Promethean
enough to write profound poetry of inner struggle will suffer torment
and will die for their art.

Another aspect of Rosalía's protofeminism is that she expresses intense anger about the condition of her culture and society. Kirkpatrick
has also shown how anger becomes Avellaneda's antidote to ambient
pressures (*Románticas* 200), but anger is still not recognized as a characteristic of nineteenth-century women's poetry. However, it is a distinc-

tive feature of the poetry of the latter half of this century, as Ostriker has shown. She writes that "Anger is psychic necessity, both emotionally and intellectually. To be conscious as a woman, is to be conscious of hurt and to demand reparation" (*Stealing* 161). Anger is an attack on culture's systemic phallocentrism, which a woman might have to explore despite the rejection it entails. Such observations as these can disinter Rosalía's latent feminism.

In the eponym of *Follas*, "*¡Hojas nuevas!* risa siento" (New leaves! I feel like laughing [trans. Barja 32, *Obras* 1:281]), Rosalía makes it clear that there is much grief, bitterness, and anger in this ironically titled book of "new leaves"—which were born in the "páramo" (desert/wasteland) of her life. These so-called new leaves of poetry are "fieras, como mi dolor" (wild beasts, like my grief [trans. Barja 32, *Obras* 1:281]); they are not demure, feminine sighs but the screams of a fiend or virago—figurative meanings for "fiera." As "¿Qué tiene?" (What's the matter with her?) asserts—all women can do today is "rabiar": "hoy el sufrir tan sólo / es rabiar día y noche" (to suffer today is only / to be raging all day and night [trans. Barja 182, *Obras* 1:410]).[58]

Perhaps Rosalía's angriest poem is "La justicia por la mano" (Taking justice into one's own hands [trans. Barja 83, *Obras* 1:332]) in which an aggrieved woman takes a scythe and murders the family that has dishonored her. This poem is surely a covert manifestation of the poet's anger that justice is blind to women, in particular to their honor: it implies that women will need to take justice into their own hands in order to achieve what is their due. Elsewhere, Rosalía is angry that there is no justice to be found; she is angry that there are so many starving beggars at her door in winter; and she is furious that Castilian invaders have felled Galicia's oak trees and leveled her forests.[59] The speaker ends the last poem, "Jamás lo olvidare!" (I'll never forget it), by recognizing that most will think her mad because the loss of trees is nothing when compared to the loss of a tower or the sacking of an estate. In the following lines, the voice of patriarchy ridicules Rosalía's concerns and asks, behind the poet's back:

¿O en mis haciendas penetrando acaso
osado criminal, ha puesto fuego
a las extensas eras? ¿Por qué gime
 así importuna esa mujer?
(*Obras* 1:609)

(Or has a brazen criminal, / sneaking perchance onto my estates, set fire / to the extensive pastures? Why does that woman persist / in stubbornly whining?)

Further indication of Rosalía's fury may be found in "Cayendo van los bravos combatientes" (The brave combatants keep on falling), a fragment appended to *Orillas del Sar*, in which she writes:

¡Vendrán!... Mas presto del vampiro odioso
destruid las guaridas,
si no queréis que los guerreros vuelvan
tristes y oscuros a morir sin gloria
antes de ver la patria redimida.

(Obras 1:728)

(Sure they'll come back!... But you should destroy at once / the lairs of the odious vampire, / if you do not want the warriors to return / in a sad and somber state and die ingloriously / before they see the redemption of their homeland.)

It is certainly legitimate to argue, as traditional criticism has done, that Rosalía is furious because of her illegitimate birth, because of her husband's infidelities, or because of the injustice she sees in Galicia. However, her fury and anger also stem from her treatment as a woman and the marginalization she suffers as a woman poet. Given the importance attributed to the expression of anger by women poets of the twentieth century, anger should now be recognized as a distinctive feature of the work of late nineteenth-century women's discourse. Space needs to be made in Rosalía criticism for interpreting her anger as a major subtext, otherwise the complexity of such an apparently simple poem as "Sin nido" (Without a nest [discussed above]) will never be appreciated. The hidden text of "Sin nido" is a palimpsest representing the abuse a woman experiences as an abandoned mother.

Given the abundance of anger coupled with the negative vision of womanhood and the woman poet, it is surprising to find that Rosalía is known as a "santiña"—a sort of dear little saint—not only by her readers but also by those who knew her. Even her daughter claimed her mother was sweet and charming and not angry at all about Castile. Obviously, a myth surrounds Rosalía like a halo. In today's critical terminology, that myth wants to keep Rosalía de Castro imprisoned in the pigeonhole marked "angel"—"ángel del hogar." But in Gilbert and Gubar's terminology, critics studying Rosalía need to see that their poet was both a "monster" and an "angel." I have no desire to deny Rosalía a place with the Saints on High, but I do want her postmodern readers to recognize that there is much "monstrous" anger in *Follas* and *Orillas del Sar.* To ignore it, because it is not "feminine," is to fail to comprehend the modernity of Rosalía de Castro as a poet.

Despite its overwhelming sense of the negative condition of womanhood, Rosalía's poetry also offers a positive gynocentric vision: she inscribes strong females within her poems, and she initiates the development of a positive female self and vision by her selection and deployment of gynocentric images and metaphors. We have already discussed the numerous strong women in *Cantares*, as well as the woman who takes justice into her own hands and murders those who have dishonored her; another commits adultery; others flout convention by running off with the men they love.[60] In addition, there are those women who always make ends meet despite terrible hardships.[61] The tone of these poems—vibrant, approbatory—is what makes one realize that Rosalía endorses these women. To the emblems of such positive women must be added "la señora de las meigas" (she of the supernatural wise women); the woman who curses men; and the cunning and guileful old woman who always gets what she wants.[62] These poems stand out as eulogies to "monster-women"—women intent on emancipation and self-determination—and they stand in opposition to the myriad negative images of frustrated and embittered "angel-women" who conform or are forced to conform by the patriarchal culture of the time.

Another feature of Rosalía's positive gynocentric vision is that she saw her poems as illuminating some small and intimate circle of reality. She characterizes her poems as clarifying intermittently a small, local, and peculiar emotion:

Pensaréis de estos versos, y es lo justo,
que son de extraña, insólita armonía,
que en ellos las ideas brillan, pálidas,
    como erráticas chispas
    que de repente estallan,
    que luego se retiran
semejándose a la bruma incierta
que en lo hondo de los huertos se desliza

y al susurro insistente de los pinos
    junto a la mar bravía.

(trans. Barja 30, *Obras* 1:280)

(You'll be right if you think these lines / are of a strange, unwonted
harmony, / for in them ideas wanly shine, / like erratic sparks / that
suddenly explode, / then drift away / resembling the uncertain mist /
that sneaks about the orchards' depths, / around the pines' insistent
rustle / along the savage sea.)

A poem such as this can be fully appreciated only if we contrast
its goals to those of a typical male poet. There is an element of nontranscendentalism in Rosalía's vision. She wishes to illuminate some
small patch (ll. 3–6), whereas the male poet would probably claim to
his readers that he was enlightening the whole of mankind or the entire world.[63]

To articulate and develop her positive gynocentric vision, Rosalía
de Castro also selects images and metaphors that center around the
concerns of a woman. For example "Los robles" (Oaks), in which the
devastation of the Galician oak trees is condemned,[64] selects a scene
of three generations of women around a fire as an image for how life
should be lived:

De la hoguera sentados en torno,
en sus brazos la madre arrullaba
    al infante robusto;
daba vuelta, afanosa, la anciana,
en sus dedos nudosos, al huso,
y al alegre fulgor de la llama,
ya la joven la harina cernía,
    o ya desgranaba,
con su mano callosa y pequeña,
del maíz las mazorcas doradas.

(*Obras* 1:593)

(Seated around the fire, / the mother would rock to sleep in her arms /
the robust infant; / the old woman would vigorously turn / the spindle
in her gnarled hands; / the young girl, by the flames' bright glow, /
would be sieving flour by now, / or with her tiny calloused hand, /
she'd be on to shelling / the corncobs' golden kernels.)

This is a loving re-creation of the past, in which women (*anciana,
madre, joven*) had their own community.[65] At the end of the poem, the

speaker apostrophizes the oak and begs it to return to restore Galicia
to its greatness; and the female poetic voice compares the oak's beauty
to a virgin's:

> y en las suaves graciosas pendientes
> donde umbrosas se extienden tus ramas,
> como en rostro de pálida virgen
> cabellera ondulante y dorada,
> que en lluvia de rizos
> acaricia la frente de nácar.
>
> (*Obras* 1:597)

(on smooth and graceful slopes / where your boughs spread out in
shade, / like the undulating golden hair / that rains in ringlets / on a
pale virgin's face / and strokes her pearly brow.)

It is unlikely that a male poet would have described a pale virgin in such
sexless terms.[66] The smoothness Rosalía foregrounds is indicative of a
different attitude toward women.

Moreover, Rosalía's descriptions of children and mothers are distinct
from the way male poets treat them. As her own child is dying, she
evokes his calm and focuses on her turbulence ("Era apacible el Día" [It
was a calm day (*Obras* 1:571)]). She also foregrounds the maternal protection she feels for her own children but concludes her reflection on
what might await them once they are grown up with this condemnation:
"Del hombre, enemigo del hombre, no puede / libraros, mis ángeles,
la égida materna" (My little angels, maternal protection cannot save
you / from man, who is man's own worst enemy [*Obras* 1:613]).[67] As the
role of the mother is foregrounded in feminist criticism, this aspect of
Rosalía's poetry merits attention. Furthermore, other discursive codes
are maternalized by Rosalía. For instance, her poems are akin to those
songs and fervent prayers ("canciones," "fervientes oraciones") which
once learned in childhood are remembered forever. The River Sar is a
child, and the inspiration the poet finds in her region is compared to
breast feeding: "como el sediento niño el dulce jugo extrae / del pecho
blanco y lleno" (just as the thirsty child extracts that sweet juice / from
the full, white breast).[68]

The sea, which for women poets in the twentieth century will frequently symbolize regeneration, is associated with death for Rosalía.[69]
However, it is a liquid womb—"la serena / y tersa superficie" (the
serene / and smooth surface [*Obras* 1:588–89])—in which the speaker
may slake her thirst once and for all: "a apagar vuestra sed inextin-

guible" (slake your inextinguishable thirst [*Obras* 1:587]). Death by drowning is a return to the maternal womb—recall the French homophony of "mère/mer"—from which the overburdened speaker first issued.

The opposite of liquidity is hardness (and dryness), and Rosalía selected several of what Ostriker later identifies as "exoskeletal" forms to arm and defend herself against sentiment and the world, as well as to manifest her split condition of "angel/monster." Ostriker found that women poets of the 1960s cultivated a hard and rational style of expression, which she called "exoskeletal." She adds: "The artist's stance in many of these poems seems to identify aggressive-defensiveness with the art of writing, and this stance is clearly ungracious, ungentle, unladylike. From the point of view of poetic reputation, so much the better. The woman poet who adopts an impermeable tone is less in danger of being dismissed as sentimental or overemotional by critics" (*Stealing* 88).[70] Ostriker adds that the selection of a hard object (stone, metal) signifies the woman poet's fragmented being which is unable to unify itself. Rosalía's symbols corroborate Ostriker's insights.

In "Yo no he nacido para odiar" (I was not born to hate), Rosalía writes of being a rock:

Como la peña oculta por el musgo
de algún arroyo solitario al pie,
inmóvil y olvidada, yo quisiera
ya vivir sin amar ni aborrecer.
(Obras 1:727)

(Like the rock hidden by moss / at the bottom of a solitary stream, / immovable and forgotten, I'd now like / to live neither loving nor loathing.)

In addition, Rosalía describes herself as having an "alma yerta" (rigid soul) and adds that "secáronse tus flores de virginal fragancia" (your flowers of virgin fragrance have dried up [*Obras* 1:567]). She describes her condition thus: "mi sien por la corona del mártir agobiada, / y para siempre frío y agotado mi seno" (my brow heavy from the martyr's oppressive crown, / my bosom drained and forever cold [*Obras* 1:568]). Dry springs and fountains and dry leaves occur throughout her mature work as emblems of her condition.[71]

Such symbols certainly indicate Rosalía de Castro's "saudade," her spiritual disposition, and the illness that was in fact devouring her. But in addition, and on a completely different level, they indicate her struggle with the self-division she feels. They can surely be read today as Rosalía's reaction to the shrinking horizons that beset her in a totally androcentric culture.

A further characteristic of Rosalía's feminist vision is that she begins criticizing—even subverting—some of the sacrosanct (i.e., male) beliefs of Western culture. Subversion may be too strong a term for this tendency, insofar as Rosalía de Castro never consciously undermines the epoch's intellectual beliefs. However, she does demystify them in numerous poems.

Orillas del Sar presents an unfavorable image of the male world.[72] The hegemonic (i.e., male) world is one of light,[73] science, and glory.[74] By contrast, the woman's world is one of shadows ("el dintel oscuro de mi pobre morada" [the dark lintel of my poor dwelling (*Obras* 1:718)]). Patriarchal religion—that is, the male God—is found to be hollow.[75]

In place of these man-made beliefs, the poet offers with conviction the world of the spirits: with its old women who are in touch with the supernatural ("meigas" [*Obras* 1:122-24]), its local spirits ("los genios propicios" [*Obras* 1:600]), and "genios misteriosos / que os llaman tan sentidos y amorosos" (its mysterious spirits / that keenly call you with such deep love [*Obras* 1:620]). Consciously or not, Rosalía shows more faith in the matriarchal religions, as may be glimpsed in the strange, quasi-traditional religious poem which begins "Si medito en tu eterna grandeza, buen Dios, a quien nunca veo" (If I meditate on your eternal grandeur, good God, whom I never see [*Obras* 1:672]), but which ends with the speaker running to church, throwing herself at the feet of Christ on the cross, and experiencing relief thus:

> que cual niño que reposa
> en el regazo materno,
> después de llorar, tranquila
> tras la expiación, espero
> que allá donde Dios habita
> he de proseguir viviendo.
> (*Obras* 1:672)

(Like the child reposing / in the maternal lap, / after a crying fit, calm / after atonement, I have hope / to go on living / there where God has made his dwelling.)

It is to be emphasized that Rosalía derives her religious consolation, such as it is, by identifying not with the dying God figure himself but with the feeling a child has in its mother's arms; with the feeling she herself might have imparted to her own son as he lay dying. What she does is mother herself back to normalcy. A male god cannot "mother" a woman back to health, for "mothering" is a woman's job and therefore women must "mother" themselves—which is what Rosalía, the prefeminist, does. Cixous implies this when she writes: "There always remains in woman that force which produces/is produced by the other—in particular, the other woman. In her, matrix, cradler; herself giver as her mother and child; she is her own sister-daughter" ("Laugh" 252]). And Rabuzzi, in her reflections on the myth of Demeter and Persephone, concludes that "the return to the mother . . . suggests . . . the maturation rather than the regression of the daughter, a condition which renders her indistinguishable from her mother. When, or if, a woman achieves this stage, she has achieved the capability of being mother to or caretaker of herself, a very significant step for any human" (*Sacred* 135).

Finally, in *Orillas del Sar* the most trenchant symbol for the subversion of male values occurs in "Desde los cuatro puntos cardinales" (From the four points of the compass), where Rosalía revises the classical (i.e., male) myth of the voyages of Ulysses, but tells it from Penelope's point of view: Penelope shrugs her shoulders at the male world of science and progress and at the modern world's blind faith in hard work:

¡Esperad y creed!: "crea" el que cree,
y ama con doble ardor aquel que espera.

Pero yo en el rincón más escondido
y también más hermoso de la Tierra,
        sin esperar a Ulises
(que el nuestro ha naufragado en la tormenta)
        semejante a Penélope,
tejo y destejo sin cesar mi tela,

    pensando que esta es del destino humano
        la incesante tarea;
y que ahora subiendo, ahora bajando,
unas veces con luz, otras a ciegas,
cumplimos nuestros días y llegamos
más tarde o más temprano a la ribera.

(*Obras* 1:713-14)

(Wait and believe!: he who believes, "creates," / and those who wait, love with twofold zeal. / Whereas I, in the most sequestered / but most beautiful corner of the Earth, / like Penelope, / but not waiting for Ulysses / (for ours was shipwrecked in the storm), / ceaselessly weave and unweave my cloth, / thinking that human destiny is / this never-ending task; / that by climbing up and heading down, / sometimes with a light, sometimes blindly groping, / we serve out our allotted time and reach / sooner or later the other shore.)

Rosalía clearly identifies with Penelope as she rewrites the Ulysses myth.[76] The revision of patriarchal myth is a distinctive feature of women's poetry, and in Rosalía's case it is another indication of her covert feminist impulse, a further sign of her clandestine struggle to deal "from a specifically female perspective" with her "female experience" (Gilbert and Gubar, *Madwoman* 72).

That Rosalía de Castro displays several distinctive features of a gynocentric vision, and that she initiates a subversion of the ideals and myths of the phallocratic Occident, and that she at times selects gynocentric images and metaphors to articulate that vision indicate why women poets in twentieth-century Spain continue to revere her and provide additional evidence of her genius as a Modern Spanish poet.

Notes

1. Mayoral comments on true and false images of Rosalía in her conclusion (*Poesía* 567–68). She writes of "una dulce y morriñosa mujer gallega que llora y se lamenta continuamente en no menos dulces y suaves versos" ("a sweet and homesick Galician woman who weeps and moans in verses that are just as sweet and smooth"), as opposed to "aquella mujer de espíritu fuerte, tantas veces áspera . . . que [habla] en un tono feroz" ("that strong-spirited woman, often harsh . . . who speaks in ferocious tones").

2. For instance, Carballo Calero's edition of the *Cantares* and studies by Alonso Montero, Kulp-Hill, Mayoral, and Poullain, and the recent three-volume *Actas do Congreso internacional de estudios sobre Rosalía de Castro e o seu tempo.*

3. For example, both Mayoral and Kulp-Hill study Rosalía's "Electra" complex—her desire to compete against her mother for her father's affections.

4. Albert Robatto's *Rosalía de Castro y la condición femenina*, in my estimation, focuses on Rosalía's presentation of the "angel" woman. She writes: "Sintetizaremos esta parte de nuestro estudio reafirmando una vez más que la capacidad de entrega, la ternura y la disposición al trabajo son tres cuali-

dades de la mujer gallega, recurrentemente expresadas en la obra de Rosalía, que nos han ayudado a precisar ese particular feminismo rosaliano" (We would sum up this part of our study reasserting once more that her capacity for giving, her tenderness and her aptitude for work are three qualities of the Galician woman, repeatedly expressed in Rosalía's work, that have helped us specify that particular aspect of Rosalía's feminism [112]).

5. See especially Stevens, *Rosalía de Castro* (who on pp. 118 and 121 makes the same point I am making here). And in the three-volume *Actas*, see Blanco García ("A problemática"), Briesemeister ("Rosalía de Castro"), Ciplijauskaité ("Cárcel estrecha"), Feal Deibe ("Sobre el feminismo"), March ("Rosalía de Castro"), M. Miller ("Rosalía de Castro"), Noia Campos "Elementos literarios"), Sánchez Mora ("Rosalía de Castro"), and Stevens ("Apología feminista").

6. Gilbert and Gubar (*Madwoman* 72) discuss how nineteenth-century women writers grew beyond the permitted bounds of female "modesty" and male mimicry.

7. I omit *La Flor* and *A mi madre*.

8. All future references to these books will be abbreviated to *Cantares*, *Follas*, and *Orillas del Sar* respectively and will be given in Spanish.

9. However, I do agree with Poullain that a bipartite trajectory does not do justice to Rosalía's complexity. Moreover, an argument could be made that attention needs to be paid to the idea that her "saudade" would have been intensified and aggravated by the fact of her being a woman writer in the nineteenth century.

10. For example, all poets toward the end of the last century were mournful and somewhat effete (decadent), and hence Rosalía's mournfulness ("saudade") is overemphasized in all criticism of her work. As early as 1890 Pardo Bazán was implying that Rosalía's poetry was decadent: "repite quejas [de] la enferma poesía lírica" ("repeats the complaints of sick, lyric poetry" [see Davies, "Rosalía" 612; and Stevens, *Rosalía de Castro* 34]).

11. For example, Davies notes that in 1885 Pardo Bazán "insisted on relegating Rosalía to the role of a minor provincial poet," and in 1891, in "La mujer española" (The Spanish woman), she "praises Avellaneda, Carolina Coronado, and Concepción Arenal" ("Rosalía" 612) but ignores Rosalía. This campaign was sustained by such figures as Núñez de Arce, Juan Valera, Tamayo y Baus, Menéndez Pelayo, and Emilio Castelar: "all [of whom] contributed to the formation of a solid block of intellectuals bound to officialdom which ostracized Rosalía de Castro" (612, 617).

12. Rosalía's vilification by her nineteenth-century peers is also treated by Cardwell ("Rosalía de Castro" 440–41), who, recognizing his own debt to Davies, notes that Rosalía's early work, which attacks the status quo, helped inspire the self-serving campaign conducted against her after 1874 and continued after her death by Pardo Bazán, Valera, Menéndez Pelayo

and others. Criticism of Rosalía and Murguía, Cardwell argues, was directed against the decentralization of Spain and the autonomy of Galicia. Such political emancipation was fiercely attacked by the supporters of the monarchy, restored in 1875, who also marginalized Rosalía's work by arguing that it reflected a decadent culture.

13. Unamuno in an article collected in *Andanzas y visiones españolas;* Azorín in *Clásicos y modernos* (1912), *El paisaje de España visto por los españoles* (1917), and *Leyendo a los poetas* (1929).

14. Jiménez told his students that in 1896 Rosalía was one of his favorite poets and that he was reading her at that time in Galician (*El modernismo* 54). Jiménez did translate a few poems from *Follas novas.* Aguirre writes that he translated "Sombra negra que me asombras" and "A [*sic*] la Habana ("Influencia" 46-47). Sánchez Romeralo says that he translated "Cuando creo que te has ido" and "Esta parte y aquella parte," which is the fifth section of "Hacia la Habana." He also notes that only the former has appeared in print, in Jiménez, *El modernismo* 302 ("Rosalía" 214 and 219).

15. See for example, Gilbert and Gubar's "Ceremonies" (esp. 26-27).

16. Alonso Montero (*Rosalía* 49) cites a letter of Murguía's, published in the *Boletín de la Real Academia Gallega* (Dec. 1950, 102-3), in which he claims that unbeknown to Rosalía he took the poems to a publisher friend in Vigo and demanded a prologue from her while they were being printed. For a month Rosalía refused, insisting "en que era mejor saliese el libro con mi nombre" ("that it were best that the book appear under my name," i.e., her husband's). In *Los precursores* (145), Murguía adds that Rosalía was obliged to write the rest of the book once the first printing was complete.

17. The collection originally ended with this poem. However, the *Obras completas* (hereafter cited as *Obras* with the volume number)—which contain thirty-eight *Cantares*—have a different order. For further analysis of this poem, see Stevens (*Rosalía de Castro* 58-60).

18. For the Galician original, see *Obras* 1:232-33. I give the Spanish because I assume that few of my readers will follow Galician sufficiently well to grasp poetic nuances.

19. For a discussion of the traditional "romance," see note 22 to my introduction above. A *romance* has lines of eight syllables, with assonance in alternate lines. In this *romance* the assonance is in o-a.

20. Critics (e.g., Mayoral) have noted that Rosalía was not physically attractive.

21. This collection of poetry in Galician, together with the *Juegos Florales de la Coruña*, marked the beginning of the Galician Renaissance. (Nothing had been written in Galician since the sixteenth century.)

22. The issue of Rosalía's command of Galician is more complex than this; see Stevens (*Rosalía de Castro* 36-48, and esp. 39).

23. She described her own heart as unfeminine in the opening poem of *Follas* (*Obras* 1:277).

24. The poem reads: "Bajo ese vínculo santo, / ¿tus ojos, niña, no ven / á la madre cariñosa / que besa con embriaguez / la rosada faz del ángel / desprendido de su ser? / ¿no ves al feliz esposo / sellar con su labio fiel / la mejilla de la esposa / lleno de amor y placer? / ¿no piensas que en estos goces / hay tal encanto y tal bien / que solamente en el cielo / mayores los puede haber? / Pues si nada de esto piensas, / pues si nada de esto ves, / *digo que no tienes alma / ni corazón de mujer*" (In this sacred bond, / do your eyes, girl, not see / the caring mother / who kisses madly / the rosy face of the angel / that sprung from her being? / Don't you see the contented husband / filled with love and pleasure / seal with his faithful lip / his wife's cheek? Don't you think that in such joy / there's such enchantment and good / that only in heaven / can there be anything better? / Well, if you think nothing like this, / if you see none of this, / *I say that you have neither the heart / nor the soul of a woman* [Trueba, *Libro* 169]).

25. However, let me note the following parallels—all from *Follas*—as they probably demonstrate her debt to him. "Todo clavo se saca / con otro clavo" (Trueba, *Libro* 78), and "Unha vez tiven un cravo" (*Obras* 1:286). Poem no. 24, "Oros sin triunfo" (Trueba, *Libro* 88) should be compared to "No hai peor meiga que unha gran pena" (*Obras* 1:355), as they concern counts and country girls. Poem no. 44 (Trueba, *Libro* 177) has a woman who kills the man who seduced her; Rosalía in "A xusticia pola man" (*Obras* 1:332) has a woman who kills a family with a scythe.

26. Trans. Barja 16; for the text in Galician, see *Obras* 1:68.

27. Additional factors of a psychological nature which would have contributed to Rosalía's marginalization are her illegitimacy and rumored marital infidelities.

28. Only poems nos. 2, 18, and 21 deal with women and/or a woman's experience.

29. To be precise, seven of the thirty-eight poems have male speakers and/or focus predominantly on a male predicament (nos. 14, 15, 22, 23, 24, 35, 38). "A gaita gallega," "Castellanos de Castilla," and "Alborada" each have a female speaker but are not really about a woman's experience.

30. For Stevens's analysis of *Cantares* in particular see *Rosalía* 36–71.

31. This ethereal woman, it should be noted, does not lead her man to perdition. Compare Bécquer, *Rimas*, Rima 11 "soy incorpórea" etc., and "Los ojos verdes."

32. This is the first stanza of a very long poem of 225 lines. It consists of fifty-five "quintillas" in abaab.

33. As will Machado in "Poema de un día—Meditaciones rurales" [128] of *Campos de Castilla* (for which see Wilcox, "Self-Referentiality"). The

resonance of Rosalía in Machado and Jiménez is astounding (and, apart from meriting a detailed study, is another testimony to her greatness).

34. Rosalía's early years are complicated. Her father, a priest, abandoned her mother. Rosalía was initially brought up by distant relatives, but joined her mother when she was about eight years old.

35. For "cantigas," see note 22 to my introduction, above.

36. Possibly written under pressure from Murguía and therefore less meditated.

37. This is an allusion to the medieval "cantiga de amigo," "Malferida iba la garza" (cited in my introduction, n. 22 above).

38. On this topic, see Stevens, *Rosalía de Castro* 96-117.

39. The fifth and final section of *Follas* is called "Viudas de vivos, viudas de muertos." For a totally different interpretation of this sequence of poems than mine, an objective one, see Poullain, *Rosalía Castro* 123-28.

40. However, in this respect, it is as well to recall Gardiner's shrewd observation, in her remarks on "seduced and abandoned women," that "lamenting a man after he has gone may be easier than conforming to his wishes when he is present" ("Mind Mother" 137).

41. See "Vivir para ver" (*Follas*, trans. Barja 302, *Obras* 1:498) and "Nadie se muere" (trans. Barja 304, *Obras* 1:500); "Cuando era tiempo de invierno" (trans. Barja 44, *Obras* 1:293) and "Allí, entre las flores, canta" (trans. Barja 126, *Obras* 1:371). In *Orillas del Sar* negative images of women are presented via women who are lovelorn ("Alma que vas huyendo de ti misma" [*Obras* 1:598]), those who are foolish enough to expect their husbands to return ("Era la última noche" [*Obras* 1:617-18]), and those who have been seduced and abandoned ("Sed de amores" [*Obras* 1:708]). There is even a young girl who married an old man; after his death, she remains so imprisoned by his memory that she is unable to love another ("Quisiera, hermosa mía" [*Obras* 1:644-49]). On this issue, see Stevens, *Rosalía de Castro* 102-6 and ff.).

42. "Con su sordo murmullo" (*Follas*, trans. Barja 44, *Obras* 1:295), "Corred, serenas ondas cristalinas" (trans. Barja 58, *Obras* 1:308), "Deja que en esa copa" (trans. Barja 62, *Obras* 1:312), "Sola" (trans. Barja 102, *Obras* 1:351), "Torres del oeste" (trans. Barja 324, *Obras* 1:519), and "Con las penas a cuestas" (trans. Barja 338, *Obras* 1:530). There are more allusions to sea and suicide in *Orillas del Sar*. See Stevens (*Rosalía de Castro* 108-16) for suicide and the sea.

43. See also "Sin nido" from *Follas*, discussed below.

44. The feminist impulse in this metaphor is easily overlooked because the second stanza of this two-stanza poem focuses the argument exclusively on loss of faith and the onset of doubt.

45. See "Los tristes" (*Orillas*, *Obras* 1:588), "Era la última noche-II" (*Obras* 1:618), and "Unos con la calumnia le mancharon-II" (*Obras* 1:611)

46. See "Tanto e tanto nos odiamos" (*Follas*, trans. Barja 254–60, *Obras* 1:462). See also "Tú para mí, yo para ti, bien mío" (*Orillas*, *Obras* 1:719–20), where marriage is lambasted. The state of marriage is in effect subverted in "Margarita," in which the title character is a strong and independent woman wrestling with the moral, spiritual, and practical problems of caring for her father all day and evening, while trying to keep her own romantic relationship alive. Her solution is to abandon her father at night while he is in bed, and sneak out to the house of her lover so that she may spend the night with him (*Obras* 1:584–86). Azorín was most impressed by this poem and in 1912 — the start of the reassessment of Rosalía — commented on it.

47. See "Quien casa tiene, tiene media vida" (*Follas*, trans. Barja 284, *Obras* 1:482–83).

48. See, respectively, "Ladraban contra mí" (*Follas*, trans. Barja 68, *Obras* 1:319), "La extranjera en su patria" (trans. Barja 92, *Obras* 1:342); "La losa encantada" (trans. Barja 240–54, *Obras* 1:454).

49. "E ben" (*Follas*, trans. Barja 136, *Obras* 1:378); "Olvidemos los muertos" (trans. Barja 278–82, *Obras* 479).

50. *Follas*, trans. Barja 62, *Obras* 1:311; trans. Barja 92, *Obras* 1:340–41; "Tengo un nido de locos pensamientos / junto al lar escondidos" (trans. Barja 320–22, *Obras* 1:515)

51. *Follas*, trans. Barja 30, *Obras* 1:279; "Mis pensamientos" (trans. Barja 300, *Obras* 1:497).

52. See, respectively, "Aturde la confusa gritería" (*Orillas*, *Obras* 1:641); "Los que a través de sus lágrimas" (*Obras* 1:673–77); "Orillas del Sar-II" (*Obras* 1:564); "La canción que oyó en sueños el viejo" (*Obras* 1:634); and "A la sombra te sientas de las desnudas rocas" (*Obras* 1:655–56).

53. And see "Una cuerda tirante guarda mi seno" (*Orillas*, *Obras* 1:710).

54. M. Miller implies this in "Rosalía de Castro" 66.

55. For Bécquer, see Poullain (*Rosalía Castro*) and Ciplijauskaité ("Cárcel estrecha"). For Trueba, see Kulp, *Manner and Mood*, and n. 25 above.

56. Kirkpatrick has shown how women in the nineteenth century withdrew from their attempts at Promethean (male) desires (*Románticas*).

57. A Freudian interpretation would go much further than this. For example, the pen would represent the appropriation of phallic discourse; the woman would fertilize herself and give birth ("blood") to her own poems.

58. Rosalía's fury is evident in the content of these poems, not in her expression. For ways Rosalía deals with anger see Stevens, *Rosalía de Castro* 89.

59. See, respectively, "¡Justicia de los hombres! Yo te busco" (*Obras* 1:707); "Cuando sopla el Norte duro" (*Obras* 1:642); "¡Jamás lo olvidaré!" (*Obras* 1:605–9), all from *Orillas*.

60. See, respectively, "La justicia por la mano" (*Follas*, trans. Barja 82, *Obras* 1:332); "Yo por vos, y vos por otro" (trans. Barja 136–42, *Obras* 1:380);

"¡Valor!" (trans. Barja 142, *Obras* 1:383); and "De horror un abismo veo" (trans. Barja 144, *Obras* 1:385).

61. See, for example, "Casiña mía, mi hogar" (*Follas*, trans. Barja 210–14, *Obras* 1:437) and "¿Por qué?" (trans. Barja 330–32, *Obras* 1:524).

62. See, respectively, "Gigantescos olmos" (*Follas*, trans. Barja 122–24, *Obras* 1:368); "Permita Dios que te veas" (trans. Barja 198–200, *Obras* 1:425); "¡La pobrecita está sorda...!" (trans. Barja 218–36, *Obras* 1:442).

63. See Stevens (*Rosalía de Castro* 87–93) for the nineteenth-century belief that women should avoid poems of a transcendent theme (i.e., of a political, social, or philosophical nature), and Rosalía's repudiation of it. Stevens (33) cites Ortner's work in support of the view that women are excluded from the "transcendent processes of culture."

64. And the male drives are symbolized by the axe ("el hacha").

65. One that probably inspired Machado in "Campos de Soria. CXIII–v."

66. In the 1880s, Rubén Darío begins one of his *Abrojos* (Thistles) with "aquella frente de virgen" (that brow of a virgin) and within ten lines has converted her into "¡la número 10!" (a 10!) (*Poesías completas* 134–35). And in the 1890s, Juan Ramón Jiménez, having described the bodies of naked women in a voluptuous manner in "La canción de la carne" (Song of the flesh), has "la pura virgen" (the pure virgin) dance with lecherous delight ("una dicha lujuriosa") (*Primeros libros* 1484–86).

67. Also in "¡Volved!" (*Orillas, Obras* 1:619), the speaker identifies with "mother" Galicia who is pained by the emigration of so many of her "Children." And in "Santa escolástica," she suddenly exclaims: "¡Majestad de los templos!, mi alma femenina / te siente como siente las maternas dulzuras, / las inquietudes vagas, las ternuras secretas / y el temor a lo oculto, tras la inmensa altura" (*Orillas, Obras* 1:665). ("The majesty of temples! in your immense height / my feminine soul / feels for you as it feels maternal gentleness, / vague stirrings, secret tenderness, / and fear of the unknown.")

68. See "Aunque no alcancen gloria" (*Obras* 1:561); "Del antiguo camino a lo largo" (*Obras* 1:600); and "Orillas del Sar–v" (*Obras* 1:567), all from *Orillas*.

69. "Los tristes" ends with this line: "las negras corrientes del hondo Leteo" (deep Lethe's black currents [*Obras* 592]); and see "¡Ea!, ¡aprisa subamos de la vida!" (*Obras* 1:725), both from *Orillas*.

70. For more on the topic of sentimentality, see also Stevens, *Rosalía de Castro* 79ff.

71. See, for example, "Ya no mana la fuente se agotó el manantial" (The fount no longer flows, the spring dried up [*Obras* 1:614]); "Si en ti secó la fuente del consuelo, / secas todas las fuentes has de hallar" (If the fount of consolation has dried up in you, you'll find all founts dry [*Obras* 1:598]); "y ya secas las hojas en las ramas desnudas" (and now the leaves on the naked branches are dry [*Obras* 1:622]); all from *Orillas*.

72. There are also negative perspectives on men and the male vision of reality. Rosalía presents negative images of the male betrayer in "Vivir para ver" (*Follas*, trans. Barja 304, *Obras* 1:498) and in "Nadie se muere" (*Follas*, trans. Barja 306, *Obras* 1:500); of man's ambition in "Aprisa" (*Follas*, trans. Barja 196, *Obras* 1:422); of male pride in "Soberbia" (*Follas*, trans. Barja 214, *Obras* 1:440); and of drunkeness in "Vamos bebiendo" (*Follas*, trans. Barja 116, *Obras* 1:362). The personification of Castile, for which she feels disgust, is also masculine—but this is much clearer in the *Cantares* and *Orillas del Sar*. In the latter, she calls the Castilians "los fieros hijos del jardín de España" (cruel sons from the garden of Spain [*Orillas*, *Obras* 1:608]).

73. "Las ondas / de luz que el espacio llenan" ("the waves / of light that fill space" [*Orillas*, *Obras* 1:564]); see also in *Follas* "luz y progreso"/"light and progress" ("¿Quién no gime?" [trans. Barja 66, *Obras* 1:317]); and "Para unos negro" (trans. Barja 160–64, *Obras* 1:397–98), where the male and female visions of life are dramatically opposed: a dying man tells his son to be astute and give offense; the dying mother tells her son to be frank and loyal, to pardon, do good, and be hospitable.

74. "Una luciérnaga entre el musgo brilla" (*Orillas*, *Obras* 1:574); "¡Oh gloria! . . . jamás te rendí culto" (*Orillas*, *Obras* 1:718). Rosalía's disgust with fame is also found in *Orillas*, *Obras* 1:581, 699, 717.

75. See "Una luciérnaga entre el musgo brilla" (*Orillas*, *Obras* 1:574–76) and "Creyó que era eterno tu reino en el alma" (*Orillas*, *Obras* 1:602).

76. Francisca Aguirre will develop this insight, as we shall see in chap. 6.

Part 2 : The 1920s

2

Ernestina de Champourcin and Concha Méndez

ERNESTINA DE CHAMPOURCIN[1] (b. 1905) and Concha Méndez (1898–1986) are not thought of as Spanish poets of the 1920s, although they did publish their first volumes of poetry during that decade and were praised and encouraged by their peers and patriarchs alike. The fame and talent of the *male* Spanish poets we have come to think of as "the poetic group of the 1920s"[2] have obscured the vision of Champourcin and the originality of Méndez, who as a result have been marginalized by the canonical anthologies and histories of Spanish literature.

They have been marginalized because the phrase "Spanish poetry of the 1920s" is synonymous with an androcentric style. That is, when students of Spanish poetry use the term "generación del 27" ("Generation of 1927," or one of its rivals—see n. 2), they are thinking of male poets and their perspectives, which are patriarchal, and their worldview, which is phallogocentric. It was the style of these male poets that was canonized, or monumentalized, and subsequently transmitted through time to today's students.[3] Alternative styles and visions of reality were displaced, or discarded, so that as readers today we are simply oblivious of their existence. Champourcin's and Méndez's early work constitute two such generally ignored gynocentric styles.[4] This was not the case in the 1920s, when they were respected by their male contemporaries and reviewed with praise when they published their early books of poetry.

Ernestina de Champourcin published *En silencio* (In silence) in 1926 and *Ahora* (Now) in 1928. Shortly afterwards she was heralded by such influential patriarchs as Juan Ramón Jiménez—who wrote the prologue to her third book of poems, *La voz en el viento* (The voice in the wind) in 1931[5]—and Gerardo Diego, who included her in his canonical 1934 anthology *Poesía española contemporánea* (Contemporary Spanish poetry) despite pressure to exclude her for being a woman (Ascunce, "Prólogo" xii).[6] In 1936 Champourcin published *Cántico inútil* (Useless canticle), her fourth volume, and married Juan José Domenchina.[7]

Concha Méndez in her youth in Madrid was part of the circle of poets that constituted the nucleus of the "Generation of 1927." She was a friend of Buñuel, Alberti, and Lorca. Her first book, *Inquietudes* (Restlessness), appeared in 1926, and *Surtidor* (Fountain), her second, in 1928; she then spent two years in Argentina, where she wrote most of her third book, *Canciones de mar y tierra* (Songs of sea and earth), published in 1930. Upon her return to Madrid, she entered fully into its literary life: Alberti mentions her in an (in)famous lecture, and Juan Ramón Jiménez wrote a lyrical portrait of this dynamic and energetic woman in 1931. In 1932, she published her fourth book of poems, *Vida a vida* (Between lives), and she married Manuel Altolaguirre, to whom Lorca had introduced her. In 1936 Méndez published *Niño y sombras* (Child and shadows).[8]

Despite the acclaim given Champourcin and Méndez in the 1920s and early 1930s, they were subsequently ignored by the canonizers of Spanish literature. As Ciplijauskaité implies, marriage to male members of their generation of poets no doubt contributed to the marginalization of Champourcin and Méndez: it reduced them to being viewed solely as their consorts' helpmates.[9] Indeed, in *Memorias habladas* (Spoken memories) Paloma Ulacia Altolaguirre has written of her grandmother, Concha Méndez, that after her marriage "los hombres se negaban a ver en ella otra cosa que la mujer de un poeta" (men refused to see in her anything more than a poet's wife [16]). Moreover, the fact that Champourcin and Méndez went into exile in Mexico with their husbands in 1939 further contributed to their obscurity as poets.[10]

A third factor in their recision from the canon is that the poetry they published prior to the Spanish Civil War does not conform to the hegemonic style and androcentric vision of what we have been "educated" to think of as poetry in Spain in the 1920s.[11] I propose to discuss five characteristics of its difference from the norm—female personae, desire, gynocentric style, nontranscendentalism, and subversion of masculine ideals—which, in my opinion, have contributed to the exclusion of these poets from the poetic canon of the 1920s. Literary historians and anthologizers have judged that these poets did not develop a sufficiently original—that is, androcentric—style and vision, but such critics have failed to record that Champourcin and Méndez produced their best poetry—of gynocentric style and vision—in the 1920s and 1930s, that is, before the Civil War decimated the Spanish Peninsula.

The personae inscribed in the poetic texts of these poets are feminist and female, and thereby run counter to what the masculine poetic worldview of the 1920s customarily reveals. Champourcin manifests an exuberant persona in two early books, *Ahora* (1928) and *La voz en el viento* (1931).[12] In "Génesis" (Genesis), the first of a series of poems on the motorcar, the speaker projects herself into the role of a navigator and imagines herself controlling the (presumably male) driver of the car:

> ¡Soy la muchacha término,
> el ancla de cristal
> que detiene las horas.
> Mis cabellos de níquel
> imantan las estrellas.
> (*Poesía* 115)[13]

(I'm the terminus girl, / the crystal anchor / that holds back time. / My nickel hair / magnetizes stars.)

This persona is sure of herself, self-actualizing, and utilizes scientific epithets to express herself.[14] In her early poems, Champourcin herself dances and describes her own steps, whereas, I suggest, male poets don't dance, they spectate, they observe "the dancer and the dance."[15] She is a seductive coquette who searches out emotions, and flirts with men and the earth ("ya me salvé de ti, ¡oh novio de la tierra!" [Oh earth boyfriend, I already escaped from you! (*Poesía* 106)]). This assertive persona achieves satisfaction and fulfillment and declares, in the conclusion to *Ahora*, in a metaphor redolent with phallic aggression, that her poems are

> cicatrices de oro, que mi pluma va abriendo
> sobre la hoja blanca.
> (*Poesía* 111)[16]

(golden scars, which my pen is opening up / on the blank, white page.)

Above all, this persona is confident of her own creative talent and has taken the initial steps on the path to self-determination:

> I   Esta vida profunda
>   que surge de las cosas,

. . . .
[g]uarda en remotos pliegues
la dulce flor secreta
5   de un pecho inexplorado,
la maravilla trémula
escondida en el sutil
desván de la conciencia.

(*Poesía* 97)

(This profound life / that arises out of things, / . . . / guards in its remote folds / the sweet and secret flower / of an uncharted breast, / the tremulous miracle / that's hidden in the subtle / attic of the mind.)

This dynamic woman—an analogy might be the "flapper" of the Roaring Twenties—was certainly in the process of freeing herself from the nineteenth-century attic, the "desván de la conciencia" of the above poem (l. 8), which her sister precursors had occupied. Jiménez in his "caricatura lírica" (lyrical caricature) of the poet, which appeared as the prologue to *La voz en el viento*, certainly thought of her as dynamic and visionary. He wonders aloud if she might not be a sibyl, "¿La pitonisa de Madrid?" (The oracle of Madrid [*Españoles* 103]).

Champourcin textualizes another persona, that of the poet as daughter. She presents the close relationship between the mother and the daughter as a positive image for the young woman. This is a relationship that is being reassessed by feminist critics, and the fact that "the mother is an important affirmative figure" certainly falls outside the parameters of hegemonic 1920s' poetic discourse.[17] In "Ojos maternales" (Maternal eyes), one of the first poems of *En silencio*, the daughter/speaker finds "toda sacrificio" (total sacrifice) in her mother's eyes, as well as an unlimited supply of care and comfort:

Sois la blanda cuna donde el alma vuela
a entibiar el frío de los desengaños;
es vuestra caricia roce que consuela.

(*Poesía* 50)

(You're the soft cradle to which the soul flies / to take the chill off the colds of deception; / your caress is a consoling stroke.)

Champourcin foregrounds the fact that the mother provides nurture and sustenance to the female of the species. She also foregrounds the notion that it is a woman who gives life. In *Ahora* she describes waking

up and giving life with her eyes and hands to all she sees and touches.
"La dulzura matinal" (Morning softness) concludes:

Fuí madre de las cosas y madre de la Vida.
Al seguir mi camino,
sentí que la ciudad se acurrucaba toda,
buscándome el regazo.

(*Poesía* 110)[18]

(I was mother to all things and mother to Life. / As I went on my
way, / I felt that the whole city curled itself up / to look for my lap.)

This foregrounding of the woman and mother as the source of all life,
because it is expressed by a woman and not a man, may have been in-
terpreted as a challenge to hegemonic discourse and therefore marginalized.

The female and feminist personae inscribed in Concha Méndez's
early work are more diverse; they reflect the jollity of Europe in
the 1920s, *entre deux guerres*. Méndez includes in the poetic register
a variety of middle-class recreational activities—sports, travel, enter-
tainments—which more than likely were dominated by men but which
"pure" male poets would have avoided as too "impure." References to
aviators and planes, swimmers, skiers and ski clubs, sailors and boat-
yards, dancers and jazz bands, fishermen/women, equestrians, sailboats,
yachts, and canoes, abound in her early work and are a striking metaphor for her own liberation and unconventional ideas.[19]

Concha Méndez does not passively identify in her early poems with
such emblems of drive and freedom as aviators, pirates, and swimmers,
she exploits the milieu and lexicon associated with the activities of
such people in order to voice her yearnings for liberation, and to inscribe a feminized self within Spanish poetry. Poems such as "El y Yo,"
"Aeronáutica" and "En avión" (He and I, Aeronautics, and In a plane)
explore the poet's nascent feelings of sexual attraction toward men. In
"Nadadora" (Swimmer [woman]) and "Noche fría" (Cold night) the
swimmer is used as a figure for her particular poetic quest; indeed,
in "Noche fría" the woman poet/swimmer acquires metaphysical dimensions. Méndez therefore appropriates these dynamic emblems of
twentieth-century sport as poetic personae that manifest her drives.[20]

In addition, the fisher-girl and the canoe (which in Spanish is a feminine noun—*la canoa*) are used as symbols for the poet's autonomy and

her independence of will. In "La pescadora" (The fisherwoman) the speaker tells a conventional fisherman:

Ni quiero la pipa curva,
ni tu pañuelo bordado,
ni las rosas—los domingos—
ni el cestillo con pescado.

Y, marcharé de este puerto
hacia otro puerto distante
para que decir no puedas:
—¡La pescadora es mi amante!
(*Surtidor* 38)

(I don't want the curved pipe, / nor your embroidered handkerchief, / nor roses—on Sundays—/ nor the frail of fish. / And, I shall leave this port / for another distant port / so that you can't claim: /—The fisherwoman is my lover!)

The speaker above makes it quite clear that she intends to take charge of her own life and not have a man dictate it to her. And in "Regata de canoas" (Boat regata),[21] it is the small boat that wins the race:

Corría ágil, ligera,
la más pequeña de todas,
la que quedó la primera.

(It ran nimble and swift, / the smallest of them all, / the one that came first.)

The poet certainly identifies most enthusiastically with "*la* piragua" (canoe) or "*la* canoa" (boat) and she turns it in to an "objective correlative" of her own self.[22] In comparison to her contemporaries—the (male) Spanish poets of the 1920s—Méndez possibly presents herself as "la más pequeña" (the smallest) of them all, but as the one most likely to succeed. Her ostensibly innocent text is therefore a palimpsest and can be read today as a veiled piece of subversion.

Moreover, "La patinadora," "La danzarina" (The [woman] ice skater, The ballerina), and the pirate—in "Raid" and "Timonel" (Raid, Helmswoman)—are used by Méndez as symbols of autonomous women, those who determine their own destinies and are independent.[23] In *Canciones de mar y tierra*, it is "la capitana" (the [woman] captain) who provides her with a more sustained metaphor for self-realization:

A todas las albas voy
a sentarme a la ribera.
No sé qué dicen que soy.
Yo sólo soy marinera.

Mi vida por ver el mar,
y cien vidas que tuviera.

Y no me quedaré en tierra,
no me quedaré, no, amante,
que me han hecho capitana
de la marina mercante,
y he de marchar en un alba
por los mares adelante.

(*Canciones* 29-30)

(At the break of every day, I go / and sit along the riverbank. / I know not what they say I am. / I'm just a sailor-woman. / I'd give my life to see the sea / and a hundred if I had them. / I shall not stay on land, / lover, I shall not, / for they've made me a [woman] captain / in the merchant navy, / and at the break of one fine day I'm to set sail / on the high seas.)

Alberti's *Marinero en tierra* (Sailor-boy on land) inspired Méndez, who as a captain symbolically navigates her self—away from the reductiveness of being perceived as the Other. She navigates her own life in "Navegar" (Sailing), her own ship in "Barca de luna" (Moon-ship), and the Atlantic Ocean of her own poetic imagination in "Trasatlántico" (Liner). The image of the captain evolves into a more sustained metaphor for her self-development because of its constant and pervasive association in her work with marine imagery: sea, ships, bathing costumes, mermaids. In "Canción" (Song), she claims she would be anything—seagull, swallow, sailor, pilot boat, fisherman—as long as she gets close to the sea:

¡Algo yo quisiera ser
que me acercara a la mar!

(*Inquietudes* 76)

(I want to be something / that gets me close to the sea.)

The sea represents liberty for her, as is implied in the following poem, "Por la escollera" (On the jetty):

Los pies desnudos
sobre la roca viva.
La piel morena
por el sol encendida.

¡Y así marchaba yo
por la escollera,
con el bañador rojo
y el alma marinera!
                    (*Inquietudes* 43)

(Naked feet / on living rock. / Dark skin / bronzed by the sun. / And
that's how I walked / along the jetty, / with my red swimsuit / and my
sailor's soul.)

The speaker is proudly defiant here, presenting her readers with the
image of herself in a red swimsuit strutting along a jetty. In "Rodando
va" (Rolling along) she makes it plain that she will subject herself to
no man:

Mi vida ha llegado al Mar.
Pide un barco submarino
que no tenga
capitán...
                    (*Surtidor* 29)[24]

(My life has reached the sea. / I request a submarine ship / that has
no / man as its captain.)

In "Canal de Bristol" (Bristol Channel) she writes of her only love:

—novia del mar me sentía
novia del mar, o su amante—
                    (*Canciones* 49).

(I felt myself to be a girlfriend of the sea, / girlfriend of the sea, or
its lover.)

In "Nocturno" (Nocturne) she also uses the ship/sea metaphor to ridi-
cule conventional attitudes toward a woman's interests:

(Una barca sin dueño
va por el río.
¿No irá buscando amores
con un navío?...)

. . . . . .
    ¡Levanten puentes altos
levanten puentes;
que desfilen los astros
más relucientes.

    Y manaña, la prensa
del mundo entero,
dirá que me he casado
con un lucero!
            (*Canciones* 143–44)

([A (female) boat without an owner / makes its way along the river. / Well, it'll be cruising to hook up / with a (male) ship, won't it?] / . . . / Raise the bridges high, / raise the bridges; / for the most glistening stars / are on parade. / And tomorrow, the press / around the world / will say that I've got married / to a star!)

Hence, objects such as ships (and the sea) and figures such as the captain (or swimmer, or aviator) are appropriated by Méndez and developed as polyvalent symbols as she proceeds to define herself as an independent woman and poet. Such autonomous self-development, coupled with the appropriation of symbols canonically patented by an Espronceda ("pirata" [(male) pirate]) or an Alberti ("marinero" [sailor-boy]), would constitute a challenge to hegemonic discourse. Hence, to defend its status, patriarchal culture would subsequently discount Méndez as a serious and original poet in her own right. Nevertheless, Méndez "persists as a kind of 'primitive,' retaining her freedom and remaining unacculturated to social conventions and unsubmissive to masculine conceptions of the feminine."[25]

In their early work Champourcin and Méndez express desire in a way that is distinct from a Guillén or a Lorca. Indeed, the fact that at that time they as women had the audacity to express sexual desire at all must in itself have contributed to their obloquy. Moreover, the desire they express runs counter to the traditional image of woman that has been canonized in the decade's androcentric texts: the sexless muse, the idealized beloved, even the whore.[26] The feelings they express are their own, and it is worth noting that "the idea that . . . one's feelings were properly and innately worth writing about was essentially a female idea" (Stanton, "Autogynography" 6–7; see also Gilbert and Gubar, "Ceremonies" 44).

Champourcin's attitude toward the expression of feelings and emotion contrasts starkly with a traditional male's adherence to analytical rationality and fixed goals. For example, in "La mañana indecisa" (Hazy morning) she indicates an openness to poetic inspiration itself, an easy give-and-take response to the life of the mind:

> Senderillo invisible, panal del pensamiento,
> ¿qué fruto darás hoy, qué mieles de silencio?
> *(Poesía 95)*

(Invisible little track, honeycomb of thought, / what fruit will you yield today, what honey-sweets from silence?)

In a similar vein, in "El ocaso destiñe" (The sunset fades) she asserts her identity with her feelings:

> ¡Yo soy el cazador sediento de emociones,
> que dispara en lo ignoto su escopeta de fuego!
> *(Poesía 103)*[27]

(I'm the hunter thirsty for emotions, / who fires into the unknown her shotgun of fire!)

A woman's identity with her sensibility, her desire to express her own emotions and feelings (rather than to distance herself from them) is now seen—for example, in Gilligan's psychological studies—as a characteristic of female discourse.[28] It is important to note this difference, because Champourcin began to write at a time when objectivity was the norm, when T. S. Eliot, certainly an influential patriarch, opines in "Tradition and the Individual Talent" that the poet who expresses less personal emotion produces the more superior artifact. Insofar as Champourcin identifies with her feelings and wants to express them directly she is "different" from the "norm"—which is established by poetry written by males and which excludes all nonconformers.

Moreover, Champourcin's expression of sensuality is distinct from that of her male counterparts. In *Ahora* (1928), a tree becomes the objective correlative for her hot/cold personality.[29] In the poem "(Hojas)" ([Leaves]), the tree itself is the speaker and likens the leaves it loses to the clothes a woman takes off:

> —Adiós mis collares
> de oro trenzado,
> adiós mis diademas
> de ricos topacios—.

. . . .
—El frío ya muerde
mis brazos morenos,
volved tibias hojas
no hagáis caso al cierzo—.
                                    (*Poesía* 92)

(Farewell my chains / of braided gold, / farewell my diadems / of rich
topazes. / . . . / The cold now bites / my suntanned arms, / return
warm leaves, / pay no heed to the north wind.)

In "Volante" (Steering wheel), the sensual connotation intensifies when
the speaker imagines herself to be the steering wheel of a motorcar
desirous of the driver's touch.[30] Champourcin appropriates a style of
the epoch—especially that of the early Salinas—to articulate her own
desires. In "Te esperaré apoyada" (I shall be waiting for you leaning
against...) she also describes how she will undress and embrace the
source of masculine inspiration to whom she directs these words:

Te esperaré encendida.
Mi antorcha despejando la noche de tus labios
libertará por fin tu esencia creadora.
¡Ven a fundirte en mí!
El agua de mis besos, ungiéndote, dirá
tu verdadero nombre.
                                    (*Poesía* 149)

(Inflamed, I shall await you. / My torch, brushing the night away from
your lips, / will release at last your creative essence. / Come and melt
yourself in me! / The water of my kisses, anointing you, will reveal /
your true name.)

The canon does not allow women to express sexual drive in so frank
a fashion. It requires them to be more decorous. Moreover, Champourcin selects the image of coitus as a metaphor for a deeper union;
the final stanza of "Voy a arraigar en ti" (I'm going to take root in
you) reads:

¿No sientes mis raíces? Tu tallo florecido,
ebrio de sí, eterniza mi cálida fragancia.
¡Irguiéndolo alzarás la copa de mi frente,
hasta volcar su zumo en los labios del sol!
                                    (*Poesía* 148)

(Don't you feel my roots? Your flowering stalk, / drunk on itself, eternalizes my warm fragrance. / By holding it high, you'll lift the top off my brow, / until it shoots its juice into the lips of the sun!)

In this sexual union, the female speaker is no passive participant.[31] In *Cántico inútil* (1936), Champourcin draws upon the woman's experience in sexual intercourse as a metaphor for ecstasy and sorrow. Two poems, "Primavera" (Spring [*Poesía* 159]) and "Sobre mi cuerpo en niebla" (On my body in mist [*Poesía* 173]), evoke the ecstasy. In the former, the poet describes nature's spirit as it touches the (female) body of the earth in spring, as if there were a physical union, a flowering, in which the speaker herself participates:

> ¡Todo vino por ti! Porque tus manos lentas
> ciñeron brevemente mi carne estremecida,
> porque al rozar mi cuerpo
> despertaste una flor que trae la primavera.
>
> (*Poesía* 160)

(It was all because of you! Because your slow hands / briefly encircled my trembling flesh, / because as you rubbed my body / you awoke a flower that spring brings.)

Later, the sorrow of sexual frustration — the denial of further touch by the hands of the partner alluded to in the above stanza — becomes a metaphor for anguish, when the speaker presents herself as "isla sin mar" (island without a sea ["Inquietud sin salida (Inescapable malaise [*Poesía* 176])]) and "una ánfora exhausta" (an exhausted amphora ["La ausencia de tus manos en mi cuerpo estéril" (The absence of your hands on my sterile body [*Poesía* 181])]).

Concha Méndez's early poetry is also notable for its exploration of female sexuality.[32] A young girl's initial attraction for a boy is presented in "La fragata extranjera" (The foreign frigate) in *Inquietudes* and in "Adolescencia" (Adolescence) in *Surtidor*; in the former, the female speaker acknowledges her desire with these lines:

> mi jadeante cuerpo
> un bañador cubría
>
> (15)

(a swimsuit covered / my panting body)

The young woman's heart is treated in several poems in *Surtidor*. In "Mi corazón" (My heart [42]) the speaker describes how she almost lost her heart to a man but dived into the waves to rescue it before it drowned. In "Aeronáutica" (Aeronautics [79–81]), the speaker is no Cinderella; she gives her heart to a man, but symbolically in the form of a "bufanda rosa" ("red scarf") which she drops from a plane as she takes off, as if to say: you may have my scarf but not my self. "By becoming an object of desire," as La Belle notes in another context, the woman "gains presence as a subject that can then convert the male into an object (of pity)" (*Herself Beheld* 55). In addition, in "Lo mismo que una granada" (Just like a pomegranate) Méndez selected the fruit as a sensual symbol for the heart's passion:

El corazón se me ha abierto
lo mismo que una granada.

Y siento caer su sangre
—mi sangre—cristalizada...
                    (*Surtidor* 25)[33]

(My heart has opened up on me / just like a pomegranate. / And I feel its blood falling /—my blood—in crystal drops.)

The pomegranate is a gynocentric symbol in that it signifies "the female principle of fertility"; also, it is "almost universally known as a womb symbol, with its red juice and numerous 'offspring'" (Barbara Walker, *Woman's Encyclopedia* 493).[34] Elsewhere, Méndez uses flowers to symbolize innocence and virginity, which the symbolic wind destroys ("Flores"/"Flowers" [*Inquietudes* 58]) or which she protects, with this warning in "¡Cuidado!" (Watch out):

navegante

. . . .

¡Cuidado,
no se deshoje, no!"
            (*Surtidor* 43).

(navigator / ... / Watch out, / don't pluck the petals off it, don't dare!)

Hence, in her early work Méndez initiates a serious representation of a (young) woman's sexual experience.

In *Vida a vida*, coitus inspires some of Méndez's metaphors and provides her with images to express mutual fulfillment and personal ecstasy. In "Recuerdo de sombras" (Memory of shadows), she foregrounds physical union:

Tú y yo en movimiento
luchando vida a vida,
gozando cuerpo a cuerpo
                    (*Vida* 39)

(You and I in movement, / fighting for our lives, / enjoying each other's bodies).

In a later poem she alludes to intercourse:

Quedarás en mí pasando
por este pasaje estrecho
del amor que me estás dando
                    (*Vida* 46)

(By passing through this narrow strait, / you shall remain in me / from the love you are giving me.)

A more dramatic poem alludes to a woman's orgasm and begins:

A tan alta presión llego
que saltará mi sangre
y se me quedará viva
y hecha de fuego en el aire.
                    (*Vida* 44)

(I get to so intense a pressure / that my blood will leap out / and leave me alive / in the air in flames of fire.)

I believe that it is important to underline the fact that Méndez selects these images and evolves them into metaphors. No other woman had used them quite so freely and naturally in Spanish poetry up to that time. The very fact that Méndez uses them so openly probably contributed to her marginalization.

Champourcin and Méndez deploy a gynocentric lexicon to articulate their visions. As such a rhetorical strategy falls outside the parameters of the canonized 1920s' poetic style, hegemonic discourse would treat its gynocentricity as devious. Anthologizers and historians of literature would no doubt consider it to be ex-centric. In Champourcin's early poetry there are uterine figures as well as metaphors inspired by the flowing of bodily fluids. In *En silencio* there are such womb-shaped objects as, for example, "cuna" (cradle [*Poesía* 52, 70]), "ánfora" (amphora [52]), and "corola" (corolla [55, 60]),[35] which contain or receive regenerating liquids, "efluvios" (effluents [55, 73]). In "Lluvia de marzo"

(March rain [*Poesía* 63–64]), the earth's soil and a parched tree are imagined to open their "wounds" to receive the rain that falls. Comparable imagery is encountered in *Ahora*, where Castilla is described as "redonda, tibia, hueca" (round, warm, hollow [*Poesía* 99]), and where a woman is figured as "cristal" (crystal [*Poesía* 89])—as opposed to *En silencio* where she is a flower that is depetaled (*Poesía* 83). In *La voz en el viento* (1931), a figure for desire or longing is "la sangre de esta herida" (the blood of this wound [*Poesía* 147]).

A part of Méndez's lexicon is also woman-centered. In a poem she dedicates to Consuelo Berges, who wrote the excellent introduction to *Canciones*, she writes:

Toma este sueño que traigo
y engárzalo a tu collar
    (*Canciones* 85)

(Take this dream I bring / and mount it on your necklace.)

The female speaker here foregrounds the fact that this poem is a gift from one woman to another, and by selecting "collar" (necklace/beads) she recalls Sappho—"and with many a flower necklace / you encircled your tender throat, / plaiting blossoms together to make a wreath" (*Sappho* 25)—and underlines the female nature of her "sueño" (dream).[36]

The noun "sangre" (blood) is used pervasively to suggest a woman's difference from men. To explain her dynamic energy, she writes to Alfonso Reyes in "Diques" (Dikes):

Mi sangre corre tanto
que no puedo detenerlo
    (*Canciones* 27)[37]

(My blood runs so quickly / I can't stop it.)

And for Carmen Conde (discussed in chapter 3 below), in "Nocturno" (Nocturne) she describes a speck in the night sky on the Atlantic Ocean (possibly the moon) as:

En el corazón del aire
una azucena de sangre.
    (*Canciones* 106)

(In the heart of the air / a [Madonna] lily of blood.)

The knowledge that she was pregnant overjoyed Méndez, as is evident in "Recuerdo" (Reminiscence):

ibas a nacer
el mundo
se afianzaba en mi sangre
(*Niño y sombras, Antología* 57)

(you were going to be born: / the world / made itself secure in my blood.)

When her first child, Juan, died at birth in March 1933, "sangre" seriously entered her poetic lexicon. In "Fue" (You went) she calls the baby "sangre de mi sangre" (blood of my blood [*Niño y sombras, Antología* 58]); she recalls him as

niño perdido
tierna flor de sangre
(*Niño y sombras, Antología* 61)

(lost child: / tender blood-flower)

she notes that

Se desprendió mi sangre para formar tu cuerpo
(*Niño y sombras, Antología* 56)

(my blood flowed free of me to form your body)

and she asserts that

mi sangre fue después
a señalar con pulso
preciso tu contorno.
(*Niño y sombra, Antología* 58)[38]

(my blood then went / to mark out with its precise / pulse your shape).

Infant mortality "helped to configure domestic reality for many . . . nineteenth- and twentieth-century" women writers (Levine and Marson, "Introduction" xviii). Méndez's willingness to address pregnancy and infant mortality in her verse is an additional reason for her poetry to have been elided from the canon.

Moreover, in the above poems she foregrounds blood in a nonstandard manner—as both the genesis and terminus of life. Blood is associated with new life, and as a mother of a stillborn child, she lost some of hers. Méndez's symbolic use of blood differs from, for example, the "sangre" Lorca envisions in his "Llanto por Ignacio Sánchez Mejías" (Lament for Ignacio Sánchez Mejías) and in some of his New York poems ("New York—Oficina y Denuncia" [New York: A criminal complaint on its workings] and "Oda al rey de Harlem" [Ode to the king of Harlem]).

A detailed analysis of the "blood" metaphor would provide us with deeper insight into the gynocentric vision of Spain's women poets. It is a symbol that reoccurs, as we shall note throughout this book, although I shall be able to focus on only a few examples. In Rosalía, blood has a nontraditional connotation of abuse and abandonment (the "dove" in "Sin nido" [Without a nest]) as well as a nonstandard connotation of creativity ("Mojo en mi propia sangre dura pluma" [I dip a stiff pen in my own blood]). In Méndez, it acquires female connotations—of menstrual blood and thereby of the primal life force. Barbara Walker writes: "From the earliest human cultures, the mysterious magic of creation was thought to reside in the blood women gave forth in apparent harmony with the moon, and which was sometimes retained in the womb to 'coagulate' into a baby. Men regarded this blood with holy dread, as the life essence, inexplicably shed without pain, wholly foreign to male experience" (*Woman's Encyclopedia* 635). To reduce the magic and the potency of this female "blood of life," men appropriated it for their own ends. As Walker goes on to explain, the discourse of the ancient patriarchs gradually erased all feminine associations from blood and made it masculine. Méndez is beginning to take back some of the prepatriarchal symbolism for blood; in her poetry, blood is both gynocentric and incipiently gynocritical. In the work of her daughter poets—Conde, Figuera, Andréu—this discourse will be extended.

Another aspect of Méndez's work is that, like many women writers of the twentieth century, she uses the sea as a metaphor for inner exploration. In London, Méndez feels alienated. Of walking through the fog one night, she writes in "Paseos" (Short walks):

Yo voy buzo por el fondo
de esta ciudad submarina
　　　(*Canciones* 58)

(A diver, I make my way through the depths / of this submarine city).

The same image, to express existential disorientation, occurs in a much later poem, "¿Dónde?" (Where?):

Buceo en el pasado
y me veo sin verme
    (*Vida* 40)

(I am diving around [delving into] the past / and I see myself without seeing myself).

Elsewhere, in "Verdes" (Greens), the pleasure of inner self-exploration is the poet's concern:

1   ¡Ay, jardines submarinos,
     quién pudiera pasear
     por vuestros verdes caminos

     hondos de líquenes y olas,
5   radiantes, y estremecidos
     de peces y caracolas.

     Y volver a la ribera:
     verdes ojos, verde el alma
9   y verde la cabellera!
       (*Canciones* 66)[39]

(Oh, submarine gardens, / would that I could take a stroll / along your green roads, / sunk in lichens and waves, / radiant, and trembling / from fish and snails. / And return to the river's bank: / my eyes green, my soul green, / and green my head of hair!)

The search within the self is not thought of as claustrophobic, as it was for earlier women writers; nor is it perceived as labyrinthine, as it has been for many male poets in the twentieth century (Machado, for example). It is seen as a potentially regenerative descent into that liquid womb of rebirth. The weight of Lorca's "Romance sonámbulo" (Sleepwalking ballad), obviously, is felt in these images (ll. 3, 8–9).[40] However, it seems to me that the influence is not negative, that Méndez draws inspiration from it, and deals with it from strength for her own imaginative purpose: to present the notion that, for a woman, descent into self can signify "green" rebirth as opposed to Lorca's "green" death.[41]

A further difference between these poets and their male counterparts is that in part their vision of the world is nontranscendental. Historically, as we noted in the introduction, philosophical discourses have excluded women from the "transcendent processes of culture." In reaction, perhaps, the woman poet may have attuned herself intuitively

to the nontranscendent and thereby have been better prepared to defamiliarize it, to articulate an immediate and spontaneous delight in
reality, to articulate a simple, childlike view of things.[42] Champourcin
and Méndez tend to eschew an idealizing or transcendentalizing weltanschauung, and the result is that their vision is not as "pura" or "desnuda" (pure or naked) as the dominant esthetic of the Spanish Generation of 1927 required.

This is a major characteristic of Méndez's early work. However, it appears intermittently in Champourcin and only then in her later books.
Méndez flaunts her down-to-earth attitude: it is as though she refrained
from transcendentalizing everyday experiences but chose to enjoy them
for the impressively simple things they are. Méndez seems less goal-
oriented than male poets;[43] when she could, she lived every minute to
the full. In "Alas quisiera tener" (I wish I had wings), she exclaims:

Hacer nido en primavera,
deshaciéndolo después.
¡Y pasar año tras año
sin recordar lo que fué!...
        (*Inquietudes* 53)

(To make a nest in spring, / dismantle it later. / And spend year after
year / without recalling what was!)

This lack of a predetermined goal, or a specific prior objective, this lack
of a need to formulate in advance a target, and to judge oneself by how
well one attains it, is one thing that may distinguish poetry by women
from poetry by the prototypical, rational male.[44] And difference from
the norm leads to obloquy.

Méndez's deployment of a child's perspective is another factor in the
immediacy of her unconventional vision. An early poem "La montaña"
(The mountain) reads:

La montaña
quiere asomarse al lago
como las flores de su orilla
y el árbol de su desmayo.

La montaña
que es verde y ocre y violeta
quiere bajar al prado...
        (*Inquietudes* 62)[45]

(The mountain / wants to peer into the lake, / like the flowers on its bank / and the tree as it trails. / The mountain / which is green and ochre and violet / wants to come down to the meadow.)

The spontaneous, nontranscendental quality to Méndez's vision indicates an ability to see ordinary things in all their newness (to defamiliarize them, as the Russian Formalists pointed out). The poem "Bañistas" (Bathers) is another example:

Horizonte. Espumas.
Azules fríos.

Salteando olas
torsos radiantes,
en líricas danzas
y acrobacias.

Aquella danzarina
del bañador verde...
Aquel gimnasta...

Las olas íntegras
son el mejor columpio.
         (*Surtidor* 106)

(Horizon. Foam. / Cold blues. / Radiant torsos / jumping over waves / with lyrical dances / and acrobatics. / That ballerina / in the green swimsuit... / That gymnast... / The waves at their peak / make the best swing.)

In addition to expressing a defamiliarized delight for the seaside, this "imagistic" poem evinces many of the characteristics of Méndez's early style. As opposed to a Platonic search for perfection, hers is a fluid, unprepossessing attitude toward reality.[46] Méndez's attitude recalls Cixous's "invocations of feminine subjectivity . . . her belief that women have a pre-conceptual, non-appropriative openness to people and to objects, to the other within and outside them" (Jones, "Inscribing Femininity" 89).

In later work (of the 1960s) Champourcin displays a similar characteristic in the way in which she talks to the Virgin Mary and to God, as if they were her equals or in her care (a technique she shares with Gloria Fuertes, as we note in chapter 5).[47] In *Cárcel de los sentidos* (Prison of feelings), published in 1964, in a poem that begins

Señora, estás en paz. Se fueron los pastores
con su alegre alboroto de rústica fragancia
(*Poesía* 243)

(My Lady, you're left in peace. / The shepherds have cleared off / with their pleasant commotion and rustic fragrance),

she imagines Mary in the stable in Bethlehem with her new baby and asks her how she felt. In *Cartas cerradas* (Sealed letters), from 1968, she talks to God in a motherly way:

No te duermas, Señor,
y cuídanos la barca.
La barca Tuya y nuestra.
Mira que va cargada
de los que Tú llamaste
y si ha levado anclas
es porque prometiste,
un día gobernarla.
(*Poesía* 302)

(Don't go to sleep, My Lord; / and look after the boat. / The boat that's Yours and ours. / Don't forget that it's loaded / with those You called to you, / and if it's weighed anchor, / it's because you promised / to govern it one day.)

In such poems as these, the poet presents abstract, complex, religious, and philosophical ideas from a nontranscendental perspective, as well as in a fresh and simple manner—an ideal postulated by Juan Ramón Jiménez in his "Notas" to the *Segunda antolojía poética* (Second poetical anthology) when he spoke of "lo sencillo y espontáneo" ("simple and spontaneous"). Perhaps because Champourcin and Méndez are more comfortable with their own feelings than male poets are, they can express themselves in so direct, simple, and nontranscendental a fashion.[48]

A further characteristic of women's poetry in Spain in the 1920s is its subversion—even tentative revision—of an androcentric view of the world. Such an anti-androcentric perspective automatically disqualifies these poets from being true members of the Generation of 1927. Ernestina's foregrounding of the mother as affirmative figure, as well as the woman as life-giver and center of the earth, is an aspect of this. Such subversion is clearly a characteristic of Spanish women's poetry of the 1920s; it is one that has been ignored.

Intentional subversion is principally an innovative feature of Méndez's poetry—for which no doubt she has been treated to the proverbial cold shoulder. In the first place, Méndez subverts certain metaphorical expressions found in major male precursors. For example, when Bécquer looks into the heart, in *Rima* (Rhyme) 47,

Yo me he asomado a las profundas simas
de la tierra y del cielo

(I have peered into the bottomless depths / of heaven and earth),

he concludes:

¡Tan hondo era y tan negro!
(Rimas 141)

(It was so deep and so dark!)

Yet when Méndez explores feelings, in "Sensaciones" (Sensations [*Inquietudes* 32]), her reaction (which intertextualizes *Rima* 47) is distinct:

Y me asomé
al abismo de tus ojos:
¡Hay algo tan profundo
en tu mirada!...

(I peered / into the depths of your eyes: / there's something so deep / in your gaze!)

Méndez encounters depth of interest, not depth of despair.

Similarly, in "Lluvia de oro" (Rain of gold), which is part of *Olvidanzas. Las hojas verdes,* when Juan Ramón Jiménez refers to the rain to symbolize the state of his soul, he focuses on its depressing, melancholy features:

Llueve, llueve dulcemente.
Tarde llueve, tarde, llora,
que, aunque hubiera un sol de aurora,
no llegaría mi hora
luminosa y floreciente...
(Primeros libros 705–6)

(It's raining, gently raining. / The evening rains, the evening, it's weeping, / for, even if there were a sun at dawn, / no luminous and flowering / hour would rise for me.)

But for Méndez, in "Lluvia en la llanura" (Rain on the prairie) rain is fertile and regenerative:

Llueve. El agua lleva
emoción de jardines,
de lontananzas,
de selvas vírgenes.

Un velo de rocío
se tiende en el ambiente.
Una tranquila luz
emerge del poniente.

Se saturan los campos.
Se sonríen las fuentes.
Y se cubren los lagos
de sueños florecientes.
                    (*Inquietudes* 46)

(It's raining. Rainwater brings with it / emotion from gardens, / from places far off, / from virgin forests. / It covers the air / in a veil of dew. / It bathes the west / in tranquil light. / It saturates fields. / It makes fountains smile. / And it covers lakes / with a bloom of dreams.)

And "Lluvia en estío" (Summer rain) concludes with this stanza:

Es la lluvia del estío,
llanto de infante pequeño.
Es la lluvia del estío,
estela de gran navío
que surca la mar risueño...
                    (*Inquietudes* 84–85)

(Summer rain is / the crying of a little infant. / Summer rain is / the wake of a great ship / that ploughs the smiling sea.)

In ancient cultures, women were believed to attract rain to the parched and sterile earth (Barbara Walker, *Woman's Encyclopedia* 348–49); Méndez's symbolic use of it recovers an element of that ancient power.

Moreover, with respect to Juan Ramón Jiménez, in *Surtidor*, Méndez has a very long poem called "El álamo blanco" (The white poplar), in which she describes dramatically how one morning a decadent aesthete is found dead below the tree. I suggest that Méndez here is tactfully signaling her difference from and her attraction toward, as well as scorn for, that languorous esthetic Juan Ramón Jiménez evolved during the first phase of his work ("la primera época").

Méndez echoes Federico García Lorca in her "Nocturno de la ciudad" (City nocturne):

1   Las luces
     beben la niebla.

     Luciérnagas de bocina
     se deslizan
5   por la tierra.

     Bajo la sombra nocturna,
     se durmieron
     las veletas.

     Por el hondo firmamento
10   se perdieron las estrellas.
                    (*Surtidor* 91)

(Lights / drink the mist. / Trumpet glowworms / slide along the earth. / Weathercocks / slept / in nocturnal shade. / Stars went astray / in the depths of the firmament.)[49]

The difference between Méndez and Lorca lies in the former's gentleness. Her lights "drink" the mist (ll. 1-2), whereas Lorca would use a more foreboding metaphor (e.g., "dientes de espuma" [teeth of surf]). Moreover, Lorca's "veleta" is ominous in its implications, whereas Méndez's (ll. 6-8) are peaceful.[50] Méndez's stars are "lost" in the firmament (ll. 9-10), but it is as though they are stored there, not devoured. It is impossible not to contrast Méndez's receptivity and calm—"beber" (l. 2), "deslizar" (l. 4), "dormir" (l. 7)—with the aggressive and negative connotations of Lorca's metaphors.

As Sharon Ugalde has demonstrated (*Conversaciones* [xii] and elsewhere), a second aspect to subversion and revision of hegemonic discourse is reappropriation of male myths and legends, their reinscription into a female discourse. Méndez appropriates the myth of Cupid—a boy—and turns it into an expression of female desire. The first verse of "A bordo (a Zenobia Camprubí)" (On board [for Zenobia Camprubí]) reads:

El pozo del corazón
se me llenó de canciones.
Las ensarté en un arpón
y apunté a otros corazones.
                    (*Canciones* 142)

(The well of my heart / filled up with songs. / I strung them along a
harpoon / and fired them at other hearts)

She also transforms myths associated with sirens and mermaids into a
symbol for her individuality as a woman. In *Surtidor* "sirenas" appear
in several poems as expressions of Méndez's desire;[51] in *Canciones* the
"sirena" in "Tú y Yo" (You and I [128]) spells out her difference from a
man who lives in "tu castillo de arena" (your sandcastle). And in *Vida
a vida* the symbol is more complexly developed, as it suggests sexual as
well as psychological levels of meaning:

No me despiertes, amor,
que sueño que soy sirena
y que eres el nadador
que va a una playa morena
a bañarse a la claror
en noche de luna llena.

¡No me despiertes, amor!
(*Vida* 44)

(Don't waken me, my love, / for I'm dreaming that I'm a siren / and
that you're the swimmer / heading to a dark beach / to bathe in the
brilliant light / on the night of a full moon. / Don't waken me,
my love!)

Before Homer gave sirens a negative connotation, they "alluded to
female sexual mysteries" (Barbara Walker, *Woman's Encyclopedia* 274).
The siren above is not the woman as Other. She is a symbol of an in-
violable female self with which the woman poet is in contact; a self that
is autonomous, not one determined by androcentric thought.

Moreover, in "Mar" (Sea), Méndez subverts our preconceived views
of Sleeping Beauty: she places her heart in a glass coffin and sends it
out to sea, where she finds fulfillment:

El viento llevó a los mares
un féretro de cristal.

¡Marinero,
si lo ves desde tu barca
encamínalo a alta mar,
que en él navega mi alma,
que murió por navegar!...
(*Surtidor* 35)

(The wind whipped off to the high seas / a coffin made of glass. / Sailor, / if you sight it from your boat, / head it further out to sea, / for my soul, which died from sailing, navigates its path.)

Méndez's Sleeping Beauty is not preserved in a cryogenic state of stupor. As she has become a sailor, she does not need to wait for Prince Charming to awaken her from her sleep, she can navigate her self toward her personal self-realization. And finally, Méndez appropriates the phoenix—a hermaphroditic bird—to describe her own rebirth as she bonds with her daughter: "Yo siento / nacerme en llama cuando estoy contigo" ("I feel / I give birth to myself in flame when I'm with you" [*Sombras* 55]).[52]

In conclusion, in their pre-Civil War poetry, Champourcin and Méndez present us with a style and vision that run counter to our "educated" expectations for poetry of that period. Is it not time to reeducate ourselves to its originality and freshness?

After the Civil War, Champourcin and Méndez continued to write and each published several volumes of verse.[53] A common characteristic of the later work of these poets is its negative perspective on the condition of an aging woman. This "geriatric" discourse enters Spanish women's poetry with Champourcin and Méndez, although it was certainly hinted at in Rosalía's "Sola he tejido mi tela" and "el nuestro ha naufragado" (discussed on pp. 58–59 and 75–76 above). In Champourcin, the voice of a scorned and lonely woman is heard. In *Cántico inútil* (1936) the speaker is hurt and offended: "¡Si yo viera el camino! / Pero lo nublas siempre / con tu palabra hostil / y tu silencio inerte" (If only I could see the road! / But you always cloud it / with your hostile word, / your sluggish silence [*Poesía* 169]). Moreover she is distraught over the hatred that she has been shown: "Y el odio se hizo carne / en aquellas palabras" (And in those words / hatred became flesh [*Poesía* 171]).

In like manner, her lover ignores and rejects her in "Inquietud sin salida" (Inescapable malaise): "¿Con qué sueñan tus manos? / Yo las espero, exhausta, / mullendo con las mías / el lino de tu almohada" (What are your hands dreaming about? / Exhausted, I'm waiting for them, / fluffing up—with mine—/ the linen of your pillow [*Poesía* 177]). In "Ya no tengo más fuerzas" (I no longer have the strength), such negative experiences leave her feeling sterile, and she curses her emotional—and biological—sterility:

¿Por qué diste a mi frente el estigma sagrado
de una pasión estéril que el fuego no consume,

por qué me condenaste como al rosal sin savia
que vive para ver la ausencia de sus flores?

(*Poesía* 183)

(Why did you brand my brow with the sacred stigma / of a sterile
passion that fire cannot consume, / why did you condemn me—a rose's
sapless briar—/ to see my flowers' *intense inane*? [emphasis added]) [54]

These poems probably reflect on one level at least the loneliness and
rejection the poet felt as a wife and lover. With *Cartas cerradas* (1968)—
written after her husband's death—the poet complains that she has
been abandoned by the male of the species as well as by God. In "En
voz baja" (Sotto voce) she writes: "Soy un grillo olvidado. / Un pobre
grillo ciego / a orillas del sagrario" (I'm a forgotten cricket. / A poor,
blind cricket / on the tabernacle's banks [*Poesía* 299]). And she complains to God of the state of uselessness in which he leaves her:

Estoy sola y sedienta
de dar lo que me diste.
Nadie cruza mi puerta,
y me dejaste tanto . . .

¿No hay nadie que lo quiera?

(*Poesía* 301)

(I'm alone and eager / to give what you gave me. / No one crosses my
doorstep, / and you bequeathed me so much . . . / Is there no one who
wants it?)

In "Evocación" (Evocation) of *Poemas del ser y del estar* (Poems of living
and being), she recalls in 1971 a visit made in 1928 to Fray Luis de
León's "huerto" (garden) in Salamanca, and concludes: "—Eramos tres
entonces: / sola en el Huerto quedo" (Then, we were three: / alone,
I remain in the Garden [*Poesía* 326]). The "huerto" is now the poet's
lonely life. [55] *La pared transparente* (Transparent wall) presents the condition of an old woman, a former emigrée, who has returned to her
native country but finds walls blocking her way everywhere (*Poesía* 387-
88). The "pared" is an exoskeletal image that expresses the poet's marginalized condition in the 1980s. [56] It is a hard object she uses to protect
herself, to fend off or distance herself from a culture she finds alien:

(La pared sueña)
Inmutable. Tan blanca
que ni siquiera el sol

la penetra y la inflama.
Y la pared querría
5   ser transparente, aupada
al trajín de la vida,
a la luz que no engaña,
a lo bueno y lo malo.
No quiere ser esclava
10   de ese espesor tupido
que la aísla y la ancla
para siempre en sí misma.

Pared, escudo, valla.
¡Desmorónate pronto,
enciéndete lo mismo
que un torrente de lava!
                                        (*Poesía* 391)

([The wall dreams.] / Immutable. So white, / even the sun can't / penetrate or ignite it. / And the wall, / buoyed by the bustle of life, / wanted to be transparent / to undeceptive light, / to good and bad. / It hates to be enslaved / by the viscous density / that isolates and anchors it / in itself forever. / Wall, shield, fence. / Please crumble soon, / set yourself alight / like a stream of lava!)

The religiously inclined poet sees the wall as the body and desires to cast it off. Yet the mature woman—who has transcended both the religious and the "flapper" personae—hints at the barriers to communication—of a social, spiritual and psychological nature—which a wall represents. In the poems entitled *The Transparent Wall*, these walls are social and metaphysical (e.g., *Poesía* 402-5). She rejects the notion of tracing her steps back ("no me gustan las huellas" [I don't like traces]) and critiques Ariadne for saving Theseus ("Ariadne / hizo un flaco servicio / al que supo perderse" [Ariadne / rendered dubious service / to a man who'd found a way to get himself lost (*Poesía* 405)]). More importantly, in "Ver otra vez" (To see again) she presents herself as an aging woman looking at her mirrored reflection in the water—as Simone de Beauvoir had done—and encountering only the void:

la mujer en el puente
contemplando el vacío
                        (*Poesía* 409)[57]

(the woman on the bridge / contemplating the void).

One almost hears the speaker's scream, as Edvard Munch captured it in his famous painting by that name. Such is the sad condition of the aging woman, one who gave so much to her art, to her man, to God, and to the world.[58] However, my reading of Champourcin is subject to revision, for, as La Belle has demonstrated, "mirror scenes in literature tell us much about feminine consciousness in its relation to body and the world" (*Herself Beheld* 9). She argues, against Lacan, that "for women, mirroring is not a stage but a continual, evershifting process of self-realization" (10), and that the various images reflected in the mirror "stimulate a woman's self-consciousness" (72). This project goes against the grain of Western metaphysics in which "to become yourself, you must be outside yourself" (50, 172, 178–80).[59] Although the poet sees the void reflected in a poem published in 1984, in subsequent work she might encounter a different image on the surface of the water or in the mercury of her glass.

Méndez's later poetry also develops a negative vision of reality.[60] In the poetry she wrote in exile, marine imagery tends to be used with a negative connotation. In "Vine" (I came), she describes her disillusionment:

Vine con el deseo de querer a las gentes
y me han ido secando mi raíz generosa.
Entre turbias lagunas bogar veo a la Vida.

Deja estelas de fango, al pasar, cada cosa...
(*Lluvias enlazadas, Antología* [Bound rains, Anthology 71])

(I came here with the desire to like the people / but the generosity in my roots has got drier and drier. / I see life sailing among muddy lagoons. / Everything leaves a wake of mire as it passes by.)

However, the two distinctive negative features of Concha Méndez's later work are an unwanted divorce and the death of her first child at birth. In such dire straits, Méndez turns to a poetic soulmate and sister precursor, Rosalía de Castro; in two poems in *Poemas. Sombras y sueños* (Poems: Shadows and dreams)—"A tu Galicia he de ir" and "Nos movió el mismo dolor" (To your Galicia I must go, and The same grief stirred us both [25–26])—she identifies with Rosalía's suffering ("¡Juntas hemos de llorar / en tu jardín, Rosalía!" [Together we must cry / in your garden, Rosalía (25)]), as well as with her "espina clavada" (driven thorn) and with the fact that Rosalía was in inner exile, "en tu tierra, desterrada" (banished in your own land), and "en tu norte, ensimismada" (in your northern [province], locked up in your own thoughts [26]). I choose to think pragmatically of Méndez's "espina" as her divorce.

However bitter the experience, Concha Méndez's response to separation and divorce is stoical. She is reminded of her own inner strength and courage: "Tan sola me has dejado, / que estoy conmigo y me basta / —igual que siempre lo he estado" (You have left me so alone, / that I'm with myself and sufficient unto myself /—just as I've always been [*Sombras* 92]). Her life keeps moving like a submarine, as it had in London in the 1920s: "Va lenta, pero segura, / venciendo el peso exterior. / Una estela va dejando, / hecha de sangre y dolor" (It travels slowly, but surely, / overcoming the weight outside. / It goes on leaving / a wake made of blood and grief [*Sombras* 93]). She thinks of her husband as "un lucero" (a bright star) that feigned at being a shining light, and concludes: "El me alejó del cantar / entrándome en la agonía" ("By entering me into agony, / he took me away from singing" [*Sombras* 95]). The self-interest of the male, to whom the poet had devoted so much of her energy, results in a diminution of the female's creative impulse.

Méndez thinks of herself as a small ship sailing "por los anchos mares / de mi soledad" (on the wide seas / of my solitude [*Sombras* 98]), with no coastline in sight. And finally, her sorrow and stoicism are apparent in the following short poem:

Campanita mía
del amanecer,
un amor tenía
y lo perdí ayer.

Larga es la cadena
y es otro eslabón
que se ha desprendido
de mi corazón.

Nuevas y anchas alas
me siento nacer.
Libertad me han dado...
¡No la he de perder!
(*Sombras* 101)

(This little bell of mine / at the break of day / used to have a love / and lost it yesterday. / Long is the chain; / and this another link / with which my heart / must part. / I feel myself born / in wide new waves. / Freedom has been given me... / That I must not scorn!)

In *Vida o río* (Life or river [1979]), the memory of her husband is still painful and preoccupies her poetic imagination. She reflects particularly on their shared experiences.[61]

In addition to divorce, infant mortality contributes to Méndez's negative vision of life. She refers to the toil of her first pregnancy as "nueve lunas" (nine moons) and "toda una angustia / de días sin reposo y noches desveladas" (a whole anguish / of days without repose and nights with lack of sleep). When her first child died at birth, she was devastated—she writes "¡Qué vacío dejaste, / al partir, en mis manos! / ¡Qué silencio en mi sangre" (When you departed, / what emptiness you left / in my hands! / What silence in my blood!). Moreover, she says, it is so painful for her to think about the baby that "una herida" (a wound) has opened up in her body.[62]

In "Por paisajes de bruma" (In misty landscapes [*Niño y sombras* (Child and shadows), *Antología* 67]), she describes the state of total disorientation she suffered during the months following the child's death, and even suggests that she felt she was going mad. A similar poem, "De distintos puntos" (From different points), is found in her next collection, *Lluvias enlazadas*, where "me llaman voces que no entiendo" ("voices I do not understand are calling me" [*Antología* 77]). In *Vida o río* she confesses in "Difícil" (Difficult) that she contemplated suicide but did not have that kind of disposition:

Por más que lo quise un día,
no pude dejar el mundo
y pasar a mejor vida.

Pienso que fueron mis astros
y la fuerza de mi sino
los que me dieron la mano
para seguir mi camino.

(Vida 94)

(No matter how much I desired it one day, / I couldn't leave the world / and go on to a better life. / I think my stars / and the force of my destiny / gave me a hand / to continue on my way.)

Today, we can conclude that the depression Méndez suffered after her baby's death did not manifest an inherent madness or suicidal proclivity; it was what we now refer to as a very serious form of postpartum depression.[63] Stanton's account of Cixous's conceptualization of maternal *jouiscience* can help us toward an understanding of the sorrow Méndez experienced: "This essential capacity to give life/love to another in an-other way is concretized through the metaphor of the pregnant body. Indeed, the delights and mysteries of interiority unknown to man, the pleasures of an expansive waiting fertile with possibilities, and the uniquely maternal experience of arrival, issue . . . , and separation number among the elements of a *jouiscience* metaphorically mined in [Cixous's writing] to delineate the feminine elsewhere" ("Difference" 168). The poet's depression is compounded by the loss of the baby and the loss of the possibility of experiencing that "feminine elsewhere."

Despite the immense strides toward emancipation and self-autonomy these poets made in the 1920s, the negative gynocentric vision of their later work has much in common with so many of their nineteenth-century sister precursors.

A further distinctive feature of the gynocentric vision in the later work of these poets is its religious impulse—very different in nature. In Champourcin, this vision is negative. In numerous later poems Champourcin presents herself as God's servant, as an empty vessel awaiting his presence.[64] In "Entrega" (Surrender) of *Cántico inútil* (1936) she is the compliant helpmate and caregiver: "Seré para tu cuerpo el lino apaciguante / que sana y que perdona" (For your body, I shall be the appeasing linen / that heals and forgives [*Poesía* 159]). In "Exigencia de amor" (Love's demanding) of *Presencia a oscuras* (Presence in the darkness) she is one who wants only to give herself, "me muero / en las ansias de entregarme" (I am dying / with desire to hand myself over [*Poesía* 198]), and in *Hai-kais espirituales* (Spiritual haikus) to be subservient, "Enséñame a tejer el hilo de tu gracia" (Teach me to weave the linen of your grace [*Poesía* 275]).

A masochistic streak also forms a part of her religious impulse (reminiscent of the "oculta inmolación" [hidden immolation] of the "beguina" [Beguine—a member of a semimonastic community of women who have not taken vows but live a life of charity and devotion], see n. 64 below). For example, she is inspired by the thought of being totally besieged by God. In *El nombre que me diste* (The name you gave me), in a poem that begins "Cercada estoy, Señor, / por Ti solo cercada" (Lord, I am enclosed, / by You alone, enclosed), she beseeches her God: "acorrálame el alma, / anula mis defensas" (corral my soul, / annul my defenses [*Poesía* 232]). Then in *Hai-kais espirituales* she claims:

"La fuente está cercada. / Igual que yo en tus manos" (The fount is enclosed. / As I am in your hands [*Poesía* 280]).[65] She even desires the total annihilation of her self. In *El nombre que me diste*, she exclaims: "Limpia este barro inquieto, / ¡haz con él un cristal / que te sirva de espejo!" (Clean this restless clay, / make a pane of glass of it / that you can use as a mirror! [*Poesía* 225]).[66] In "Hora santa" (Sacred hour) of *Presencia a oscuras*, she writes of herself as "esta nada" (this nothingness) and continues:

Soy un agua sin cauce. Deténme en tu pozo. Cíñeme en
tus lisas paredes invisibles. Conténme en Ti. Aprisióname.
                                                    (*Poesía* 211)

(I'm a waterflow without a bed. Stop me in your well. Surround me with / your smooth, invisible walls. Contain me within You. Imprison me.)

Cárcel de los sentidos indicates that the poet was left dried up by her experience, not fulfilled, for she asks the "Señor" (Lord) to whom she has given all not to abandon her:

Te doy gracias, Señor,
por haberme destruido.
Ahora no abandones
este surco sin trigo;
esta fuente reseca,
este árbol sin nidos...

y siembra lo que quieras
en mi campo baldío.
            (*Poesía* 261)

(I thank You, Lord, / for having destroyed me. / Do not now abandon / this furrow with no wheat; / this parched fount, / this tree with no nests... / and sow whatever you like / on my waste land.)

Subservience and self-denial are gladly embraced by devoutly religious people as steps on the road to mystic fulfillment, and Champourcin's religious metaphors do suggest a deep-seated desire to comply with the traditional expectations of her culture, in which the model of the devout believer was one of the few molds approved for a woman's self-realization. But it should be noted that in general Champourcin is not torn asunder by the patriarchal norm for women of her time; she does struggle to discover another aspect of herself within it. The thought in her poetry is sincere and her feelings authentic.[67]

In Méndez's later work, where there are numerous expressions of unconventional religious belief, the religious vision is positive.[68] It is as though the poet reverts to the type of religious feeling that permeated pre-Christian civilizations, in which a "Goddess of Regeneration" was worshiped. Méndez frequently expresses her belief in spiritualism. In *Vida o río* she writes: "Siguen llegándome voces / no sé de qué mundo extraño" (Voices from I know not what strange land keep coming to me [89]).[69] Linked to this belief in the life of spirits is the poet's desire to be free of her conscious mind. In "Isla" (Island) of *Vida o río* she imagines herself as an island:

A veces quisiera ser
árbol en isla desierta
y vivir bajo aquel sol
bajo las altas estrellas,
como árboles que
se ven cubiertos de hiedra,
y así sentir el frescor
del traje que me cubriera.
                    (*Vida* 59)[70]

(At times I want to be / a tree on a desert island / and live under that sun, / under those high stars, / like trees / you see covered in ivy, / and thereby feel the freshness / of the clothes that cover me.)

In "El día que me siembren" (The day I'm sown), this empathy with nature inspires her to ask questions about reincarnation:

¿Qué nacerá de mí
el día que me siembren?
¿Serán rubias espigas,
alguna flor silvestre,
o un árbol solitario
bajo la luz celeste?

¿O será puro polvo
que algún viento
se lleve?

¿Qué pasaré yo a ser
el día que me siembren?
                    (*Vida* 65)

(What will be born from me / the day I'm sown? / Will it be fair
spikes, / a wild flower, / or a solitary tree / under sky blue light? / Or
will it be pure dust / that any wind / may carry off? / What will I move
on to be / the day I'm sown?)

Champourcin and Méndez react to religious belief in opposite ways.
Champourcin is intent on complying with internalized patriarchal expectations, while Méndez explores her personal religious intuitions,
which include prepatriarchal forms of worship.

Méndez also offers a novel twist to the discourse on mothering. We
have already mentioned Champourcin's foregrounding of the mother-
daughter relationship as well as her frustration at never having moth-
ered her own children. In addition, we observe Rosalía's negative por-
trayal of motherhood in such poems as "Sin nido." Concha Méndez's
work on this topic is more extensive and articulates a positive vision
of mothering. As today's feminist psychologists consider that bonds
between women are paramount in female self-development,[71] this is
another distinctive feature of Méndez's work and probably one that is
an additional reason for her exclusion from the canon. Her opus contains reflections on being a mother to children and to her own mother.
With respect to the solitary experience of pregnancy, Méndez writes in
"Recuerdo" (Reminiscence): "(La madre va siempre sola / quien quiera
que la acompañe; / el mundo es un desierto / y el hijo en él un oasis)"
([The mother always goes alone / no matter who accompanies her; / the
world is a desert / and the child an oasis within it] [*Antología* 57]). With
respect to her dead baby, she notes in "Se desprendió mi sangre" (My
blood flowed) that she forever remains a living testimony to his birth:

Mi corazón que es cuna que en secreto te guarda
porque sabe que fuiste y te llevó en la vida,
te seguirá meciendo hasta el fin de mis horas.
(*Niño y sombras, Antología* 56)

(My heart is a cradle that retains you in secret / because it knows you
existed and that it carried you in its life, / it will go on rocking you
until the end of my days.)

With respect to her daughter—Paloma (b. 1935)—Méndez's sense of
maternal pride and joy is expressed in numerous poems (*Sombras* 80–
86), in which she portrays her young daughter as her companion as well
as her charge. Méndez continued to take delight in children, especially

the bronzed beauty of the children in Mexico and Brazil,[72] as well as in the memory of her own childhood.[73]

A significant concern of Méndez's later work is her mother's death — the subject of the dozen poems that bring *Poemas. Sombras y sueños* to a close. Amongst the painful expressions of disbelief, anger and denial, grief and mourning — for a death the poet did not expect, and from which she was separated by the Atlantic Ocean — the poet's sense of physical attachment to her mother stands out, and recalls the way a baby is bound to its mother. The poet feels that she will become a mother to her mother, because her mother, alone in death's kingdom, seems like a defenseless child: "y yo casi tu madre" (and I almost your mother [*Sombras* 108]). As Cixous has written: "Woman is always in a certain way, 'mother' to herself and other" (Stanton, "Difference" 161).

Méndez claims that the mother forms a child's being and that, as a consequence, some of that being perishes when the mother dies. She addresses her dead mother as "madre de todo el ser que dispongo" (mother of all the being I have at my disposal [*Sombras* 106]) and claims: "todo lo encarna la madre / que nos dió el ser que tenemos" (the mother who gave us the being we have incarnates all [*Sombras* 105]). As Méndez believes that her identification with her mother is physical as well as emotional, she feels that a part of her has also died with her mother. For instance, throughout her adult life, the poet has felt cared for by her mother, just as she was cared for in her childhood ("como allá en mi niñez, por ti amparada" [protected by you, just as I was way back in my childhood (*Sombras* 109)]). The poet now senses that this aura of protection has been taken away. Moreover, in "Parece que los montes" (It seems that the mountains) the speaker feels that a form of spiritual death has also occurred within herself:

Aquel ser que creó luz en mis ojos,
que me dió manos y me dió existencia,
al reino de las sombras se me ha ido
dejándome sin alma en esta ausencia.

(*Sombras* 111)

(That being who created light in my eyes, / who gave me hands and gave me existence, / has left me for the shadow-kingdom, / leaving me soulless in this absence.)

In addition to our soul, she claims, "a light" goes out when our mother dies: "Y de nuestra raíz última / algo se desprende. El aire / tampoco nos llega al cuerpo / como nos llegaba antes" (And something falls off /

our last root. / Nor does air / reach our bodies / the way it did before);
we are left "como seres mutilados" (like mutilated beings [*Sombras*
115]). It is as if Méndez feels her childhood going into oblivion with
her mother's death, and that she remains bereft of both the person and
a part of herself.[74] The following poem brings together many of these
ideas and feelings:

Dicen que el quince de Octubre
y que fué de madrugada.
Dicen que no murió sola,
sino bien acompañada.

Yo he venido de su sangre
y al quedar su sangre helada,
no sé como aquí en mi sangre,
no he sentido su llamada . . .

Debió dolerme la vida,
sentir espino en la almohada...
Pero la distancia grande
de un mar que nos separaba
hizo que yo no sintiera
la hora que te llevaba.

(*Sombras* 112)

(They say that it was on the fifteenth of October / and in the early
morn. / They say she did not die alone, / but well companioned. / I
have come from her blood, / and now her blood is frozen / I don't
know how it is that here in my blood, / I've not felt her call . . . / Life
should have made me feel the pain, / a hawthorn in my pillow . . . / But
the great distance / of a sea that separated us / meant that I could not
feel / the moment they took you.)

In its breathless syntax and rhythmical intertextualization of earlier
Spanish elegies, this poem articulates the intense grieving, the profound shock and acute sense of guilt Méndez experienced when she
heard the news of her mother's death.

The work of Méndez and Champourcin challenges our androcentric view of Spanish poetry of the 1920s. We have glimpsed, I believe,
as Sydney Janet Kaplan observes, that "Studying groups of women
writers within a particular time-frame . . . may actually lead to a redefi-
nition of periods in literary history"; she adds that the "predominant
preoccupations" of a period may be "reassessed if it is studied through

the perspective of women writers" ("Varieties" 48). Moreover, Gilbert and Gubar conclude that "when we foreground women's increasingly successful struggle for autonomy in the years from, say, 1880 to 1920, we find ourselves confronting an entirely different modernism" ("Tradition" 203). I hope that Concha Méndez's modernity might be appreciated by today's readers, so that she may rise, phoenix-like, from the ashes of oblivion. She deserves more sustained attention, for with her early books of poetry the horizon of women's poetry in Spain was stretched and expanded: air and light, as well as vast expanses of earth and sea, entered what had hitherto been a claustrophobic space for a gynocentric weltanschauung. As for Ernestina de Champourcin, who fortunately has her devotees today, masked by her more traditional inclinations, there is embedded in her work the discourse of an autonomous subject and liberated woman, one who today in Spain—in her nineties and living in Madrid—continues to inspire poets and readers by her example.

Notes

1. "She has never accented her surname, since it is of Provençal origin" (Landeira, "Ernestina de Champourcin" 141).

2. Such poets as Lorca, Guillén, Salinas, Alberti, Cernuda, Aleixandre, Prados and Altolaguirre, Alonso and Diego, Domenchina and Moreno Villa who, depending on one's preferences, belong either to the "Generación del 27," the "Generación del 25" or "grupo poético de los años 20."

3. On this issue, see Quance, "Entre líneas" (esp. 84–95).

4. Ignored, that is, except by a few devoted scholars who recently began to recuperate this body of work. For Champourcin, see Espejo Saavedra's detailed analysis of love sonnets included in Diego's anthology, *Poesía española contemporánea*; Debicki's study ("Dimensión olvidada") of avant-garde poetic techniques in *Ahora, La voz en el viento*, and *Cántico inútil*; Villar's overview of Champourcin's work and life in "La vida con las palabras"; and most recently, Ascunce's "Prólogo." For Méndez, see Ciplijauskaité ("Escribir"), Bellver ("Exile"), and Miró ("Preliminar").

5. See Jiménez, *Españoles de tres mundos* 103.

6. In Diego's anthology Champourcin railed against the word "poetisa" (poetess): "En la actualidad no puedo oír mi nombre, acompañado por el horrible calificativo de poetisa, sin sentir vivos deseos de desaparecer, cuando no de agredir al autor de la desdichada frase" (Today I cannot bear to hear my name, accompanied by the horrible epithet "poetess," without feeling a real wish to disappear, if not to set upon the author of the wretched phrase [*Poesía española contemporánea* 460]).

Josefina de la Torre was the other woman selected by Gerardo Diego for inclusion in *Poesía española contemporánea* (527-34). De la Torre published *Versos y estampas* (Verses and vignettes) in 1927—when she was seventeen—and *Poemas de la isla* (The island poems) in 1930, for which she had the honor and encouragement of being proclaimed by Pedro Salinas, who wrote the prologue to her first collection. Since 1930 she has published only *Marzo incompleto* (Incomplete March [1968]), but in 1989 (see Miró, "Poetisas" 4-5) her "complete poems" were published by the government of the Canary Islands (using the title of her first volume of verse). Her work does not offer the trajectory of sustained growth, of waxing and waning, I am able to describe in Champourcin's and Méndez's and therefore cannot be considered here. Nevertheless, it deserves study. I wish to thank my colleague José Ignacio Hualde for providing me with a photocopy of her *Poemas de la isla* (1930).

7. Information on Champourcin was limited for some time to Villar ("La vida con las palabras") and Landeira ("Ernestina," in Galerstein), and the dust jackets of her books. However, we now have Landeira ("Ernestina de Champourcin," in Levine) and Ascunce ("Prólogo"). Ascunce remarks that "sobre su persona y en torno a su obra se han impuesto un silencio y una especie de oscurantismo incomprensibles" (There has settled on her person and about her work a silence and sort of incomprehensible obscurantism [xi]).

8. My original source for all information on Concha Méndez's life was Miró, "Preliminar." Later, I was able to consult Bellver's studies ("Exile" and "*El personaje presentido*") and Ulacia Altolaguirre's account of Méndez's *Memorias* (*Concha Méndez*). For Argentina, see chap. 7 of *Memorias*. She met Buñuel in San Sebastián and he introduced her to the members of the Residencia de estudiantes (*Memorias* 39-40, 56-57). For Lorca and Alberti see chap. 2; and for Cernuda, on whom there are many observations, see esp. chap. 15. For her marriage, see chap. 9 (on her subsequent separation, see 121ff.). The wedding was attended by Rosa Chacel, J. R. Jiménez, Lorca, Guillén, and Cernuda. For Alberti's lecture, see *La arboleda perdida* (282ff.). For Jiménez's "retrato lírico," "*Y Concha*," see *Españoles de tres mundos* (131-32).

9. Writing of Champourcin and Méndez, Ciplijauskaité observes: "al casarse, adoptan a los amigos y el modo de vivir de sus maridos," and later concludes, "las dos mujeres poetas consideradas aquí habían renunciado ya a una parte de su personalidad al casarse y nunca pretendieron lucir en las candilejas" (When they marry, they adopt their husbands' friends and style of life . . . the two women poets considered here had already renounced a part of their personalities by marrying and they never tried to play to the footlights ["Escribir" 120, 126]).

In his 1995 introduction to a very limited selection of Méndez's poems (despite its promising title), Valender states that Méndez did not begin to write her best poetry until she met Altolaguirre (1931), and that when he left her (1944), the quality of her work diminished (32, and see 16–17). Consequently, the selection called *Poemas: 1926–1986* includes only nine of the poems of *Inquietudes, Surtidor,* and *Canciones de mar y tierra,* books I foreground in the present study, and it consigns them to the back of the anthology in a section called "Otros poemas (1926–1940)." Valender implies that Cansinos-Assens's review of *Canciones,* written probably in 1930 or 1931, in which he said that Concha's poetry evinced signs of "active virginity," brought her to her senses and made her realize that she should get married and to cease to articulate "virginity" in her work—or in Cansinos-Assens's words, cease to "take refuge against love" ("Introducción" 16, 39 n. 6).

10. In fact, Méndez and Altolaguirre lived first in Cuba, from 1939 to 1943.

11. I say "educated" but González del Valle is more precise when he writes that "el canon está en relación directa con lo que a uno se le enseña," and when he adds that "el canon es ideológico y político" (The canon is in direct relation to what one is taught . . . the canon is ideological and political [*Canon* 30, 31]).

12. *La voz en el viento* contains poems written between 1928 and 1931. I suspect the poems that interest me were written around 1928 as they are similar to those that appear in *Ahora.*

13. Although I completed my study of Ernestina some years before Ascunce's edition of her poetry appeared (*Poesía a través del tiempo,* abbreviated to *Poesía*), my page references are to his edition.

14. Pedro Salinas is credited in Spanish poetry for this style, which the Italian Futurists made famous. For Champourcin's experimentalism, see Ascunce Arrieta's "La poesía de Ernestina de Champourcin."

15. I say that male poets don't dance, they spectate, in the sense that Yeats *observed* the dancer (and could not tell her from the dance). Yeats's poem, "Among School Children," is included in the 1928 collection, *The Tower* (*Collected Poems* 214). Kazantzakis's Zorba clearly is the exception.

16. Compare Rosalía's "mojo en mi propia sangre dura pluma" (chap. 1, p. 67 above).

17. I quote from *The Johns Hopkins Guide* (244). For Chodorow, Cixous, and Irigaray's "valorization of the maternal," see Stanton, "Difference" 160; and Jones, "Inscribing Femininity" 100. I believe that we must now begin to take mother-daughter relationships into account in our assessments of poetry written by Spanish women and, in due course, contrast the attitudes revealed by male poets toward their mothers.

18. See also "Vida-Amor" (Life-love) of *Cántico inútil* (1936), where she explains her ability to help God and declares: "¡Soy la raíz primera de todos

los amores! / ¡Mi vida es el aliento supremo de la Vida! / Nada logra su ser sin el zumo que fluye / por mis venas exhaustas" (I'm the primary root of all love! / My life is the supreme breath of Life! / Nothing manages to come into being without the juice that flows / through my exhausted veins [*Poesía* 158]).

19. For this facet of Méndez and how it fits with Europe of the 1920s, see Valender ("Introducción" 12–13).

20. Unfortunately, there is no edition of Méndez's complete poetry. Page references are to first editions of individual works—which are extremely hard to come by. In her 1981 collection, *Entre el soñar y el vivir* (Between dreaming and living), she was still asserting her dynamism: "quiero vértigo ser a todas horas" (I want vertigo-being at all times [56]).

21. The context suggests that Méndez is not referring to what today we call canoes but to a type of rowing boat, possibly with a small outboard motor ("canoa automóvil").

22. For "objective correlative," see T. S. Eliot's essay on *Hamlet* (*Selected* 145). Debicki studies Champourcin's use of this technique ("Dimensión olvidada" 56, 60 n. 12).

23. See, respectively, *Inquietudes* (69, 81) and *Canciones* (109, 133). For her interest in skating, see *Memorias* (145), and in the sea, *Memorias* (65).

24. See also "Amante, sólo del mar" (*Surtidor* 46)

25. La Belle, in a very different context (*Herself Beheld* 139).

26. I have in mind Juan Ramón Jiménez's idealizing of "la mujer desnuda" (e.g., *Libros* 555), Guillén's intellectualizing in "Salvación de la primavera" (*Aire nuestro I* 103–13), and Lorca's foregrounding of the unfaithful wife in "La casada infiel" (García Lorca, *Obras* 406–7).

27. In *Presencia a oscuras*, written in the middle of her life (1952), she expresses reservations about the intensity of her emotions: "me pierdo en el dédalo de mis propias pasiones" (I lose myself in the thimble of my own passions [*Poesía* 206]). Then late in life, in *La pared transparente* (1984), she insists again on the importance of sentiment and interiority, although her metaphor is now intellectualized (and *juanramonicized*): "cultivad las raíces / que se alzan por dentro" (cultivate roots that rise up inside [*Poesía* 405]).

28. In relation to which Ciplijauskaité writes: "Estudios psicológicos recientes han demostrado que los hombres imponen una orientación teleológica a su vida e insisten más en la ejecución de sus proyectos que en relaciones íntimas. Las mujeres, al contrario, se esfuerzan por establecer una red de comunicaciones aún frecuentemente siendo más introvertidas" (Recent psychological studies have demonstrated that men impose a teleological orientation on their lives and put more emphasis on the execution of their projects rather than on their intimate relationships. Women, on the other hand, despite the fact that they tend to be more introverted, make

an effort to establish a network of communications ["Escribir" 120]). And Bellver observes: "Nancy Chodorow maintains that 'the basic feminine sense of self is connected to the world, the basic masculine sense of self is separate' [and that] Carol Gilligan similarly suggests that psychic wholeness depends for women on affective attachment and for men on worldly achievement" ("Exile" 169).

29. In reference to Conde, Cabello writes: "As an archetype the tree is preeminently a feminine symbol. Jung notes that 'the tree may have been, in the first instance, a fruit-bearing genealogical tree, and hence a kind of tribal mother'" ("Carmen Conde" 28).

30. "¡Dame tus dedos, acres / de olor a gasolina. / Esos dedos cerrados / que precintan la oscura / mercancía del vértigo./ ¡Ellos me harán correr / hasta encontrar mi vida! (Give me your fingers, acrid / from the smell of petrol. / Those closed fingers / that put their seal on the dark / commodity of vertigo. / They will make me run / until I find my life! [Poesía 124–25]).

31. Cano Ballesta alludes to this when he writes of Ernestina and La voz en el viento: "canta el amor con voz apasionada, directa, sin falsos pudores," and he adds that she was breaking "con los tabús que tradicionalmente impedían el vuelo de toda lírica femenina" (she sings of love with a direct and passionate voice, without false modesty; [breaking] with the tabus that traditionally prevented the flight of all feminine lyrics [Poesía española 69]). But Debicki warns his readers not to read "los deseos de la amada de modo demasiado literal" (the beloved's desires in too literal a manner ["Dimensión olvidada" 56). Ascunce even claims that "the sensual component" has disappeared almost completely from La voz en el viento ("Prólogo" xxxix n. 38).

32. Male sexuality is symbolized in "el viento" ("wind"), which is almost always phallic. In Inquietudes, see "Viento de primavera" (38), "Flores" (58), and "Traje de luna" (51–52), from which I take these lines: "El viento marero y suave / que acaricia dulcemente . . . Y plegará mi vestido" (The smooth wind from the sea / that softly caresses . . . And will crease my dress). In Surtidor see "Alas" (21) and "Canción" (44). In addition, Méndez turns an "automóvil" into a phallic symbol: "gusana . . . reptil . . . que . . . se desliza" ("worm . . . reptile that slithers along" [Inquietudes 13]). In Vida a vida male sexuality is "tu espada" ("your sword" ["Te vi venir presintiéndote" 42]).

33. See also "En la alborada" (Inquietudes 77)

34. See my introduction (p. 27) for the anonymous Egyptian text in which the pomegranate symbolizes female sensuality. In this respect, it is interesting to find a Chinese communist woman poet, Li Chü (mid-twentieth century), rebutting such ideas; she describes women harvesting "wheat" and writes that "Round, round wheat, [is] better than pomegranate seeds" (Barnstone and Barnstone, Book of Women Poets 155).

35. Later in *Cántico inútil* (1936), she refers to "el surco": "el surco cali-ente de mi pecho dormido" (the warm furrow of my sleeping breast [*Poesía* 180]). In *Poemas del ser y estar* (1974), this becomes "otro surco incapaz de guardar la semilla" (another furrow incapable of keeping seed [*Poesía* 135]).

36. And see "cuentas de largos collares" (accounts of long strings of beads [*Entre el soñar* 36]).

37. See also "¡Como galopa la sangre!" (*Sombras* 73).

38. Ciplijauskaité has written of Concha's subsequent pregnancy and successful delivery of a daughter: "el tema de la maternidad como una ex-periencia vivida produce versos que son únicos en el repertorio de la gene-ración. Incluso éstos representan una variación *sui generis* sobre el tema del exilio: el exilio de la alegría de verse madre" (the theme of maternity as a real experience gives rise to poems that are unique in the genera-tion's repertoire. They also manifest a sui generis variation on the theme of exile: the exile of the joy of finding oneself a mother ["Escribir" 123]). In *Poemas. Sombras y sueños*, written during the years of the Spanish Civil War and Second World War, blood signifies personal pain ("sangrante pena" [bleeding grief (*Sombras* 59)]) and universal disaster ("la mar de sangre" [sea of blood (*Sombras* 52, and see "Llantos que venís a mí" 66)]).

39. Compare that very different sea of creation and destruction, being and nonbeing, which is filled with all nature of creatures, in Vicente Aleixandre—for example, "Mar y noche" from *Ambito* (1928): "El mar bi-tuminoso aplasta sombras / contra sí mismo" (The bituminous sea crushes shadows against itself [*Obras* 131]).

40. "Romance sonámbulo" (García Lorca, *Obras* 400–403) is from the mid-1920s and this poem appeared in 1930.

41. For an illuminating interpretation of Annis Pratt's "green world," see Sherno ("Gloria Fuertes' Room").

42. By "childlike," I mean fresh and spontaneous, defamiliarized from the accretions of traditional perceptions. I do not see this nontranscen-dentalism as an indication of female subjugation. Unlike women in the nineteenth century, neither Méndez nor Champourcin are perceived to be, or conceived of themselves as being, children. For the belief in the biologically inferior woman, the equation of the intellectual capacities of woman and child, and the disdainful conception of the feminine intellect, see chap. 6 of Dijkstra's *Idols*.

43. And see n. 28 above.

44. I think of J. R. Jiménez's attitude to poetry (between 1913 and 1939): "Quisiera clavarte, hora, / igual que una mariposa, / en su corazón." (I'd like to prick you, time, / like a butterfly, / through your heart [*Libros* 174]); "No más soñar; pensar / y clavar la saeta, / recta y firma, en la meta / dulce de traspasar" (Dream no more; think / and shoot the arrow, / straight and firm, into the goal / of piercing through to the sweet beyond [*Libros* 428]).

45. In *Inquietudes* see also "Paisaje" (47), "La noche y el viento" (48), and "Camino alto" (50)

46. See also "¿Nunca habéis sido payaso?" and "Paisaje Tropical" (*Entre el soñar* 16, 19-20).

47. In the 1960s, Ernestina published four books—*Cartas, Cárcel, Hai-Kais, El nombre*—in Mexico with (Alejandro) Finisterre, Juan Larrea's son.

48. Chodorow says that men are socialized "to be aggressive, non-empathetic and *affectively repressed*" (my italics, quoted in Gardiner, "Mind Mother" 134). To which I would add: abstract and analytical, goal-oriented and detached.

49. There are, I am assured, 1,100 species of Lampyridae (fireflies, glowworms). Trumpet firefly or glowworm could well be a local name.

50. For "Veleta" see García Lorca, *Obras* 7-8, 72-73; for "dientes de espuma," *Obras* 111-12.

51. See especially "Navegando" (47), "Nocturno en el mar" (57), and "Nubes" (87).

52. See also *Entre el soñar* (61).

53. Champourcin has published ten collections of poetry between 1952 and 1991, Méndez five. Ciplijauskaité's "Escribir" is a study of the poetry both women wrote in exile. Bellver's "Exile" also studies this phase of Méndez's poetry.

54. "Intense inane" is Shelley's phrase for "nothingness."

55. "Huerto" also alludes—for instance—to Christian faith and ideals, to Christ's preaching to his disciples, and to the Garden of Gethsemane. Its use here also indicates the complex overdetermination of Champourcin's mature poetic sign.

56. For further commentary on the symbol of the wall, see Ascunce ("Prólogo" xxiii, xlviii-xlix, lx).

57. For important insights into the mirror for women's self-realization, and its difference from the "Narcissistic" male mirror, see Ciplijauskaité (*Novela femenina* 78-80); and La Belle (*Herself Beheld* esp. chap. 2, 41-55).

58. However, for a different perspective, more optimistic, on Ernestina's latest poetry, see Ciplijauskaité's "Yo invisible," which concludes: "mientras que la voz de [sus coetáneos masculinos] adquiere matices irónicos y escépticos hacia el final de la vida, la curva de los versos de Champourcin es ascendente; la voz, admirablemente firme y afirmativa. El *yo* se extiende por el recuerdo y la fe; se vuelve completamente interior, pero en comunicación con todo lo que le rodea" (While the voice of [her masculine peers] acquires ironic and skeptical overtones toward the end of their lives, the curve of Champourcin's verse is ascendant; her voice, admirably firm and affirmative. The self ranges through memory and faith; it becomes completely interior, but remains in communication with all that surrounds it").

59. I have not been able to develop a serious analysis of the mirror in Spain's women poets, but it should be done. For example, Josefina de la Torre, in "Mi falda de tres volantes" (My skirt with three flounces)—which appeared originally in *Poemas de la isla* and which Gerardo Diego chose for his anthology—uses gynocentric imagery to articulate a young woman's feelings of pride in her own attraction and beauty. This witty poem begins: "Mi falda de tres volantes / y mi blusa desprendida, / que me adornan andares / y brazos del aire libre. / ¡Cómo se ondea mi falda / desde el volante primero, / perseguida curva eléctrica, / hasta la orilla firme! / Y mi blusa desprendida, / viento y calma, sol y sombra, / como juega y se persigue / desde el hombro a la cintura. / ¡Ay que me gusta mirarte, / espejito biselado, / cristales de las esquinas, / gafas de los estudiantes! / ¡Qué bien me veo pasar, / remolino de las brisas, / pequeña y grande, confusa / huella blanca en el asfalto!" (My skirt with three flounces, / and my unfastened blouse, / which endow me with sure steps / and uncovered arms. / How my skirt flutters / around the first flounce, / a chased electric curve, / up to the firm border! / And my unfastened blouse, / wind and calm, sun and shade, / how it plays and is chased / from shoulder to waist. / Oh, I love to look at myself, / beveled compact mirror, / corner windows, / students' glasses! / I see I look so good as I pass by, / swirl of breezes, / little and big, confused, / white footprint on the asphalt!" [*Poemas* 89-90]). The young female lyrical subject of this poem looks at her own beauty in various mirrors—including her reflection in the sunglasses of male students—and in effect subverts the patriarchal manner in which Spanish poetry traditionally perceives women. Rossetti also uses the mirror for self-analysis, as we shall note.

60. A perspective already intimated in *Vida a vida*, in a poem titled "Insomnio" (Insomnia): "¡Qué angustiosa cárcel ésta / de hierro por todas partes, / con las ventanas al mundo / a las sombras, a la nada!" (What an anguished prison is this / of iron on all sides, / with windows on to the world, / on to shadows, on to nothingness [*Vida* 47]). This poem would have been written between 1930 and 1932, which otherwise were years of fullness and success for the poet.

61. In *Vida a vida y Vida o río*, see "Encuentro" (78), "Ausencias" (83), "Recuerdo" (85), "Diferentes" (99), "Tarde en Toledo" (103), "Aquel día" (103), "Era verano" (107), "Cuando te sueño" (109), and "Calle lejana" (111). In *Entre el soñar*, she has forgiven him, even excusing his abandonment of her, blaming it on the fact that their son died at birth (71).

62. See "Se desprendió mi sangre," "Hacia qué cielo," "Que no venga" (*Niño y sombras, Antología* 56, 57, and also 57 respectively); and see also "Me levanté" (*Antología* 73, where she draws on a metaphor from the Renaissance, that life is a wounded deer).

63. Chap. 16 of *Memorias* gives an account of her attempts to commit suicide.

64. Champourcin manifests a fascination for the traditional religious way of life in her first book. In "La ciudad muerta" (The dead city [*Poesía* 57-58]) she focuses on the "beguinas" and the type of quiet and retiring life they lead behind a window. (See Barnstone and Barnstone for a discussion of the thirteenth-century Dutch poet Hadewijch, who "was probably the head of a *beguinage*" [*Book of Women Poets* 341]). The "beguina" is perceived as a potential role model, a strong influence on the speaker, and one the poet sees as attractive as well as somewhat repulsive ("oculta inmolación . . . sudario de la ilusión" [hidden immolation . . . shroud of illusion]). (Compare Lorca's "La monja gitana" [García Lorca, *Obras* 404-5] for similar hidden feelings of conflict.) In other poems of *En silencio*, the speaker expresses her inclination for a chaste life. In "Renunciación" (Renunciation) she tells the Lord that "mis rosas" (my roses) are chastened by "tus lirios tristes" (your sad lilies [*Poesía* 65-66; and see 51, 56, 74, 76, 83]). Traditionally, the rose symbolizes sensuousness and the lily "feminine purity," and the one is opposed to the other. Register explains Leslie Fiedler's antithesis of the Rose and the Lily. The former is "the dark-haired, sensuous, unsubmissive woman" and the latter "the Fair-haired Maiden, the woman-as-muse who flourished in European Romantic literature" ("American Feminist Literary Criticism" 4-5). Ernestina's vacillation between the sensuous and the chaste reflects a desire to comply with the expectations of her culture: preparing herself to be a "bride" for God, while at the same time becoming a "lover" (and "mother") to man. Indeed, her sensuous impulse is frequently tempered by a chaste ideal (see, for example, "Romance de otoño," *Poesía* 200).

65. See also *En silencio* (*Poesía* 66, 67-68, 75), *Ahora* (*Poesía* 96, 104-5), *Cántico inútil* (*Poesía* 159, 178-79), and *Presencia a oscuras* (*Poesía* 209).

66. The poem begins "¡Levántame del suelo! (Raise me from the floor! [*Poesía* 225]). I mention it in particular because "barro" (clay) becomes so important a symbol for Angela Figuera.

67. For Ernestina's concern with "divine love," see Ascunce, "Prólogo" xliv-xlvii, liv.

68. There are absolutely no conventional expressions of religious belief in Méndez's work. Chap. 15 of her *Memorias* gives an account of her contact with spirits.

69. In *Sombras* see 21, 33, 66; and in *Vida o río* see also "Sombras" (79) and "Ruidos" (112).

70. In *Vida o río* see also "Octubre" (112), and in *Sombras* see 50, 61, 87, 89.

71. See n. 28 above.

72. In *Vida o río* see "Niños (México)" (59), "Niña" (60), "Retrato (óleo)" (64), and "Negrita brasileña" (99). Several poems of *Entre el soñar* express horror that today's world is an inhospitable place for children.

73. In *Vida o río* see "Castillo" (*66*), "Recuerdos" (*72*), "Mi alma y yo" (*76*), "Recuerdo" (*77*), and "La Granja (España)" (*95*). It may be that in certain poems she also expresses maternal feelings for her husband.

74. This comment is inspired by Angela Carter, *Wise Children* 164.

Part 3 : The Franco Era

3

Carmen Conde and Concha Zardoya

IN THE NEXT TWO CHAPTERS, I turn to the work of four women—Carmen Conde, Concha Zardoya, Angela Figuera, and Gloria Fuertes—who matured as poets between the end of the Spanish Civil War in 1939 and the death of Francisco Franco, the Spanish dictator, in 1975. The Civil War (1936–39) devastated the literary and cultural life of Spain. As we noted, Champourcin and Méndez went into exile and, as we shall note, Zardoya's parents left for Chile, where she herself was born. All major poets of the preceding generation either died (Machado and Lorca) or went into exile (Jiménez, Alberti, Guillén, Salinas, and Cernuda). Furthermore, the new dictatorship of Francisco Franco imposed strict censorship on those who remained behind: Figuera's *Belleza cruel* was published in Mexico in 1958 but not until 1978 in Spain. In this climate, the work of conservative artists was rewarded. Sensitive poets who remained behind on the Peninsula began to confront the catastrophic state of the society in which they lived. The dictatorship, coupled with the lamentable condition of Europe during and after the Second World War, brought to the fore brutality, injustice, oppression, and lack of freedom.[1]

In historical studies, Conde, Zardoya, Figuera, and Fuertes are considered to be members of the "first generation" of post–Civil War Spanish poets, and there is a general consensus of opinion on calling this generation "Social Poets."[2] Although Conde, Zardoya, Figuera, and Fuertes may be included by perspicacious critics in a discussion of that "first generation," they always receive less attention than their male peers: Gabriel Celaya (1911–91), José Hierro (b. 1922) and Blas de Otero (1916–79).

In point of fact, Carmen Conde (1907–96) published her first book, of poetic prose, in 1930. However, it was not until 1945, with *Ansia de gracia* (Longing for grace), that her first collection of poetry was published to great acclaim.[3] Concha Zardoya (b. 1914) published her first book of poetry, *Pájaros del Nuevo Mundo* (Birds of the New World), in 1946. Angela Figuera (1902–84) published her first book, *Mujer de barro* (Woman of clay), in 1948, and Gloria Fuertes (b. 1918) published hers, *Isla ignorada* (Ignored island), in 1950. They are very different poets indeed. In general, Conde and Zardoya are concerned with more traditional poetic ideals, whereas Figuera and Fuertes develop critical visions of the patriarchal culture in which they lived. The former pair meditate positively on mothering and use it as a metaphor to develop nascent gynocentric views; the latter critique a condition that enslaves mothers (and women generally). Conde and Zardoya subtly deflate the male drive for supremacy, whereas Figuera denounces it, and Fuertes mocks it with irony and glee. Together this group of four poets articulates a gynocentric vision that has been influential in the second half of the twentieth century.

Carmen Conde is the first woman to have a book of poetry published by the prestigious *Adonais* collection (*Ansia de gracia*), and the first ever to be elected, in 1978, to the Royal Spanish Academy; she is an important symbol as well as a poet: a model to every other woman who has written poetry in Spain during the second half of the twentieth century. Her "complete" poems to 1966 (*Obra poética: 1929–1966*) brought together sixteen volumes of verse.[4] Since then she has published a further nine books.[5] Embedded within this vast opus, there is the muted, almost silent discourse of a woman who is conscious throughout her life of being different from others, different because she is a woman, and different because she is a bluestocking—a woman who thinks and writes. Her *Mujer sin Edén* (Woman without Eden [1947]) certainly foregrounds this discourse, but perhaps because it was not followed by any sustained feminist meditation on culture, it now seems atypical of her work. However, over a decade later, in *Derribado arcángel* (Archangel overthrown) Conde initiated an agonic struggle, undertaken "hasta que vuelva a hallarme en una mujer nueva" (until I find again that I've become a new woman [*Obra* 680]),[6] in which she reconnects with her womanliness: "¡Es mejor ser mujer!" (It's better to be a woman! [692]).[7] The poet is still waging this struggle in 1984, where she finally exclaims "¡Si ya no soy quien fuera! / Acabo de parirme" (But I'm no longer the woman I was! / I've just given birth to myself [*Obligado* 31]). Clearly, then, there is a feminized consciousness and impulse running through Conde's opus, in certain poems that textualize a state of womanhood that is not found in poetry written by men.[8]

Like Conde, Concha Zardoya (b. 1914) must be a model to other women poets of the Peninsula, in the sense that she has published over thirty volumes of poetry between 1946 and 1994.[9] Unlike Conde, Zardoya was born in Chile, of Spanish parents, and did not resettle in Spain until 1977.[10] In 1981, she selected as her poetic alter ego Diotima, described by Barbara Walker as "Priestess of Mantinea, famous Pythagorean philosopher, teacher of Socrates: another once-renowned *alma mater* later forgotten by patriarchal historians" (*Woman's Encyclopedia* 239). In recuperating Diotima, Zardoya signals her own intellectual credentials: she is a Platonist, her God is Beauty, and her philosophy of love is Plato's.[11] But these ideals did not prevent her, in 1993, from appreciating Fanny Rubio's poetry of "dichas libertarias" and "distorsión": "¡actitudes que ahogan / mi antiguo platonismo!" (libertarian delights . . . distortion: attitudes that drown / my old Platonism [*Don* 59]).

Zardoya's work is a meditation on the traditional concerns of intellectual poets—love, death, solitude, memory, art, history—and as such has been admirably studied by Rodríguez Pequeño. Zardoya's idealism situates her squarely within the logocentric tenets of Western culture, and she sees her reflection on its goals as a self-education: "Tú quieres explicarte lo explicado por otros / siglo a siglo" (you want to explain to yourself what's been explained by others / century after century [*Ritos* 7]). In her reflection on these goals, Zardoya derives her inspiration from a host of male poets and painters of the past and present: "No te vale nadar contracorriente" (it does you no good to swim against the current [*Diotima* 191]).

However, despite the traditional parameters of her fundamental beliefs, and despite the androcentric source of her inspiration, Zardoya chose in her selection of Diotima to reaffirm what she had much earlier asserted: "¡Soy yo, mujer de carne . . . que sale de mi vida / para incendiar el mundo!" (It is I, woman of flesh . . . who leaves my life / to set the world on fire! [*Hermosura* 130]). Moreover, like that of her contemporary Carmen Conde, Zardoya's vast opus features the muted and intermittent discourse of a woman who is reflecting on womanhood (on motherhood and marginalization) and who chooses gynocentric metaphors to express that condition and her reservations with the patriarchal status quo.

Like Champourcin and Méndez, Conde reflects on mothering. She foregrounds the daughter's positive relationship with the mother; she also meditates extensively on pregnancy and on postpartum depression; she maternalizes her ancestors; and she alone initiates a revisionary reading of the biblical Eve.

Conde's reverence for the mother is voiced intermittently throughout her work.[12] Of particular interest is the fact that the poet presents her mother as someone who was a more natural being than nature herself. She perceives her mother to be an earth goddess of unbounding strength and energy. In *Ansia de la gracia*, in "Madre" (Mother), the poet claims that "Una madre es la cueva de donde arranca el río. / Una madre es la tierra por donde corre el agua" (A mother is the cave from which the river sets off on its course. / A mother is the earth through which the water flows [*Obra* 284]), lines that recall Champourcin's "Ojos maternales" ("Sois la blanda cuna donde el alma vuela"). In a poem significantly titled "Mis otros yoes" (My other selves), Conde foregrounds her mother's strength and asks: "¿De qué bosque cortarían / la madera de tu cuerpo" (From what forest could they have cut / your body's wood? [*Monólogos, Obra* 576]). When her mother dies, which is when the speaker feels like a "huérfana irremediable" (*Voz, Obra* 796), she likens her to a tree, and death becomes the hole that a tree leaves in the earth: "Memoria del árbol arrancado por Ti" (Memory of the tree pulled up by You [*Voz, Obra* 797]). The nature metaphor, to foreground the strength and endurance of the mother, persists throughout her work.

The poet's mother remains a figure of strength for her, even though in "Madre" (Mother) Conde had once to nurse her back to health:

¡Pesas poco, madre!
En mis duras piernas yo te mezo,
en mis brazos te recuesto como a una hija.
Te responden maternales
las entrañas que me diste.

(Ansia, Obra 282)

(You weigh little, mother! / In my firm legs I rock you, / in my arms I lay you down like a daughter. / The entrails you gave me / respond maternally to you.)

In nursing her mother back to health, Conde began to assume her own mother's powers,[13] and makes that "very significant step" of becoming "mother to or caretaker of herself," as Rabuzzi observes of women in general in her commentary on the Demeter/Kore myth (*Sacred* 135).

In "Mis otros yoes" Conde also exclaims: "Has sido fuerte. Ven-
ciste / a la loca que fui yo" (You were strong with me. You conquered /
the madwoman I was [*Monólogos, Obra* 575]). This implies that Conde
saw her mother as both nurturing and disciplining her: as molding her
character and as rescuing her from her wild impulses. In one of the
broader contexts of this study—the madwoman in the attic paradigm—
it appears that Conde's mother provided her with a positive role model
for success, as opposed to the negative role model that might drive a
sensitive woman to retreat into the "madness" that beset or characterized many earlier women artists. The strength and grandeur Conde
perceived in her mother helped save the poet from the predicament of
women poets in the late nineteenth century.

A second feature of Conde's meditation on mothering is a reflection
on her own imminent motherhood. Like Concha Méndez, she experienced both pregnancy and the death of the baby, a daughter who died at
birth.[14] In the first poem of *Derramen su sangre las sombras* (Shades shed
their blood), a mother-to-be talks to her "hij*o*" (son) directly, a baby
of whose coming she had despaired (*Derramen* 13); soon, the mother is
looking forward to "la eterna / mujer con el hijo entre los brazos" (the
eternal woman with her child in her arms [15]). The mother's "vientre"
(womb) is thought of as fertile ground (16), and also as the tunnel of
death, into which she'll follow her own mother (17-18).[15] She describes
her body as being split into two, self and *other:* "la realidad doble / que
es mi vida en transcurso" (The double reality / of my life in its course
[19]), and she delights in thinking of herself as being doubled in another
person, "con gozo / nuevo de verme en otros ojos míos, / de mis ojos
hechos, / de mi sangre coloreados, / ¡ay!, de toda cuanta soy" (with joy /
anew to see myself in other eyes of mine, / made by my eyes, / colored
by my blood, / oh! by everything I am! [19]).

As the pregnancy advances, the mother addresses her "Hij*a*" (daughter) and confides in her that her presence inside has helped her—the
speaker—believe in herself (21). She then describes the joy of feeling the
child alive (22, 26), and she turns in her imagination to her own mother,
asking her if she remembers "la alegría" (happiness) of feeling her—
the speaker—inside her (30). The final poem, written before the child's
birth, is totally self-abnegatory: "Yo soy suya . . . toda te pertenezco"
(I am your [life] . . . I belong to you [fem.] totally [34]). This is a poem
that gives us insight into and corroborates those studies of women's
attitudes that claim that women are less ego-bound and self-oriented
than men. As Conde experiences maternity, a mother who is giving

birth sees her self as less important than the self of the *other* within. The second section of *Derramen su sangre* is called "Desencanto" (Disenchantment). It was written after the baby girl was stillborn: "Dentro de mí, muerta" (Inside me, dead [40]). The poems express anger, grief, and self-laceration, feelings associated with what today we call severe depression. The child was a girl, "porque era, acerté, una niña, como yo esperaba" (because it was, I was right, a girl, as I hoped) and the poet would have called her María del Mar (Mary of the Sea [50]). The speaker also expresses her desire to have died with the child she did not ever have a chance to know ("hija que no conozco" [daughter I do not know (41)]). She curses herself and her body:

> ¡qué mísero mi vientre
> que no ha querido
> dejarte vivir fuera de él!"
> . . . .
> ¡Horrible amor el de mis entrañas,
> creándote y deshaciéndote cuando ibas a abandonarlas!
>
> (*Derramen* 42, 48)

(how wretched is my womb / that did not want / to let you live outside it! . . . Horrible love of my entrails, / creating you and unmaking you just as you were about to abandon them!)

As her body has proved to be barren, and because she as a female person is thereby rendered useless, she will devote her art to the dead daughter (43).

The following lamentation epitomizes the nadir of the poet-mother's depression: "He aprendido un suspiro que me retumba cual un viento en habitación vacía. Ese suspiro es tuyo, como mis lágrimas, y en él descanso pensando que tú me esperas al otro lado de la muerte" (I've learnt to know a sigh that rolls around inside me like a wind in an empty dwelling. That sigh is yours, like my tears, and I lay myself to rest inside it thinking that you await me on the other side of death [44]). The poet is devastated by the fact that she could have touched the girl, seen her eyes, felt her heart beat: "te faltó la flor de un beso mío en tu pura frente sin sol y sin vida! / Ese beso me envenenará por siempre todos los besos" (you didn't even feel the flower of one of my kisses on your pure sunless and lifeless brow! That kiss will embitter every kiss for me forever [48]). She had lived in expectation of "el día dichoso en que mi ser se abriera en dos" (the grateful day on which my being would open up into

two [49]); but the poet is left with the memory of physical pain and anguish and with the emptiness of the self: "Y después del dolor tremendo
de su presencia desgajándose de mi carne, el espantoso vacío dentro de
mí; el oscuro silencio de su llegada; ¡el río de sangre inútil, sin rumbo,
que mana de toda yo sin encontrarla a ella!" (And after the dreadful
grief of her presence tearing itself away from my flesh, the appalling
emptiness inside me; the dark silence of her arrival; that river of useless
blood, on no true course, that flows from the whole of me without ever
finding her here at all! [49]). As a poet, she is also left with "el inmenso
vacío, la desolación de mis versos" (the immense emptiness, the desolation of my verse [51]). As she sits with her breasts full of milk, "ajenos,
ignorantes, distanciados de la tragedia que tuvimos tú y yo, hija" (alien,
ignorant, distanced from the tragedy you and I suffered, daughter [53]),
she thinks of that tiny body and heart in the ground as something that
awaits her when she herself dies (52).[16] Conde will write from the "white
ink" of her useless milk, to adapt Cixous's metaphor ("Laugh" 251).

A third aspect of Conde's preoccupation with mothering is her maternalization of her ancestors. This is manifested through the metaphor
of weaving. One of the recurring metaphors found in poetry by women
is derived from the art and craft of weaving, as Showalter explains:

> For at least the past decade, too, metaphors of pen and needle have been
> pervasive in feminist poetics and in a revived women's culture in the
> United States. The repertoire of the Victorian lady who could knit, net,
> knot, and tat, has become that of the feminist critic, in whose theoreti-
> cal writing metaphors of text and textile, thread and theme, weaver and
> web, abound. The Spinster who spins stories, Ariadne and her labyrin-
> thine thread. Penelope who weaves and unweaves her theoretical tap-
> estry in the halls of Ithaca or New Haven, are the feminist culture
> heroines of the critical age. Furthermore, metaphors of the female web
> of relationship have taken on positive associations with psychology; as
> Carol Gilligan observes, women's place in man's life cycle has been that
> of nurturer, caretaker, and helpmate, the weaver of those networks of
> relationships on which she in turn relies. ("Piecing" 224–25)[17]

Conde was developing such a metaphor as early as 1947. She addresses
her dead ancestors and, selecting the "telar" (loom) as her metaphor,
she asks in "El pesar de la criatura" (The child's burden) if they sense
her as their prolongation:

¿sentís que vuelvo a ser joven y dura
encima del telar donde os prolongan?

¿O estáis ya sin conciencia vegetal,
despúes de la sangría de la muerte?
                                        (*Fin, Obra* 314)

(Can you feel that I become young and firm again / over the loom
where they prolong you? / Or, after death's bleeding, / did your
vegetable consciousness leave you?)

The speaker of the poem intuits a certain connectedness—of genealogical incandescence ("Semilla incandescente")—which the "loom"
keeps reweaving. Conde later focuses on the connectedness that she
senses with her intellectual and artistic forebears, claiming that she
carries the seed of generations in her "intellectual" blood in order to
write. Each morning she goes to her study to meet them ("por reunirse
consigo" [to meet with you]); she addresses herself and tells herself
that the act of sitting and writing: "Son sus ejercicios de encuentro con
la idea / que hace siglos sembrara en su sangre / ardorosas simientes"
(They're your exercises that let you unite with the idea / that burning
seeds / must have sowed in your blood centuries ago [*Noche* 85]).[18]

A fourth aspect of Carmen Conde's meditation on the mother is her
development of Eve into a metaphor to critique androcentric values.
Conde is the only woman poet of her time to have written a sustained
critique of the male Logos, *Mujer sin Edén* (1947).[19] As "masculine
desire" has dominated "speech" and has relegated woman to a state of
inexistence (Jones, "Inscribing Femininity" 83), Conde's long poem is
an important—and early—document in twentieth-century woman's articulation of self and appropriation of language. Judith Richards and Jo
Evans, who both have written penetrating commentaries on this book,
provide exemplary and illuminating applications of postmodern reading strategies to convince us of *Mujer sin Edén*'s revisionary originality.
Richards claims that it subverts and revises "the well-known Biblical
events" of Adam and Eve's expulsion from the Garden of Eden; she
notes that the book itself is "focalized almost entirely from a female
point of view," and that Eve "makes her voice rather than her sexuality the principal source of her power and the impetus of her subversive strategy" ("Word without End" 71). Richards continues: "The
displacement of the traditional narrator, and the demystification of his
right to narrate reveals the former text to be no more than a narrative
and linguistic event" (72). Evans writes that "The female speaker, Eve,
rejects the popular image of silent and submissive femininity personi-

fied in the ideal of the Virgin Mary," and that Eve's mere expression
of "displeasure with the symbolic order . . . is an attack on patriarchal
monotheism" ("Carmen Conde's *Mujer*" 75). She continues: "If these,
then, are the premises for Edenic bliss then woman has no place in
Eden" (77). The postmodern reader in me wants to subscribe fully to
this interpretation of *Mujer sin Edén* — and Richards's and Evans's argu-
ments here and throughout are compelling — but the traditional reader
in me remains finally unconvinced. Evans tends to agree, for, as she
concludes her perspicacious analysis, she observes that within the text
there are "two images of femininity [Virgin/Whore that] exist simultaneously, one giving meaning to the other" (80), and that as a result
"the work acquiesce[s], in its final lines, to a stereotypically female form
of inarticulacy" (81). However, probably because I am male, my reading of *Mujer sin Edén* (and of the rest of Conde's poetry) convinces me
of the poet's basically traditional vision: she subscribes to the androcentric myths of Western culture, and specifically to the myth of God.
In the first stanza of this very long poem, Eve describes Adam's body —
from which God plucked her — as "mi patria única" (the only fatherland
I have [*Obra* 373]). Moreover, Eve as lyrical protagonist of the book
sees God as superior, complains against His might and injustice, genu-
flects to beg His forgiveness for making her a woman. Eve still thinks
of herself as an inferior aspect of the Creation and complains about it.
In my opinion, such attitudes detract from the emancipation and self-
autonomy for which Carmen Conde and the speaker of *Mujer sin Edén*
search. Hence, I see Conde as having initiated the possibility for corrosive demythification within twentieth-century Spanish women's poetry
but not as having realized it as successfully as Richards and Evans would
have me believe. I agree with Ugalde that in *Mujer sin Edén* "strides
were made toward the inscription of an authentic female identity," and
that in it "the protest against imposed voicelessness is piercingly felt"
("Feminization" 171-72).

There is a poem in *Mujer sin Edén* titled "Junto al mar" (By the
sea), in which, Richards writes, "Eve replaces the Garden of Eden with
the womb-like sea, suggesting immanence instead of transcendence"
("Word without End" 77). The imagery suggests that Eve unites with
God made mortal (as Sea) in carnal union, which allows the text to
portray "an androgynous vision of *human* identity" (78), human, that
is, as opposed to the dichotomous male/female identity that has been
used by religion to condemn woman as sinful and incapable of enlight-

enment. Again, I wish I could subscribe fully to this novel reading, but I see Eve's joy as originating in a mystical loss of consciousness, as she has been reabsorbed into God's womb from which she came:

> Metiéndome yo en él, ya no soy Eva.
> No pienso, no me muevo, me abandono...
> Flotándolo me entrego y se me entrega
> en un largo tomar que me desangra.
> La fuerza que contiene en su sustancia
> renace y muere en sí. Es Dios el mar.
> ¡Es el mar áspero, criatura
> de Dios eterna: su morada!
>
> .   .   .   .
>
> ¡Y entrándole frenética
> me coge con sus ondas que no acaban,
> deshace mis cansancios; me adormece!
>
> .   .   .   .
>
> ¡Déjeme en el mar,
> que me penetre siempre el mar!
>
> Mecida dulce o brutalmente; poseída
> o rechazada sin soltarme de sus brazos.
> ¡Oh mar de Dios, mar desatinado y mío,
> mar que abrasas
> mi cuerpo avaricioso de tu cuerpo!
>
> (*Obra* 404–5)

(By easing myself into it, I'm Eve no more. / I do not think, I do not move, I abandon myself... / By floating in it, I yield myself and it yields itself to me / in protracted possession that drains the blood from me. / The power of its material essence / comes back to life and dies in itself. The sea is God. / The rough sea, eternal creature / of God, is his dwelling! . . . And furiously entering it, / it grasps me with its waves that never end, / dissolves my weariness; lulls me to sleep! . . . Leave me in the sea, / let the sea penetrate me forever! / Rocked softly or brutishly; possessed / or rejected without its ever freeing me from its arms. / Oh, you sea of God, reckless sea, but mine, / sea that burns my body / voracious for your own!)

This poem certainly evokes the "fluidity, softness, movement, life" which Cixous posits as "antithetical to masculine solidity, hardness, rigidity, and death" (Stanton, "Difference" 170), but its speaker's hearkening after her desired God and her foregrounding of his phallic power deflect my attention from female *jouissance/jouiscience*. *Mujer sin Edén* is not as corrosive a demystification of androcentric Western myth as it promises, as it first seems to be, and as the postmodern reader in me would have wished it to be, but Conde's *gynomorphization* of the Genesis myth is unique and reveals to her daughters in Spanish poetry the potential for revisionary mythmaking.

Concha Zardoya's reflections on mothering are both similar to and distinct from Conde's. In the first place, Zardoya's sense of attachment to her mother and grandmother is strong. As Diotima, she does not want to leave the maternal womb; she depends on that "dulce leche materna" (sweet maternal milk) and on "el seno de tu madre" (your mother's bosom [*Diotima* 18, 20, 23]). From her grandmother she has learned the virtues of the "ángel del hogar": to be "abnegada," "dadivosa," "modesta," "generosa," and to practice "paciencia" and "esperanza" (self-denying, giving, modest, generous, patience, hope). She has also learned the importance of "quehaceres sencillos, cotidianos" (simple, daily tasks) and that a modest woman allows only a small light to shine, "con tu pequeña lámpara de aceite" (with your little oil-lamp [*Diotima* 45–46, 85–86, 116]). The poet appreciates her traditional upbringing and she utters no complaint. Moreover, from her grandmother and "la maestra" (the school mistress, see the poem by this title in *Forma* 59), she has acquired her love of poetry: in "Ariadna" she tells how her grandmother taught her and Ariadna, her playmate, the "Romance del Conde Arnaldos" (Ballad of Count Arnaldos), and told her "cuentos / que aprendiste de niña en tu Montaña" (tales you learnt as a girl in your Mountain [*Debajo* 33]). When Zardoya herself was a kindergarten teacher she taught her children that same "Romance del Conde Arnaldos" (*Diotima* 46, 82). Clearly, Zardoya perceives her matrilineal heritage as a positive influence on her life.[20]

Like Ernestina de Champourcin, Zardoya reflects on the frustrations of not being a mother. In an early poem, "Muñeca" (Doll [1953]), she confesses a desire for her doll to be her daughter and, gazing at it, she asks the following rhetorical question: "¿O mis ojos descubren / lo que anhela mi vida?" (Or are my eyes discovering / what my life desires [*Hermosura* 40]). In a much later poem, "Sin nadie" (Without anyone), published in 1986, there are no rhetorical evasions, just the bald statement:

Una niña tú fuiste
que jugaba a ser madre.
Por ser fiel te quedaste
con un hueco en los brazos:
sin nadie.

(*Altamor* 66)

(You were a girl / who played at being a mother. / For being faithful,
you were left / with a hollow in your arms: / without anyone.)

Zardoya's maternal impulse may have been biologically frustrated but
it has been displaced onto nature and people. Appreciating the beauty
of leaves on a tree, she exclaims: "Maternal, yo renuncio a cortar una /
por no oír el gemido de su muerte" (Maternal, I refuse to cut one /
so as not to hear its death moan [*Engaños* 57]). Moreover, she mothers
her elders. She writes of herself that "Tú padre es hijo tuyo abandonado / en tu España solar y desdichada" (Your father is a son of yours
abandoned / in your wretched ancestral Spain [*Desterrado* 62]); and her
elegy, "Y tú bajaste al sur" (And you came down South), on Gabriela
Mistral (who traveled to New Orleans to visit her) includes these lines:

Eras niña otra vez y de la mano
te llevé por la senda luminosa
de los parques a ver las ardillitas.
Tú querías jugar... y yo lloraba.

(*Elegías* 65–66)

(You were a child again and I took you by the hand / to lead you along
the luminous path / of the parks to see the little squirrels. / You
wanted to play... and I cried.)

Another manifestation of Zardoya's maternalization of others is her
assertion—comparable to Conde's—that her family and loved ones live
on in her work. In "Como si los muertos míos" (As if my dead ones),
she writes:

Los muertos míos, mis muertos
a la luz vuelven en los versos
que me susurran sin voz,
en las leves cancionillas
que balbucean mis labios.

(*Corazón* 41)[21]

(These dead of mine, my dead ones, / return to the light in the lines / that, without a voice, whisper themselves to me, / in the light little songs / my lips babble.)

Linked to this is the poet's maternalization of the earth: throughout her work she figures the land, the sea, and the sky as a vast female spirit that consoles the living and calms the dead. She selects nouns such as "seno," "vientre," "regazo," and "madre" (bosom [of a woman], womb, lap [of a woman], mother) and adjectives such as "virgen" and "maternal" (virgin, maternal) to gynomorphize the planet.[22] The poet finds this maternal instinct in nature. For example, in "Madre" (Mother) she transforms a fig tree into her mother:

Ya te dejo mi boca...
¡Ciega sed de dulzura!

He bebido, cantando,
fresca savia que alumbra.
Viva luz por el labio,
hacia dentro se oculta.

Te proclamo mi madre.
Sangre arbórea que es tuya,
va por dentro del alma:
¡para siempre nos una!

(*Hermosura* 72)

(Now I leave you my mouth... / Blind thirst for sweetness! / By singing, I have drunk / of fresh sap that sheds light. / Living light for the lip / hides itself well within. / I proclaim you my mother. / Arboreal blood that is yours / runs inside my soul: / let it unite us forever!)

Meditating on "la noche" (the night) she writes in "Atalayas" (Watchtowers):

La «madre de los dioses» te llamaron
los antiguos: oscuro vientre, madre,
de los mundos creados, de las cosas.

(*Engaños* 73)

("Mother of Gods" the ancients / called you: dark womb, mother, / of created worlds, of things.)

In "Tierra Profunda" (Profound earth) she evokes the cemetery where she has chosen to be buried:

Maternal, me has tendido tu mano vieja y tierna,
abrazando mis penas, mi soledad desnuda.
. . . .
Mollar, tu tierra aguarda que mis huesos descansen
en su regazo virgen de madre siempre joven.

(*Retorno* 81)[23]

(Maternal, you've offered me your soft old hand, / embracing my
sorrows, my naked solitude. / Boneless, your earth awaits for my bones
to rest / in its virgin lap of an ever-young mother.)

Elsewhere, "Perséfone" (Persephone) is personified as alone bringing
the earth back to life in spring (*Patrimonio* 51). Hence, in her gynomorphization of the planet and her own loved ones, Zardoya develops her
particular gynocentric vision of the world.

A negative gynocentric vision is encountered in both Conde and
Zardoya when their speakers reflect on the marginalized status of
woman. Conde experiences marginalization because of her exceptional
abilities as a young woman, because of the aging process, and as a result
of her widowhood.[24]

It appears that because of her exceptional talents and intellectual
abilities Carmen Conde was perceived to be abnormal. In "Contra-
punto de destinos" (Counterpoint of destinies) of *Monólogos*, her own
mother admonishes her for not being a traditional woman: "Yo quisiera
que aprendieras / lo que una mujer precisa: / el arreglo de la casa, / el
coser y la cocina" (I would want you to learn / what a woman has to
know: / taking care of the house, / sewing, cooking [*Obra* 554]). The
poet replies: "si soy como tú dices, / es porque lo manda Dios" (If I'm
what you say, / it's because God decrees it [554]), but she then adds:

Sobran mujeres sencillas
y sobran más, complicadas;
que cosan, laven, cocinen,
que trabajen y que paran.
Déjame con mis delirios,
déjame que no te estorbo.
Soy más pequeña que tú.
Tú eres un trago; yo, un sorbo.

(555)

(There are plenty of simple women, / and there are even more complicated ones: / let them sew, wash, cook, / let them work and let them

give birth. / Leave me with my deliriums, / leave me alone for I don't get in your way. / I'm smaller than you. / You're a draught; I, a sip.)

Carmen Conde seems to have been very conscious of her difference from the "real" woman who was her mother, and from those women who took to housework. She feels alienated from her own sex.

As a mature poet, Conde expresses the yearnings and frustrations of a barren and aging woman. In *Los Poemas de Mar Menor*, for example, the poet's inability to conceive a child is mentioned when she writes to her husband: "Huelo tu simiente / y, pobre Sarah que soy, no te devuelvo / lo que me vienes a dar" (I smell your seed / and, poor Sarah that I am, I do not repay you / with what you come and give me ["Comprobación" *Obra* 748]). Sarah is the biblical symbol of infertility — and hope — and the poet identifies with her here and elsewhere, as in *Humanas escrituras*, when she reflects on Gabriela Mistral (*Obra* 920). It is clear that, like her sister Ernestina de Champourcin, the poet is pained by own infertility, the failure to leave offspring. When one of her siblings dies, she writes in "In Memorian": "Tú dejas buena siembra en hijos que tuviste. / Yo a nadie dejaré que sangre nuestra lleve" (You're leaving a fine sowing in the children you had. / I shall leave no one who carries our blood [*Desde nunca* 25]).

Conde also meditates on widowhood. In fact, her poetry develops in a novel way the discourse on widowhood initiated by her sister precursors. For Champourcin and Méndez, as we noted, widowhood was a bitter experience; their consorts had abandoned them after they had given the best of their lives. However, for Conde there is no recrimination but a desire to be with the dead partner. After her husband's death in 1968, the poet finds herself in an abyss: "Pongo las manos donde las ponías tú / por si arañaran algún rescoldo que no se hubiera apagado / y pudiera incorporármelo al mío tenaz de ti" (I place my hands where you put yours / in case they can scrape up some embers that had not died down / and can stir them up with mine, which are ingrained in you [*Corrosión* 21]). She knows that her search for him is in vain, but draws as imaginatively close to him as she can:

Pero sigo acariciando los brazos de tu sillón mío ahora
en el que te morías gota a gota ante mi angustia
infinitamente volcada.
Perduro quieta, arregazándome en tu vacío
porque, a ojos cerrados, te tengo en mí.

(*Corrosión* 21).

(But I keep on caressing the arms of your easy-chair, mine now, / in which you were dying drop by drop in the presence of my anguish / infinitely shed. / I quietly endure, tucking myself up in your emptiness / because, when I close my eyes, I hold you inside me.)

In her dream, she embraces her dead consort as he gives her "una incesante rama de flores" (a never-ending bunch of flowers [*Corrosión* 60]). In "Pausa ante el origen, VIII" (Pause for the origin) she also replights her troth to him:

Soy la tuya que tuviste, como nadie
tuvo jamás su criatura
de pasión; de cuánta fe
y esperanza entre las lumbres.

Oh nuestra mar contenida en viejos saberes ciertos,
conmigo concurre ahora a todo lo abandonado.

(Corrosión 66)

(I'm yours, the one you had, as no one / ever had his creature / of passion; one who in those flames blazed / with so much faith and hope. / Oh, our sure sea of abiding understanding / gathers with me now around all that's left behind.)

These poems are not marred by sentimentality. They are a direct and moving expression of a widow's desolation.[25] Assessments of mid-twentieth-century poetry in Spain have as yet not taken such a discourse into account.

Concha Zardoya is similar to Rosalía de Castro in the articulation of her sense of marginalization. She does not belong to "el otro mundo /—el de los hombres" (the other world, / the one that belongs to men [*Casa* 27]); she leads a solitary life and hers, like that of other women, is sunless (*Casa* 33, 91). With the unicorn she concludes: "acepto / de mi prisión los límites" (I accept / the limits of my prison [*Casa* 94]).[26] Later, in her meditation on sewing and writing, "Doble símbolo" (Double symbol), she tells herself that because "has nacido mujer" (you were born a woman):

sabes que todos menosprecian
la voz de la mujer o se sonríen
si su palabra apunta hacia lo alto
o penetrar procura las tinieblas.

(Corazón 21)[27]

(you well know, all despise / a woman's voice, or smile / if her word aims high, / or tries to penetrate the shadows.)

But Diotima's "Muñeca" (Doll) provides the most trenchant metaphor of marginalization:

Sus ojos
no miran,
inmóviles.

Su boca
cerrada,
silente.

Dormida.
Despierta.
Dormida.

No anda.
No llora.
No canta.

Desnuda.
Vestida.
Descalza.

En ella,
costuras
ensayas.

Imagen
de niña
pre-viva.

Imagen
de niña
pre-muerta.
(*Diotima* 56–57)

(Her eyes / don't look, / immobile. / Her mouth, / closed, / silent. / Sleeping. / Waking. / Sleeping. / She does not walk. / She does not cry. / She does not sing. / Naked. / Dressed. / Unshod. / In her, / seams, / rehearsals. / Image / of a girl / before she's brought to life. / Image / of a girl / dead-in-life.)

The doll's muteness would horrify the poet; its dependency would offend the independent woman; the text's rigid verticality suggests a straitjacket. In retrospect, for Zardoya, her doll foreshadows the marginalized life of a woman in a patriarchal world.

Moreover, Zardoya frequently selects the older female figure to imply the liminary position of women in society.[28] For instance, her evocation of the fishermen at San Sebastián ends abruptly with the following subtle touch: "las mujeres / han plegado la red con manos lentas" ("the women / have folded up the net with slow hands" [*Corral* 73]). The widow, "sonámbula . . . devastada" ("sleepwalker . . . devastated") with her "suspiro infinito" ("infinite sigh") appears and reappears in her work,[29] as does "la pobre mujeruca que mendiga" (the poor and filthy woman who begs [*Corral* 71]), as well as Goya's witches (*Retorno* 52, 58, 63). The symbolic female moon covers its eye "para no ver el llanto de las madres" (not to see the mothers' crying), weeping caused by the triumph of so much death (*Ceniza* 9). The curse in the mouth of the wife in Picasso's *Guernica* "es justicia y fuego" (is justice and fire [*Manhattan* 33]), and the poet applauds the fact that Goya painted two women smirking at a man who was masturbating (*Retorno* 57). In fact, she praises Judith and all other "matronas" (matrons) and "mozas" (lasses) who used "el femenino ardid" (a female ruse) to achieve their ends (*Retorno* 50). Zardoya is acutely aware of a woman's marginalized status in a patriarchal culture. She expresses no rage, but delicately manifests her disapproval intermittently throughout her work.

An additionally distinctive feature of the work of Conde and Zardoya is that their poetic visions are gynocentrized by the actualization of lexicon, image, and metaphor that articulate a woman's concerns. By drawing upon nontraditional, nonpatriarchal images and metaphors, Conde expresses a view of life which is distinct from that found in the work of her male peers. We have already noted how in her early poetry she focuses on aspects of a woman's life and experience that tend to be ignored by traditional, canonized verse. In particular, we have noted that she confronts the pain of stillbirth ("un parto brutal, cuando se muere el hijo" [a brutal delivery, when the child dies (*Iluminada*, *Obra* 455)]), and that she deals with pregnancy ("No se aprende a perder el amor / aunque cien mil veces se pierda. / Se aferra a las entrañas como hijo" [One would not learn to lose a love / even if one were to lose it a hundred thousand times. / It clings to your entrails like a child (*Desde* 89)]). Moreover, Conde refers to women's breasts, especially in *Ansia de gracia* (*Obra* 283) and *Vivientes de los siglos* (*Obra*

531), and breasts continue to inform her imagery: "Lastimadas colinas de los senos / adolescentes, la actitud inestable / de las muchachas ante el amor" (Injured hills of adolescent / breasts, the unstable attitude / of girls confronted with love [*Desde* 23]).[30] She focuses on naked girls (*Iluminada*, *Obra* 433-34), and on virgins who feel sexual ardor ("en celo" [in heat (*Vivientes*, *Obra* 520)]). In *Los monólogos de la hija* (A daughter's monologues), like Concha Méndez, she imagines her poems bejeweling her mother's neck ("Tengo un collar de palabras / que nunca ceñí a tu cuello" [I have a necklace of words / that I never draped round your neck (*Obra* 573)]).

Also like Méndez, Conde selects blood as a metaphor, but whereas for Méndez it is negative, associated with the death of her son at birth, for Conde it is regenerative. Conde expresses the desire to use her blood to fertilize the barren earth, to be unfaithful to God and to give herself to humanity: "volcarse / en lagos de sangre ajena / fertilizándola noble" (to wallow / in lakes of alien blood, / nobly fertilizing it [earth] [*Fin*, *Obra* 309]). And in "Canto funeral por mi época" (Funeral song for my time), she offers herself as a sacrificial victim: "¡Abridme como res que todos matan, / sacad mi sangre entera, destruidme, / que quiero deshacerme entre vosotros!" (Open me up like a beast that's slaughtered by everyone, / extract all my blood, destroy me, / for I want to pull myself to pieces among you! [*Fin*, *Obra* 321]). In metaphors such as these, Conde is alluding to the Primal Mother's menstrual blood and its magic power to endow life and effect regeneration. Irigaray speaks of this when she writes of the "desire-need . . . to make blood flow in order to revive a very ancient—intrauterine, undoubtedly, but also prehistoric—relation to the maternal" ("This Sex" 100).

And as with Méndez, the sea offered Carmen Conde a sustained gynocentric vision of life. From the beginning of her work, she saw the sea as a friend who empathized with her troubles.[31] In 1962, she published an entire book, *Los poemas de Mar Menor* (Poems of Mar Menor), devoted to the bay near Cartagena (in the province of Murcia). In "Ante ti" (In your presence) the poet steps into this sea for reassurance: "Me abandono en tu mar" (I abandon myself in your sea)—she tells her native region—"me dejo tuya / como darse hay que hacerlo para serte" (I leave myself to you / because the only way to become you is to give oneself up [*Obra* 745]). And in a poem entitled "Incorporación a tu esencia" (Incorporation into your essence), the sea is presented as a liquid womb that envelops the woman and protects her: "Densísimo, que sin moverme apenas / dentro ya de ti, sostienes mi andadura / cargada de pesantez" (Once I'm inside you, you hardly move me, / so very dense, you sustain / my heavily loaded steps [*Obra* 747]). This sea also "mothers" the poet: "Para aliviarme de este peso de mí / entrego a tu densor fabuloso / completa inmovilidad. Y ando" (To unburden myself of this weight that I am, / I yield complete immobility / to your fabulous thickness. And I walk [*Obra* 747]). The poet becomes part of a regenerative womb and derives inspiration from it: "¡Ojos los míos que se abren ciertos / dentro de ti; videntes de ti, tuyos / y realizados ojos de la inmortal espera!" (Mine are eyes that open surely / inside you; your seeing eyes, your very own / immortally waiting eyes come true! [*Obra* 747]).[32]

Around the middle of the 1970s, the sea also incarnates a death wish in her work. The poet's suicidal impulse is to be noted when she writes of her "body" ("el cuerpo") adding: "Quiere / deshacerse en el voluminoso líquido / sin dejarle mancha ni trazo ni espuma. / Incorporársele íntegro / quisiera el cuerpo" (Wants / to dissolve in the voluminous liquid, / leaving neither stain, nor trace, nor foam. / Wholly to incorporate itself / is what the body wants [*Corrosión* 118]). Later the sea is envisioned as a topography for death's journey. The speaker is shedding life's baggage and contemplates the sea and what will be hers: "para ganar / dentro de muy poco espacio / toda la mar para ti" (to gain / in a very short space of time / all of the sea for you [*Cita* 40]). And in another poem, she exclaims: "Si los ojos las manos las piernas / volviéranse al agua donde nacieron" (If only my eyes, hands, legs / could return to the water where they were born [*Cita* 49]).

In "Nacimiento último" (Last birth of all [*Desde*]), she claims that she would be the happiest woman in the world if she could possess the sea. She deserves—at the end of her life—to consummate the marriage act with the elements, and she claims that a "nombre callado que no es nombre" (silent name that's not a name) could emerge from these nuptials, that it would not be an Aphrodite but a stone that could be worked on. These nuptials would "segura / de salvarme de mí ya realizada" (save her from herself); she therefore wishes to be abandoned to the sea: "a la mar que me hizo y que me tiene / en su voz de las mares de la Tierra" (to the sea that made me and holds me / in its voice of the seas of the Earth [38]). A detailed analysis of sea imagery in Conde's extensive opus would no doubt determine that her aquatic metaphors of *Mujer sin Edén* foreshadow her feminization of water in subsequent work.

Concha Zardoya's maternal relationship with nature and people is also reflected in numerous gynocentric images, occurring throughout her work, in which she feminizes concrete objects and abstract concepts. "El llano" (the plain) becomes a naked woman and its sand dunes her breasts (*Pájaros* 19); the air and earth are virgin (*Pájaros* 66, 71); "gracia de niña" (charm of a girl) characterizes a squirrel and water (*Hermosura* 53, *Ceniza* 25). Houses are maternalized: the poet's window becomes "aya vieja," "abuela," "madre joven" (old nanny, grandmother, young mother [*Debajo* 7–8]), and a mansion in the Deep South of the United States becomes "madre generosa" (generous mother [*Hondo* 35]). Time is figured as "la Medusa" (the Medusa [*Hondo* 43]);[33] the years as "abuela" (grandmother [*Corazón* 29]); and the poet's own shadow as "hija y hermana, / quizás madre" (daughter and sister, mother perhaps [*Corazón* 68]). Music contains a "virgen aureola" (virgin halo [*Forma* 48]).

Sewing also becomes a dominant metaphor in Zardoya's work. She recalls it with pleasure,[34] but it is a metaphor that signifies discipline and writing. "Sombra Mía" (Shadow of mine [*Diotima* 34–35]) is devoted to her memory of her mother and the long hours the poet herself spent sewing:

Al principio, fue un juego: imitar divertía.
Mas después fue insinuando su verdad trascendente:
el nivel doloroso de los arduos oficios,
la fatiga y el sueño enlazados vivían.
Mi conciencia de niña, silencioso testigo.

(*Diotima* 34)

(At the beginning, it was a game: to imitate was amusing. / But later its transcendent truth was gradually intimated: / the level of pain in hard tasks, / fatigue and sleep were experienced knit together. / My awareness as a girl, silent witness.)

Sewing is observation and imitation; it prepares the child for the painstaking work of her future.[35] Zardoya also transforms sewing into a metaphor for writing poetry. The tentative "el libro se pregunta / si alguien tejerá con sus palabras / un nido para el ser" (the book wonders / if anyone with its words will weave / a nest for their being [*Engaños* 130]) becomes in "Doble símbolo" the declarative: "Escribir y coser ¿no son lo mismo? / Hilo y tinta devánanse viviendo" (Sewing and writing, aren't they one and the same thing? / Thread and ink spin themselves into life [*Corazón* 21]).[36] Zardoya's attitude contrasts with that of Elizabeth Barrett Browning, who some hundred years earlier had expressed her complete contempt for sewing and for all the "arts" at which an accomplished woman was supposed to excel ("Mother and Poet," in Cora Kaplan, *Salt* 121-23).

Related to her appreciation of the dexterity of weaving and sewing, Zardoya's poetry transforms hands—"las femeninas, suaves manos" (smooth, feminine hands [*Dominio* 39])—into a person's effort to transcend limits and scientifically prescribed barriers. When she touches a man's hand, she gets a fuller sense of the Old South (*Hondo* 74-75). She exclaims that "nuestras manos son alas" (our hands are wings [*Ritos* 60]), and writes in the "Post scriptum" to that collection: "El poeta—ante el frío, la miseria y la represión—siente ansias de evadirse: su huida, imaginariamente, le lleva al reino de las aves: sus propias manos—encadenadas—aspiran a ser pájaros" (The poet—faced with the cold, misery, and repression—feels a longing to escape: her flight carries her in her imagination to the kingdom of the birds: her own hands—shackled—aspire to become birds [*Ritos* 68]).[37]

Despite the transcendent urge inherent in that desire, a nontranscendental impulse is also to be encountered in Zardoya's worldview. We noted that Concha Méndez's poetic vision avoids the abstract concerns of the androcentric world and concentrates on concrete, sensuous reality. Zardoya also creates a space within her texts for such nontranscendentalism.[38] As a poet, she values "las más menudas gracias de la vida" (life's slightest charms [*Don* 19]), a talent she foregrounds in the poem she devotes to Juana de Ibarbourou. From her grandmother the poet has learned, as we noted, the importance of "quehaceres sencillos, cotidianos" (*Diotima* 45). Zardoya also believes that "en el vivir sencillo" (in simple living) one cheats time out of its victory (*Casa* 84); elsewhere she adds that "hay lazos sencillos que nos unen / a la vida, al amor, en gran corriente" (there are simple bonds that merge us / with life, with love, in their strong current [*Engaños* 90]). In expressing her admiration for Jorge Guillén, she transvalues basic household objects: for example, in "Jarra" and "Cenicero" (Pitcher, Ashtray [*Hermosura* 11, 18]). Her transformation of the olive-oil bottle (in "*La* alcuza") includes this observation: "Eres madre callada, / una vida que ignoran / las miradas altivas" (you're a mother who keeps silent, / a life / haughty glances overlook [*Hermosura* 20]). Zardoya asserts in "Actos Sencillos" (Simple acts) that such acts are "Historia femenina inacabable, / que viene del ayer y va al manaña" (never-ending female history, / which comes from yore and heads for the morrow [*Corazón* 17]).

Related to the simple and unassuming nature of such mundane objects and acts, there is Zardoya's figure for her individual poetics: not the consecrated panpipe ("la flauta") but the rustic flute, "la siringa" (*Hermosura* 46). In addition, the unpretentious violet—recalling Rosalía's "margarita" (daisy ["Cuido una planta bella"])—is her favorite: it is fragile (*Hermosura* 79), lachrymose (*Mirar* 82), and humble ("Os oigo" [I hear you]):

Susurran las violetas en el bosque
la suave melodía del perfume
que exhalan, delicadas, entre helechos,
entre agujas de pinos o entre jaras.

Os oigo murmurar esos secretos
que el bosque guarda, fiel, en su espesura.
Los ignoran los mirlos y picazas,
la frágil mariposa del verano.

Vosotras dialogáis y son humildes
las palabras nacidas: el coloquio
a mis oídos llega, discretísimo,
con su mensaje tímido y fraterno.

Enunciáis la verdad y es convivencia
que preludiáis, sensibles. Yo os oigo.

(Forma 19)

(Violets in the wood / —delicate, among ferns, / pine needles or thickets—/ whisper the gentle melody of the perfume / they exhale. / I hear you murmuring those secrets / that the wood keeps, faithfully, inside its thickets. / Secrets not known to blackbirds and magpies, / to the fragile summer's butterfly. / You talk and the words born / are humble: the conversation / reaches my ears, very discretely, / with its shy and fraternal message. / You state the truth and, sensitive as you are, / you herald good fellowship. As for me, I hear you.)

Like her poetic great-great-grandmother, Rosalía de Castro, Zardoya perceives herself as attuned to nature and empathetic toward that which is oft overlooked.

A further characteristic of the gynocentric visions of Zardoya and Conde is the criticism they direct against androcentric values and phallocratic power. Carmen Conde is sensitive to suffering in all human beings regardless of their sex. However, her critique of war—unlike Figuera's and Fuertes's, as we shall see—is not directed against the male hegemonic power structure. Her vision displays a general empathy and sympathy for the suffering of humankind as a whole.[39]

Nevertheless, a small space is reserved in Conde's poems for a critique of the way women are abused in a patriarchal and phallocratic world. In "Mientras dormimos todos" (While all of us are sleeping) men treat women as their mares: "Jinetes delirantes a sus corceles doman. / Mujeres sometidas desnúdanse en lamentos" (Delirious horsemen break in their steeds. / Mastered women keen and undress [*Mundo, Obra* 617]). In "Los que lloran" (Those who weep) women are reduced to their biological selves—procreating: "En los prados, en los ríos, las colinas, / las mujeres parían nuevos hombres" (In the meadows, in the rivers, the hills, / women give birth to more men [*Mundo* 647]), whom they must eventually bury. Conde's attitude toward the wretched condition of woman is complex (and conflicted). She knows they are abused, but in "Por viejos campos nuestros" (In our old fields) she also empathizes with the wretched lives most men live:[40]

> Las mujeres cantan a pesar de todo:
> saben que su voz consuela a los hombres.
> Dan su pecho escuálido, racimo de leche
> que le ayuda al hijo a sobrevivir.
> Muchos hijos mueren por desnutriciones
> de alimentos, alma, sonrisas o besos.
> Las madres los lloran y hasta se resignan
> con parir a otros que les sustituyan.
>
> (*Desde* 32)

> (In spite of everything, women sing: / they know that their voices console men. / They give their squalid breast, dose of milk / that helps their child survive. / Many children die from being malnourished / on food, spirit, smiles, or kisses. / Women weep for them and even resign themselves / to delivering others who can take their place.)

The poet sees how women help men and her sympathies do finally lie with the former, for the basic reason that wives and mothers are never fully appreciated. She captures the real horror of their condition in this line: "no basta a los hombres / que mujeres siervas entreguen placer" (it's not enough for men / that women-servants hand them pleasure [*Desde* 32]). Despite all the effort a woman makes as wife and mother, she remains unappreciated.

Conde, like Angela Figuera, as we shall see, insists on the fact that women are doomed to bury the men they raise. In "En la fosa" (In the grave), she speaks for "las madres de estos jóvenes soldados" (the mothers of these young soldiers) and exclaims:

Vayamos con los picos y las palas...
¡Animo mujeres! ¡Id al campo!
La cosa es bien sencilla: se reduce
únicamente a enterrarlos.

     (*Mundo, Obra* 664)

(Let's get going with picks and shovels... / Let's go to it, women! Out
to the fields! / It's really very simple: it just comes down / to
burying them.)

In "A los que van resignados" (For those who are resigned) she also
sees women as giving birth to crows, emblems of death:

Las madres con los ojos desgajando
llantos que nadie atiende, porque música
o porque vicio o la codicia, el desprecio
acorralan su cuerpo, paridor de cuervos
las más de las veces.

     (*Tiempo* 46–47)

(Mothers plucking tears out of their eyes /—tears no one heeds—
because music / or because vice, greed, scorn / pound their bodies,
whelpers of crows / more often than not.)

In reference to the Civil War and its aftermath, her critique of patriarchy is more bitter in "Las víctimas no hablarán" (The victims will
not speak):

Las madres y las esposas
vestidas de muertos callan

· · · · · · · · ·
¿Por qué es hombre el que mata?

     (*Mundo, Obra* 640)

(Women and wives / dressed with their dead keep quiet. / ... / Why is
it men who kill?)

In the same collection, she declares: "¡Qué raza ignominiosa, muchachos, son los hombres / que aplastan implacables los hombres que ven-
cieron!" (Lads, what an ignominious race are men, / they relentlessly
crush the men they've conquered! [643]). In another collection, she is
extremely sarcastic about the phallocratic need for arms. In "Han dicho
armas" (They said arms) she writes:

Cuando a los hombres exigen los hombres
hay que escucharles, servirles las armas.

El fuerte las necesita: acabar con el débil.
El débil por defenderse del fuerte.

(Obligado 19)

(When men call for men, / they have to be listened to and served
arms. / The strong need them: to finish off the weak. / The weak, to
defend themselves against the strong.)

In "Eso" (That's the problem), the male of the species is presented as
incapable of seeing itself for what it really is: "Lo triste e intolerable—
¡convéncete, hombre!—, / es que tú no te ves, que sólo miras / enfrente
de ti, desaprobándolo todo" (Accept it, man! the sad and intolerable
thing / is that you do not see yourself, for you only look / in front of
you, frowning on it all [*Mundo* 667]). In Conde's work we also find
a philosophical reservation about the compatibility of the sexes ("son
dos mundos ajenos que nunca se penetran" [they're two alien worlds
that never come together (*Iluminada, Obra* 440)]). About this condition, the speaker confesses to feeling only "angustia" ("anguish")—the
poem's title—not fury, rage, or anger.

More trenchant criticism of the patriarchal order is expressed in
"Evidencia" (Proof) when the poet advises God to end it all, as she sees
no evidence of creation:

Los hombres miran allá y no ven hombres.
Las mujeres solamente ven niños.
Los caminos se cubren de madres viejas,
de madres muertas,
de madres clamando a Dios
porque sus hijos
seguirán estallando las noches.

No se abrirán muchachas.
No crecerán muchachos.
. . . .
Ellas siguen pariendo, aunque lo saben.
Las madres viejas y secas
con rugosos pezones que gimen,
saben que el abismo se ha vuelto a abrir.
Y que a él, a la nada sin luz,
vamos todos jadeándonos.

Es por ello tan sólo, Señor,
que mi voz sin ventura te invoca:
que detengas la vida, la ciegues, pues Tú
ya conoces el Caos.

(*Iluminada, Obra* 493–94).

(Men glance over there and do not see men. / Women see only
children. / The roads are covered with aging mothers, / dead
mothers, / mothers crying out to God / because their sons / will keep
on blowing the nights apart. / Girls will not unfold. / Boys will not
grow up. / . . . / Even though they know all this, they go on giving
birth. / Mothers old and dry / with wrinkled, whining nipples, / know
that the abyss has opened up again. / And that, gasping for our breath,
all of us / are heading toward it, a nothingness devoid of light. It's for
that reason only, Lord, / that my unhappy voice invokes you: / that
you stop life, blind it, for you / already know Chaos.)

Despite a few clearly antipatriarchal comments, Conde's vision is
not—in my opinion—subversive. She criticizes the malevolent effects
of power without identifying its origin in the masculine drive for supremacy at all costs.

We have already glimpsed in Zardoya's images of marginalized
women her reservations about the horrors and injustice caused by an
androcentric culture. However, the butt of Zardoya's critique is God.
The suggestive "Tú vas dejando yertamente / la blanca indiferencia de
tu huella" (You go on rigidly leaving / the white footprint of your indifference [*Dominio* 94]) becomes "Dios descansa, / olvidado del mundo y
de las aguas" (God rests, / oblivious to the world and the waters [*Mirar*
68]), and is later stated as: "Jesús . . . redentor inútil para el hombre"
(Jesus . . . useless redeemer for man [*Corazón* 46]).[41]

The poet's critique of the male drive for supremacy is expressed
more graphically. Men are "crueles cazadores ya no púberes" (cruel
hunters who are no longer adolescents [*Pájaros* 66]).[42] They pattern
themselves on rays of lightning: "el hombre prometeico . . . mata por
matar, impunemente" (Promethean man . . . kills for killing's sake,
with impunity [*Corazón* 76]). Hence their love of weapons (*Tiempo* 48)
and the atomic bomb (*Hondo* 152), which Zardoya lambasts. Zardoya is
never irreverent of her male precursors. Her difference from Espronceda, who claimed in "Canción del pirata" (The pirate's song) that "mi
única patria [es] la mar" (my only homeland is the sea), is signaled thus:
"Es mi única patria la palabra" (My only homeland is the word [*Corral*

121]). However, she is most certainly irreverent in the use to which she puts the "nanas infantiles" (lullabies).

Her lullabies are subversive and revisionary: they undermine the status quo and teach the listeners (young and old) an alternative world-view. In *Corral de vivos y muertos* (Pound of dead and living) they deal with Franco's Spain. In *Hondo Sur* (Deep South) they deal with the unjust treatment of southern blacks. Her two dozen lullabies on post–Civil War Spain refer to hunger, the dead, the devastation of the land, the lack of freedom. One of the shortest is "Nana de la niebla" (Lullaby of the mist):

> Velo de llanto, la bruma
> hambre, miserias oculta.
>
> Casi lluvia, gris, silente,
> cubre penas, cubre muertes.
>
> Triste sudario de España,
> guarda muertos, casi blanca.
>> (*Corral* 43)

(Veil of tears, the mist / hides hunger, squalor. / Almost rain, gray, noiseless, / it covers grief, it covers deaths. / Sad shroud of Spain, / it retains its dead, almost white.)

A traditional lullaby would probably have the mist envelop with protection the house in which the baby sleeps, whereas the mist here is covering up crimes and poverty. The moon in *Hondo Sur* is black ("Luna negra" [Black moon]), and the poet suggests that if there were a true moon, black children would seem white:

> Si hubiera luna, niña,
>> serías blanca.
> Si hubiera luna, niña,
>> blanca de cara.
>
> Si hubiera luna, niña,
>> reina del alba.
>> (*Hondo* 103).

(If the moon could shine, little girl, / white you'd be. / If the moon could shine, little girl, / white of face. If the moon could shine, little girl, / queen of the dawn you'd be.)

The fact that there is no moon—paradigmatic symbol of the feminine—in this lullaby signifies the hopelessness and lack of protection afforded the blacks. However, in a traditional lullaby no doubt the moon would watch over the sleeping baby.

Zardoya like Conde is careful and considered in her critique of the hegemonic power structure. She is esthetically incapable (superb formalist that she is)[43] of a devastating critique of those structures; as a woman she is disinterested in fully developing a feminist view of reality and female vision of womanhood. Nevertheless, within her extensive opus she chooses to reserve a space to express her concerns as a woman in a male world and to develop gynocentric metaphors to articulate that particular vision.

Finally, the discourse on female desire is developed in Conde's meditations (but is not part of Zardoya's concerns). We have noted that Champourcin and Méndez express their desire as women in audacious metaphors; Carmen Conde continues this tradition. In her early books, *Ansia de la gracia* (1945) and *Iluminada tierra* (Illuminated earth [1951]), Conde textualizes the ecstasy of the lover and the joy she as a woman feels at giving her body to an *other*. As that *other* can be nature or man, these poems by Conde are reminiscent of Champourcin. "Lo infinito" (Infinite) alludes to such ecstasy and concludes: "Ser mujer y tuya, ¡qué inefable / fundirse la conciencia entre tus brazos!" (To be a woman and yours, how ineffable / the melting of my awareness in your arms! [*Ansia, Obra* 255]).[44] Later, she refers to herself as "la impaciente enamorada" (the impatient woman in love) and dreams of her lover as: "hombre que me vencía / para cogerme suya, sometida y secreta" (man who conquered me, / submissive and secret, to take me for his own [*Iluminada, Obra* 438]). Although readers today may very well object to such manifestations of willing enslavement on the grounds that they encourage and enforce a traditional and stereotypical state of womanhood, it is worth recalling that these poems were written in that hierarchical Spain of the 1940s—for which fact alone they are daring and ground-breaking in their own right. Furthermore, by inscribing their desire, they challenge the masculine domination of speech and declare that "Woman does indeed exist."

Even more defiant is the fact that to express a woman's pleasure of coitus Conde, in the 1940s, textualizes orgasm. In this respect her poems recall Méndez's. In "Primer amor" (First love) Conde graphically describes the impact of her lover on her body as "Esta dicha de fuego que vacía tu testa, / que te empuja de espaldas, / te derriba a un abismo / que no tiene medida ni fondo" (This joy of fire your head empties out, / that thrusts you from the back, / knocks you into an immeasurable, / bottomless abyss [*Ansia, Obra* 268]).[45] In "Conocimiento" (Knowledge) orgasm is described from a woman's awareness: "De antes de la sangre que me hizo / viene este resuello sin reposo" (From before the blood that made me / comes this unrequited panting [*Ansia* 276]). In a later poem, "Deseo" (Desire), she uses coitus as a metaphor for transcendence: she would be a shadow among shadows and proclaims:

> Aunque en éxtasis de fuego me vistiera
> uno de vuestros cuerpos
> —siempre el más hermoso—,
> para olvidar mi espíritu.
>
> (*Iluminada, Obra* 454).

(Even if one of your bodies /—always the most beautiful—/ were to dress me in an ecstasy of fire, / to forget my spirit.)

A second feature of Conde's articulation of desire is that it inscribes the sexual frustrations of a mature woman. In this respect, Conde is developing the geriatric discourse which emerged with Champourcin and Méndez. In "Cántico" (Canticle), the poet surprises us—that is, shocks the traditional male in me—by expressing her sexual desire for young, athletic males. She expresses her desire for a young boy in the full innocence of his youth and confronts her own desire for physical contact ("el indomable anhelo" [indomitable desire (*Devorante* 831)]). Even though she conceives of the boy as a phallus—"Agil muchacho esquivo, / impreciso y cierto, vulnerable y duro / como una palabra que no me atrevo a decirte..." (Agile, elusive boy, / vague and sure, vulnerable and hard / as a word I dare not speak to you [833])—she recognizes that her possession of him would be fatal to his youthful energy, innocence, beauty.

A further aspect of the desire of an old or aging woman is that she is less or no longer attractive to the opposite sex. In *Enajenado mirar* (Enraptured gaze [1962-64]), she plays the role of "amada" (beloved)—"Sólo soy tu amada" (Only I am your beloved [*Obra* 907])—and she decks herself out sexily—"mezclaré con mis cabellos flores rojas" (I shall mingle with my hair red flowers)[46]—in a way that makes it obvious that she knows that she is this god's second choice and that he has come to her because he has got nothing better to do—"la que buscas / cuando no tienes a nadie y te destrozas a ti mismo, / porque tienes que volver a mí" (the woman you search for / when you have no one else and tear yourself apart, / because you must return to me [907]).

In conclusion, Carmen Conde is not Spain's first female poet with a gynocritical vision of culture. She does open a small textual space in her vast poetic opus to the articulation of a woman's concerns and she does deploy an arsenal of novel gynocentric metaphors to initiate an undermining of androcentric structures. When Conde looks back on her major women precursors, Rosalía de Castro, Gertrudis Gómez de Avellaneda, and Carolina Coronado, as she did on just two occasions,[47] her portraits are of conventional figures, the ones literary history has canonized. Her Avellaneda and Coronado are not the women poets Susan Kirkpatrick uncovered, nor the Rosalía I discussed earlier in this book. Nor does Concha Zardoya offer a gynocritical vision of reality, but there are numerous gynocentric insights embedded within her sustained meditations on Western culture's long-held androcentric ideals that manifest the repressed feminist that she was/is—she lives quietly today in a remote suburb of Madrid, busy weaving her creations (and unstitching my observations, I trust).

Notes

1. See Debicki, *Spanish Poetry* (55–97) for a complete account of this period.

2. For instance, Daydí-Tolson's *Post–Civil War Spanish Social Poets.* The label "first postwar generation" is José Luis Cano's. For a fuller discussion, see Debicki (*Spanish Poetry* 63–80, 80–89).

3. See Newton ("Discurso" 61) for a review of Conde's success.

4. Conde's *Obra poética: 1929–1966* contains the following books *Ansia de la gracia* (Longing for grace [1945]); *Mi fin en el viento* (My end in the wind [1947]); *Sea la luz* (Let there be light [1947]); *Mujer sin Edén* (Woman without Eden [1947]); *Iluminada tierra* (Illuminated earth [1951]); *Vivientes de los siglos* (The centuries' living beings [1954]); *Los monólogos de la hija* (The daughter's monologues [1959]); *En un mundo de fugitivos* (In a world of fugitives [1960]); *Derribado arcángel* (Archangel overthrown [1960]); *Los poemas de Mar Menor* (Poems of Mar Menor [1962]); *En la tierra de nadie* (In nobody's land [1960]); *Su voz le doy a la noche* (Your voice I give to the night [1962]); *Jaguar puro inmarchito* (Jaguar pure and unstained [1963]); *Devorante arcilla: Inédito* (Devouring clay: Unedited [1962]); *Enajenado mirar: Inédito* (Estranged gaze: Unedited [1962–64]); and *Humanas escrituras* (Humane writings [1945–66]).

5. *A este lado de la eternidad* (On this side of eternity [1970]); *Corro-*

sión (Corrosion [1975]); *Cita con la vida* (Appointment with life [1976]); *El tiempo es un río lentísimo de fuego* (Time is a very slow river of flame [1978]); *La noche oscura del cuerpo* (The dark night of the body [1980]); *Desde nunca* (Never ever [1982]); *Derramen su sangre las sombras* (The shades shed their blood [1983]); *Del obligado dolor* (From unavoidable grief [1984]); and *Hermosos días en China* (Beautiful days in China [1985]).

6. The title *Derribado arcángel* (1960) was possibly inspired by Angela Figuera's *Vencida por el ángel* (Vanquished by the angel [1950]).

7. And: "Ser mujer es llamar y oírse llamada siempre / por voces que no nacen de mis labios..." (To be a woman is to be called and to hear oneself always called / by voices that are not born of my lips [*Derribado VII, Obra* 692]).

8. Quance cites Susan Cabello, who wrote that in 1947 Conde claimed that a woman must write "desde sus esencias femeninas, desde sus entrañas" (from the female essence, from her entrails ["Entre líneas" 79, n. 2]).

9. Zardoya's collections include: *Pájaros del Nuevo Mundo* (Birds of the New World [1946]); *Dominio del llanto* (The power of weeping [1947]); *La hermosura sencilla* (Simple beauty [1953]); *Los signos* (Signs [1954]); *El desterrado ensueño* (Banished illusion [1955]); *Mirar al cielo es tu condena* (Your sentence is to look at the sky [1957]); *La casa deshabitada* (The uninhabited house [1959]); *Debajo de la luz* (Under the light [1959]); *Elegías* (Elegies [1961]); *Corral de vivos y muertos* (Pound of dead and living [1965]); *Donde el tiempo resbala* (Where time slips up [1966]); *Hondo sur* (Deep South [1968]); *Los engaños de Tremont* (The deceits of Tremont [1971]); *Las hiedras del tiempo* (Time's ivies [1972]); *El corazón y la sombra* (Heart and shadow [1977]); *Diotima y sus edades* (Diotima and her times [1981]); *Los ríos caudales* (Abundant rivers [1982]); *Manhattan y otras latitudes* (Manhattan and other latitudes [1983]); *Retorno a Margerit* (Return to Margerit [1983]); *Poemas a Joan Miró* (Poems for Joan Miró [1984]); *Ritos, cifras y evasiones* (Rites, ciphers and evasions [1985]); *No llega a ser ceniza lo que arde* (What burns does not become ash [1985]); *Forma de esperanza* (Form of hope [1985]); *Los perplejos hallazgos* (Perplexing discoveries [1986]); *Altamor* (Altamor [1986]); *Gradiva y un extraño héroe* (Gradiva and a strange hero [1987]); *La estación del silencio: Elegías* (Season of silence: Elegies [1989]): *Un dios que nos domina* (A god who overpowers us [1992]); *Patrimonio de ciegos* (Heritage of the blind [1992]); *El don de la simiente* (The gift of seed [1993]), and *Marginalia* (Marginalia [1994]).

10. In 1932, under the Republic, Zardoya's parents moved back to Spain. She remained there until 1948, when she moved to the United States as a professor.

11. See, for example, *Diotima* 88, 96, 102, 127; *Ceniza* 17.

12. An entire book, *Los monólogos de la hija*, expresses the poet's deep

faith in the filial relationship itself (*Monólogos, Obra* 579-81) and reflects the depth of love the poet feels for her own mother (565-66).

13. Nevertheless, Conde continues to aggrandize her mother and remains incapable of believing that her own mother was once a mere "niña" ("La niña ocultada," *Monólogos, Obra* 565).

14. In 1983, Editorial Torremozas—whose original goal was to issue poetry by women—published Conde's *Derramen su sangre las sombras*. At first glance, *Derramen su sangre* seems to be an anthology of Conde's poetry to date, because its early poems are from the 1930s and its later ones from the 1960s and 1970s. Upon closer inspection, however, one realizes that the early poems had never been published before, and that the later ones can be fully understood only if they are provided with their due context. That context is the nine months in the life of a pregnant woman—who sheds her blood ("derramar . . . sangre") when she gives birth. But in this particular case, the woman also loses her child at birth. Hence, in these poems, which Carmen Conde refrained from publishing at the time they were written, the poet reflects on the joy that she felt when she discovered that she was pregnant, and then on the horror she experienced when the baby girl died at birth. The shadows ("las sombras") of memory, and the "shades" of the dead, continue to haunt the poet for the rest of her life.

15. In "Motherhood according to Bellini," Kristeva has written: "By giving birth, the woman enters into contact with her mother; she becomes, she is her own mother; they are the same continuity differentiating itself" (*Desire in Language* 239).

16. And the book closes with a cluster of poems that had been included, but decontextualized, in her published volumes (*Su voz, A este lado, Corrosión*). Quance, citing Cabello, notes that Conde remarked: "Sea o no madre efectiva, la mujer sabe de la maternidad" (whether or not she is in fact a mother, a woman knows about maternity ["Entre líneas" 79 n. 2]).

17. On Freud's interpretation of weaving (wool=pubic hair that hides a woman's "genital deficiency"), and Hillis Miller's naming of this as the "mock phallus," see Nancy Miller's "Arachnologies" (*Subject* 80, 97 n. 3).

18. See also *Desde* (52), which seems to be based on washing clothes and wringing them out.

19. The book has five cantos and comprises more than fifty pages of poems.

20. See also "Si no fuera por ti fracasaría" (*Engaños* 18), which eulogizes her mother.

21. See also "Herencias" (*Corazón* 16), "Unitaria Sangre" (*Forma* 56), and "Sangre" (*Dios* 39).

22. For example: "la tierra es un regazo" (earth is a lap [specifically, a woman's lap] [*Dominio* 36]); "al alba lavará maternalmente" (the dawn will

wash maternally [*Ceniza* 43]); "la niebla . . . como una madre tierna que acaricia / a los dormidos hijos en su cuna" (the mist . . . like a tender mother who caresses the children sleeping in their cots [*Altamor* 27]); "Estamos en la mar: es nuestra Madre" (We're in the sea: she's our Mother [*Altamor* 29])

23. For a comparable figure, see her early elegy on Miguel Hernández (*Pájaros* 57); also *Dominio* 49–51 and 67–69, *Diotima* 177, and her elegy on Vicente Aleixandre (*Altamor* 93).

24. As a child and young woman, Conde voiced no sense of alienation. Her world was charged with potential (see *Iluminada*, *Obra* 486). Later in life, her perspective changed. In *La noche oscura del cuerpo* (1980), speaking of herself as an *other*, she confesses that previously she had always felt hemmed in: "Nunca tuvo estancia como la que tiene hoy / para ir recorriéndose por dentro: / siempre espacio limitado bajo techo que aplasta" (You never had a dwelling like the one you have now / for ranging around inside: / always limited space under a roof that squashes one down). And she asks of that *other* which is self "¿Por qué hubo de vivir tan oprimida" (Why did you have to live in such an oppressed manner? [*Noche* 87]). Conde's empathy for the totally marginalized woman can be seen in "A vosotras tres" (*Del obligado dolor* 39) in which we witness the pathos of a woman driven mad by the injustice society has dealt her. The mad woman, totally marginalized from society and loveless in the world, may stand for all that the woman and the poet might have become. The mood of this poem is "there but for the grace of God go I." Another factor in Conde's sense of marginalization is political. The book in which she describes this alienation is significantly titled *En la tierra de nadie*. Because Carmen Conde refused to side with one group or another, she was rejected: "Quisiera que supieran que las amo / aunque nunca me una a sus debates. / Quisiera que entendieran que soy libre / de amarlos a distancia, desde el margen" (I wish they could know I love them / even though I don't join in their debates. / I wish they could understand that I'm free / to love them at a distance, from the sidelines [*Tierra*, *Obra* 778]). But the speaker is not understood and is left with the pain of being marginalized: "Me duele que me nieguen o me ignoren" (It hurts me that they deny me or ignore me [778]).

25. For a widow's funerary verses, see *El tiempo es un río* (79–80, 93, 94, 102). Seven years after *Corrosión* (1975) Conde continues her lament in *Desde nunca* (1982). "Distancia" (Distance) expresses the closeness she still feels to her long-dead husband ("Te retengo en mi ser igual que a sangre" [I retain you in my being like blood" (*Desde* 20)]) even though they are distant from each other. In "Entonces" (Next), her soul is his tomb ("tu yacija" [your grave (*Desde* 60)]), and her body a landscape of desolation in which she searches for him. In "Invitación" (Invitation), she dreams only of him ("este sueño de ti que me ha crecido / voraz enredadera entre los brazos" [this dream of you which has grown / into a voracious creeper in

my arms (*Desde* 74)]); and she ends by informing her readers that "He cerrado las puertas a mi vida" and by warning them: "aprende / que mata más el amor que el llanto" (I've closed the doors on my life; learn / that love kills more than tears [74]).

26. For unicorn, see also *Tiempo* (43–49). Hunters knew that it was easy to slay the unicorn because of its desire to place its single horn in a virgin's lap (Barbara Walker, *Woman's Encyclopedia* 279).

27. Compare Rosalía's advice, in "encierra el alma humana," to the "niña" who would think (chap. 1, p. 67).

28. Younger female figures—"vírgenes," "novias," "muchachas," "niñas," even "mujeres" and "madres," all of which are present throughout her work—are frequently positive.

29. *Dominio* 83–84 and *Signos* 60. And see *Desterrado* 89 and *Ritos* 24.

30. See also *El tiempo es un rio* (88), where a pubescent girl realizes she's going to develop breasts.

31. E.g., "La turba de la espuma se conduele / de amor junto a mi amor sin su criatura" (The mass of foam sympathizes / with love alongside my love without its child) in "Tres poemas al mar cantábrico" (Three poems on the Cantabrian Sea [*Mi fin, Obra* 298]).

32. The fertility of the sea—"viejo vientre potente de semillas" (potent old womb of seeds)—is noted in a later book (*Corrosión* 95), and again the referent is "Mar Menor." It is now perceived as an eternal womb that swallows the good and the bad. In addition, the sea takes her body (and worried mind) and gives respite: "entregarme indefensa a la mar, / a la mar mía" (yielding myself defenselessly to the sea, / sea of mine [*Corrosión* 116]).

33. "Medusa" (*Patrimonio* 8) is also a pretext to satirize feminine guile.

34. *Debajo* 33, *Forma* 58; especially as it was a task she shared with her mother (*Altamor* 75).

35. See also "La Lanzadera" (*Corazón* 19).

36. And see "El hilo que bordas" (*Corazón* 23).

37. For further development of this metaphor, see *Corral* (105–12 [nos. 6, 11, 24, 26, 45], and "Con nuestras manos" 141–42), *Hondo* (168), *Diotima* (148), and *Retorno* (77).

38. With Carmen Conde it tends to be a praise of "quotidian pleasures" ("placeres cotidianos," as Gabriel Celaya dubbed them). She praises simple food and honest friends (which in Conde's work are tantamount to life in "el levante" [the southeast coast of Spain]). "Bodegón" (Still life) begins: "Sobre mi mesa diaria, aprestada sobre el mar, / hay los peces preparados por Alberto / y los peces adobados por Fuensanta" (Every day on my table, set out to overlook the sea, / there are fish prepared by Alberto / and fish dressed by Fuensanta [*Poemas, Obra* 759]).

39. For example, in 1963 she wrote of the suffering in Nicaragua (*Jaguar puro inmarchito*), and in her 1984 book, *Del obligado dolor,* she describes suf-

fering in Biafra and Lebanon. In point of fact, in *Del obligado dolor* she is giving birth metaphorically to the nearly fifty years of hidden grief and suffering that she had been gestating since the Civil War of 1936: "me refiero a las matanzas, / a las cárceles, exilios, la miseria, el hambre, / y la inmunda persecución" (I refer to the killings, / to the prisons, exiles, misery, hunger, / and the filthy persecution [*Obligado* 29, and see two poems from 1937 "El Grao" and "Heroísmo" which are included in this collection (44-45)]). The Spanish Civil War meant the loss of youth for her and her husband (*Obligado* 48), and—as explained in a riveting poem—the loss of the beloved Miguel Hernández (*Obligado* 51-55).

40. E.g., in "Por viejos campos nuestros" she states that sexual intercourse for men is the only pleasure in an otherwise wretched life (*Desde* 32).

41. See also *Dominio* (93, 95-96), *Hermosura* (140), *Hondo* (111, 117), *Engaños* (183-86), and *Forma* (31). For Zardoya, the poetic word itself is her only God; see "La palabra es un dios" (*Dios* 61).

42. An edenic landscape in *Pájaros* is figured by the delightful absence of the male of the species (*Pájaros* 27, 67).

43. Her four volumes of criticism on Hispanic poets are *masterly*.

44. See also "Hallazgo" (Discovery): "Desnuda y adherida a tu desnudez. / Mis pechos como hielos recién cortados, / en el agua plana de tu pecho" (Naked and espoused to your nakedness. / My breasts like cubes of recently cut ice, / on your breast's level water [*Ansia*, in *Obra* 256]).

45. See also "Sueños de la enamorada II" (*Iluminada*, *Obra* 442-43).

46. Compare María Josefa in Federico García Lorca's *La casa de Bernarda Alba*.

47. See *Tiempo* 114-17, for Rosalía, and *Noche* 70-71, for the three.

4

Angela Figuera

IN PREVIOUS CHAPTERS, we have observed that poets express anger toward society for marginalizing them as women and artists. Angela Figuera develops this discourse on oppression by confronting her self-doubt as a poet and as a woman. We have also observed that the poets under study have tended to respond with empathy to the prospect of motherhood (or maternalization). Angela Figuera confronts the idealization of motherhood by describing the reality of the debased female who is abandoned to rear the Cainite male of the species. Figuera's articulation of desire and her demystification of cultural and literary myths is analogous to that of her precursors, but her treatment of the latter is more trenchant. Her work manifests little sympathy for the pleasures that accrue from intimacy and nontranscendental concerns. On the contrary, Figuera identifies with the oppressed and the working classes and develops an exoskeletal style to combat and denounce the hostility of her phallocratic time and milieu. So, despite her protestations to the contrary, hers is a gynocentric and gynocritical vision.[1]

Angela Figuera Aymerich (1902-84) was forty-six when she published her first book of poetry in 1948; however, between 1948 and 1962 she published eight additional volumes. Her first books, *Mujer de barro* (Woman of clay [1948]) and *Soria pura* (Soria the pure [1949]) focus on herself, in communion with nature, as lover and mother. She is reminiscent of Méndez at this time in her concern for mothering, while in her response to nature she recalls Champourcin and Conde. However, her vision is far more gynocritical than theirs. Her subsequent major books—*Vencida por el ángel* (Vanquished by the angel [1950]), *El grito inútil* (The useless cry [1952]), *Víspera de la vida* (The evening before life [1953]), *Los días duros* (Harsh days [1953]), *Belleza cruel* (Cruel beauty [1958]), and *Toco la tierra: letanías* (I touch the earth: Litanies [1962])—reflect on the social and political depredation of her age, the inauthenticity of established religion, and the frustrations and power-lessness of woman as writer and mother.[2] The hatred, injustice, suffer-ing, and hunger she witnessed horrified her, and she saw herself as using her poetry—a painfully useless scream ("grito inútil")—to protest that evil state of affairs and to denounce the injustice inflicted on the down-trodden classes with which she identified. Figuera's lamentations and condemnations manifest her desire to challenge and modify the phallo-cratic status quo and revise the androcentric vision of her culture. Hers are "social" poems, but with a difference—one that the "aesthetic uni-versal" has elided.

Figuera engages the discourse on female desire. In *Soria pura*, the female speaker discovers her own sensuality and articulates her own sensual and sexual satisfaction with life. In the context of Spanish poetry of the 1940s, this is both daring and unique. "Cañaveral" (Bed of reeds) evokes the poet's personal sexual fulfillment:

Entre las cañas tendida;
sola y perdida en las cañas...

¿Quién me cerraba los ojos,
que, solos, se me cerraban?

¿Quién me sorbía en los labios
zumo de miel sin palabras?

¿Quién me derribó y me tuvo
sola y perdida en las cañas?

¿Quién me apuñaló con besos
el ave de la garganta?

¿Quién me estremeció los senos
con tacto de tierra y ascua?

¿Qué toro embistió en el ruedo
de mi cintura cerrada?

¿Quién me esponjó las caderas
con levadura de ansias?

¿Qué piedra de eternidad
me hincaron en las entrañas?

¿Quién me desató la sangre
que así se me derramaba?

...Aquella tarde de Julio,
sola y perdida en las cañas.
(94)[3]

(Lying in the reeds; / alone and lost in the reeds... / Who closed my
eyes, / which of their own accord were closing? / Who, without a
word, sipped / juice of honey from my lips? / Who pushed me down
and held me / alone and lost in the reeds? / Who knifed with kisses /
the bird in my throat? / Who shook my breasts / with a touch of earth
and ember? / What bull charged in the ring / of my closed waist? /
Who puffed up my hips / with the leaven of yearning? / What stone of
eternity / was thrust into my entrails? / Who unleashed my blood / for
it to sprawl on me? / That evening with Julio, / alone and lost in
the reeds.)

Figuera's choice of verbs certainly evokes images of male dominance,
but she simultaneously creates a sense of sufficiency where the presence
of another seems less important than her own sensuality. Moreover,
what male poet could relate the shock of immersing himself in icy-cold
water to the delights of orgasm, as Figuera does in "Río" (River)?

Entro en el agua, dura de tan fría,
que me coge del talle;
que me ciñe y envuelve
con apremios de amante...

¡Qué grito por el aire esplendoroso
al tener que entregarme!
(77)

(I enter the water, so cold that it's stiff; / it catches hold of my waist, /
encircles and subjects me / to a lover's urgent entreaty... / Such a
shriek struck the magnificent air, / the second I surrendered!)

By expressing her own sexuality in female terms, Figuera is of course
also challenging the status quo.

Moreover, Figuera mounts an implicit challenge to traditional views
on love and loving in a few early poems in which a young female
speaker details the conflicts that arise with her male lover as that love
develops. For instance, for the man love becomes a desire to control,
whereas for the woman it remains a gift: "Tu amor es de presa, de

ofrenda es mi amor" (Your love is a seizure, mine an offering ["Darse" (To give oneself) 30]); without a word the man's hands set upon the woman's warmth and are transformed into tenacious "claws of fire" as they grasp at her flesh ("Tus manos frías" [Your cold hands] 32). In "Deseo" (Desire) the sexually frustrated woman perceives her lover as a cold, mute stone, whereas she is alive with fire:

> Tú, quieto, como piedra. Tú, frío, como piedra.
> Yo, con mi brasa oculta por un velo ¡tan tenue!
> que el roce de tus labios lo hubiera destrozado...
>
> (32)
>
> (You, silent, like a stone. You, cold, like a stone. / I, with my live coal hidden by a veil—so tenuous! /—the stroke of your lips could shatter it.)

The speaker of this poem also feels within her the grounds for ecstasy ("la perfecta llamarada del éxtasis" [the perfect flaring-up of ecstasy (32)]), and she pities her man for being unaware of it.

A second distinctive feature of Figuera's gynocentric vision is negative. In mid-career she articulates the sense of futility and despair she experienced with respect to her own talents as a woman poet in an androcentric culture. Rosalía de Castro, as we noted, suffered a serious loss of confidence in herself as a poet, and Figuera expresses comparable feelings but in greater depth. Such feelings have been linked to the condition of Spain in the 1950s but never to the fact that Figuera was a woman in such a hostile, male-centered environment. However, feminist critics have made us aware of the fact that in such a state women experience loss of confidence and self-worth, which in turn undermines their potential for development. When, for example, a woman poet senses that she is not taken as seriously as her male counterparts, she may begin to experience a lack of faith in her own talents.[4]

In "Mundo concluso" (World concluded), the speaker complains of her condition in the following terms:

> ¿Por qué he de ser mujer repetida de Eva
> escudriñada en toda mi triste anatomía,
> sin un gesto que niegue los rituales muestrarios?
> ¿Por qué he de parir hombres iguales a otros hombres,
> abrumadoramente monótonos e iguales?
>
> (149)

(Just by being a woman, why must I be a repetition of Eve, / scrutinized o'er all my sad anatomy, / without even a gesture that belies the ritual of checking out samples? / Why must I give birth to men who are the same as other men, / mortifyingly monotonous and alike?)

As Roberta Quance has argued, the despair expressed here stems in part from Figuera's condition of being a woman at that particular time and in that particular place, and it also devolves from the fact that she is a woman poet with little or no recognized female tradition in literature and myth to inspire her.[5] Moreover, the fact that the poet realizes that she is "scrutinized in all my sad anatomy," foregrounds her disgust at being reduced to an object by the power of the male gaze. Irigaray, arguing that "woman's desire . . . does not speak the same language as man's," has observed that the "discrimination of form, and individualization of form, is particularly foreign to female eroticism. Woman finds pleasure more in touch than in sight and her entrance into a dominant scopic economy signifies . . . her relegation to passivity: she will be the beautiful object" ("This Sex" 101).

"El grito inútil" (Useless cry) further manifests a woman poet's loss of self-confidence. This poem, like many other of Figuera's "social" poems, is normally read—quite rightly so—as a powerful denunciation of the sociopolitical depredation inflicted on Spain by the Franco regime. It begins with a series of questions:

1   ¿Qué vale una mujer? ¿Para qué sirve
     una mujer viviendo en puro grito?

     . . . .

     ¿Qué puedo yo con estos pies de arcilla
     rondando las provincias del pecado,
5   trepando por las dunas, resbalándome
     por todos los problemas sin remedio?

     ¿Qué puedo yo, menesterosa, incrédula,
     con sólo esta canción, esta porfía
     limando y escociéndome la boca?

10   ¿Qué puedo yo perdida en el silencio
     de Dios, desconectada de los hombres,
     preñada ya tan sólo de mi muerte,
     en una espera, lánguida y difícil,

edificando, terca, mis poemas
15   con argamasa de salitre y llanto?

(171)

(What's a woman worth? What's the use / of a woman living as a mere cry? / . . . / What can I do with these clay feet / traipsing round the provinces of sin, / scaling the dunes, slipping / on all the unsolvable problems? / Needy and incredulous, what can I do / with just this song, this persistence / grating and smarting in my mouth? / What can I do lost in God's silence, / disconnected from men, / pregnant now with nothing more than my own death, / in a languid and difficult waiting period, / building, in my stubborn way, my poems / from plaster made of saltpeter and tears?)

A traditional reading of this poem would note its biblical echoes, and in particular that its opening lines—an allusion to Proverbs 31.10–11 "Who can find a virtuous woman? Her price [worth] is far above rubies"—hint at a woman's subordination in patriarchal civilizations. As Cixous argues in "Sorties": "There is an intrinsic bond between the philosophical and the literary," in that they found themselves on "the abasement of woman, [the] subordination of the feminine to the masculine" (92). A traditional reading of these stanzas would also note that this is the cry of an artist who feels his[6] art is of little use in combating the social degradation and political tyranny that beset him. However, postmodern readers will note that Figuera selected at least two gynocentric metaphors to express her frustration: "feet of clay" (l. 3) and "pregnant . . . with death" (l. 12). "Feet of clay" is an intertextual reference to the poet's first book of poetry, *Mujer de barro*, where "barro" connoted the clay of life, the mud of generation and sustenance. In contrast to that positive marking, "feet of clay" here acquires a negative meaning and implies the opposite of the spontaneous and energetic vision of *Mujer de barro*; it represents the condition of a woman who drags herself around, aimless, lost, one who is unsure of herself and her situation in her culture. In the early 1950s, therefore, Angela Figuera had begun to despair of her talent and her worth.

The second metaphor—from pregnancy ("pregnant now with my own death" [l. 12])—is even more indicative of the despair and loss of purpose the poet has experienced. The speaker is not pregnant with children but with death, because, as "Madres" (Mothers) makes clear, she will give birth to sons who will be sent to die for phallocratic ideals. This is also the rhetorical cry of a woman who feels (subconscious) guilt for not performing the roles sanctioned and assigned to her by her culture: those of mother, childbearer, wife, and lover. For this reason she feels pregnant with death: useless and inferior. As her confidence and self-respect are eroded, she feels she has no right to shout, complain, denounce.

The woman poet's despair stems from a double disenfranchisement: for being a wòman and a poet. Her "grito" on behalf of the powerless and disenfranchised, her denouncement of the status quo, is "useless" because it is uttered by a woman. Hence, the woman poet's only function can be to scream and weep over the abysmal state of affairs. "El grito inútil" is not just a "social" poem; it attests to the marginalized condition of the woman poet in mid-century Spain; it is an indication of the desperation felt by a woman who sensed she was ignored as an artist by the patriarchal system, which always has its subtle ways of eliding those voices that do not speak from within its intellectual and cultural parameters. Gilbert and Gubar's reflections are pertinent to this issue: "as Lévi-Strauss has suggested, writing may always have been associated with class oppression, but as feminist theorists from Woolf to Beauvoir have argued, the situation of woman goes beyond class: no matter what their socioeconomic status, those that produce the species have never controlled the production of culture" ("Ceremonies" 22).

Another distinctive feature of Figuera's negative gynocentric vision is the fact that she confronts her own anger and articulates it in her poems. The bitterness Figuera expresses in her mature poetry of the fifties has been discussed—uncomfortably—by a few critics.[7] As traditional readers, we view anger and bitterness as a lapse of good taste because our culture has developed no reflex strategy to cope with an angry woman. But Ostriker has argued, as we noted, that a woman poet has an intellectual and emotional need to explore her anger, and that "to be conscious as a woman, is to be conscious of hurt and to demand reparation" (Stealing 161). In retrospect, Figuera's expression of anger and bitterness can be read as a strategy for self-survival as a poet in an androcentric culture.

Many of Figuera's poems are conscious manifestations of female rage and anger, turned inward and resulting in a sense of guilt, egotism (see "Egoísmo" [Selfishness] 111–12), and uselessness. In "Habla" ([Speak] 139–40) she implores God to make her suffer; in "El grito inútil" (171–72), as we noted, she believes that as a woman she is a useless object, impregnated now only with her own death; and in "Posguerra" ([After the war] 174–75), she sees her state as that of an animal that has escaped slaughter. And following Carmen Conde, she goes to the extreme, in "La sangre" ([Blood] 161), of offering herself as a woman—"Sangre de la mujer, cáliz abierto" ("Woman's blood, open chalice")—as a sacrificial victim.[8] Like the prepatriarchal Mother-Goddesses, her desire is to renew this fated earth with her own blood:

Cuando yo me muera, abridme, desatadme
las frágiles esclusas de las venas.
Verted mi sangre toda. Derramadla.

(161)

(When I die, open me up, untie / the fragile sluices of my veins. / Pour out all my blood. Shed it.)

But self-laceration is not the only strategy adopted by Figuera. She also directs her anger against the institutions that oppress her and all women, and by expressing it she hopes to inspire other women to action. In "Esta paz" ([This peace] 114), she unmasks the alleged peace Spain "enjoyed" after 1939 and Europe after 1945: "esta paz de ahora, enmascarada / entre papel y tinta mentirosa" (this peace of today, masked between paper and lying ink [is not peace (114)]). She continues:

Paz de niños con hambre
que no han sabido nunca
cómo se clavan los menudos dientes
en un mullido pan de blanca miga
bajo un crujir dorado de cortezas.

(114)

(Peace of hungry children / who've never known / how little teeth can bite / into real white, fluffy bread / with a golden crunching of crust.)[9]

In "Bombardeo" ([The bombing] 119–22), the speaker wraps her arms around her belly to protect her unborn child from the bombs, a gesture that clearly implies her own disgust with the loveless inhumanity of the triumphant, patriarchal oppressors. In "Madres" ([Mothers] 132), she implores the mothers of this world to protest the horrendous treatment that awaits the fruits of their wombs: "¿Qué rabias, qué codicias, qué rencores / harán brotar espinas de sus ojos" (What rage, what greed, what resentment / will it take to make thorns sprout from your eyes? [133]).

In her final book, anger is alluded to in the powerful sonnet "Aunque la mies más alta dure un día" (Although the tallest stalk of wheat lasts just a day). Here the speaker describes anger in a detached manner, formulating it in retrospect as a poetic strategy:

Mujer de carne y verso me declaro,
pozo de amor y boca dolorida,
pero he de hacer un trueno de mi herida
que suene aquí y ahora, fuerte y claro.
(284)

(Woman of flesh and verse I declare myself to be, / well of love and grieving mouth, / but I must make a thunder of my wound / that it resound loud and clear, here and now.)

Figuera's anger and the despair she felt as a woman and as a woman poet in an unsympathetic culture frustrated her, but it did not reduce her to silence. On the contrary, the exoskeletal poetics she developed, as we shall see, helped her to respond to her predicament.

We have been observing just how intensely critical Figuera is of her milieu and her condition as an artist. Indeed, it can be said that in her work a truly gynocritical vision establishes itself in Spanish poetry. She completely demystifies the discourse on mothering initiated by her predecessors, she also subverts a phallocratic worldview as well as the poetic ideals of her male precursors.

Angela Figuera's putative "maternal" impulses have been foregrounded by well-meaning critics (see Bosch, "Poesía," and Mantero, "Angela Figuera"),[10] but in effect she confronts the discourse on mothering of her sister precursors and peers (Rosalía, Champourcin, Méndez, Conde) and stands it on its head. In "Madres" ([Mothers] 132–33), Figuera subverted the traditional view of mothers as "úteros fecundos (fecund wombs) by maintaining that copulation and orgasm are not just euphoric experiences for a would-be mother. For women, making love can be a sobering and depressing event, because they know that the children they bear will be enslaved by or sacrificed to phallocratic ideals. The poem ends with this couplet: "Madres del mundo, tristes paridoras, / gemid, clamad, aullad por vuestros frutos" (Mothers of the world, sadly giving birth, / rail, wail, and howl for your offspring [133]). Besides giving life and providing care, mothers must attempt to influence the culture into which their children are released.

In addition, in "Destino" ([Fate] 141–42), Figuera addresses God, the "hermético alfarero" (hermetic potter), and accuses him of deceit and fraudulence. He leaves the male of the species free to roam the earth, but he enslaves woman: "me encadena / al ritmo y servidumbre de la especie" (enchains me / to the rhythm and servitude of the species [141]). Mothers are enchained by God, and they are also enslaved by God's Church on earth, as Figuera makes clear in many other poems. As we shall note, Figuera delineates a deliberately unorthodox posture in her poems in which women take on an active role in order to do those very things Christ taught his (*male*) followers to do.

Figuera's most sustained demystification of motherhood is found in her great poem "Mujeres del mercado" (Market women):

1   Son de cal y salmuera. Viejas ya desde siempre.
Armadura oxidada con relleno de escombros.
Tienen duros los ojos como fría cellisca.
Los cabellos marchitos como hierba pisada.
5   Y un vinagre maligno les recorre las venas.

Van temprano a la compra. Huronean los puestos.
Casi escarban. Eligen los tomates chafados.
Las naranjas mohosas. Maceradas verduras
que ya huelen a estiércol. Compran sangre cocida
10   en cilindros oscuros como quesos de lodo
y esos bofes que muestran, sonrosados y túmidos,
una obscena apariencia.

Al pagar, un suspiro les separa los labios
explorando morosas en el vientre mugriento
15   de un enorme y raído monedero sin asas
con un miedo feroz a topar de improviso
en su fondo la última cochambrosa moneda.

Siempre llevan un hijo, todo greñas y mocos,
que les cuelga y arrastra de la falda pringosa
20   chupeteando una monda de naranja o de plátano.
Lo manejan a gritos, a empellones. Se alejan
maltratando el esparto de la sucia alpargata.

Van a un patio con moscas. Con chiquillos y perros.
Con vecinas que riñen. A un fogón pestilente.
25   A un barreño de ropa por lavar. A un marido
con olor a aguardiente y a sudor y a colilla.
Que mastica en silencio. Que blasfema y escupe.
Que tal vez por la noche, en la fétida alcoba,

sin caricias ni halagos, con brutal impaciencia
30   de animal instintivo, les castigue la entraña
con el peso agobiante de otro mísero fruto.
Otro largo cansancio.

(178)

(They're made of lime and brine. Women who've been old forever. /
Rusty armor stuffed with rubbish. / Their eyes are hard like cold
sleet. / Their hair withered like trodden grass. / And rancid vinegar
flows through their veins. / They do their shopping early. They ferret
through the stalls. / Almost scratching at them. They select bruised
tomatoes. / Moldy oranges. Mashed greens / that already smell like
manure. They buy cooked blood / in dark, cheese-like cylinders of
mud, / and the type of lights that—pink and swollen—are / obscene to
look at. / When they pay, a sigh parts their lips / as they poke
sluggishly around in the filthy recesses / of an enormous, threadbare,
strapless purse, / scared stiff of suddenly coming across / in its depths
their last, stinking coin. / They've always got a child with them, all
matted hair and snot, / who drags behind them and hangs from their
greasy skirt / sucking an orange or banana skin. / They shout at it,
push it around. They move off / dragging the *esparto* of their filthy
rope-soled sandals on the ground. / They go back to a fly-infested
patio. With little kids and dogs. / With neighbours who fight. To a
pestilent stove. / To a basket full of dirty clothes. To a husband / who
smells of cheap brandy and stinks of fag-ends. / Who chews in silence.
Who curses and spits. / Who perhaps during the night, in the stinking
bedroom, / without caress or flattery, with the brutal impatience / of
an instinctive animal, punishes their entrails / with the oppressive
weight of another wretched offspring. / Just one more long,
exhausting job.)

The male patriarchal order is clearly delineated in this text in which the
poet encounters a stunning objective correlative for her anger and despair. The atrocious condition of motherhood is graphically described
in dramatic detail as the poor woman desperately pillages the market
stalls like an animal to make ends meet for her brood of unappreciative males ("un hijo" [l. 17], "un marido" [l. 25]). These women are
no decorative flowers or jewels made of *mother*-of-pearl (a metaphor
she subverts in "Morena," discussed below). The poverty described is
an implicit indictment of the authoritarian power structure of Franco's
Spain. The text (which recalls Rosalía's "Como venden la carne en el
mercado") exemplifies the gynocritical fire of her poems: "frutos en-

vueltos en la pulpa caliente de mi carne" (fruit wrapped in the hot pulp of my flesh [54]).

In addition to the demystification of the discourse on mothering, Figuera subverts several tenets of the androcentric worldview and phallocratic system. Three butts of her ire are the male's subjugation of the female; the phallocratic, totalitarian power structures; and the Church.

Los días duros (Harsh Days [1953]) denounces the male's subjugation of the female in such poems as "Madres" (Mothers) and "Destino" (Fate). To protest the oppression of the male-dominated culture, the speaker in "Madres"—as we mentioned—maintains that orgasm is no mere frenetic thrill: "Para vosotras, madres, no fue sólo / amor un ramalazo por los nervios, / un éxtasis fugaz, una delicia / derretida en olvido" (For you, mothers, love was not just / a whipping for the nerves, / a fleeting ecstasy, a delight / melting into oblivion [132]). Love, "Madres" says, is a greater pain for women because they learn that the fruit of their wombs will become fodder for wars, and for the slavery of the factory.

This metaphor is developed in "Destino," where coitus is presented as no simple pleasure for a woman because her fate is to live with the consequences of its pain and suffering:

Libre el varón camina por los días.
Sus recias piernas nunca soportaron
esa tremenda gravidez del fruto.

Liso y escueto entre ágiles caderas
su vientre no conoce pesadumbre.
Sólo un instante, furia y goce, olvida
por mí su altiva soledad de macho;
libérase a sí mismo y me encadena
al ritmo y servidumbre de la especie.
                    (141)

(Freely the male strides through each day. / His strong legs have never supported / such a tremendous weight of fruit. / Smooth and neat between agile hips / his belly knows no affliction. / Only in an instant, of fury and enjoyment, does he forget / through me the haughty solitude of his masculinity; / he frees himself for himself and enchains me / to the rhythm and servitude of the species.)

Comparing the separate realities of men and women, Figuera here critiques the male's because the patriarchal culture subjugates and enslaves the female of the species.

Another feature of Figuera's subversion of phallocratic culture is her unflinching criticism of totalitarian power. She directs her anger and irony against the sociopolitical, military, and religious structures erected under the dictatorship of Francisco Franco.[11]

Belleza cruel (Cruel beauty)—which was not published in Spain until after Franco's death—manifests her desire to subvert the Francoist, patriarchal order, particularly as in many poems Figuera foregrounds the condition of downtrodden women, thereby implicitly condemning the society that thwarts and fails them. Like Carmen Conde, whom she cites in her poem "Guerra," Figuera has learned that Spain's women give birth to internecine warfare; the poem ends "Parí la GUERRA" (I gave birth to the WAR [222]). The speaking subject in this text identifies with the masculine power structure the better to undermine it, for implicit in this text is a denunciation of the patriarchal culture that uses women for its own ends. In reaction to the lifeless state Franco has created, Figuera urges in "Puentes" ([Bridges] 241-43) the building of bridges to the world outside, symbolic bridges of union with self and other, Spaniard with foreigner, which Francoism—in its male isolation—had burned after the Civil War. Figuera's criticism of the self-interest of the powerful remains trenchant and uncompromising.

An additional feature of Figuera's subversion of androcentric culture is her relentless denunciation of the Church. In *Los días duros* she presents herself as a vessel awaiting God's bidding, implying that the ecclesiastical powers are no longer capable of heeding His word. Figuera sees herself as living metaphorically amidst the stink of unburied dead—those the Church has refused to honor with Christian burials. She totally condemns this situation but affirms the possibility of renewal from her own unorthodox but Christian viewpoint. Many poems in *Vencida por el ángel* (1953)—possibly Figuera's most powerful book—subvert religion.[12] The speaker of "Vencida por el ángel" (113) has been "conquered" ("vencida") by the Old Testament's "angel" of death, anguish, and grief; that angel, the poet implies, has been nurtured by Franco's authority and flourishes within the culture he has created. In opposition to the untenable hypocrisy of the official, established religion of her country, the poet suggests one that she perceives as truly Christian. Elsewhere, Figuera sarcastically claims that His angels are too perfect to interfere in this world ("Miedo" [Fear] 211-12), and she compensates for their neglect by foregrounding the plight of poor, downtrodden women whom the poet's imaginative angels shower with reward and beauty once they are in their graves. "La justicia de los ángeles" ([The angels' justice] 231-32) describes the very different deaths and burials of a rich, important man and an impoverished woman, Petra. The latter died caring for her nine illegitimate children, and to reward her for her unsung devotion, a host of angels during the night remove the flowers from the rich man's grave and deposit them on Petra's. Figuera is punning on her own Christian name ("ángela" [the woman angel]), and implicitly revises the "ángel del hogar" syndrome. The angel "Angela" captures and transmits God's true messages and suggests how they should be implemented in the impoverished society of mid-century Spain. Her point is that orthodox and traditional religions—or the "Christianity" practiced by the established church—are callously displaying neglect toward those for whom they should care.[13] By denouncing church, state, and armed forces, Figuera fights against what Mary Daly calls androcentric death worship: "The true religion of mankind . . . is death worship. Masculine power, sterile in itself, survives by ruthless suppression of whatever is organic and sensitive, within and outside itself. It creates a God in its own authoritarian likeness to whom woman submits in her own despite, trapped in her own gentleness, by her own avoidance of power."[14] Beneath Figuera's ironical allegories lies the belief that the Church is controlled by men who interpret its doctrines, totally ignore the true spirit of motherhood, and assign women a passive role. Figuera disassociates spirituality from theology, and thereby insists in her feminist manner on the injustice and futility of her country's authoritarian and patriarchal religion.[15]

Added to her demystification of phallocracy, there is Figuera's subversion of the male poetic canon. Figuera's early poetry mounts a subtle challenge to the dominant male poets of her time. One of her first poems is titled "Mujer" (Woman):

1   ¡Cuán vanamente, cuán ligeramente
      me llamaron poetas, flor, perfume!...

      Flor, no: florezco. Exhalo sin mudarme.
      Me entregan la simiente: doy el fruto.
5   El agua corre en mí: no soy el agua.
      Arboles de la orilla, dulcemente

los acojo y reflejo: no soy árbol.
Ave que vuela, no: seguro nido.

Cauce propicio, cálido camino
10   para el fluir eterno de la especie.

(26)

(How vainly, how flippantly / did poets call me flower, perfume!... /
Flower, no: I do the flowering. I give off a scent without changing
shape. / They hand me the seed: I provide the fruit. / The water runs
inside me: I'm not the water. / As for the trees on the river bank,
sweetly / I embrace and reflect them: I'm not a tree. / Nor am I a bird
that flies: I'm a safe nest. / Propitious river bed, warm path / for the
eternal flowing of the species.)

The female speaker above (ll. 1-2) refers sarcastically to poets—certainly male—who in their vanity, haste, and lack of profundity reduce the woman they apostrophize in their verse to a beautiful object, a decorative piece, an adornment (flower, perfume, bird [ll. 2, 8]). In opposition to such stereotyping, the central body of the text (ll. 3-8) proceeds subtly to subvert the notion that woman as beloved is a passive object, an intransitive recipient of admiration. The female artificer of this poem has deliberately selected verbs that denote an active and transitive condition: "I do the flowering (l. 3), the exhaling (l. 3), the fruiting (l. 4), the flowering (l. 7)." Hence in the concluding couplet (ll. 9-10)—the bed through or over which the future of the species must flow—woman is seen not as a passive mold but as an active participant in the act of procreation.

A stance of subtle revisionism is also to be detected in a few other poems of this time. In "Morena" ([Dark-haired girl] 27), Figuera implies that woman is not a configuration of hallowed poetic clichés: "ni soy nácar ni azucena" (I'm neither mother-of-pearl nor Madonna lily); she is "barro" (clay, earth, mud) which is fertile and provides sustenance ("Barro" [Clay] 27, "Tierra" [Earth] 34).

Such a latent feminist poem should be read in conjunction with another poem from Figuera's early period, whose title is "El fruto redondo" (The round fruit [offspring]):

1   Sí, también yo quisiera ser palabra desnuda.
     Ser un ala sin plumas en un cielo sin aire.
     Ser un oro sin peso, un soñar sin raíces,
     un sonido sin nadie...

5   Pero mis versos nacen redondos como frutos,
     envueltos en la pulpa caliente de mi carne.

(54)

(Yes, I'd also like to be a naked word. / A featherless wing in an airless
sky. / A weightless streak of gold, a rootless dream, / an incorporeal
sound... / But my verses are born round like fruit, / wrapped in the hot
pulp of my flesh.)

In this text the poet reflects on her own poetics and in so doing intertextualizes Juan Ramón Jiménez. The phrase "palabra desnuda" above
(naked word [l. 1]) is an explicit allusion to the esthetic of "naked"
poetry made famous by Jiménez.[16] Moreover, the title "El fruto redondo" alludes to a poem entitled "El otoñado" (Replete with autumn
fullness) which Jiménez published in *La estación total* (The total season)
two years prior to Figuera's in 1946.[17] In "El otoñado" Jiménez likens
his poetic maturity to a ripe fruit or sphere gracefully circling through
infinite space. The imagery Figuera selects for the first stanza of her
poem—"featherless wing," etc. (ll. 2–4)—is a tactful but parodic echo
of Jiménez, from whom she distances herself in her concluding couplet. Hers is a more immediate poetics, more in touch with humanity.
Whereas his appears mental, cold, and abstract, hers is passionate,
warm, and physical (ll. 5–6). She gives birth to poems the way women
give birth to children. This difference in Jiménez's and Figuera's poetics parallels the one Ostriker (*Stealing* 132–35) finds between the sub-
jective and corporeal metaphors women use to describe their art, in
contrast to the logical and inorganic imagery selected by men.

As we have been observing, Figuera's gynocentric style is apparent in her selection of image and metaphor. Another of her standard
metaphors is the female figure. For her socially committed poetics,
she deliberately selects imagery that is woman-centered. Unlike other
social poets in Spain, she uses the female figure (woman, mother,
child) to transmit her antiphallocratic messages. Her poems insist that
a woman is not as the "vain poets" of "Mujer" (26) stereotype her—
"flower, perfume, bird"—nor as male lovers want her to be—"mother-
of-pearl, Madonna lily" ("Morena" 27). In "Egoísmo" (Selfishness)
Figuera notes the horrors (hunger, lies, pain) at her doorstep, and exclaims:

Fuera, las madres dóciles que alumbran
con terrible alarido;

las que acarrean hijos como fardos
y las que ven secarse ante sus ojos
la carne que parieron y renuevan
su grito primitivo.

(111)

(Outside, docile mothers who give birth / with terrible shrieks; / those
who drag kids round like bundles / and those who, seeing before their
very eyes / the flesh they bore dry up, renew / their primitive screams.)

The expressionistic images above (reminiscent again of Munch's painting), as well as being an implicit and powerful denunciation of the
political system that tolerates such abuse, are most effective because
they establish a link between the cries uttered by the mother at the birth
of her child with those she emits at its death.[18] "Rebelión" ([Rebellion]
179–80) begins with the line "Serán las madres las que digan: Basta"
(Mothers must be the ones to say: Enough [179]). In effect, Figuera
declares in this poem that to effect change, mothers of the world will
have to rebel against the patriarchal oppressors.

"Bombardeo" ([The bombing] 119–22) associates pregnant women
with the Virgin Mary and thereby foregrounds the unique, even transcendent, roles women play in transforming the world. By implying
that her pregnancy is akin to the Mother of God's, the feminist speaker
of the poem reminds readers of a woman's regenerative postion in culture.[19] She also manages to denounce political, military, and ecclesiastical establishments, by implying that the armed forces (the Fascists) are
destroying the very institutions (the Church) they claim to be defending. The victorious forces are transformed into symbols of selfishness
and masculine hegemony—forces that result in the dehumanization of
society.

Figuera's final thematic twist with this rhetorical knife appears in
Belleza cruel and it concerns infertility. In numerous poems she describes the land in which she lives—Spain—as an infertile country, arid,
dry (219, 221, 235, 238) where seeds (especially those of liberty) cannot
grow. What Figuera does in these poems is to turn the tables on the
metaphor of infertility. Traditionally it is women who are dubbed infertile; but Figuera in these poems shows that the male establishment
is sterile because it has created an infertile culture. If future generations are to turn things around and make the land fertile once more—
"saneada tierra / para sembrar a pulso la simiente" (drained land / to
be seeded by dint of sheer hard work [249])—they must not imitate

the model provided them by their fathers and grandfathers. In effect, Figuera chooses to advise her son and his generation that they should not meekly submit to that infertile, phallocratic society; they should wrest power from it.

We have been noting how Figuera selects gynocentric metaphors to develop her gynocritical vision. A second feature of her gynocritical style is her exoskeletal poetics. Figuera has hardened herself against the oppressive culture in which she lives and she has toughened her poetics accordingly. She selects hard, cold images and cultivates an aggressive form, not primarily to guard against sentimentality but to defend herself, to denounce the pervasive injustices of her era, and to articulate the divisions such injustice creates inside her.

"Los días duros" (Harsh days) expresses her emboldened stance. It indicates that age and experience have made the speaker more aware of the strengths of women. At the outset the speaker repudiates her early esthetic for being naive, for looking at the world through rose-tinted spectacles:

> No. Ya no puedo estar, como solía,
> oculta en matorrales de madreselvas,
> de musgo delicado, de jazmines
> que perfumaban la ilusión precisa
> 5 de mi vivir aparte, preservada.
> . . . .
> Bien lo sabéis cómo era yo de tierna.
> Cómo canté mi arcilla y mis claveles.
> . . . .
> Siempre extasiada en descuidado gozo
> como una niña al borde del sendero.
>
> 10 Hoy ya no puedo. He de salir. Alzarme
> sobre mi dócil barro femenino.
> Gritar hacia las cosas que me gritan
> con labios erizados, con garganta
> hostil y azuzadora.
>
> 15 Los días duros, agrios, se levantan
> como árida montaña. Hay que treparlos
> en puro afán, dejando bien ceñida
> a su áspero contorno, viva, roja,
> la hiedra de la sangre derramada.

20   Hay que vivir a pulso los minutos
      sin rémora, sin miedo, cabalgando
      en la delgada arista del presente.

(125-26)

(No. I can no longer remain, as I was wont, / hidden in clumps of honeysuckles, / of delicate moss, of jasmines / that perfumed the precise illusion / of my living apart and protected. / . . . / You well know what I was like at a tender age. / How I sang about my clay and my carnations. / . . . / Always enraptured in carefree joy / like a girl at the edge of the path. / Today, I can no longer do it. I must go outside. Rise up / above my docile, female clay. / Shout—with prickly lips, / with a hostile, rabble-rousing voice—/ at things that shout at me. / Harsh and bitter days rise up / like an arid mountain. One must climb them / with sheer hard work, and leave / their rough terrain girt / with the ivy of shed blood—living and red. / One must live the minutes the hard way, / without drawing back, without fear, riding / on the thin edge of the present.)

The first lines above (ll. 1-5) suggest that in the fifties the speaker thought of her earlier volume *Soria pura* as a mistaken vision of life. "My clay" (l. 7) is an equally deprecating allusion to the idealism and joy of *Mujer de barro*, her first book of poetry. There follows (ll. 8-9) a criticism of the self for its escapism (an unjustified critique, in my opinion).[20] Then with "today, I can no longer do it" (l. 10) the poet begins to articulate her tough and hard poetics: in response to a bitter, harsh, and arid environment, she will shout and express her point of view in an aggressive manner. She sees life as an arid mountain and herself (ll. 21-22) as having to ride along one of its precipitous ledges without falling off.

The poem continues by revealing that the speaker is a middle-age woman who feels herself to be in a psychologically weak and vulnerable position:

Ya no es escudo el hijo entre los brazos.
Ya no es sagrado el seno desbordante
de generoso jugo, ni nos sirven
los rizos de blasón.

(126)

(The child in our arms is no longer a shield. / Our breasts overflowing with generous juice / are no longer sacred, / and our heraldic curls / no longer get us by.)

The clear implication of these lines is that patriarchal society has contributed to the woman poet's tough stance by marginalizing her because
she is now old and has lost her beauty (and in this respect the poem
alludes to the geriatric discourse we observed in Champourcin, Méndez, and Conde). However, the self inscribed in this text is determined
to fight against such oppression:

> A la embestida seca de los machos
> que olvidan la pulida reverencia,
> la rosa, el madrigal y aquellos besos
> en el extremo de la mano esquiva,
> hay que oponer lo recio femenino.
>
> (127)

(To the abrupt charge of the males / who forget the polished bow, / the
rose, the madrigal and those kisses / at the tip of the elusive hand, /
one must oppose female toughness.)

In these hard times ("los días duros") woman must be tough and
robust ("recio"); she cannot allow her "docile, feminine clay" (l. 11
above) to be trampled on. When she was young, she could rely on
the fact that the softness of the clay out of which she was fashioned
("barro") would be appreciated, but now that she is older, she needs to
make that clay tough and strong to counteract "la embestida seca de los
machos" (the males' abrupt and callous charge). This emboldened self
will oppose "lo recio femenino" to pitiless, patriarchal obduracy, and
closes the poem by resolving "no puedo desmayarme blanda" (not to
swoon like a softie [127]). As a "poeta" (poet [134]) she states her de-
termination to remain alert to the world's harshness; and elsewhere declares "has de pisar sin miedo barro impuro" (you must tread fearlessly
on impure mud ["Poeta puro" (Pure poet) 310]). Figuera's hard and
tough poetics respond both to the lamentable condition of society and
to the condition of woman in mid-century twentieth-century Spain.

Moreover, in a poem only recently collected, Figuera inveighs against
the soft prissiness of Spain's women poets who utter only "suspirillos
rimados, como pájaros bobos" (little, rhymed sighs, like silly birds).
She asks "mis hermanas poetisas" (my sister poetesses), "Porque, amigas, os pasa que os halláis en la vida / como en una visita de cum-
plido" (For, friends, your problem is that you live life / as if you were
paying it a courtesy call). She then sarcastically exhorts them to act
and, among other things, to meditate on the twists and turns of the
woman's body during orgasm. In her "Exhortación impertinente a mis

hermanas poetisas" (Impertinent exhortation to my sister poetesses) Figuera seeks to shock them with her own tough perspective on life, when she advises:

y dejad que la vida poderosa y salvaje
os embista y derribe como toro bravío
al caer sobre el anca de una joven novilla.
No queráis ignorar que el amor es un trance
que disloca los huesos y acelera las sienes;
y que un cuerpo viviente con delicia se ajusta
al contorno preciso donde late otro cuerpo.

(302)

(and let this powerful and savage life / charge at you and knock you down like a wild bull / as it falls on the haunches of a heifer. / Do not forget that love is a trance / that dislocates bones and quickens temples; / and that a body living with delight adjusts itself / to the precise contours within which the other body beats.)

Figuera concludes by urging them to become the true daughters of Eve and bite the symbolic apple of knowledge and sin:

Eva quiso morder la fruta. Mordedla.
Y cantad el destino de su largo linaje
dolorido y glorioso. Porque, amigas, la vida
es así: todo eso que os aturde y asusta.

(303)

(Eve wanted the fruit to bite it. So bite it. / And sing the fate of her long, / painful and glorious lineage. Because, girls, that's what life's about: / everything that frightens and dumbfounds you.)

As Figuera directs this poem to her "sisters in poetry," it is clear that she believes that women poets have to harden and toughen themselves in order to articulate a responsive, poetic vision.

In this context, the poetics of Figuera's best-known book, *Belleza cruel*, can be better appreciated. When Figuera describes beauty—the beauty she did find in her country—she sees it as "cruel" ("belleza cruel"). She glimpses it in the hunger of the poor and the workers; in the day laborers and farmhands who break their backs and never glimpse a blue sky; and in the women of poor families for whom giving birth to warmongers is presented as the harshest cruelty of all. Such brutal realities require a harsh and tough poetics. Moreover, in her last book, *Toco la tierra*, alluding again to the fact that her poems have grappled with harsh cruelty and injustice, she adds in "En tierra escribo" (I write on earth): "Mi reino es de este mundo. Mi poesía / toca la tierra y tierra será un día" (My kingdom is of this earth. My poetry / touches the earth and will be earth one day [254]). She sees her work as nontranscendental; her poetry, rooted to the land, "wrapped in the hot pulp of her flesh," avoids idealistic flights of fancy and empathizes with those who have to sweat to survive each day.[21]

Hence, in addition to the undeniable social content of Figuera's poetry, its vision and style are informed by an exoskeletal female perspective of hardness and toughness.

Figuera, like many women, as Ostriker has noted in a different context, makes poetry "for and from the lives of lost women, the insulted and injured of present and past history" (Stealing 191). Indeed, what Ostriker has written of today's women poets, we can say of Angela Figuera: as she examines herself in contrast to those she sees about her, she begins to assume in her work "an almost mystic responsibility for the lives of others" (178).

In the foregoing remarks I have described some of the feminist patches that form part of the "quilt" that is the Figuera text.[22] They are attitudes that tend to be obscured when her poetry is read in conjunction with that of her male peers. If they are recognized, the power of her work will be better appreciated.

Notes

1. In Ramos (Literatura 17), she asserts: "Yo no creo en el feminismo" (I do not believe in feminism).

2. In Belleza cruel, Bosch argues, the poet can be seen "to be searching for a point of equilibrium between exaltation and lugubriousness" ("Poesía" 6). It was published in Mexico in 1958 but did not appear in Spain until 1978, three years after Franco's death, probably because the theme of Spain—its cruelty and beauty—is overtly textualized.

3. All quotations are from Figuera, Obras completas; page references are included in parentheses after each quotation.

4. See Ostriker, Stealing, chap. 4, "Herr God, Herr Lucifer: Anger, Violence, and Polarization."

5. Quance, "Mujer" and "Angela Figuera"; and see below n. 19.

6. I am deliberately using the traditional possessive adjective here.

7. Conde in Poesía femenina española writes of "un fiero . . . acento" (a wild . . . tone [18]). Cano (Poesía española 521–22) and Torrente Ballester (Panorama 397) insist that she is a "Christian" poet, even though she ac-

cuses and condemns, as Cano writes, "the injustices and pain in today's society" (521).

8. Conde's poem is from her 1947 *Mi fin en el viento.*

9. In Spain at this time, black bread was the staple.

10. These male critics tend to idealize her maternal impulse. A further indication of the unease with which we men approach poetry by women—and re-create it in our own image—is Carlos Alvarez's 1978 introduction to *Belleza cruel* in which he argues, to the virtual exclusion of all else, that even though Figuera is a woman her poetry is virile (and see Quance, "Entre líneas" 80).

11. For example, in *El grito inútil* (1952) Spain is a prison ("La cárcel" [193]); all its land lies fallow and infertile ("Regreso" [196]). The survivors of the Civil War suffer "the quiet vengeance of millions of dead people" ("Posguerra" [174–75]) and perceive both themselves and their country as sterile.

12. *Belleza cruel* is considered to be Figuera's best work. In my opinion, *Vencida por el ángel* is superior.

13. In addition, in these poems Figuera effectively subverts the role of priests: as they are too pure to dirty their hands with the problems of this world, she herself does those very tasks she believes they and God's angels should assume (besides "La justicia de los ángeles," see "Me explico ante Dios" [I explain myself before God] 266–67).

14. Quoted by Ostriker (*Stealing* 138).

15. In answer to a questionnaire, Figuera wrote: "Católica. Practicante hasta 1936. Luego, no" ("Catholic. Practicing until 1936. Afterwards, no."). In Lechner, *Compromiso* 2:165.

16. See "Vino, primero, pura, / vestida de inocencia" ("She came, first, pure, / dressed in innocence") in Jiménez, *Libros* 555.

17. See Jiménez, *Libros* 1140.

18. As a member of the middle class, Figuera in this poem identifies herself with the sociopolitical order that tolerates such injustices.

19. "Bombardeo" begins: "Yo no iba sola entonces. Iba llena / de ti y de mí" (I was not alone at that time. I was filled / with you and me). Later it continues: "Iba llena de gracia por los días / desde la anunciación hasta la rosa. / Pero ellos no podían, ciegos, brutos, / respetar el portento. / Rugieron. Embistieron encrespados. / Lanzaron sobre mí y mi contenido / un huracán de rayos y metralla. / . . . yo colocaba, dulce, mis dos manos / sobre mi vientre que debió cubrirse / de lirios y de espumas y esas telas / que visten, recamadas, los altares" (I was filled with grace in those days / from the annunciation to the rose. / But, blind, brutes, they could not / respect the portent. / They bellowed. / They hunched themselves up and charged. / They hurled on me and my content / a hurricane of thunderbolts and shrapnel. / . . . softly, I placed my two hands / over my belly which should

have been covered / with lilies and foam and those embroidered cloths / that dress the altars [119, 120]). For Figuera's revision of biblical myths, see Quance's important studies (n. 5 above). In particular, in "Angela Figuera" Quance argues that Figuera rejects the notion of God as the "hermético alfarero" and repositions herself as an artist into an "hacedora."

20. Line 9 implies that she thought of herself as too much under the influence of J. R. Jiménez, and line 10, A. Machado. For further discussion of this issue, see my "Impresiones."

21. In her "Poéticas," Figuera also expresses a hardheaded attitude toward life. She explains that she does not write for posterity, pleasure, or beauty; she writes out of necessity, when she is moved by an event, in the hope that one single human being might be touched or consoled. She mentions people's meanness of spirit, but adds that she has tried to make the world somewhat better.

22. I take the metaphor from Tornsey's "The Critical Quilt."

5

Gloria Fuertes

GLORIA FUERTES IS PROBABLY the most widely read woman poet of mid-twentieth-century Spain. Her language is direct; her style entertaining and accessible to a broad gamut of readers; her humor and wit, which are attractive and corrosive, draw on her Madrid culture for their pique.[1] She was born in Madrid in 1918 into a working-class family, which sets her apart from the bourgeois background of the male writers of her generation. In an "Autobio" (Autobio[graphy]) published in 1995, she writes:

> Comprendo que los poetas
> que han nacido en un seno y ambiente burgués
> tengan un cierto sentido de culpabilidad.
> No es mi caso.
> Yo nací en un seno de hambre y pobreza
> de chabola (aunque era una buhardilla).
> Me crié en una chabola a ras de tejado,
> no había luz eléctrica ni agua en mi buhardilla
> retrete sí,
> con una cortina de sábana vieja pieceada
> —exquisitamente decorativa.
>
> *(Mujer 59)*[2]

(I understand that poets / who were born into the lap of bourgeois luxury / have a certain sense of guilt. / That's not my case. / I was born into the heart of hunger and poverty, / of a shack (although it was an attic). / I was raised in a shack that was level with the roof, / there was neither electric light nor water in my attic / lavatory yes, / with an old, pieced-together sheet for a curtain / exquisitely decorative.)

Fuertes's working-class roots could well have contributed to her sense of marginalization, and to her constant expression of solidarity with the poor, the downtrodden, and oppressed. They may also have contributed to her ironical reflections and sarcastic asides on wealth and power, no matter where they exist: "En Estados Unidos / hacen vídeos para gatos, / hoteles para perros... / Pero todavía no hacen amor / para hispanos y negros" (In the United States / they make videos for cats, / hotels for dogs... / But they still don't make love / for hispanics and blacks [*Mujer* 67]).

Fuertes published her first book, *Isla ignorada* (Ignored island), in 1950. She continued to publish every decade at regular intervals and all her work—*Obras incompletas* (Incomplete works), *Historia de Gloria* (Gloria's history), and *Mujer de verso en pecho* (Woman with verse on her chest)—is readily available today, collected by Editorial Cátedra, which in itself is an indication of the magnetism she exercises on her readers.[3]

Gloria Fuertes has received sustained and illuminating commentary from sympathetic critics.[4] Carmen Conde saw her as early as 1954 as "barojiana y goyesca . . . impura" but with "enorme ternura caliente, maternal" (Barojian and Goyesque . . . impure . . . enormous warmth and tenderness, maternal ["Introducción" 21]). Bellver has studied her social consciousness ("Gloria Fuertes"). Recent trends in reading Fuertes focus on her humor, her linguistic strategies, and her feminism. Persin analyzes her humor for its production of meaning ("Humor como semiosis" and "Gloria Fuertes").[5] Debicki reveals that the inclusion of seemingly unpretentious events in her poems and her deployment of nonstandard language oblige her readers to participate actively in decoding the poem (*Poetry of Discovery* 81-101). Fuertes's feminism has been perceptively studied by Persin, and recently by Sherno and Marson—whose acute observations I corroborate here.[6]

Fuertes's gynocentric vision is almost exclusively gynocritical and contains most if not all of the features we have observed in the poetry of her percursors. In the first place, her style and perception of the woman poet are gynocritical.

Fuertes presents the woman poet as a marginalized creature. "No dejan escribir" (Writing is not allowed) foregrounds a woman who works in a newspaper office, but "soy sólo mujer de limpieza" (I'm only the cleaning woman). The female speaker of this poem adds:

Sé escribir, pero en mi pueblo,
no dejan escribir a las mujeres.

                                  (*Obras* 72)

(I know how to write, but in my village / they don't let women write.)

In 1954—more than twenty years before *The Madwoman in the Attic* —Fuertes selected the metaphor of the attic or loft ("buhardilla") to articulate her own marginalization as a woman and as a woman poet. In "Nací en una buhardilla" (I was born in a garret), Fuertes describes how her own mother marginalized her early as more or less "mad" because she was like her uncle, that is, like a man rather than a woman: "qué tonterías dices y qué locuras haces" (what stupid things you say and what mad things you do [*Obras* 58]).[7] Later, Fuertes echoes Rosalía when she writes:

—Ahí va Gloria la vaga.
—Ahí va la loca de los versos, dicen,
la que nunca hace nada.

                                  (*Obras* 254)[8]

(There goes Gloria the space-cadet. / There goes the madwoman with her poems, they say, / the one who never does a thing.)

Clearly, Fuertes identified and sympathized with her poetic great-great-grandmother's "madness."[9] Her difference from Rosalía, however, is her appealing capacity for self-irony, a trait that contributes to the highly developed sense of humor that characterizes her work in its entirety, and a strategy she deploys to counteract her marginalized status as a poet. For example, in "Nací en una buhardilla" Fuertes writes that her mother did not want her—"nací cuando mi madre pensaba en un muchacho" (I was born when my mother was thinking about a boy); she then goes on to explain how she began to perceive herself as alienated from her society:

Cuando yo era pequeña un pájaro muy raro,
venía a estar conmigo a mi clara buhardilla,
yo le contaba cuentos y le echaba pedazos
de pan y algún guisante y así me entretenía.

                                  (*Obras* 58)

(When I was little, a very rare bird / would come to keep me company at my bright dormer window, / I told him tales and threw him bits / of bread and the odd pea, and that's how I amused myself.)

Henceforth, the poet observed reality from her window (*Obras* 84), and reality for its part looked at her as if she were mad: "¿No ves la noche que me mira como tonta?" (See the night that looks at me as if I'm stupid? [*Obras* 89]). This is the first glint I personally have detected of the attic's being transformed from a space of literal confinement into a space for figurative exploration. In later poets, Janés, Rossetti, Andréu, the attic will become a metaphor—for plumbing the depths of the unconscious as well as the subconscious mind—but Fuertes does not make that jump. However, in her work for the first time marginalization is confronted and the negativity of its vision is subverted.

In "Estaba un pajarito" (A little bird was), Fuertes contrasts the anger of the caged bird—a symbol selected by earlier women to signify their marginalized condition—to the happiness of one free to choose the people and places it will grace with its singing (*Obras* 104). She views positively her own condition as one who lives in a "casa *sin amo* [my italics]" (house *without a master*), which, she exclaims, is haunted: "¡Mi cuarto de soltera está embrujado!" (My spinster's room's bewitched [*Obras* 83]).[10] She likens her loneliness to a prostitute's—"como buena puta" (like a good whore [*Obras* 186]). Much later, the condition of otherness ("prisionero") has imprisoned her in herself:

Estás prisionero.
Hay una reja
que no te deja,
entrar en ti.
La cárcel eres tú.
    (*Historia* 322)

(You're a prisoner. / There's a grille / that will not let you / enter yourself. / You yourself are the prison.)

And in another poem she writes: "la única salida de mi prisión . . . es hacer poesía con lo que vomita mi corazón" (the only exit from my prison . . . is making poetry with what my heart throws up [*Historia* 125]). Therefore Fuertes, from the beginning of her career, has felt herself to be imprisoned, marginalized, ostracized—"*atticized*"—as woman and poet, but she has used that state of confinement for creative ends: "Al calor del silencio se maduran mis versos" (From the heat of silence, my verses mature [*Historia* 308]). Fuertes's work textualizes the negative effects of the condition of being a "Nobody"—"y los hombres se creen que no soy nada" (and men believe for themselves that I'm a nothing [*Obras* 49])—but subverts them with her imagination.

Unlike her precursors, Fuertes struggles with negative conditions—
"No sé por qué me quejo" (I don't know why I complain [*Obras* 115])—
and prevails. Fuertes's gynocentric vision is overwhelmingly positive.
She sees herself as involved in the construction of the prison that incar-
cerates her; and she adjusts to her situation: "¡Vivo como una reina! /
(ahogada)" (I live like a queen! [a stifled one] [*Historia* 107]). The vision
she projects overall is not that of the marginalized poet because she
connects with the world outside and reveals that she lives in symbiotic
dependence with it.

One of the steps Fuertes takes to confront marginalization is to
totally reject traditional notions of what a poet is reputed to be and
do. Her most persistent metaphor for the poet is "puta" (prostitute).
In "Nací para poeta o para muerto" (I was born to be a poet or to
be dead [*Obras* 160]) the poet is transformed by parallelistic structure in three consecutive stanzas from *poeta > puta > nada* (poet >
prostitute > nothing). In "Maletilla" (Peripatetic rookie bullfighter),
she states that the establishment considers her to be a "nieta de puta"
(granddaughter of a whore [*Obras* 168]), and she identifies herself to
her readers as a "poeta/puta": "siento . . . que mis versos hayan salido a
su puta madre" (I'm sorry . . . if my poems emerged from their smash-
ing mother [*Obras* 293]).[11] For Fuertes, the poet does not illumine the
darkness with *his* transcendent discoveries, *she* gives warmth, affection,
company, to those who are desperate.

The poem "Cabra sola" (Single nanny goat) not only demythifies the
notion of what it is to be a woman poet, it turns back the insult on the
person who called the poet a goat. It is indeed a fact that, in addition
to the sympathetic critical reception noted above, Gloria Fuertes regularly receives insults of this type from her male contemporaries.[12] The
poem begins:

> Hay quien dice que estoy como una cabra;
> lo dicen, lo repiten, ya lo creo;
> pero soy una cabra muy extraña
> que lleva una medalla y siete cuernos.

> (There are those who say I'm like a nanny goat, / that they say it and
> repeat it, I well know; / but I'm a very strange nanny goat / who sports
> a medal and seven horns.)

The speaker then goes on to describe the self-reliance and ingenuity of
this "cabra . . . que no quis[o] cabrito en compañía" (nanny goat who
refused to be accompanied by a kid [boy]), and concludes:

Y vivo por mi cuenta, cabra sola;
que yo a ningún rebaño pertenezco.
Si sufrir es estar como una cabra,
entonces sí lo estoy, no dudar de ello.
                    (*Obras* 212).

(A single nanny goat, I march to my own tune; / for I belong to no
flock. / If to suffer is to be like a nanny goat, / then I certainly do,
don't doubt it.)

Fuertes rejects literary fame and renown as a poet, "no por reco-
mendaciones / escribo por meditaciones" (I write from meditations, /
not from recommendations [*Obras* 332]);[13] she writes "para ahora y
para luego" (for now and then [*Historia* 64]). She declares, "mi volun-
tad siempre ha huido / de la ambición" (my will has always fled / from
ambition [*Historia* 263]), and later adds, "y a una corona de laurel / prefiero tus manos en mi sien" (and to a laurel crown, / I prefer your hands
on my temple [*Historia* 303-4]).

Hence, Gloria Fuertes subverts and demythifies traditional notions
of poet, poem, and poetry. She sees herself first as a person and second as a poet: the poppy, she writes, beautifies the field of wheat, then
dies—not me:

Yo no me conformo como la amapola,
antes que poeta soy una persona,
no he nacido mártir
quiero otra amapola.
                    (*Historia* 182)

(Unlike the poppy, I don't conform, / I'm a person before a poet; / I
wasn't born a martyr, / I want another poppy.)

In "La linda tapada" (Pretty woman in a djellaba), she declares that
she'll find poetry wherever it happens to be:

No te tapes Poesía
te reconozco en las cosas pequeñas
y en las casas grandes,
allí donde estés, daré contigo.
Te huelo poesía,
te presiento en el alto y en el bajo,
en el monte y en el burdel,
en el mar y en el borracho,

en la alegría del mar
y en el dolor del mal.
No te tapes poesía que te veo,
no me tientes a retóricos sonetos,
vamos a hablar como siempre,
¡o te mando de paseo!

(*Obras* 283)

(Don't cloak yourself, Poetry, / I know you in the little things / and in the big houses, / there I'll find you out, wherever you may be. / I smell you, poetry, / I sense you up high and down low, / on the mount and in the brothel, / in the sea and in the drunk, / in the gaity of the sea / and in evil's grief. / Don't cloak yourself, poetry, for I see you, / don't tempt me with rhetorical sonnets, / we're going to speak just as we always do, / or I'll tell you to go to blazes!)

Fuertes's relationship with poetry is therefore intimate, immediate, and familiar—as if it shares her *piso* (flat) and her *barrio* (neighborhood). With Gloria Fuertes poetry becomes an everyday activity. It is not Keats's sacred urn that immortalizes lovers, nor is it a beautiful statue to be placed on a pedestal and worshiped. It is not a spiritual quest, a transcendent goal, an impossible longing—as, for example, Bécquer perceived it in *Rima 5*: "Espíritu sin nombre, / indefinible esencia" (Nameless spirit, / indefinable essence [*Rimas* 106]). Nor is it an artifact written with an eye to history, in preparation for its canonization in the mausoleum of literary tradition. Gloria Fuertes sells poems the way others sell flowers or cigarettes on the street. In "El vendedor de papeles o el poeta sin suerte" (The paper seller or luckless poet), she equates herself with hawkers and balladeers: the speaker sells her wares on the sidewalks ("vendo versos, / liquido poesía" [I sell poems, / I liquidate poetry]), virtually giving them away—"regalo poesía" (I make presents of poetry)—because she believes that poetry is the best gift of all: "Para la madre, / para la novia, / el mejor regalo / un verso de amor!" (For your mother, / for your girlfriend, / the best gift, / a line of love! [*Obras* 52]).

Fuertes's strategy of demystification should not blind her readers to the fact that she loves and respects the poem, the poet, and poetry. As she writes in "Prologuillo" (Little prologue):

Este libro está escrito día a día,
a ratos perdidos,
a amigos perdidos.

Los poemas (¿son poemas?)
no tienen orden ni concierto,
—sé que a veces desconcierto—
pero están escritos con cierto amor.
Esto no es un libro, es una mujer.

(Historia 57)

(This book is written day by day, / in spare moments, / for lost
friends. / The poems—if they're poems?—/ have no order or array,/
—at times I know they disarray—/ but they're written with a certain
love. / This isn't a book, it's a woman.) [14]

And the woman, who embodies herself "with a certain love" in her
poems, selects a vulvular as opposed to phallic metaphor—an oyster—
to designate her poetic activity:

Sola como una ostra,
me escondo para escribir.
Pensad que en su soledad
piensa en vosotros la ostra
y después os da su perla
hecha en tristeza y a solas.

(Historia 99).

(Alone like an oyster, / I hide away to write. / Think, in its solitude /
an oyster has you in mind; / then offers you its pearl, / made by itself,
in gloom.)

The immediacy of the relationship Gloria Fuertes imagines for herself
and poetry is captured in the above lines: like a fetus in the womb, it is
in contact with her and she with it. Poetry for her is not an *other*—it is
a part of the *self*. She maintains a symbiotic as opposed to disjunctive
relationship with it, and it with her. [15]

Fuertes does not write impersonal, Modern poems in the manner of
an Eliot or a Valéry. The implication is that she participates uncon-
sciously in that until-recently ignored current of women's literature—
now studied by feminist criticism—which tends to find expression only
in diaries and letters. [16] In one poem she states, "Mi poesía es una confesión. / Es un secreto a voces" (My poetry is a confession. / It's a well-
known secret [*Historia* 325]). In "Algo es algo" (Something is better
than nothing), she declares:

Mi lucha no ha sido en vano,
con escribir «mi diario»

no he vencido,
he distraído
a los chicos de mi barrio.
¡Algo es algo!

(*Historia* 267)

(My rumble has not been in vain, / by writing "my diary," / I haven't surmounted, / I've titillated / my *barrio*'s boys. / I take what I can get!)

In symbiotic struggle, Fuertes transforms her self, her personal life, and her surroundings into a gynocritical poetics. Her dominant metaphors reveal that stance. They also reveal how she confronts the negative conditions of being a woman and a woman poet, and how she transforms them with the aid of her sharp sense of humor and her surprising and unique gynocritical perspectives.

A second distinctive feature of Fuertes's vision is that to counteract her marginalization she develops a very strong sense of self-sufficiency and self-dependency. She likes to pun on her surname, which means "strong," and one of her confessions in "Lo confieso" (I confess) is:

voy consiguiendo todo sin el llanto,
que soy la mujer *fuerte* que se viste
y medita mirando al calendario.

(my italics, *Obras* 98)

(I accomplish all without weeping, / for I'm the woman called "the strong," who gets dressed / and reflects with a schedule in mind.)

"Miradme aquí" (Take a look at me here) dramatizes the lonely condition of the artist and describes the pressure the writer feels from being thrown back on the self to struggle with the phantom within. It begins:

Miradme aquí,
clavada en una silla,
escribiendo una carta a las palomas.
Miradme aquí,
que ahora podéis mirarme,
cantando estoy y me acompaño sola.
Clarividencias me rodean
y sapos hurgan en los rincones,
los amigos huyen porque yo no hago ruido
y saben que en mi piel hay un fantasma.
Me alimento de cosas que no como,

echo al correo cartas que no escribo
y dispongo de siglos venideros.
(Obras 120–21)

(Look at me here, / stuck in this chair, / writing letters to the doves. /
Look at me here, / for now you can look at me, / I'm singing and alone
I create a companion for myself. / I'm pounded by intuitions / as toads
rummage through my drawers. / Friends take flight because I make no
sound; / they just know there's a phantom inside my skin. / I feed off
things that I don't eat, / leave letters in the mail that I don't write: /
I've got the future on time's doorstep.)

Though hard to bear, the artistic gift and impulse—and phallocracy's
disdain—certainly make Fuertes more self-reliant. Much later, she
writes:

Hace tiempo que la felicidad
no me viene del exterior,
me la tengo que inventar dentro
como si fuera un poema.
(Historia 181)

(For years, happiness / has not come to me from without, / I've had to
invent it from within, / as if it were a poem.)

Furthermore, Fuertes recognizes in her work that a woman has no
one to look after her, to care for her in the way women traditionally
care for others, and that therefore she must learn to rely on herself,
develop that sense of care and love from within herself by embracing
and cultivating her own body.[17] In a poem significantly titled "Canción
de las locas" (The madwomen's song) she describes the horrors of life
and exclaims in compensation: "En mi cuerpo tengo una fuente / y si
quiero bebo" (Inside my body I have a fount, / and if I want I drink
[*Obras* 105]). For this reason, when she is sick and tired, and there is no
one to "mother" her (my choice of word, not hers), she writes "Carta
a mí misma" (Letter to myself [*Obras* 189]), telling herself to go see a
doctor, to take care. In "Si te sientes como una bayeta" (If you feel like
a floor-cloth), her advice to those who feel depressed because someone
has insulted them is that they should nurture themselves:

Si eres bayeta,
colilla
o cáscara

¡siémbrate en tí!
Y vuelve a florecer en un cuadro,
en un poema,
o si cáscara,
en el manjar de un niño hambriento.
(Así hice yo.)

(*Historia* 126).

(If you're a floor-cloth, / fag end, / or bit of rind, / plant your seeds
inside yourself! / And flower next time in a painting, / a poem, / or if a
scrap of peel, / in the favorite dish of a hungry child. / [That's what
I did.])

Fuertes reacts to being a marginalized, lonely woman and an artist
by developing a strong sense of self-worth, which she expresses in her
work. A further instance of her self-sufficiency is "Algo dentro de mí
me quiere mucho" (Something inside me loves me a lot), which reads:

Mi corazón, otra vez en candelero.
Mi rico y acaramelado corazón.
Mi pobre corazón destartalado
por el tantarantán que le has metido
con tu frase tanguera
de: «No me quieras tanto»;
—mi dominguero corazón ardiente
está de viernes santo—.

Y susurrea mi corazón amigo:
Tú ganas, Gloria,
quien no te quiere está perdido.
¡Quítate la tristeza y ponte otro vestido,
que es fin de año y te lo juro, maja,
que yo te haré tragar tus doce lágrimas.
(Algo dentro de mí me quiere mucho.)

(*Historia* 298-99)

(My heart, in the limelight again. / My rich and cloying heart. / My
poor heart dilapidated / by the bam-bam-bam you give it / with that
tango phrase of yours: / "Don't love me so much"; /—my passionate,
Sunday-heart / is on its Good Friday kick. / And my friendly heart
whispers: / You're the winner, Gloria, / those who don't love you are
the losers. / Take off your sadness and put on another dress; / it's year's

end and, sport, I swear, / I'll make you swallow your twelve tears. / [Something inside me loves me a lot.]) [18]

Fuertes's inner strength leads her to assert "Mi yo soy yo, / y estoy en mí" (My self is I, / and I am in myself [*Historia* 324]); and "Me quiero. / Yo soy mi hija, / y decidí no quedarme huérfana" (I love myself. / I'm my own daughter, / and I decided not to remain an orphan [*Historia* 326]).[19] Clearly, it is not just that she is an artist that has stimulated her to develop her sense of self-reliance and self-worth, it is also that she is a woman, marginalized by her culture. This particular psychological self-boost, I suggest, will not be found in poetry written by men, probably because men are provided by their society with care, attention, and encouragement, both as poets and as human beings. Moreover, Fuertes's psychological independence and self-determination is an important advance when contrasted with the despair of talent and loss of confidence we have noted in Rosalía de Castro and Angela Figuera. The model she provides for her sisters is positive.

A third distinctive feature of Fuertes's gynocritical vision proper is her metapoetics: she consciously distances herself from a number of her male precursors and peers, whom she does conceptualize as the *other*. In my particular reading of *Obras incompletas* and *Historia de Gloria*, I find her alluding to Gustavo Adolfo Bécquer, Antonio Machado, Juan Ramón Jiménez, Jorge Guillén, and Gabriel Celaya. Her intertextual reflection on and rejection of these *others* is quite extensive, as the following remarks indicate.

Bécquer is revised in the following text:

Gracias, amor
por tu imbécil comportamiento
me hiciste saber que no era verdad eso de
«poesía eres tú».
¡Poesía soy yo!

(*Historia* 71)

(Thanks, my dear, / for your stupid behavior; / you made me realize that it's not true that / "poetry is you." / Poetry is me!)

The reference is, of course, to *Rima* (Rhyme) 21:

"¿Qué es poesía?", dices mientras clavas
en mi pupila, tu pupila azul.

"¿Qué es poesía?" ¿Y tú me lo preguntas?
Poesía . . . eres tú.

(*Rimas* 122)

("What is poetry?" you say as you fix / your blue pupil on mine. /
"What is poetry?" And you're asking me? / Poetry . . . is you.)

The effects of this intertextual rebuttal are numerous. In general terms,
Fuertes is distancing herself from late Romanticism and self-centered
sentimentality;[20] but she is also challenging the notion that a woman's
function is to be a male poet's muse—the more beautiful and passive,
the better. Second, she is foregrounding the fact that she herself makes
poetry, is actively involved in its production. Third, she is underlining
the importance of her own life, her biography, in the development of
her verse.

Rosalía de Castro's "cravo" (nail) and Antonio Machado's "espina"
(thorn) are modified in "La esquirla" (The splinter [chip]):[21]

Una vez me clavé
una esquirla de hielo en el corazón,

y cuando ya me iba a morir,
el hielo se desheló.

(*Obras* 263)

(Once I stuck / a chip of ice in my heart, / and just as I was about to
die, / the ice melted.)

The late Romantic reification of egoism, sentiment, and lost illusions,
and the importance Romanticism attached to discovering self through
love, are demythified here in that witty and unpretentious melting of a
chip of ice.

Fuertes distances herself from Juan Ramón Jiménez in a more defiant manner in the following poem:

Por fin,
ya no destrozo la Poesía;
me gusta más la violada realidad
que la santísima pureza juanramoniana.

(*Obras* 332).

(Finally, / I no longer destroy Poetry; / I prefer violated reality / to the
holy purity of Juan Ramón Jiménez.)

The allusion is to the perceived purity of Juan Ramón's "segunda época" ("second epoch," as Sánchez-Barbudo christened it [*Segunda época*), which the poet himself describes as "naked" as opposed to "pure" work. The reality Fuertes engages is not that of Jiménez's "naked" female muse but one that has been "violated," with the probable hint of rape. Indeed, in a later poem, "Rapto" (Abduction/Rapture), she echoes Jiménez's "médium sonámbulo" (somnambulistic medium) when she writes:

La poesía se apodera de mí
y yo me entrego.
La asisto y la resisto,
me dicta y me conmueve;
después,
escribo lo que ella quiere.
(*Historia* 347)

(Poetry takes hold of me / and I surrender. / I assist it and resist it, / it dictates to me and moves me; / afterwards, I write what she wills.)

Compare Fuertes's relatively amorous verbs with the aggression and violence implicit in Jiménez:

Poder que me utilizas,
como médium sonámbulo,
para tus misteriosas comunicaciones;
¡he de vencerte, sí,
he de saber qué dices,
qué me haces decir, cuando me cojes;
he de saber qué digo, un día!
(*Libros* 901).

(Power that utilizes me, / for your mysterious communications, / like a somnambulistic medium; / I must conquer you, yes, / I must know what you say, / what you make me say, when you seize me; / I must know what I say, one day!)

Moreover, in "Domesticar al destino" (Domesticating fate) the metaphor Fuertes selects for the type of reality that holds her imagination is "la puta realidad" (damnable reality [*Historia* 247])—another probable refutation of Jiménez's "la realidad invisible" (invisible reality).

Her intertextual dialogue with and differentiation from Juan Ramón are developed elsewhere. "La hervida realidad" (Boiled reality) begins,

Manjar de dioses,
hervida realidad,
yo la prefiero
a la mentira de la dulce alondra.

(Dish of the gods, / boiled reality, / I prefer it / to the lie of the
sweet lark.)

and it ends,

Lo otro, la imaginada fantasía,
¡mentira pura!
(sólo salvable en un chiste de rosa
o en un cuento de niños).
                              (*Historia* 250)

(The other, imagined fantasy: / pure lie! / [only salvageable in a soppy
joke / or in a children's tale].)

It seems—to me—that Fuertes has selected words such as "alondra,"
"imaginada fantasía," "pura," and possibly "rosa" to allude to Jiménez's
poetics. The rose and purity are his hallmarks and the lark occurs at the
beginning of his "segunda época" to announce his new poetic vision of
reality.[22] Hence, Fuertes not only rejects the poetics Jiménez canonized, she opposes it with a gynocentric poetics of her own—one that is
"puta" and "violada" as opposed to "desnuda." Fuertes engages a poetic
reality of which she is fully conscious, as opposed to many Modern
poets who perceive themselves as plumbing the unfathomable depths
of the unconscious mind.

Fuertes also distances herself from Jorge Guillén, and therefore
from the dominant esthetic of the 1920s in Spain. However, her refutation is subtle and shows no animosity. Compare Guillén's *décima*
"Beato sillón" (Blessed armchair)—which begins "¡Beato sillón! La
casa / Corrobora su presencia" (Blessed armchair! The house / corroborates your presence), and contains the famous phrase "El mundo
está bien / hecho" (The world is well / made), with Fuertes's poem "Las
cosas" (Things):

Las cosas, nuestras cosas,
les gusta que las quieran;
a mi mesa le gusta que yo apoye los codos,
a la silla le gusta que me siente en la silla,
a la puerta le gusta que la abra y la cierre

como al vino le gusta que lo compre y lo beba,
mi lápiz se deshace si lo cojo y escribo,
mi armario se estremece si lo abro y me asomo,
las sábanas, son sábanas cuando me echo sobre ellas
y la cama se queja cuando yo me levanto.
¿Qué será de las cosas cuando el hombre se acaba?
Como perros no existen sin el amo.

                                    (*Obras* 215–16)

(Things, our things, / like me to love them; / my table likes me to lean my elbows on it, / the chair likes me to sit on its seat, / the door likes me to open and close it, / just as the wine likes me to buy it and drink it, / my pencil falls apart if I grasp it and write, / my wardrobe trembles if I open it and peer inside, / sheets are sheets when I lie on them / and the bed complains when I get up. / What will become of things when man is no more? / Like dogs, they don't exist without a master.)

Unlike Guillén, Fuertes does not exalt the reality that surrounds her, she takes care of it, as if every part of it were like a pet dog. Such a nontranscendental attitude of caring is found throughout her work.

   Therefore, it is not surprising to find Fuertes distancing herself from her peer Gabriel Celaya in a poem called "Poética" (Poetics). Recall Celaya's famous dictum, from *Cantos íberos* (Iberian songs [1955]), that "La poesía es un arma cargada de futuro" (poetry is a weapon loaded with futurity), with the following statement:

La poesía no debe ser un arma,
debe ser un abrazo,
un invento,
un descubrir a los demás
lo que pasa por dentro,
eso, un descubrimiento,
un aliento,
un aditamento,
un estremecimiento.
La poesía debe ser
obligatoria.

                                    (*Historia* 313).

(Poetry should not be a weapon, / it should be a hug, / an invention, / a form of discovery for the rest of the world / of what happens inside, /

that's what it should be, a revelation, / a breath, / a complement, / a vibration. / Poetry should be / compulsory.)[23]

In rebutting her male precursors and distancing herself from her peers, Fuertes is developing her own poetics, one in which her concerns as a woman are articulated: she rejects transcendental esthetic idealism; she is conscious of her body, conscious of her daily reality, conscious of the fact that she shares that reality with the people and things that surround her. She would have agreed with Figuera that poems are "fruit wrapped in the hot pulp of my flesh." Fuertes's is a nontranscendental vision of art and life.

A fourth distinctive feature of Fuertes's gynocentric/gynocritical vision is its corrosive and derisive demystification of androcentric self-interest. In "Mal humor" (Bad mood), an early poem, she writes that she detests

Los fríos,
Los Samueles,
los sabuesos,
los adustos,
los contables,
los machos,
los guerreros,
los pedantes,
los que dicen:
—la mujer mi esclava.
            (*Obras* 59)

(The cold ones, / the Samuels, / the sleuths, / the stern ones, / the accountants, / the machos, / the warriors, / the pedants, / those who say: / my slave the woman.)[24]

Men are personified as animals, neanderthals, robots, dried-up trees. An early poem states "los hombres son tigres" (men are tigers [*Obras* 61]), and a much later one, "La tierra nunca fue joven" (The earth was never young), asserts:

—en Canarias tenemos flores iguales
a las de hace millones de años—,
en la tierra tenemos hombres iguales
a los primeros rumiantes,

—se siguen matando entre ellos
igual que los primeros habitantes—.
(Historia 221)²⁵

(—in the Canaries we have flowers the same / as those of two million years ago—, / on earth we have men the same / as the first ruminants, / —they keep on killing each other off / the same as the first inhabitants—.)

Fuertes is a declared pacifist ("en mi laboratorio de pruebas / trabajo en desinventar la guerra" [in my test-laboratory / I work at disinventing war (*Historia* 327)]), and like Angela Figuera she lambasts warmongers—all male—in many poems: "el macho oscuro / con hombros de ataúd" (the dark male of the species / with his coffin-shoulders [*Historia* 203]).[26]

The poem "El robot Nazi" (The Nazi robot) demythifies in one fell swoop the male of the species and the established order personified by him:

Al andar extendía las patas en línea
sin jugar con la rodilla,
el brazo derecho le alzaba bruscamente
y le dejaba caer como un rayo
que no sólo exterminaba a judíos,
sino a todos los que no andaban como él.
(*Historia* 72)

(To walk, he moved his feet forward in a straight line / without trifling to use his knees, / he abruptly raised his right arm / and let it fall like a thunderbolt, / which exterminated Jews / and anyone else who did not walk with him.)

Like María de Zayas, Fuertes—by means of her goose-stepping Nazi robot—critiques the egocentric single-mindedness of the sociopolitical order which the male of the species has erected. The latter is a structure from which women and other disenfranchised groups, such as the poor, are excluded merely for forming part of the dispossessed: they are proscribed from "falling in" with it or him, for reasons of ideology, religion, gender, or class.[27]

In a very early poem, "Aviso" (Warning), she warns her readers of the lifelessness of businessmen and bureaucrats:

Está seco, sus ramas sin hojas,
su tronco sin ojos,
sus cables sin savia,
se mueve sin amor.
Está seco.
   Nada le estremece,
por nada hasta blasfema.
La Bolsa y el Negocio
sólo le hacen vibrar.
Está seco.
   Se mete en Ministerios,
administra guardillas,
rebaja los jornales,
que su vida es así.
   Y le he visto,
os advierto:
Enterrad a ese hombre cuanto antes.

(Obras 97)

(He's dry: his branches, without leaves; / his trunk, without eyes, / his
wires, without sap; / he moves without love. / He's dried up. / Nothing
thrills him; / he curses at the slightest pretext. / The Stock Market and
the Business Deal / are the only things that make him tick. / He's dried
out. / He gets into Ministries; / he's an administrator of lofts; / he
lowers the daily wage; / for that's what his life's about. / And I've seen
him, / I warn you: / Bury that man as soon as possible.)

And in a much later poem, "El monstruo" (The Monster), Fuertes
focuses on another aspect of male dessication, the inability to express
feeling:

Yo estaba en el bar,
entró un hombre corriente,
se sentó enfrente,
le miré distraída pensando en mis cosas,
— ¡me espanté! —
tenía cara de no haber dicho «te quiero» en toda su vida.

(Historia 90).[28]

(I was in the bar, / a regular guy entered, / he sat down in front of
me, / I looked at him absentmindedly for I was thinking about myself,

/—I was appalled!—/ he had the face of one who never in all his life
had said: "I love you.")

Related to her corrosive demystification of the male of the species is
Gloria Fuertes's irreverent view of established religion. God is part of
her world (*Obras* 121), and she addresses Him as an equal, not as if he
were her superior, a trait we noted earlier in Ernestina de Champourcin.[29] Her "Oración" (Prayer) includes:

> Haz que me acostumbre a las cosas de abajo.
> Dame la salvadora indiferencia,
> haz un milagro más,
> dame la risa,
> ¡hazme payaso, Dios, hazme payaso!"
> (*Obras* 128).

(Make me abide by things below. / Grant me redeeming indifference, /
perform one miracle more, / give me laughter: / turn me into a clown,
God, turn me into a clown!)

Her "Oración para ir tirando" (Prayer to keep on going) begins: "Padre
nuestro que estás en los cielos / ¿por qué no bajas y te das un garbeo?"
(Our Father who art in heaven, / why don't you come down here and go
for a spin? [*Obras* 228]). Fuertes finds God in the quotidian events of
her "barrio" (neighborhood [*Obras* 124]), and she treats Him as one of
her own: "Y yo le doy, / pellizcos a sus manos, / disgustos a sus curas, /
y le pago con deudas" (And I / nip on his hands, / upset his priests, /
and repay him with debts [*Obras* 72]).[30]

However, Fuertes's attitude toward biblical truths is less playful,
more deadly serious.[31] In "Está claro" (It's obvious), she states:

> Cuando el mundo el paraíso era,
> le habitaba una sola pareja
> —hasta se saben sus nombres...
>
> Y si esto verdad fuera,
> descendemos del incesto y el incesto degenera...
> (*Obras* 268)[32]

(When the world was paradise, / a single couple inhabited it /—we
even know their names... / And if this were true, / then we're
descended from incest and incest entails degeneration.)

Her strongest subversion of the Church and patriarchal biblical myths
is called "Otra versión" (Another version):

Al principio.
Era la era del paraíso.

Jugaban por los valles
trepaban por los riscos,
y todo era posible,
y todo permitido.

Y Adán se convirtió en manzana
y Eva se convirtió al catolicismo.
(*Historia* 370).

(In the beginning. / It was the age of paradise. / They played in the
vales, / climbed the cliffs, / and all was possible, / all allowed. / And
Adam became [Adam's] apple / and Eve was converted to Catholicism.)

Paradise was destroyed by the patriarchs who confected the Bible, and
by the Fathers of the Catholic Church who have had a monopoly on interpreting and establishing its so-called truths. Hence, Fuertes likes to
poke holes in Old and New Testament teachings ("Tú lo sabes" [You
well know] *Historia* 150 and *Historia* 90, 361).

Fuertes is not antireligious, nor even anti-Christian. In fact, she
draws on the Bible to preach her own small sermons.[33] The love Fuertes
has—for humankind and God—is not that inspired by androcentric institutions. Another "Autobio" (Autobio[graphy]) reads:

Nunca vi claro lo del clero,
ni siquiera de niña en el colegio
cuando te lo crees todo.

Cuando era pequeña
tampoco me creí lo de la cigüeña.
(*Historia* 61)

(I was never quite sure about the clergy's ideas, / not even when I was a
girl in college / when you swallow everything whole. / When I was
little / I didn't believe in the stork either.)

Asked if she believes in fidelity, she replies: "No. Un no rotundo" (No.
A resounding no [*Historia* 59]). Infidelity is positively valorized in her
poems (*Historia* 89, 196, 316).

Fuertes's amorous and religious sentiments are more humane than those accepted by patriarchal society and permitted by the Church and its Fathers (*Obras* 361). Nor does she assume that God is a man: "Porque El lo sabe todo de antemano, / El o Ella, quien sea, se lo sabe" (Because He knows it all beforehand, / He or She, whoever it might be, already knows it [*Obras* 207]). Indeed, she entertains the notion of a female deity. She notes that "La mujer fue anterior al hombre" (Woman preceded man [*Historia* 244]); and in "Anginas justicieras" (Righteous anginas), she writes: "No soy feliz . . . por amar a todo el mundo como Dios manda; / y para ser feliz sólo tienes que amar a una persona / como manda Madame Naturaleza" (I'm not happy . . . from loving everyone as God commands, / and to be happy one has to love just one person / as Madame Nature orders [*Obras* 260]). Fuertes's irony and humor make it hard for a reader to categorize her exclusively as adhering to one particular idea, for she is comic and serious in her pronouncements. However, she concludes "No reiros de nada" (Don't laugh about anything) with this stanza:

Todo mal quedará al fin disipado;
el mundo no estará apolillado,
cuando por fin
algún [*sic*] gallina-madre
ponga un huevo cuadrado.
                    (*Obras* 326)

(In the end, all evil will be dispelled; / the world will not be motheaten, / when finally / some mother hen or other / lays a square egg.)

Fuertes's sympathies are certainly clear, but she is not programmatic in her assertions. Her religious instinct is characterized by giving, by going out toward others and the world; it manifests "care for and sensitivity to the needs of others" (Gilligan, *Different* 18). Throughout she places emphasis on the "heart" and not the "head" ("Si mi corazón" [If my heart] *Obras* 95; "Yo en la gloria" [Me in glory] *Historia* 100; "Dictador particular" [Private dictator] *Historia* 367). Fuertes proposes a holistic or integrationist stance for human beings, as opposed to the divisiveness androcentric culture has fostered.[34] "Tenemos que" (We have to) reads:

Reencontrarnos
reencantarnos
reemocionarnos

reilusionarnos
reintegrarnos
rehabilitarnos.
¡Releñe!
Reimplantarnos
la armonía.
Todo parejo,
cada almeja
con su almejo.
        (*Historia* 320)

(Reencounter ourselves, / reenchant ourselves, / reexcite ourselves, / rethrill ourselves, / reintegrate ourselves, / rehabilitate ourselves. / Rescrew! / Reimplant / harmony in ourselves. / Every Johnny with his Jane, every Jane with her Johnny.) [35]

Fuertes sees herself as comparable to an old female deity replete with love to give ("Curada de espanto" [Cured of fright] *Historia* 2226), and in opposition to Santa Teresa de Jesús, she declares herself a "Mística terrenal" (Earthly mystic):

—«Que muero porque no muero»—(Santa Teresa)
—Que vivo porque no vivo—(yo)
—«Vivo sin vivir en mí»—(Santa Teresa)
Vivo porque vivo en ti—(yo)
                          (*Historia* 253)

("I die because I do not die"—[Saint Theresa]. /—As I'm alive, why shouldn't I live [Me]. /—"I live without living in myself" [Saint Theresa]. / I live because I live in you—[Me].)

Linked to this is Fuertes's attitude toward Death—"¡Esa insulsa que nunca sabe a nada!" (That dull dame who never tastes of anything! [*Obras* 277]). While her male peers and precursors generally stand in awe of death or mythologize it out of mind, in "A la muerte" (For death) Fuertes insults it as if it were an old bitch:

Ubre de palidez,
leche de cera,
solapada sin sol,
¡hipocritilla!
—sabes lo de después
y no lo dices—,

haces más daño al vivo que al que matas,
llevándote los vivos de los muertos.
Amiga de lo ajeno,
¡lame tumbas!
loquita filahuésica incansable,
apañada trapera delincuente,
viciosa tejepena.
. . . .
¡Vete!
archivera asquerosa de partidas
de defunción y de las otras.
¡Muerta!

(Obras 143)

(Udder of pallor, / milk of wax, / sunless sneak, / you hypocritical little
woman! / —you know what happens afterwards / but say nothing—, /
you do more harm to the living than to those you kill / by taking the
dead away from the living. / Girlfriend of whatever is not yours, /
tomb-licker! / tireless, bone-collecting, mad midget, / tricky,
racketeering ragwoman, / vicious sower of grief. / . . . / Clear off! /
loathsome archivist of death certificates / and other such things. /
Dead bore!)

As an early poem states: "Es obligatorio tener mitos / y yo gustosa
desobedezco" (It's incumbent on us to have myths / and I gleefully
disobey [*Obras* 136]). French feminists have made us aware of how the
male's preoccupation with "the life and death of the penis" is "projected
into other aspects of culture," in particular on to "the need for immortality and posterity" and on to "the fear of death." Like them, Fuertes
likes to "poke fun" at male desire, subvert its phallic need for transcendent ideals, and its "impossibility of living in the here and now" (see
Marks and Courtivron, "Introduction III" 36).

Fuertes's gynocentric style will by now be apparent to the reader,
and a fifth distinctive feature of her work is its foregrounding of gynocentric images and metaphors. Like Angela Figuera, Fuertes deploys
womanhood as a recurrent metaphor. She focuses on those women who
are poor and abject, exploited and downtrodden: "Dios está . . . en la
madre que pare . . . en la mujer pública" (God is . . . in the woman
who gives birth . . . in the public woman [*Obras* 43]); "o alguna señorita de aborto provocado / o alguna prostituta con navaja en la ingle"
(or some young woman forced to abort, / or some prostitute with a

knife in her groin [*Obras* 167]).[36] The prostitute is one of her favorites, always viewed from an empathetic point of view (*Obras* 64, 167, 250, 326; *Historia* 291, 365). The condition of women who hang around bars (*Historia* 194) and women singers and starlets (*Historia* 183, 371), whose lives might seem glamorous from afar, is demythified. And in one delightful subversive revision, "La maja de Solana" (Solana's girl), a tart, possibly a prostitute, takes revenge on a john, or on her pimp:

La maja de la plaza de la Paja,
cuando el chulo se la raja,
se desgaja
                la refaja,
saca y pule
                la navaja,
corta y taja,
¡Es Pepa la Desparpaja!
                                            (*Obras* 287)

(When the spiv stabs / the downtown tart, / she rips open / her skirt, / draws and shines / her knife, / hacks and cuts: / three cheers for Magnificent Maggie!)[37]

One of Fuertes's constant selections concerns women whose bodies have been racked by childbirth and hunger. For example, when she writes, "Las flacas mujeres . . . siguen pariendo en casa o en el tranvía" (Skinny women . . . keep on giving birth at home or on the tram [*Obras* 67]), and "estas locas son muertas, / que las sigue latiendo el corazón / debajo de las tetas" (these madwomen are dead, / for their hearts keep on beating / beneath their breasts ["Paliduchas" (Wan women) *Obras* 86]), she brings to mind her peer, Angela Figuera. The fact that Gloria Fuertes creates a space in her poetic texts for such gynocritical social commentary is another clear indication of her feminist vision.[38]

In addition to foregrounding a woman's condition in her poetry, Fuertes—like numerous other women poets—selects imagery—such as the sea, fish, and witches—to articulate her femaleness. In "A no ser en tus manos" (If I'm not in your hands), she exclaims, "donde mejor me encuentro es en el mar" (where I feel best is in the sea [*Obras* 192]). She perceives the sea's waves as involved in childbirth: "Morir pariendo como las olas / para que el mar perdure" (To die giving birth like the waves / so the sea may endure [*Obras* 176]). And in "Tu presa" (Your dam) she sees herself as flowing:

Ya sé lo que me pasó:
Yo era agua,
estaba en tu presa,
abandonaste la empresa
y elevaste las compuertas...
Hoy me quieres recoger...

Yo era agua.
Yo soy agua,
—quiero y no puedo volver—.
                    (*Historia* 247–48)[39]

(Now I know what happened to me: / I was water, / I was in your
dam, / you raised the sluice gates / and reneged on your plan... / So
now you want me back... / I was water. / I am water, / —I'd like to
return but can't—.)

But the fish is her preferred symbol (*Obras* 88, 95; *Historia* 208), and
"Cada uno copula como pueda" (Everyone copulates however they can)
delightfully explains why:

Los peces,
se reproducen sin «hacerlo».
La hembra suelta los huevos
en el mar,
y el macho atraído y excitado
por aquella pedrea,
los «padrea».
Viven en armonía
con las corrientes de su entorno.
Quisiera ser como los peces.
                    (*Historia* 326)

(Fish / reproduce without "doing it." / The female drops the eggs /
into the sea, / and the male, attracted and excited / by that spurt of
lava, / becomes their "father." / They live in harmony / with the
currents that surround them. / I'd like to be like fish.)

Fuertes also textualizes sewing—"zurciendo estoy mi alegría, / se me
había apolillado" (I'm darning my joy, / it had gone moth-eaten on me
[*Obras* 317]). In "Poema para un desconocido" (Poem for an unknown
person), she recalls Zardoya: "mi corazón es un ovillo / y mi lápiz la
aguja, / vamos a restañar lo descosido" (my heart is a ball of wool / and
my pencil's the needle, / let's stanch the unstitched [*Historia* 341]).[40]

Moreover, Fuertes identifies with the monster-woman, not the angel, by symbolizing her self and related activities as a female animal: "loba," "cabra," "yegua" (she-wolf, she-goat, mare [*Obras* 90; *Historia* 95; *Historia* 262, 339]).[41] In addition, she refers to witches to describe her activity: "las brujas tejen telarañas en mi sobacos" (witches weave webs in my armpits [*Obras* 300; *Historia* 271]). When she dramatizes her inspirational animus/anima, she perceives it as a phantom or ghost (*Obras* 214). My point in choosing to comment on such imagery is not just to argue that it is more forceful and convincing in expressing a gynocentric vision but also that it is not found in poetry written by men. Hence, part of Fuertes's originality is that she develops in her work a woman-centered lexicon.

A sixth distinctive feature of her work, as we have noted, is that it textually foregrounds Gloria Fuertes's self and her personal condition as a woman and as a woman poet in mid-century Spain (e.g., "Autobio" [*Historia* 176–77]). In pragmatic terms, she puts herself into her text, as Cixous urged, "as into the world and into history—by her own movement" ("Laugh" 245). The first poem of her *Obras incompletas* is "Nota biográfica" (Biographical note), which begins:

Gloria Fuertes nació en Madrid
a los dos días de edad,
pues fue muy laborioso el parto de mi madre
que si se descuida muere por vivirme.
A los tres años ya sabía leer
y a los seis ya sabía mis labores.

(*Obras* 41)

(Gloria Fuertes was born in Madrid / when she was two days old, / for my mother's delivery was very laborious: / if she'd've been careless, she'd've died to let me live. / By three, I knew how to read / and by six I'd learned my jobs.)

"Autobiografía" (Autobiography) continues this direct line of presentation of the self; it begins, "A los pies de la Catedral de Burgos, / nació mi madre" (On the doorstep of Burgos Cathedral, / my mother was born [*Obras* 71]). But Fuertes's readers encounter more than autobiography in her poems, for the poet takes advantage of her female condition to play with and subvert traditional reactions to normal situations. For example, in the following short poem she describes directly her pleasure—which is distinct from what traditional women would feel or dare express: "¡Cuando me sonrieron los chavales de las chabo-

las, / sentí como si todas las campanas del mundo / tocaron a Gloria!"
(When my chums in the slums smiled at me, / I felt as if all the bells
in the world / played the Gloria [*Historia* 84]). We also encounter a direct presentation of her disappointment; in "Soy sólo una mujer" (I'm
only a woman)[42] she confesses:

> Yo quisiera haber sido delineante,
> o delirante Safo sensitiva
> y heme,
> aquí,
> que soy una perdida
> entre tanto mangante.
>
> (*Obras* 256)

(I would like to have been a draughtswoman, / or a sensitively delirious
Sappho, / but here / I am, / a loser / among a bunch of loafers.)

Clearly, culture thwarted such professional aspirations but to compensate the poet turns her writing into a therapeutic session.[43] In "Nota a
mí misma" (Note to myself)—selecting again a vulvular metaphor—
she tells herself that she is not a mollusk, but could become a fish and
use her gills (*Historia* 208). In "No sé" (I don't know) she grudgingly
accepts her womanhood:

> No sé de dónde soy.
> No he nacido en ningún sitio;
> yo ya estaba
> cuando lo de la manzana,
> por eso soy apolítica.
> Menos mal que soy mujer,
> y no pariré vencejos
> ni se mancharán mis manos
> con el olor del fusil,
> menos mal que soy así...
>
> (*Obras* 79)

(I don't know where I'm from. / I was born in no place in particular; /
I was already around / when the apple fell, / hence, I'm apolitical. / It's
just as well that I'm a woman, / that I won't breed swifts, / that my
hands won't be stained / with a rifle's smell, / it's just as well that I'm as
I am.)

At times her self-presentation is not as direct. For example, "Yo" (I) reads:

Yo,
remera de barcas
ramera de hombres
romera de almas
rimera de versos,
Ramona,
    pa' servirles.
                    (*Obras* 223)

(I, / rower of boats, / whorer of men, / romany of souls, / rhymer of verses, / Raymunda, / at your service.)

The self that writes poetry is symbolically foregrounded here, as it is elsewhere. One poem begins: "Hago versos, señores, hago versos, / pero no me gusta que me llamen poetisa" (I compose verses, gentlemen, I compose verses, / but I don't like being called a poetess [*Obras* 137]). "En retaguardia" (In the rearguard)—which expresses her guilt at not fighting in the war—ends: "la gente se está matando / mientras yo escribo sentada—, / bien herida, mal amada" (people are killing each other / while I sit writing—, / well wounded, badly loved [*Historia* 88]). A later poem reads:

Difícil, por ahora, ser demente,
porque yo no escribo de mente
escribo de corazón,
de ojos,
de manos,
de un ser,
—o de varios—.
Escribo de ovarios
(inclusive).
                    (*Historia* 272)

(Difficult, at this moment, to be out of my mind, / because I don't write with my mind, / I write with my heart, / with my eyes, / with my hands, / with my being, /—or with several—. / I write with my ovaries / [as well].)

As is obvious from the choice of "ovarios," Gloria Fuertes's poetics is gynocentric in that it textually foregrounds imagery of a woman's body

which it develops into metaphors of female thoughts and feelings. Elsewhere her breasts are foregrounded—"bastante bien mis senos" (my
breasts are pretty good [*Obras* 245])—often to emphasize the loneliness of her life. "Cena fría" (Cold supper) probably puns on a voiceless
sibilant pronunciation [s] for "cena" to identify it with "seno":

¡Qué inútilmente descubres tus senos
en las reuniones,
vuelves a casa con ellos
lacios tristes
desnudos de miradas de ternura!
Cómo tiritan tus senos
en las locas noches musicales sin una sola nota
de amor.

(*Historia* 214)[44]

(How you waste your time showing off your breasts / at meetings, / to
return home with them, / limp, sad, / denuded of tender glances! /
How your breasts shiver / on wild, musical nights, without a single
note / of love.)

She also refers to the umbilical cord: "el cordón umbilical de la tristeza"
(the umbilical cord of sadness [*Obras* 155]); "la mala vida y la buena
gente / me ha cortado el cordón umbilical / del llanto. / (Me plagio)" (a
bad life and good people / have cut my umbilical cord / of tears./ [I pla-
giarize myself] [*Historia* 289]). In "No es lo mismo" (It's not the same)
she uses her body to foreground her difference from prudish women,
and the difference of her sexual pleasure from a man's: "Es diferente, /
estar sobre un hombre / a estar bajo un hombre" (It's different / being
on top of a man / to being underneath a man [*Historia* 294]). Fuertes's
inscription of the body, when judged by the ideals of French feminists,
is literal; it certainly does not attain the figurative resonance and eman-
cipatory power of Clara Janés's. Nevertheless, Gloria Fuertes's work
takes the first step in confronting the taboo surrounding the inscription
of female body parts and thereby offers future poets the opportunity
of continuing the march forward.

   In conclusion, Gloria Fuertes's gynocentric vision is feminist both
in its protest over the marginalization of women and in its advocacy
for change. It is also female in its articulation of self-reliance and self-
textualization, and in its foregrounding of gynocentric metaphors. Her
vision is also gynocritical in its pervasive demystification of androcen-

tric self-interest, in its undermining of the male poetic canon and the traditional view of the poet, as well as its subversion of desire. The gynocentric and gynocritical visions inherent in Gloria Fuertes's work reveal the originality of her talent and her uniqueness as a poet of the Franco era.

Notes

1. See Daydí-Tolson, *Post–Civil War;* González Muela, *Nueva poesía;* and Ynduráin, "Prólogo."

2. Page references are given in the text with the following citations: *Obras* (*Obras incompletas* [Incomplete works]), *Historia* (*Historia de Gloria* [Gloria's Story]), and *Mujer* (*Mujer de verso en pecho* [Woman with verse on her chest]). However, the latter appeared much too late—spring 1995— for any serious inclusion in the following comments; in broad terms, it is a continuation of, not a radical departure from, her previous work.

3. Her first book, *Isla ignorada,* is not included in either *Obras* or *Historia.* See Sherno's "Gloria Fuertes' Room" for an illuminating analysis.

4. For a complete overview of all criticism to date, see Cappuccio, "Gloria Fuertes"; for a sound critical overview, see Marson, "Gloria Fuertes" 203–5.

5. See also Rogers, "Comic Spirit."

6. E.g., Persin's "Gloria Fuertes"; Sherno's "Poetry of Gloria Fuertes" and "Gloria Fuertes' Room"; and Marson's "Gloria Fuertes."

7. First published in the 1954 *Antolgía y poemas del suburbio* (Anthology and poems from the suburbs).

8. This poem, "Yo, en un monte de olivos" (I, on a mount of olives), also alludes to Christ's passion.

9. Rosalía de Castro's "Dicen que no hablan las plantas."

10. See also "Cuarto Oscuro" (*Obras* 246).

11. The expression is a pun. It could also imply "their fucking mother."

12. For example, during a roundtable discussion at a symposium held at the University of Wisconsin, Madison (Sept. 1989), Jaime Siles and Guillermo Carnero vehemently attacked Fuertes and her work and ridiculed the person who lectured on it. The lectures, not the discussion, were published in Ciplijauskaité, *Novísimos.*

13. See also "Me pedían unos versos para el concurso de floricultura" (*Historia* 183–84).

14. Compare Rosalía's "Yo cantar, cantar, canté" ("mas donde gracia me falta / el sentimiento me sobra").

15. The liquid/solid opposition implicit in this imagery is found also in Irigaray, in whose writing, Stanton explains, "the rigid hardness . . . the

solid that the penis represents . . . is contrasted to an intrauterine, amniotically fluid sexuality, which Irigaray identifies as specifically feminine" ("Difference" 169).

16. For which, see Mandlove, "Letter Poems." Smith-Rosenberg's essay ("Female World") pioneered this line of inquiry. Showalter notes that the essay "examines several archives of letters between women, and outlines the homosocial emotional world of the nineteenth century" ("Toward a Feminist Poetics" 131-32).

17. Recall Cixous: "woman is always in a certain way, 'mother' to herself and other" (quoted in Stanton, "Difference" 161). And "*in* her, matrix, cradler; herself giver as her mother and child; she is her own sister-daughter" ("Laugh" 252).

18. On New Year's Eve, Spaniards swallow twelves grapes as midnight is chimed in.

19. See also "Tengo miedo de tener miedo" (*Historia* 350). And see n. 17 above.

20. The lexicon and cadences of "Ojalá sea mentira" also seem to rebutt Bécquer's stance and Machado's metaphysics. It begins: "¡Ojalá sea mentira ese rumor que corre sobre el río / donde peces de plata mueren sin ser pescados!" (I wish it were a lie this murmur that runs on the river / where silver fish die never having been fished [*Historia* 61]).

21. For Rosalía, see "Unha vez tiven un cravo" in *Follas* (trans. Barja 36-37; *Obras* 1:286). For Machado, "Yo voy soñando caminos" (*Poesías* 11).

22. In "Canción de despacho" from *Estío* he exclaims: "¡Bien por la alondra del oriente! / ¡No hay más que mirar y ver / la verdad resplandeciente!" (Good for the lark from the east! / Now just look and behold / the shining truth! [*Libros* 105]). See my *Self and Image* 74-76. For further resonances, see "Cuestiones fúnebres" (*Obras* 81), "El valiente" (*Obras* 96), and "¿Qué sería de Dios sin nosotros?" (*Obras* 225).

23. See also "Con pluma no con plomo" (With pen not with lead [*Mujer* 85]).

24. Compare Conde's "no basta a los hombres / que mujeres siervas entreguen placer" from "Por viejos campos nuestros."

25. See also "El sireno" (*Obras* 230-31), in which the male's "señorito" tendencies are satirized together with his rejection of his origin in the female of the species. And "Aviso": "Los dinosaurios, / andaban con dos pies antes que el hombre, / pero no les creció el cerebro / y no pasaron a más" (Dinosaurs / walked on two feet before man did, / but their brain didn't grow / and they progressed no further [*Historia* 327]).

26. See also "Bomba" (*Obras* 268-69), "Contra la atómica" (*Historia* 73), "Hay frases" (*Historia* 80), and "A buenas horas" (*Historia* 287).

27. See also "Multinacionales—El Presidente" (*Historia* 373).

28. Fuertes is not exclusively anti-male, she is also against the limited

attitude of the female of the species. For example, in "Poema para niños adúlteros" she writes: "No creer todo lo que os digan, / el lobo no es tan malo como Caperucita" (Don't believe all they tell you, / the wolf is not as bad as Little Red Riding Hood [*Historia* 65]). And see "Hay tantas..." (*Historia* 322).

29. Champourcin's poems are earlier, in *Cárcel de los sentidos* (1964) and *Cartas cerradas* (1968).

30. See also "Ahora habla Dios" (*Obras* 253-54); "El camello" (*Obras* 240-41), in which the Baby Jesus rejects the Wise Men's gifts and takes the camel; and "Jueves Santo" (*Obras* 325). On Fuertes's radical feminist perspective toward God and prayer, see Umpierre, "Inversión."

31. Compare her irreverence toward the stories children are told about where babies come from (*Historia* 78).

32. See also "La clase" (*Obras* 204-5).

33. For example: "Ya que no tenéis valor, / categoría y fuerza / para amaros los unos a los otros, / procurad haceros menos la puñeta / los unos a los otros" (Seeing as you have neither courage, / class nor strength / to love one another, / try to screw it up less / for one another [*Historia* 316]). In *Mujer de verso* her tendency to sermonize and to delineate her particular view of God has increased.

34. Mary Daly also argues that the man-made is death.

35. Fuertes's puns are impossible to translate. "Releñe" probably alludes to "leñe" as "coño" or "leche" (semen). The phrase "todo parejo, / cada almeja / con su almejo" plays with "cada oveja con su pareja" (every sheep with its companion), as well as with "almeja" meaning "clam" and "cunt." Indeed, the double entendre of these lines is: "every Jane with her Jane, every Johnny with his Johnny."

36. Her sympathies also lie with umarried women who have to make do with other women's husbands (*Obras* 64); and with the horrendous condition of married women (*Historia* 69).

37. The insistent interior and end-rhymes of this poem as well as the colloquial connotations of its lexicon make it impossible to translate. To give the reader a somewhat better idea of its force, I take my cue from an old Beatles' song, inspired by a folkloric whore of Liverpool's Lime Street, who charged only sixpence to turn a trick (so I was told, when I was a schoolboy in Liverpool): "Maggie May of Lime Street, when jostled by a John, draws a knife from out her drawers and gashes him for life. Good old Maggie, smartest of the lot!"

38. See also *Obras* 46-47, 148, 240.

39. See also *Historia* 185, 218.

40. Zardoya's poem is from 1977, *El corazón y la sombra*. Fuertes's *Historia de Gloria* was published in 1981.

41. However, in a self-satire, she describes herself as a bull (*Historia* 63).

Also compare Rosalía's "¡Hojas nuevas!" where poems are "fieras, como mi dolor."

42. On this, see Valdivieso, "Significación."

43. See also "Me sigue persiguiendo la poesía," "Los problemas," and "Adobado con ternura" (*Historia* 262).

44. See also *Obras* 81—"Quién coserá mis senos."

Part 4 : The Post-Franco Era

6

Francisca Aguirre, María Victoria Atencia, Clara Janés

In the remaining chapters, I study the work of women poets for whom the end of the dictatorship of Francisco Franco proved to be a stimulus and inspiration. The three studied here—Aguirre (b. 1930), Atencia (b. 1931), and Janés (b. 1940)—in fact published during the Caudillo's reign; the others—studied in the next chapter—first published during the 1980s, that is, well after Franco's death in 1975. Spain experienced slightly more freedom of expression and liberty of conduct during the late 1960s, but it was not until after 1975 that the country had full access to the rights and liberties the rest of Europe had taken for granted for decades.[1] These factors encouraged individual expression and, in particular, resulted in the publication of books by women poets at a rate never witnessed in the past.

Francisca Aguirre published three books of poetry during the 1970s—in 1972, 1977, and 1978—and has not been heard of since. María Victoria Atencia did publish two slender volumes in 1961, however it was not until 1976, one year after Franco's death, that she—like one of her precursors, Ernestina de Champourcin (Ascunce, "Prólogo" xxii)—broke a fifteen-year silence with *Marta & María* (Martha and Mary) and revealed her true poetic voice.[2] Since *Marta & María* she has published ten volumes of poems. Atencia today commands a respected readership, whereas Aguirre is unknown. Clara Janés, one of the most admired poets of contemporary Spain, published two books between 1964 and 1973, but it was not until 1975 that her authentic voice began to be heard; in the 1980s, she published six books of poetry.

Atencia, Aguirre, and Janés should belong to the "second post-civil war generation" of Spanish poets.[3] In fact, Aguirre is married to Félix Grande, an important member of that particular group, a fact that no doubt contributes to her obscurity.[4] Angel González (b. 1925), Jaime Gil de Biedma (1929-90), José Angel Valente (b. 1929), Francisco Brines (b. 1932), Claudio Rodríguez (b. 1934), and Félix Grande (b. 1937) are key members of the group of poets that dominated the Spanish poetic scene until the early 1970s. There is no consensus of opinion on what distinguishes this group of poets from their immediate predecessors, but Andrew Debicki's title for them, "Poets of Discovery" (*Poetry of Discovery* 1-19; *Spanish Poetry* 99-118, 120-26), captures the creativity they displayed toward language, life, and poetic self. In general, their poems are more concerned with existential, philosophical, and esthetic matters. However, the gynocentric visions of Francisca Aguirre, María Victoria Atencia, and Clara Janés are very different from the androcentric visions of their male peers—and from each other's. Aguirre's vision is certainly tinged with social commitment; Atencia's is private and intimate; Janés's is sensual and liberating. Each in her own way foregrounds the female self and subverts androcentric ideals.

◆

Francisca Aguirre (b. 1930) began to publish at the end of the Franco era in Spain. She was forty-two before her first book appeared, and she has published just three books of poetry: *Itaca* (Ithaca [1972]), *Los trescientos escalones* (The three hundred steps [1977]), and *La otra música* (The other music [1978]).[5] Aguirre is little known, but she deserves critical attention precisely because she provides an antagonistic vision of a woman in the patriarchal Spanish society of the 1960s and 1970s. Her gynopoetics challenge the androcentric vision of her culture and reflect on the need to modify phallocratic dicta. Her first book, *Itaca*, is a revisionary reading of the *Odyssey* from Penelope's point of view; it is consciously female in the sense that Aguirre uses the persona of Penelope for "self-exploration, self-projection, self defense" (Ostriker, *Stealing* 22).[6] The poems in *Itaca* are narrated by a depressed and disillusioned Penelope, alone and abandoned on the island of Ithaca after Ulysses has set sail on his personal odyssey. This barren isle reflects the hollowness and pointlessness of life sensed by a woman in the mid-twentieth century, a woman who is oppressed by the image Spanish bourgeois society holds up to her eyes. In reaction, Penelope/Francisca strips away all the certainties and so-called Truths her culture has implanted in her mind. Aguirre's subsequent books are unified by no such overarching metaphor, but they do evince similar anguish and a comparable vision of life. The world is perceived as empty, as vicious and full of vengeance, but the isolated, creative artist discovers strength in women (Rosa Chacel, Olga Orozco, her own mother), in her immediate family, and in literature and art.

One of the most distinctive features of Francisca Aguirre's gynocentric vision is masochistic marginalization. It is as though her anger, whose negative effects we have observed in some of her precursors, turns inward, splits her poetic persona apart, and reduces her to silence.

Several years before the publication of Gilbert and Gubar's crucial *Madwoman in the Attic*, Aguirre had already examined in her verse the effects of marginalization, claustrophobia, and masochistic self-destruction. *Itaca* presents an image of a woman who has been reduced to a state of mental illness by the actions of a patriarch, who became free to transform himself into the (male) legend Western culture lauds. As Aguirre's poems evolve, the island of Ithaca becomes a spatial metaphor for the prison (psychological, emotional) in which Penelope is confined. In fact, the second section of the book is called "El desván de Penélope"—Penelope's "attic."

Ithaca is described initially as a lifeless, empty place: "mantiene el eco de voces que se han ido" (holds the echo of voices that have parted [*Itaca* 14]). It is a deserted island on which no strangers in their right mind will land: "Itaca es sólo el mar / y un cielo que la aplasta" (Ithaca is only sea / and a sky that crushes it [*Itaca* 17]); "aquí nadie viene voluntariamente . . . sólo llegan los náufragos" (no one voluntarily comes here . . . only those who've been shipwrecked [*Itaca* 18]). Those who do arrive cannot stand it: "se quedan mudos" ("end up mute") and become "un cortejo disgregado, / un arenal en marcha" (a disbanded procession, a sandpit on the march [*Itaca* 19]). Ithaca, which conditions Penelope, is barren and empty, a silent void, whose few inhabitants wander about as if they were part of a funeral procession. And all this, Aguirre implies, emblematizes the space women inhabit in the present era.

The figural meaning of such an island—a prison of psychic space—takes on novel dimensions in "El muro" (The wall):

1   Pensó: qué espantoso vacío,
    un desierto es la tierra;
    si ahora echara a correr
    podría salirme de ella totalmente.
5   Miraba a su alrededor
    y miraba también dentro de sí

y no encontraba nada:
ni el más pequeño promontorio.
Comprendió que iba a ser muy fácil,
10   se trataba sencillamente de correr,
y en ella había, sin duda,
una necesidad de correr sin descanso.

Meditaba, aturdida:
tal vez llegue a algún sitio
15   o puede que por fin salga de todos.

Ingenuamente tomó una decisión.
Y de pronto vio el muro.

Se alzaba ante ella a poca distancia;
lo contempló con estupor;
20   no era muy grande y, sin embargo, parecía rodearla;
más aún: parecía abrazarla.
Giró vertiginosamente la cabeza
mientras algo muy antiguo dentro de ella golpeaba
con un sonido hermoso.
25   Y muy despacio se sentó en el suelo
y comenzó a llorar con gratitud
aceptando con humildad los pañuelos
y las voces que amorosamente la protegían.

                                      (*Itaca* 80–81)

(She thought: what a frightful emptiness, / the land is a desert; / if I were now to begin to run / I could get away from it all completely. / She looked around her / and she also looked inside herself / and she found nothing: / not even the smallest promontory. / She realized that it was going to be very easy, / it was simply a matter of running, / and in her there was, undoubtedly, / a need to run flat out. / She pondered, in bewilderment: / perhaps I'll reach some place / or maybe finally I'll get away from them all. / Naively she made her decision. / And suddenly she saw the wall. / It rose before her a little way off; / she contemplated it with astonishment; / it wasn't very big but, nevertheless, it seemed to surround her; / what's more: it seemed to embrace her. / She spun her head around in a daze / while something really ancient inside her beat / with a beautiful sound. / And very slowly she sat down on the ground / and began to weep with gratitude / accepting with humility the handkerchiefs / and the voices that lovingly protected her.)

These are Penelope's thoughts and they come to us in a deliberately unassuming "free indirect style."[7] The speaker sees her exterior space as a wasteland (ll. 1–2). She contemplates running away from it (ll. 3–15), but notes a wall which seems to surround her (l. 20), against which she seems to bang her head (ll. 22–23). She accepts this condition with gratitude and humility, taking it for a loving protection, possibly reminiscent of the womb ("algo muy antiguo . . . con un sonido hermoso" [ll. 23–24]).

The self-destructive tendencies which can be observed in "El muro" are examined in other texts in which Penelope displays masochistic symptoms.[8] Although each moment Ulysses is away tests her fidelity ("mi constancia"), she remains bound to him and the desolate island on which he has left her, and to which she confesses in "Las instancias" (Suits):

aspiro sólo a preservar
el ínfimo tendón
que me sujeta
a tu desolación
como una triste sanguijuela.
                    (*Itaca* 64)

(I aspire only to preserve / the tiniest sinew / that keeps me tied / to your desolation / like a sad leech.)

Women are brainwashed by patriarchal culture into a state of such mental masochism. In other poems the speaker convinces herself that the life of a woman is a living death. For instance in "La confianza" (Trust) the speaker simply asks Penelope:

¿cómo has sido capaz de presenciar la muerte
sin comprender que te contaminaba?
                    (*Itaca* 65)

(how could you have witnessed death / without realizing that it contaminated you?)

A stunning characterization of the self-destructive condition of woman —one into which she is impelled by her culture—is contained in "El escalón" (The step):

1   Como el caballo de lidia que en la pica
     va hacia el toro con los ojos vendados
     conducido por una mano oscura

que no podrá asociar a aquella otra
5   que le palmea el cuello con afecto
mientras le acerca hasta los belfos
algún terrón de azúcar,
así voy yo, torpe animal,
sin comprender la mano que hoy me hiere
10   y sin reconocerla en esa otra
que con sabiduría cuida de mis heridas.
Como el caballo ciego que no sabe
y sin embargo esquiva la embestida
así yo, bestia que tantea, husmeando,
15   me vuelvo hacia el rincón de la desdicha
intentando esquivar el asta absurda,
intentando retroceder hasta mí misma,
hasta el rincón que sólo visita mi angustia,
hasta ese hueco que a nadie reconoce,
20   intentando bajar el escalón que un día subiera,
intentando volver hacia la madriguera fría
y esconder en sus sombras
el corazón retrocedido y triste.

(*Itaca* 67–68)

(Just as the fighting horse during the goading / goes with its blinkered eyes toward the bull / led by a dark hand / that it cannot associate with that other / that claps it on the neck with affection / as it holds to its lips / a cube of sugar, / so go I, dumb animal, / without understanding the hand that wounds me today / and without recognizing in it that other / which wisely takes care of my wounds. / Like the blind horse that does not know / and nevertheless dodges the charge / so go I, beast that sniffs and gropes, / back to the corner of unhappiness / trying to dodge the absurd goad, / trying to withdraw toward myself, / to the corner that only my anguish visits, / to that hollow that recognizes no one, / trying to walk down the step that one day I might walk up, / trying to return to the cold den / and hide in its shadows / my sad, recoiling heart.)

The first lines (ll. 1–7) portray, in a seemingly objective and unassuming manner, the condition of the picador's horse, a state that the speaker's monologue presents as both hers and the condition of woman in general—"dumb animal" (l. 8), "beast that sniffs and gropes" (l. 14). The speaker thinks of women as being ushered into masochism by caring hands (l. 11); she also presents women as so hopelessly conditioned that their instincts impel them to return to unhappiness (l. 15), anguish (l. 18), darkness (l. 22). Aguirre therefore shares with some of her poetic mothers the view that a woman is psychologically conditioned to act as if she lived in a "madhouse."

Despite the apparent negativity of this vision, it soon becomes apparent that the speaker of these texts is rejecting and subverting some of the dominant thoughts and values of the prototypical male of Western culture. Ulysses' odyssey surely symbolizes, on one level, Western civilization's belief in ultimate goals, grand schemes, great causes, the search for Truth, Beauty, for an all-encompassing view of life, a vision of totality. By describing the negative impact of such a quest, Aguirre is deflating the quest itself. Other such ideals are demystified in Aguirre's work. When a woman is threatened by phallocentric discourses, "corrosive demystification" — Ostriker claims (*Stealing* 162) — is "her mode of conquest."

"El espectáculo" (The spectacle) deflates the notion that the male of the species sacrifices his life for his beloved and his country. The speaker of this poem warns Penelope that the men she beholds are not dying for her, that they see in her only a refuge or resting place. The speaker interjects: "Míralos: van a morir por algo que no existe," and then adds "no les niegues su industriosa mentira" (Look at them: they're going off to die for something that doesn't exist . . . don't deny them their industrious lie [*Itaca* 32]).

Against the androcentric belief in ultimate goals, Aguirre's work opposes the notion that everything is "provisoria y mudable" (provisional and changing [*Trescientos* 16]). With respect to the belief that we should strive for a vision of totality, her work insists on the notion of fragmentation. When she reacts to the vision of a Picasso or a Klee, she opposes their all-encompassing designs to "una fragmentación dinástica" (a dynastic fragmentation) which she as a woman sees on earth (*Trescientos* 56–57). We are "lagartijas" (lizards) says the speaker of one poem, not a congregation but "una segregación tanteando en el vacío" (a segregation groping in the emptiness [*Itaca* 55]). Life is not "una fortaleza" (a fortress), the speaker of "El equilibrio" (Equilibrium) insists, but "porción, fragmento, parte / nada más" (portion, fragment, part / nothing else), hence she concludes:

y a este retazo no hay por que pedirle
que abarque una totalidad que no le pertenece.

(*Trescientos* 31–35)

(and there's no need to ask of this remnant / that it comprise a wholeness it doesn't have.)

Clearly, Aguirre wants to undermine masculine visions of control, totality, and analytic rationality: life is not a soldier's fort, it's a scrap of cloth, a remnant from a piece of rag.[9] Aguirre therefore engages the discourse of nontranscendentalism we have discussed in her precursors to debunk philosophical verities of the Occident.

"Esta vida, hay que ver, qué desatino" (This life, you'd never guess, is a right farce [*Trescientos* 61–63]) summarizes her philosophy toward life. It employs the metaphor of old clothes—perhaps in contrast to the idealistic philosophy implied in Jiménez's "Vino, primero, pura, / vestida de inocencia" (She came, first, pure, / dressed in innocence [*Libros* 555]). The speaker of Aguirre's text is a poor woman who has to make ends meet as best she can. Here are a few of her lines:

Esta vida tan remendada,

. . . .

me parece un vestido tan raído,
un traje de segunda mano,
algo que nunca fue estrenado,
algo que usaron otros
y que yo, pobre desde siempre,
hundida en la miseria desde siempre,
lavé y planché, cosí, zurcí agujeros
hasta dejarla decentita,
hasta darle un aspecto de decoro
y lucirla con esa dignidad
que sólo son capaces de poseer los pobres,
aquellos que han conocido la carencia
desde mucho antes de nacer.

(*Trescientos* 61)

(This terribly patched-up life, / . . . / seems to me a really threadbare frock, / a secondhand dress, / something that has never been shown off, / something that others used / and that I, forever poor, / foundering in wretchedness from the start, / washed and ironed, sewed, darned up its holes / until it was decent enough, / until it looked acceptable / and could be worn with the type of dignity / that only the poor are capable of possessing, / those who have known want / from even before they were born.)

Grand schemes, such as life's goals and ultimate design, are cut down to size by Aguirre's minimalist tone and language. A little later in the same poem the speaker adds:

Señor, qué vida la de algunos, tan escasa,
tan reducida a una maceta, a un costurero,
tan dada la vuelta
como aquellas americanas
que mi abuela minuciosamente cosía:
lo de adentro hacia afuera
y los pespuntes en el mismo sitio:
una obra de arte, como nueva.
                              (*Trescientos* 62)

(Lord, what a life some live, so skimpy, / so limited to the size of a flower pot, a sewing box, / turned so often / like those jackets / my grandmother used to stitch meticulously: / front to back / and the backstitches in the same place: / a work of art, like new.)

The scheme of life may be cut down to size, but life is still perceived by Aguirre as "a work of art." It can therefore be shown that Francisa Aguirre's sharp wit is directed at deflating the grand illusions of the Occident, and that hers is a minimalist philosophy of life. As she exclaims in an aside in a poem reminiscent of Vallejo, "Suceden estas cosas" (These things happen [*Trescientos* 24]), "esto no es la roca Tarpeya" (this is not the rock of Tarpeia)—from which women did affect the course of history.[10] For Aguirre, such grand causes belong to the myths of the past; legends written by men in which women are denatured and from which the gynocentric had been erased.

A further distinctive feature of Aguirre's gynocritical vision is that, just as she debunks Western philosophies of life, she subjects art to a feminist revision. To distance her poetics from that of the high Romantic and Modern poets of our culture, whose conviction was that their art illuminated life on earth, brought light to mankind, Aguirre calls poetry—in a poem to her husband—an "oficio de tinieblas" (a shadowy task):

este oficio tan ambicioso como escaso,
tan de tanteo, tan de sombras
que persiguen la luz como un ahogado.
                  ("Oficio de tinieblas," *Trescientos* 43)

(this job's as ambitious as it's unproductive, / so much groping, so much a play of shadows / pursuing the light like someone who's drowning.)

In addition, Aguirre alludes to male precursors to signal her difference. For instance, in deliberate contrast to Juan Ramón Jiménez's self-centeredness—"...Y yo me iré. Y se quedarán los pájaros / cantando" (...And I shall go away. And the birds will stay here / singing [*Tercera antolojía* 212])—Aguirre notes: "me moriré / de un silencio mayor que yo" (I'll die / from a silence greater than myself [*Trescientos* 11]).

One of the more sustained metaphors Aguirre uses to deflate Western poetic ideals—and inscribe a gynocentric vision within Hispanic poetry—is to conceive of art as weaving or spinning, which she shares with Conde and Zardoya. As we see in "Esta vida, hay que ver, qué desatino," Aguirre transformed her grandmother's sewing into a metaphor for living. The connection with weaving is first made by Penelope in a poem entitled "Monólogo" (Monologue). She tells herself that she wove "para cubrir aquellas tus heridas," and that her weaving was "un manto de palabras / inútiles y hermosas" ("to cover those wounds of yours . . . a blanket of beautiful and useless words" [*Itaca* 33]). The goal of her art is not, for example, to capture those Platonic absolutes, such as Truth and Beauty, but to fashion something simple to wrap around the self. The spinner metaphor is taken up again in *La otra música*,[11] in for instance "Música de la distancia" (Distant music), where music is a weaver or sewer whose effect is to make people rejoice:

1   Su destino es negar la geografía.
     Acerca, siempre acerca esa música infinita.
     Es artesana
     y con su aguja y su dedal
5   y un hilo como el tiempo
     zurce los huecos que segrega la lejanía.
     Une los horizontes
     con canciones de coros infantiles
     y en su sencilla faltriquera
10   esconde un cañamazo
     que despliega un paisaje sin límites.
     Fabril y cuidadosa
     devana un alfabeto catecúmeno.
     Ella es aquel atajo cuaternario
15   que guió hasta el encuentro. Alguien

debió cantar ante la luz
y conducidos por ese hilo de música
llegaron otros que se unieron
a celebrar el mundo con el canto.

(*Música* 23)

(Her fate is to negate geography. / She brings things near, always
brings that infinite music nearer. / She's a craftswoman / and with her
thimble and needle / and a thread like time / she patches up the holes
that distance separates. / She unites horizons / with songs from
children's choirs / and in her plain handbag / she hides a piece of
canvas / that displays a limitless landscape. / Hard working and
careful / she spins a catechumenal alphabet. / She's that quaternary
shortcut / that led surely to the meeting. Someone / must have sung in
front of the footlights / and, guided by that thread of music, / others
arrived who came together / to celebrate the world with singing.)

Art is minimalized by being converted into a sewing woman (ll. 3–6,
9, 13) who unpretentiously keeps busy at her task, a task that favors life
and inspires others (l. 19) to celebrate it. For Francisca Aguirre, art is
not a "well-wrought urn" but a communal "quilt."[12]

A further metaphor which Aguirre appropriates for feminist poetics is the myth of Prometheus. Legend has it that Prometheus's entrails
were eaten out by vultures as a punishment for his hubris. Likewise,
in "Autofagia" (Self-immolation) Aguirre's speaker confesses to being
beset (devoured) by that which is external to her (such as vultures), but
she ends her poem with these exclamations:

Es como si el entorno me redujera hasta mí misma,
como si me empujara desde mis manos y mis ojos
hacia el negro agujero de mi sangre.
Es como si las cosas me obligaran a una horrible autofagia:
soy a la vez huesos y perro.
En una pieza Prometeo y el buitre.

(*Itaca* 59)

(It's as if my surroundings had limited me to my own body, / as if they
had shoved me with my hands and eyes / down into the black hole of
my blood. / It's as if things had forced me to a horrible self-
immolation: / I am both bones and the dog. / Prometheus and the
vulture.)

The speaker preys on her own battered flesh (a metaphor we have noted
earlier in Rosalía and Champourcin). This is certainly a negative ver-

sion of poetic creation, but postmodern readers will understand that it articulates a psychologically valid truth for the woman poet. Whereas the Modernist credo was to subdue such harsh feeling and forego distasteful expression (*pace* Ostriker, *Stealing* 124), the articulation of emotional and intellectual extremities becomes a psychic necessity for certain women poets (161); it inspires them to create.

In a later book, Aguirre subjects the notion of "autofagia" to further revision.[13] In "El paraíso encontrado" (Paradise found), a homage to the French primitive painter Douanier Rousseau, the speaker of the poem describes everyday household objects as if they were part of a jungle from which wild animals suddenly spring and devour parts of her body. As Aguirre struggles with her inner power, her space—to adapt Cixous's description in "Laugh of the Medusa" (258)—is jumbled, disoriented; the furniture is changed round; things and values are dislocated and broken up; structures emptied; and propriety turned upside down. As a result of her struggle, the speaker of "El paraíso encontrado" discovers the strength from within to turn her jungle into a positive experience and to subvert the oppressive milieu that hems her in. The poem ends this way:

1   Entonces, con una de las manos que aún conservo,
    arranco de la estantería como del árbol de la ciencia
    un volumen repleto de semillas—palabras—
    y mientras oigo a los reptiles acercarse
5   voy dejando que crezcan hasta el pelo,
    envolviéndome la cabeza,
    versos y flores, polen de música,
    una humedad de llanto y de rocío
    alimentando versos trepadores,
10 versos y versos como madreselvas
    tejiéndome una mágica guirnalda,
    rebrotándome, reanimándome como a una estatua triste
    a la que hicieran una silente transfusión de savia.

                                                    (*Trescientos* 48)

(Then, with one of the hands that I still have, / I pull from the shelves as from the tree of knowledge / a volume replete with seeds—words— / and as I hear the reptiles getting closer / I go on letting them grow up to my hair, / enveloping my head, / verses and flowers, musical pollen, / a humidity of tears and dew / feeding climbing verses, / verses and verses like honeysuckles / weaving a magic garland for me, /

sprouting from me, resuscitating me like a miserable statue / to which
they'd given a silent transfusion of sap.)

Here, the entrails, which in the Prometheus myth are forever being devoured, grow profusely to indicate that the female speaker has tapped
her inner strength and inspiration.[14] "Reserva natural" (Natural reserve [*Trescientos* 70]) uses the same metaphor of a forest to imply that
the woman artist creates a "natural (game) reserve" within herself on
which she can draw for her artistic inspiration.

The implication of such thoughts is, to put it bluntly, that as there
are fewer role models for women poets, they will likely be thrown back
onto their own resources, their own inner strength and imagination
in order to articulate a vision with which they can feel satisfaction. In
addition, as Ostriker argues, unlike male poets who valorize spirit over
nature and matter, Aguirre and other women poets present nature as a
positive equal (Ostriker, *Stealing* 15–28); nature is that in which humankind is embedded, and spirit should celebrate not subdue it (107–14).

Aguirre therefore hints intermittently at positive female forces,
which are manifest in some of her gynocentric metaphors. She herself
uses the oxymoron "espantosa dulzura" (frightful sweetness) to articulate what positive notions she encounters—a notion that recalls W. B.
Yeats's "tragic gaiety."[15] In the poem "Espantosa dulzura," which begins "A veces este mundo me parece un gran circo triste y alucinado"
(At times this world seems to me to be a huge, sad, and deluded circus),
she observes "la fusta del domador amado" (the riding whip of the beloved [male] trainer), before she looks at "las amazonas en sus caballos
blancos" (the Amazons on their white horses [*Música* 25]). The horror
or fright the male trainer provokes (to which the woman has grown accustomed) is contrasted with and compensated for by the impressive
self-sufficiency of the horsewomen and their white horses.

The sea constitutes a further "frightful sweetness" in Aguirre's work.
In "Testigo de excepción" (Exceptional witness) the sea is like a womb
—as it was for Conde—in which the speaker would immerse herself for
consolation and regeneration:

1   Yo sólo quiero un mar:
     yo sólo necesito un mar.
     Un agua de distancia,
     un agua que no escape,
5   un agua misericordiosa
     en que lavar mi corazón

y dejarlo a su orilla
para ser empujado por sus olas,
lamido por su lengua de sal
10   que cicatriza heridas.

(*Trescientos* 44) [16]

(I only want a sea: / I only need a sea. / A water with distance, / a water that will not escape, / a compassionate water / in which to wash my heart / and leave it on its bank / to be pushed by its waves, / licked by its salt tongue / that heals wounds up.)

A further positively marked metaphor is the heart. It provides the speaker with sustenance. The heart's irrationality and wildness ("locura") is championed against "la lógica" of mankind, which always prevails in Western civilization (*Trescientos* 15). Pragmatism, a philosophy concerned with use, with ends and means—as is our male-dominated Western culture—is subverted by the speaker's insight in this poem.[17] In another poem, a homage to Machado and to the regenerative powers of "la tarde" (the evening) the speaker refers to "mi corazón de brújula" (my compass-heart [*Trescientos* 23]), and implies that *it* not her head guides her through life and teaches her to appreciate insignificant intangibles: "lo mínimo . . . despojos . . . memoria" (the minimum . . . scraps . . . memory). And in "Nosotros" (Us), a poem dedicated to her family in which the speaker recalls moments of shared fulfillment—of intimacy and communal epiphany—she introduces the metaphor of a "successive heart," akin to an eternal memory or "intrahistoria":

Todo se aúna reuniendo
en un tiempo sin tiempo el sucesivo corazón
mientras volvemos, como el movimiento último
de la sinfonía de Schubert que no puede acabar.

(*Música* 53–54)

(All combines by reuniting / the successive heart in a timeless time / while we return as in the last movement / of Schubert's symphony that cannot end.)

For Aguirre, as for other women poets of the twentieth century, fellowship with others, especially one's family, is an important experience. Gilligan, we noted, speaks of "connection with others" and "interdependence of love and care" as hallmarks of a woman's "conception of adulthood" (*Different* 17). Juhasz argues that poetry written by women displays "relationship, communication, and identification as poetic devices" (*Naked and Fiery Forms* 141). Aguirre's gynocentric vision manifests similar preferences.

Aguirre's gynocritical vision undermines a teleological (male) view of life. Life is not a race to the finishing line; it is an experience to be enjoyed the best "we" can. Reality is not a quest for absolutes, it is an appreciation of the small and humble patch "we" are.[18] In another poem, the speaker urges her readers to understand and accept the humble decoration that life is, and that they/we are.[19] It is possible that because of Aguirre's unconventional perspectives, some of whose feminist aspects I have described above, her work has been ignored by students of the period. However, the perspective she has brought as a woman to mid-twentieth-century Spanish poetry should in future be given more careful consideration.

↫

María Victoria Atencia (b. 1931), like Aguirre and like Angela Figuera, only acquired the full confidence to publish her work when she was a woman in her forties. Despair of talent affected the three of them. In fact, Francisca Aguirre ceased publishing in 1978, just six years after the appearance of her first book. Atencia did publish her youthful poems in 1961 but then fell into a fifteen-year silence. That silence was broken in 1976, since which time she has published several volumes at frequent intervals. Unlike Aguirre, Atencia did overcome her despair, her "posible desgajamiento" (Ugalde, *Conversaciones* 6)—the possibility that she would never write poetry again. Atencia's vision of life and art is the polar opposite of Aguirre's. Whereas the latter's inspiration was not fettered by the poetry of social commitment, Atencia's certainly was: her intimate, interior world was inimical to the poetry of Spain in the 1950s and 1960s.[20]

To read the poems of María Victoria Atencia—most of which were recently collected in *La señal* (The sign)[21]—is to indulge in a regressive fantasy for this male reader.[22] He is conducted into a heavily decorated drawing room of the end of the nineteenth century where a lady of perfect composure, erudite culture, exquisite taste, and impeccable breeding is serving tea to her chosen friends—serving tea is a metaphor Atencia herself uses—friends to whom she imparts her passion for the world and to whom she stoically intimates her reservations. For Atencia, her room, her home, her garden, her immediate environs in Málaga are a sanctuary. However, her *locus amoenus* is not created out of powerlessness, as was the case with her nineteenth-century sister precursors; there are no images of confinement that reflect her ineffectuality; no "sanctuary" poems to protect her hurt and violated self and to provide some respite from the oppressions of the world.[23] As her poems demonstrate, Atencia frequently leaves her sanctuary to journey throughout Europe, the United Kingdom, the United States; she travels not to flee but to enrich her spirit with the cultures of the past. She returns to her "private realm" to foster intimacy and interpersonal engagement. Not without good reason did Jorge Guillén christen her "María Victoria Serenísima" (Atencia, *Señal* 101).[24]

Serenissima, ma non troppo, for there is another image of Atencia: that of the pilot of a plane. Sharon Ugalde informs us: "She was the mother of four young children and an aviator with a private pilot's license, flying routes that spanned distances from Stockholm to Tangier and from New York City to Cologne" ("María Victoria Atencia" 55). But Atencia gave up flying after her instructor died in a crash and her parents died shortly afterwards. These events impressed on her the vulnerability of her children (Ugalde, *Conversaciones* 12). Atencia's serenity is a foil to her acute sense of mortality (first manifested in her 1961 *Cañada de los Ingleses* [English gully]) and her sensibility toward time's pitiless toll. As Vicente Aleixandre remarked, in her poetry there is both "splendour" and "darkness."[25]

In contrast to earlier women poets, Atencia finds liberation in interior spaces. For her, the room is a metonym for the contiguous spaces that she loves and cares for—home, garden, Málaga, especially the Paseo de la Farola and the port—spaces she meditates into order, drawing out their fullness and beauty. This world is "totalmente suyo" and "va revelando su más íntimo ser" (totally hers [and] reveals her most intimate being [Ciplijauskaité, "Compromiso" 96]).[26] Her defamiliarization of quotidian time and space lends a novel twist to the technique first described at the beginning of the twentieth century by the Russian Formalists. The effect is that we, her fortunate readers, see anew the analogous spaces in which we ourselves myopically labor each day:

EL MUNDO DE M. V.

Si mi mano acaricia la cretona de pájaros
inglesa y he encendido el quinqué y hay un lirio
en la opalina y huele a madera la casa,
puedo llegarme al verde y al azul de los bosques

5   de Aubusson y sentarme al borde de un estanque
cuyas aguas retiene el tapiz en sus hilos.

Me asomo a las umbrías de cuanto en esta hora
dispongo y pueda darme su reposo: también
este mundo es el mío. Entreabro la puerta
10   de su ficción y dejo que sobre este añadido
vegetal de mi casa, por donde los insectos
derivan su zumbido, se instale una paloma.

                                     (65)

(M. V.'s World. / If my hand caresses the English / bird-chintz and I've lit the oil lamp and there's a lily[27] / in the opalescent vase and the house smells of wood, / I can reach the green and blue of the woods / of Aubusson and sit on the edge of the pond / whose waters the tapestry holds back in its threads. / I gaze into its shady spots with all that at this hour / is left of me so it might give me its repose: also / this world is mine. I half-open the door / of its fiction and permit that above this vegetable / addition to my house, around which insects / direct their droning, a dove install itself.)

The iridescence of a sensual interior—touch, sight, smell (ll. 1–3)— is linked parallelistically to a harmonious exterior: the ordered, natural universe of an Aubusson tapestry (ll. 4–6). The poet partakes of that exterior's "reposo" (l. 8) and her metapoetic imagination (ll. 9–10) draws from it a symbolic "paloma" which she "installs" within (l. 12). As Ugalde has observed, the room is "logically a symbol of women's imprisonment within the bounds of servile domesticity," but Atencia like Emily Dickinson transforms it "into a space for self-realization through the power of her poetry" and re-creates "an authentic identity" for herself ("María Victoria Atencia" 58).[28]

For the poetic persona that orders home and garden, Atencia chooses the name Martha, from the volume *Marta & María* (Martha and Mary) published in 1976 after a silence of fifteen years. If Martha cares for the concrete reality, Mary invests it with abstractions from the realms of culture and spirit.[29] Martha's appreciation, love, and care for metonymic interiors is a distinctive feature of Atencia's work.[30] She writes of "bienestar diario" (daily comfort [10]); that "palparé uno a uno los lomos de mis libros" (I shall fondle one by one the spines of my books [44]), and that "proseguí en el rito usual de dar forma a mi nuca" (I proceeded with the usual ritual of giving shape to the nape of my neck [340]), and succinctly proffers "andar es no moverse del lugar que escogimos" (to walk is not to move from the place we've chosen [95]). Concurrently, the imagination of the spiritual Mary transmutes these interiors into poetic insights ("agonistically" savoring of "mermelada inglesa" [English marmalade] 334), and into philosophical observations on the human condition (taking issue with Herrick's injunction to "gather ye rosebuds while ye may" [240]). Much later in her work, Atencia's home makes her think of encroaching death ("Trastero" [Box Room (*Intrusa* 38)]). The room, as Showalter observes, can cease to be a womb and become a tomb.

Atencia's sense of intimacy and closeness is extended to the outside world. Seagulls with their joyful sounds "salvan / la llegada del día" (rise above / the arrival of day) and greet the poet in "Gaviotas" (Seagulls):

Pues venís a mi encuentro,
torno, como los peces,
mi juventud en plata.
Sólo estremeceréis
la mar de mis pupilas.

(181)

(Since you come to meet me, / I turn, like fishes, / into my silver youth. / Only you could ripple / the sea of my pupils.)

And when a "convoy extranjero" ("foreign convoy") leaves the port of Málaga, she responds: "y aún le duele el vacío de su marinería / al costado más débil de los muelles, y al mío" ("the emptiness left by [the departure] of its crew still hurts / the weakest side of the quays, and mine" ["Convoy extranjero" 241]). A cargo ship, "Lady Eva," is gynomorphized into a pregnant woman:

Bajo un trajín de grúas
tu línea se sumerge
y en tu vientre los trigos
se aduermen al calor
de una preñez triunfante.

(183)

(Under the hustle and hauling of the cranes / your line is submerged / and in your belly the wheat / goes to sleep in the heat / of a triumphant pregnancy.)

Under Atencia's gynocentric gaze, the female "line" and "belly" are perceived as triumphantly fertile.

An additional feature of Atencia's gynocentric vision is her reflection on motherhood. Atencia's concern and love for her own mother and her children is frequently manifested. She remains imaginatively connected to both ("Hija y madre" [Daughter and mother] 167). Motherhood is the axis of the early *Cañada de los Ingleses* (see 389, 390, 397, 398). Later, when she beholds "una joven dormida" (a young woman asleep), her impulse is to "velarte" (keep watch over you [268]),[31] and her pragmatism (coupled with her refined sense of irony) is expressed thus: "debiera ser tan sencillo como sanar un niño de la rubeola" (it should be as simple as curing a child of the German measles [348]). Atencia remains imaginatively connected to her own mother. In an early poem, she wishes to be returned "al pecho caliente de mi madre" (to my mother's warm bosom [23]); later she sees her mother as a "niña" (girl) in the "pupilas rotas" (broken pupils) of a drowning horse (*Pared* 13). Atencia's sustained meditation on motherhood is undertaken in *Trances de Nuestra Señora* (Critical moments in Our Lady's life), where she identifies with the Virgin's conception and pregnancy. What Atencia told Ugalde about this book is important: "No es propiamente un libro de poesía religiosa. O no sólo eso. Está allí la Virgen, siempre tan venerada por mí, tan presente en mí. Pero también estoy yo, con mis perplejidades y mis sorpresas; yo, como novia, como esposa, como embarazada, como madre. En los *Trances* estoy yo, trascendida pero siempre con suficientes testimonios de mi personal identidad" (It's not really a book of religious poetry. Or not only that. There is the Virgin, always so adored by me, so present in me. But also I am there, with my bouts of bewilderment and surprise; I, as a fiancée, as a wife, as a pregnant woman, as a mother. I am in *Trances* transmuted, but my personal identity is always sufficiently in evidence [*Conversaciones* 14–15]).[32] Just as interior spaces are not prisons for Atencia, motherhood is not a curse but a condition that allows her to explore aspects of her authentic self.

As we have just noted, women and the female figure are foregrounded in Atencia's work. She uses them to question and define her identity as a female. She remains on intimate terms with the "niña" that she was, a "niña" who is part mother to the woman. One of the poems of *Arte y parte* (Muse and memoir), published in 1961 when the poet was thirty years of age, begins: "de un espeso tejido me rodea tu mundo / por todos los contornos" (with a thick weave your world surrounds me / in every shape and form [373]). Indeed, the dreams, charms, and desires of the girl inform the imagination of the young poet (e.g., 371, 376,

381, 382). The older poet tries to open "otro paraguas más pequeño / y mío, de colores,[33] de cuando yo era niña" (another umbrella, smaller / and mine, with colors, from when I was a child [57]), and she wants the musky aroma of dried fruit and lemons displayed in frails to return her "a la infancia" (to infancy ["Vendeja" (Goods for sale) 185]).[34] When she encounters Andrew Wyeth's painting, *Christina's World*, in the Museum of Modern Art in New York, she recalls the self that she was versus the anxious self she is ("El mundo de Cristina" [Christina's world] 246). Moreover, in her 1992 books, her concern for the "niña ausente" (absent child) has reemerged.[35]

Throughout her work there are numerous memories of her intimate friendships with other women, alive and dead, real and imagined (e.g., Rosalía de Castro [21]). Atencia's cultivation of such bonds is manifested in her first book ("Mirando hacia arriba" [Looking upwards] 377–78). In "Anita" it is expressed in concrete gynocentric images: "quiero / destrenzarte y soltarte el curso de las crenchas, / embadurnar mis dedos en aroma y aceite, / presionarte la nuca y aliviar tu cansancio" (I want / to take out your plaits, tousle your parts, / daub my fingers in scent and oil, / massage your nape and soothe your weariness [83]).[36]

Atencia consciously connects herself with other members of her matrilineal group. There are memories from childhood of friends (14, 394), of the women who surrounded her just after her birth (25), of Blancanieves who died in childhood (22, 39), of contemporary female friends (192, 345), and sister poets (204, 347, 352). Her "abuela" (grandmother) and her legacy are important (32, 54), and the memory of her own mother is strong:

COLOR DE ROSA

Me siento, para darle compañía, a los pies
de la cama. Me enseña su caja con botones,
su collar de azabache, la mantilla de blonda
con que acudía a misa de privilegio en Santo
Domingo, su camisa de malteado georgé...
Madre está enferma. Madre va enseñándome cosas
del armario con quieto silencio entristecido,
hasta que llega el traje color de rosa pálido,
y entonces se incorpora, renovada, a ponérselo
delante de mí misma, me coge de la mano

y saltamos felices. Su cara de muñeca
inglesa antigua evoca la cera levemente.

07.12.75 (56)

(Rose Color. / I sit down, to keep her company, at the foot / of the
bed. She shows me her box of buttons, / her jet necklace, the lace
mantilla / with which she went to private Mass at Saint / Dominic's,
her malt-colored, georgette slip... / Mother is sick. Mother continues
to show me things / from the wardrobe with a calm, glum silence, /
until she gets to the pale-pink-colored dress, / and then she gets up,
with renewed strength, to put it on / in front of me, she grasps me by
the hand / and we jump about for joy. Her face of an antique English
doll / recaptures some of its former softness. July 12, 1975)

The frail, sad beauty of her aging mother, and the pleasure her mother
experienced from such exquisite clothes, is movingly foregrounded as
the poet-daughter shares with her mother the happiness that once was.
Hence, when Atencia contemplates the beauty of young women, she
foresees the ominous threats that lie in wait for them as they mature
(137, 140, 272).

But the largest portion of women in her poems are taken from myth,
art, and literature (as was the case with Wyeth's Christina): Lot's wife
(239); Eve (263, 355); the Virgin Mary (277, 289–307); Emily Dickinson (245); Portia (225); Ophelia and Desdemona (38, 268, *Puente* 30);
Goya's countess of Chinchón and duchess of Alba (255, 256); Paolina
Borghese (261); Mme. Dupin and Clara Schumann (*Intrusa* 23, 26).[37]
Her duchess of Alba is a meditation on passion spent; the countess of
Chinchón hints at marginalization: "desde el sillón prestado contem-
plas la comedia" (from the borrowed armchair you contemplate the
farce [255]). Each of these cultural women—these "historic and mythic
heroines" (Ostriker, *Stealing* 22)—stimulates Atencia to discover aspects of her own female self, to reflect on the historical marginalization
of women, and to subtly change the historically determined perceptions her readers have held of women in art, literature, and culture.

Atencia also manifests the concerns of an aging woman: "mi ardiente
vientre inútil" (my useless and burning womb [237]), "mi cintura vacía"
(my empty waist [352]), "muchacha fui también y caña soy" (I also
was girl and now am reed [*Intrusa* 37]).[38] "La fiera" (Wild woman and
beast) becomes an objective correlative for the displacement of sexual
passion:[39]

Cuando salía iba paseando a una fiera
por el jirón de tierra que el ojo de mercurio
ilumina en el puerto, y la joven belleza
del muchacho afirmaba los buques en su amarre
y cruzaba suspensa por la raya del mar.

Una noche escuchamos cómo aullaba la fiera.

(320)

(When he set out he was taking a wild beast [woman] / for a walk
along the strip of land the mercury-eye / lights up around the port,
and the young beauty / of the lad steadied the ships in their moorings /
and cruised in a state of suspension along the edge of the sea. / One
night we listened to how a wild beast howls.)

With subtle irony, which is typical of her style, Atencia distances herself from the wild beast's feelings for the young sailor, only to include
herself in the poem's closure—a separate verse that we may or may not
relate to Atencia's female condition.

By now it will be quite clear to the reader that Atencia utilizes a
female lexicon, and that she selects gynocentric images and metaphors
to articulate and develop her vision. She foregrounds the female body:
the nape of the neck (251, 340); her heels (*Puente* 19); her own body
when undressing or naked (10, 90). She selects parts of the female
body—"seno" (bosom [10]), "útero" (uterus [89, 150, 171]), "pechos"
(breasts [121]), "sienes" (temples [136]), "vientre" (belly [*Intrusa* 44])
—often as metaphors for nature (10, 121, 136) and to express protection ("útero maternal bajo el agua" [maternal womb under the water
(89)]). She turns women's clothes (29, 54), jewelry (93), and accessories
(67, 130) into symbols of the female condition, and of the condition of
nature ("collar de escarcha" [necklace of frost (41)]), and of her own
poetics ("el chal de natural seda fuscia cubría / mi intención de palabras" [the raw silk fuchsia shawl cloaked / my words' intended meaning
(*Intrusa* 24)]). She turns her dolls into emblems of her state (24, 217,
Intrusa 18).[40] For Atencia, water—lakes, lagoons, the sea—is a skein of
pleasure and protection (51, 89): "tómame una vez más, mi desdeñoso
amante, / mientras las algas ponen / un collar en mi cuello" (possess
me one more time, my scornful lover, / while seaweed sets / a necklace
round my neck [164]). Entering a lagoon, she explains: "Levanté con
los dedos el cristal de las aguas, / contemplé su silencio y me adentré en

mí misma" (With my fingers I lifted / the waters' crystal, / I contemplated its silence and entered into myself [244]).[41]

Atencia is critiqued for being neo-Parnassian. However, by selecting precious forms she distances herself from the intensity of her feelings; they function as objective correlatives. Atencia displays the "exoskeletal" style of contemporary women poets: the deliberate selection of cold, hard objects, which allow the woman poet to explore her self-division and which are a defense against the accusation of gushing sentimentality. Her "Rosa de Jericó. *Anastatica hierochuntica*" (Rose of Jericho. *Anastatica hierochuntica*) reads:

Tantos años, y más, dejada en el armario,
con luz escasa y sed y savia detenida,
un vaso de cristal de Suecia interrumpe.
Tersos rasgos se yerguen
que asaltan con sus brincos de nuevo los gorriones,
ajenos a esta tregua entre la sed y el agua.

(333)

(After so many years, and more, left in the closet, / years of little light, of thirst and arrested sap, / a Swedish crystal vase bursts onto the scene. / Glossy growths stiffen and stand up straight / that hopping sparrows again attack, / oblivious to the lull between thirst and water.)

A rose of Jericho, whose Latin name includes the word "resurrection" (*anastatica*), is "a fernlike desert plant that forms a tight ball when dry and unfolds and blooms under moist conditions"[42]—Atencia's wry reflection on the female condition.

Atencia's perception of her own work is unassuming and unpretentious—unlike that of many male poets. She perceives herself as doing no more than playing blindman's-buff in her life and with her art (42); she asserts that "carencia es plenitud" (scarcity is fullness [265]); and she hints that the ephemeral beauty of a mere flame can "give light to" a poem (274). Like some of her precursors and peers, Atencia engages the discourse on nontranscendental beliefs.

Atencia is also committed to the revision of androcentric myths, as Jaffe has most persuasively argued ("Gender"). Death is merely the seventh, uninvited guest at dinner (30); Count Dracula is a lover to whom she gives her peace "a borbotones" (in torrents [59]); and she stands on its head the phallocentric perspective on Lady Godiva (94).[43] She reinscribes Greek myth within a female tradition. She states that she is the mother of Hector and that she is proud of it and him; what she doesn't say is that Hector's mother, Hecuba, killed to avenge the murder of one of her sons (138). When Jupiter accosts Leda—"con blanda pluma y tibio / borbotón de ternura" (with soft feather and warm, / tender gushing [148]), he does so because he's welcomed.[44] Her most sustained (and ongoing) revision is reserved for the figure of Ophelia (38, 268, *Puente* 30), where as Ugalde ("Feminization" 167–70) reveals, Atencia is struggling against "the imprisonment of female subjectivity" and suggesting "a way out" ("Feminization" 167–70, quotation on 169). In her 1992 volume *El puente*, Atencia reproaches the Czechoslovak poet Vladimir Holan (whom Clara Janés translated into Spanish) for believing that Ophelia's body was eaten up by water rats; on the contrary, Atencia insists that Ophelia "preserva / su maternal secreto río abajo" (preserves / her maternal secret below the water [*Puente* 30]).

In conclusion, it is with a sure hand and a cool gaze that Atencia is in the process of inscribing a female identity within Hispanic poetry. As Ciplijauskaité says, Atencia is a woman who "understands and wants to transmit femininity" ("Compromiso" 102). As we have observed, several distinctive features of her gynocentric and gynocritical visions indicate that she belongs in the female phase of self-discovery Showalter described in *A Literature of Their Own*. Although she has been "hitherto unjustly neglected" (Debicki, *Spanish Poetry* 185), that oversight will be redressed when the poetry of twentieth-century Spain is viewed more dispassionately.

᭣

Clara Janés (b. 1940) is recognized today as one of the most original poets of the last twenty years.[45] In the dedicatory poem to *Lapidario* (Lapidary [1988]), Helena Paz says that Janés carries her readers "a la mesa de los hombres, la mesa redonda; donde se reparten el pan y la sal" (To the men's table, / the round table; / where bread and salt are served out [7]). In "Dos palabras" (Two words), Rosa Chacel reacts to Janés's first books by heralding her as a "profetisa" and "sacerdotisa" (prophetess and "priestess" [Janés, *Kampa* 98]).[46] In 1989, Ciplijauskaité judged Janés's poetry to represent "una nueva esencialidad" (a new essentialism) in the contemporary Spanish lyric ("Hacia una nueva esencialidad").

Janés published her early poems between 1964 and 1973; they bear the stamp of existential angst and alienation.[47] Her vision is not gynocentric at that time, for she tends to perceive the whole of humankind as marginalized from their true selves. However, with her poetry of the mid- to late seventies—*En busca de Cordelia y Poemas rumanos* (In search of Cordelia and Rumanian poems [1975]) and *Libro de alienaciones* (Book of alienations [1980])—she rejects social and human limitations and begins to inquire into the essence of things, an exploration that has led and still leads her to the inscription of a female self within her work.[48] The latter is a distinctive feature of the numerous books of poetry Janés has published since 1980. But perhaps her most distinctive feature is the exploration and articulation of female sensuality which she begins in *Eros* (1981) and accomplishes in *Creciente fértil* (Fertile crescent [1989]).

Janés's vision is both gynocentric and gynocritical, as can be seen in her inscription of a female self. She initiates this inscription in the 1970s with an investigation of her Rumanian roots.[49] *En busca de Cordelia* is an analysis of the poet's uninscribed femaleness: the traumas of childhood and adolescence. It is a long poem in free verse, some 640 lines; its themes are as ambitious as they are diverse; the style surrealist, or postsurrealist.[50] By means of a string of poetic personae—Cordelia, the Old Woman, the dead father, Tristan, Othello, Fafnir—the poetic speaker confronts her existential anguish and begins to explore her mental chaos, her emotional frustration, and the tormented state of her entire being.[51]

The poem is enticingly complex and merits extensive analysis in a separate study. Suffice it to say that Fafnir is her guru, and that the Old Woman represents the obligations (tinged with love and hatred) that the speaker feels toward the person who had taken care of her since she was a child. Othello is her dog and—as a Shakespearian allusion—may well signify Janés's intellectual defiance and subjugation of male jealousy. Cordelia—Shakespearean symbol of honest, filial love—represents the youthful spirit that the adult poet repressed; to gain her personal freedom, the adult woman needs to rediscover and reconnect with the Cordelia she knows is drowning within her.[52]

From the perspective of a gynocentric vision, it is curious that the text's protagonist encloses herself—in 1975—in a "buhardilla" (attic/loft) and is thereby considered to be a "loca" (madwoman). Paradoxically, it is during this period of self-enclosure that the speaker finds inner freedom for herself. Keats teaches her his concept of "Negative Capability," [53] that is, the ability to live in a state of uncertainty and mystery, the ability to dispense with the need to adhere to preestablished goals, those dictated by the patriarchal, rational ego. Janés's inner search in *En busca de Cordelia* is undertaken without any preconceived knowledge of what she wants to attain and where she wants to be at its conclusion. Thus, Janés differentiates her quest from the prototypical masculine search—which tends to direct itself toward a rational and external goal (such as fortune and fame).

Janés's search within herself—of an exploratory, aleatory, and fortuitous nature—as it is pursued in *Isla del suicidio* (Suicide island) and *Libro de alienaciones* (1980)—turns into an encounter with the poet's femaleness. The island in *Isla del suicidio* is literally one of the Balearic isles ("Pitiusa" [*Libro* 26]), and metaphorically the female body (*Libro* 12); it is also the speaker's psychic state—"un paisaje mental / lapidario y desierto" (a deserted, lapidary / and mental landscape [*Libro* 26]), as the island was for Francisca Aguirre. On this island, the female speaker discovers Tanit (*Libro* 23 and 28), a Phoenician goddess related to Astarte; that is, she comes into contact with a pre-Christian goddess who endlessly creates and destroys. Janés is pointedly identifying with gynocentric myths, and in so doing provides and asserts a model for woman's behavior that is distinct from the one patriarchal Western culture promotes: that of the passive woman who always attends to and nourishes her loved ones.

Moreover, Janés describes the condition of woman in the midtwentieth century. Woman is "depositario de todo sufrimiento" (repository of all suffering [*Libro* 73]) and she affirms and sustains, in "En vano en la tierra" (In vain on the earth), the path that *she* must follow:

Tal vez si pudiera penetrar mi propia entraña,
llegar a reengendrarme,
ser capaz de tomarme en los brazos y de darme calor
como a un niño aterrado
que sólo busca acurrucarse junto al fuego...

Huérfana soy en medio de una estepa.

Jamás el hombre me podrá dar cobijo.

(*Libro* 90)

(Perhaps if I could penetrate my own core, / manage to reengender myself, / be able to take myself in my arms and warm myself up / like a frightened child / who just wants to curl up in front of the fire... / I am an orphan in the middle of a steppe. / Man will never be able to shelter me.)

A woman must care for and coddle herself—as we noted earlier with Fuertes—for no man can "mother" her. It is in her exploration of female desire that Janés will discover how she alone can emancipate her true self.

A further path Janés explores on the road to emancipation is her identification with the witch or sorceress. She identifies with the monster-woman in order to pursue her personal liberation. Her lyrical persona speaks in the voice of a witch and vindicates the witch's point of view. In the poem of the same name, the poet offers us a series of "hechizos" (charms [*Eros* 53–63]), for example to oblige men who have neither desire nor interest in it "para hacer amar" (to make love). The fact that Clara Janés has made use of this knowledge is another aspect of her prophetic side, which Rosa Chacel spotted in 1978. Also, the more Janés searches within herself, the more she identifies with millenarian female wisdom. This is significant because the occult wisdom of the witch has been proscribed by our civilization. Phallocratic Western culture has persecuted witches and has suppressed their arcane secrets—under the pretext that witches are irrational and subversive, and that their knowledge is unscientific.[54]

Another feature of Janés's self-emancipation is her foregrounding of and delight in objects, people, and places of quotidian reality. It is here that the nontranscendental aspect of her poetic vision is to be glimpsed. In *Vivir* (Living [1983]), she writes in praise of daily life—of nourishment, of animals, and of historical buildings.[55] The woman poet averts her gaze from the phallogocentric transcendent, the male ego's preoccupation with exterior goals and ultimate schemes, and focuses on the simple but sensual beauty of the immanent, on that which is here and now. This is a current in Spanish women's poetry that we have already observed in Rosalía, Méndez, Zardoya, and Aguirre. It is also one that Ostriker studies in contemporary women poets. It represents a movement away from alienation, and toward synthesis with nature and with each other. By praising matter, as Janés does in *Vivir*, she is signifying her connectedness with—as opposed to separation from—materiality and humanity.[56]

A further distinctive feature of Janés and her work is that inscription and emancipation of self are manifestly intertwined. Janés is conscious of developing her own gynocentric style. At first, her insights are traditional. In *Vivir* she reflects on the essence of poetry and develops her particular poetics, capturing fullness in the transitory, uncovering hidden truths.[57] Her "Nota 11" (Note 11) on poetry foregrounds spontaneity:

sobre unos versos que nacieron
espontáneos

A veces el poema es el objeto o don
y con más evidencia
pone de manifiesto ese propósito:
dar luz a una palabra
sin quitarle su magia
o ser depositario
de una visión o de un sentir
que toma cuerpo
en sílabas contadas.

(*Vivir* 58)

(on some lines that were born / spontaneously. / Sometimes the poem is an object or gift / and makes that purpose known / with more clarity: / to give life to a word / without depriving it of its magic / or it's the repository / of a vision or a feeling / which takes form / in a few syllables.)

In future work, it is the "feeling" and the "vision" of which Janés's poems will be the "repository." *Kampa* (1986), based on an ingenious intuition, develops an idea inherent in today's reader-response literary criticism. *Kampa*'s poetic speaker acquires life and meaning insofar as she reads Vladimir Holan. By means of her complete and utter love for Holan's ideas and words, *Kampa*'s lyrical subject feels herself reincarnated into a being she had earlier desired to be.[58] In one poem, for example, the lyrical subject feels herself reincarnated into the body of the beautiful and young Juliet (*Kampa* 38). As a result, in her imagination she gives her body totally to Holan, the poet-loved one, in order that he may ward off death for a few more days.

A later characteristic of Janés's ingenious poetics is found in *Lapidario* (1988). Each of the thirty texts in this book claims to be a meditation on a precious stone or jewel; that is, Janés selected for scrutiny adornments traditionally worn by women. With her arcane knowledge and ingenious mind, Clara Janés transforms each of those thirty precious stones into an exoskeletal reflection on poetics.

The poems of *Lapidario* are divided into two parts. The first, in prose, is a citation or a historical-folkloric description of the jewel or precious stone. The second, in verse, is Janés's revisionary poem. I cite as an example one of the shorter texts:[59]

PIEDRA DEL RAYO

Junto a las fuentes, después de la tormenta—contra la que protegen, al decir de los druidas—aparecen las hachas neolíticas, siempre que un rayo, con su línea quebrada de fulgor, haya delimitado dos distintas mitades en la cúpula opaca.

Signo de fuego en la frente del aire, indicios de humedad en un bramido que el alentar arrastra de la tierra, ¿vence a los insumisos elementos ese filo pulido por el hombre?

(*Lapidario* 28-29)

(Close to the founts, after the storm—against which they protect it, according to the druids' saying—the neolithic axes appear, provided a ray, with its line of radiance broken, has marked out two distinct halves on the opaque cupola.)

(Lightning Stone. / Sign of fire on the air's brow, / traces of humidity in a roar / the glowing draws from the earth: / does this blade, polished by man, / vanquish the unsubmissive elements?)

On one level, "el filo pulido" (the polished blade) represents the poem. It has been "pulido por el hombre" (polished by man) who has traditionally controlled the pen/phallus. The "fuego" (fire) is Janés's strategy to appropriate the phallus-pen-poem, and to capture within it her particular plenitude, the vision of which lies hidden from androcentric eyes. Her lightning bolt is a reappropriation of the myth of Prometheus; unlike her nineteenth-century sisters, she will succeed whereas they, as Kirkpatrick demonstrated, were doomed to failure.

Ugalde has shown that, in *Lapidario*, Janés pursued her inscription of the female self. Janés's selection of the hardness of stone and jewel is her strategy to escape from the ghetto of sentimentality and anti-intellectualism to which patriarchal culture would proscribe her. The stone allows Janés to express her "self" through and with the hard "other." The hard form was a way to objectify the self unsentimentally, "erase every trace of direct intimacy," and to "reveal in all its nakedness her most intimate being." Janés's being flows into that otherness, just as her reading of Holan—in *Kampa*—effected this "flowing of one being into another." In her appropriation of the "Garnet" ("Granate"), Ugalde writes, Janés "lives to the full the essence of the 'garnet' as if it were her very own, and the dividing line between the mortal and the eternal disappears." Hence, Janés's conception of the ego is fluid, and stands in stark contrast to the autonomous male ego; it impels her to interrelate with others, as mother does with fetus/daughter ("La subjetividad" 512–13, 519–21).

The fact that Janés selected the (exoskeletal) hardness and sensuousness of jewels and precious stones as objects, through which she would explore her sense of esthetic beauty and fully manifest her own self, is another indication of her gynocentric vision.

To the above must be added the fact that, with *Creciente fértil*, Janés's style became undulatory, that is, repetitive and cumulative rather than linear:

> Mira mi pie que ondea acercándose a tus labios,
> es un fruto que entre velos te ofrece la danza,
> mientras todo mi cuerpo va dibujando dunas
> y oleajes, los brazos en gesto de palmera
> se extienden, y el cabello simula la caricia
> del aire.
>
> *(Creciente 23)*

(Look at my foot which undulates as it approaches your lips, / it's a fruit the dance offers you amongst its veils, / while my entire body keeps depicting dunes / and swells, my arms with a palm tree's gestures / stretch out, and my hair simulates the caresses / of the air.)

In writing her body, Janés, consciously or not, employs the discursive style of French feminist thought.

Indeed, the most distinctive feature of Janés's gynocentric and gynocritical visions is her exploration of heterosexual female desire. *Eros* (1981) is a woman's sensual and erotic canto to love. In this text love starts not with illusions but when "El hombre y la mujer se reconocen" (Man and woman recognize each other [for what they are]). And what the man and the woman recognize is that "La atroz desolación ata sus miembros" (atrocious desolation binds their limbs [*Eros* 18]). Although Janés's poetic voice searches here for "un lugar no abismal" (a non-abysmal place [*Eros* 27]), she knows that she must give up hope of finding such a "lugar no abismal" in the prototypical beauty of the young male adolescent—"de él se enamoran / todas las muchachas / cegadas por el fugaz desnudo de su ser esquivo" (every girl, / blinded by the fleeting nakedness of his elusive being, / falls in love with him [*Eros* 29]). On the other hand, in "Eso dicen las voces de mis venas" (The voices in my veins say), tell the poet:

huye del fugitivo,
del que no toca tierra con sus plantas,
y mírate en el rostro de las horas
despiadada.

(*Eros* 29)[60]

(flee from the fugitive, / from him who does not touch the earth with
his soles, / and look at yourself in the face of the hours / mercilessly.)

In addition, Pasero has observed that the book elaborates "in specific,
sexual terms . . . on sexual pleasure and erotic discovery" and that it
contains numerous "references to female body parts" ("Clara Janés"
236). Thus, in *Eros* an older woman, who is the mature poetic voice of
these poems, confronts her adult sensuality and reflects upon its advan-
tages and limits.

Bécquer's dramatic poem—"Yo soy ardiente, yo soy morena" (I am
ardent, my skin is dark [*Rima* 11])—is revised by Janés's gynocritical
perspective in "No sé" (I don't know):

Soy hermosa y mi piel es suave
y el viento del mar me devuelve rocío
de tiernas tersuras.
Mi cabello perfumo y adorno de áurea madreselva
y mi pecho es redondo y casi virginal.
Tuve un amante que ensalzó mis caderas
y mi forma de amar intensa y silenciosa.
Podría ser aún como un río de luz en tus brazos.
No sé que te retiene, si furtivo, he visto
un destello de ardor en tu gesto al pasar.

(*Eros* 34)

(I am beautiful and my skin is smooth, / and the sea-wind gives me
back a dew / of tender smoothness. / I perfume my hair and adorn it
with golden honeysuckle / and my breast is round and almost
virginal. / I had a lover who extolled my hips / and my intense and
silent way of loving. / I could still be like a river of light in your arms. /
I don't know what holds you back, so furtive, I saw / a flash of ardor in
your gesture as you passed by.)

The sensuality apparent in the above poem, together with its celebra-
tion of the female body and the frank expression of female sexuality, are
the hallmarks of *Creciente fértil*, where Janés fully develops her eroticism and articulates female desire.[61] To express her own desire, her

desire for the male, and her requirements of the postures he and she assume, the poet draws on the sensual mystery of the Middle East by speaking through the masks of the "queens of ancient Sumerian, Hittite, and Babylonian civilizations" (Pasero, "Clara Janés" 238). Also, as part of her expressive arsenal, Janés draws upon the work of "arábigo-andaluz" (Hispano-Arabic) and medieval Spanish women poets. Like Florencia Pinar, she uses the emblem of the partridge to express her body's lust (*Creciente* 38). She also revises the *jarcha* that refers to an explicitly erotic posture, "No te amaré." However, instead of describing pain, as did the *jarcha*, Janés focuses on—and I translate freely—her leonine desire when her body is bent back from the waist so that the tips of her toes stroke the smooth lobes of her ears ("Leones acompañan mi deseo / dispuesto al salto / cuando mi talle doblas y rozan mis puntas / los lóbulos suaves"). Her lover's sexual organs ("parvas") are wheat or grain that is being threshed into flame; their orgasm is a curve of joy, a fusion of bland whiteness, and the lover's sperm ("frost") reaches the lost nape of her neck ("Un trillo de fuego irrumpe en la selva, / dos llamas en fuga / prenden en tus parvas, / en blanda blancura se funde / la curva del goce / y alcanza la nuca perdida en la escarcha" [*Creciente* 32]). In addition to reconceptualizing medieval poetry, Janés echoes Ernestina de Champourcin in her use of coital metaphors.

Janés's imagery is explicitly erotic: "un sátiro de bronce, / con el pene candente, ronda mi oscura sed" (a bronze satyr, / with a red-hot penis, prowls around my dark thirst [26]); "Yo con los pies por alto, / adopta tú la forma de algún ave: / cala muy de repente, picotea furioso, / roba el rubí escondido" [I with my feet up high, / you adopt the shape of any bird: / penetrate all of a sudden, peck furiously, / steal the hidden ruby (30)]). As a self-determining and active lover, she takes on the forms of the earth or of nature; she is even a building to be entered by her lover:

> Soy la cúpula azul de la mezquita de Ahmet,
> doscientas ventanas sostienen mi luz.
> Para que alcances a cubrirme
> haré arder tu cuerpo de cedro
> hasta que como incienso te esparzas
> y te eleves, y colmes mi desmayo.
>
> (*Creciente* 18)

(I am the dome of the Ahmet mosque, / two hundred windows sustain my light. / So that you will manage to cover all of me / I shall make your body of cedar burn / until like incense you spread out / and rise up, and fill to the brim my swoon.)

As a bee, she aggressively pursues the prince she wishes to seduce:

Soy la abeja enviada en pos de ti, ¡oh Telipinu!
En ebrio vuelo emprenderé el acoso;
tomaré cera y lavaré tu cuerpo
melado como el ámbar;
te picaré en las manos y en los pies,
despertaré insolente tu capullo
y podré al fin libar.
Y de una gota desataré una fuente
con labios deslizantes,
cubriéndote a batidas
hasta enjutar tu orto,
para que sometas
exangüe a mi dominio.

(*Creciente* 24)

(I'm the bee sent after thee, oh Telipinu! / In inebriated flight I'll embark on the pursuit; / I shall take wax and I shall wash thy body / as honey-colored as amber; / I shall sting thy hands and thy feet, / I shall insolently awaken thy bud / and I shall finally be able to suck. / And from a drop I shall unleash a fount /—with slithering lips—, / covering thee with [the] beats [of my wings] / until I dry up thy rising, / so that drained thou wilt submit to my dominion.)

As has been demonstrated by this poem, Janés's articulation of desire is daring, breath taking, and stunningly original. Elsewhere, the poet expresses her body (e.g., "flor de magnolio negro / que se abre en mi carne / desplegando la noche" [flower of black magnolia / which opens in my flesh / to unfold the night (28)]), and actively incites her lover to penetrate it ("hunde aún más el filo, / apura ya la pulpa, / desgarra dos corolas" [sink the blade further in, / now drain the pulp, / crush two corollas (28)]). With her movement, Janés interjects herself into her texts, as Cixous urged women to do. By writing with her body, and by articulating its desire, passion, and *jouissance*, she frees herself from all inhibitions and attains a state of self-liberation unequaled by her precursors and peers. Exultation is the mood of the final poem:

Yo cabalgo la torre de Gálata
mas la torre en mi cuerpo

se convierte en un sauce
agitado por el viento
e inicia un juego que me funde.
Me transformo en rocío en sus hojas,
apreso en mi transparencia
los destellos de su noche...
Todo es oscuridad,
un fluir de oro entre las piernas
y un cóncavo abandono a sus halagos,
mientras aún erecta la torre en mí sumida
vuelve a soltar
su desbandada de cometas.

(*Creciente* 52)

(I ride astride the Galatian tower, / but inside my body the tower / is
transformed into a willow / shaken by the wind / and initiates play that
fuses me [to it]. / I am transformed into dew on its leaves, / I capture
inside my transparency / the flashes of its night... / All is darkness, / a
flowing of gold between the legs / and a concave yielding to its
gratification, / while the tower sucked inside me still erect / sets free
again its rush of comets.)

Vulvular and phallic symbolism is fully developed here, in combina-
tion with natural and celestial imagery, to articulate the poet's *jouissance* and *jouiscience*. *Creciente fértil* is surely the most liberatory vision
of female desire that exists in Spanish poetry. Indeed, it seems that
Janés has achieved what French feminists postulate in their theoretical
writings. By writing "the marvelous text of her self," she has emancipated her self and discovered plenitude. Her writing in fact returned
her to the "immense bodily territories" of the female where she recovered a woman's "goods, pleasures, organs." By articulating the voice of
the uterus, she has dispatched masculine desire from the podium it has
occupied for ages and has shown that—despite Lacan—woman does
indeed exist. She has demonstrated that the vagina's pleasures, of an
intrauterine and fluid sexuality, are superior and liberatory when contrasted to the brief delights of that rigid and solid penis, whose joy is in
immortality, posterity, organization, escaping death and fleeing from
the here and now.[62]

Hence, the originality of Janés's vision is that it follows a woman's
struggle with alienation through to an encounter with her gynocentric
roots, then on to a discovery of her mythical, matrilineal heritage, and

beyond that to a full understanding of desire. In her work she has re-appropriated traditional symbolism—tree, flower, bird, female body—which her gynocritical discourse has recontextualized and endowed with a feminized polyvalency of meaning. Hers is a fully developing gynocentric and gynocritical vision, and one that will be watched with keen interest for the new spaces it chooses to traverse. Rosa Chacel was herself clairvoyant when she selected the words "profetisa y sacerdotisa" (prophetess and priestess) to describe Janés's project.

In conclusion, Janés, Atencia, and Aguirre developed distinct poetic visions during and immediately following the dictatorship of Francisco Franco. In comparison with Janés's female vision of self-discovery, Francisca Aguirre's is feminist in its articulation of protest and advocacy. However, Aguirre manifests numerous insights into female self-determination. Atencia has no interest in protest. Hers is a female vision of discovery and exploration of the traditional woman: but unlike her precursors of the nineteenth century and earlier parts of the twentieth, Atencia in her texts is not in the least inhibited or constrained by patriarchal, phallocratic, and androcentric expectations.

Notes

1. See Debicki, *Spanish Poetry* (98–99, 134–35).

2. Ernestina's silence lasted from *Cántico inútil* (1936) to *Presencia a oscuras* (1952), during which time she worked as a translator to support her husband and herself. In addition, Valender ("Introducción" 28) points out that Concha Méndez published nothing for over thirty years (between 1944 and 1979).

3. For this title, see García Martín, *Segunda generación*. However, the English reader may wish to consult Wilcox, "Spanish Poetry from the Mid 1930s to the Mid 1980s: An Introduction." Of María Victoria Atencia, Ciplijauskaité notes: "no pertenece a ningún grupo literario: no cabría en uno sólo" (she does not belong to any literary group: she would not fit in to only one ["Serena plenitud" 7]). But Debicki suggests that Atencia's "immediacy" and her work's "wider implications" connect her with her generation, whereas her "artfulness" links her to the 1970s and 1980s (*Spanish Poetry* 170–71, 235 n. 27).

4. We noted the same factor in the fates of Champourcin and Méndez.

5. I use the following abbreviations when citing from these books: *Itaca, Trescientos, Música*. Page references follow each quotation.

6. Compare Rosalía de Castro's revision of Penelope in "Desde los cuatros puntos cardinales."

7. By which I mean an elliptical splicing of those voices (of various poetic personae) the text actualizes. For example, the thoughts of the speaker and those of the poet.

8. Ostriker, *Stealing* chap. 4, has studied the phenomenon of anger's turning into self-destruction.

9. Compare Gimbutas's remark that goddess-centered cultures "did not . . . build forts" (*Language of the Goddess* 321).

10. Tarpeia was the daughter of the governor of the fortress built by Romulus on the banks of the Tiber (i.e., Rome). She desired the gold in the bracelets of the Sabine women and to get it she opened the fortress gates to the Sabines' king—whereupon they killed her. Moreover, the Sabine women did stop the war that ensued by running between the opposing armies.

11. Music's positive force in this book often finds expression in metaphors related to the woman: "priestess" (16), child-bearing (33), and akin to the fascination a wild beast exercises (15, 27).

12. As noted earlier, I take the quilt metaphor from Tornsey. The "urn" is the metaphor Cleanth Brooks chose for his study of Romantic and post-Romantic poetry.

13. For the much broader context of "autofagia," the interested reader should consult Ilie, "Autophagous Spain."

14. Compare Kirkpatrick's observations on the failure of nineteenth-century women poets to sustain the Promethean battle.

15. See Yeats, "Lapis Lazuli," *Collected Poems* 291–93.

16. See also "Salutación," (*Trescientos* 67).

17. Penelope's heart displays similar characteristics: "respeto hacia todo lo que vive" (respect toward all that lives). It teaches her to smile: "ante este hermoso árbol / que misterioso crece / justificando inútilmente al mundo" (before this beautiful tree / which grows mysteriously/ justifying the world in its useless way [*Itaca* 40]).

18. In his postmodern, late period W. B. Yeats called this "patch" "an acre of green grass" (*Collected Poems* 299). In his mid period, he called it an acre of stony ground.

19. See "Si supiésemos amueblar nuestro corazón": "If only we knew how to furnish our heart, / our Plato's cave, / our life's projection pit / with what is proper to its territory. / If only we knew how to run round that greenhouse / recognizing its plastic flowers / and grouping all of them together with the tenderness that we'd dedicate / to old orthopaedic members. / If only we knew how to set the segregation to one side without slipping, / without turning ourselves into witnesses for the prosecution. / If we were so really and truly *us* / that we could not establish / that sterile distance between *us* / and the nostalgia we call *others*. / If we had the courage to be that restlessness / and not another thing, / that impotence and not its

history. / Perhaps we would rest on that impulse / and for once we would be happy / with our scanty, awkward and humble scenery" (*Música* 53–54).

20. On the effect of social poetry on Atencia, see García Martín ("Introducción" 17 and n. 19).

21. However, approximately one-half of the poems of *La pared contigua* and *De la llama en que arde* were not included in *La señal;* for this reason, "señal" may be used here with the meaning of "token" (selection). Moreover, in 1992 Atencia published *El puente* and *La intrusa*. Unless otherwise indicated, references are to *La señal* and are given as page numbers only.

22. I say this because I suspect that males might idealize Atencia (just as Figuera's reputed maternal impulse was aggrandized by earlier male critics). See for example Alvar's comments, cited by García Martin in *Antología* (20). As will become clear, I suspect that Atencia encourages us to regress: to be young boys again and be cared for in the space she orders and over which she reigns.

23. For the home as a space of "sacredness" and "centeredness," see Rabuzzi, *Sacred* 63. For "sanctuary," see Cheryl Walker, *Nightingale's Burden* 50 ff. Walker also studies (43–49) how a woman's lack of effective power is manifested in images of confinement, imprisonment, escape.

24. For original, see Guillén, *Final* 311.

25. Aleixandre, "Unas palabras," in Atencia, *Ex libris* 7. Quoted in Ciplijauskaité, "Serena plenitud" 7, and Ugalde, "Time" 7. The "cañada de los Ingleses" is a ravine in Málaga. It contains on one of its sides the "English cemetery" where Jorge Guillén is buried.

26. For a thorough stylistic analysis of this "mundo," see Ciplijauskaité, "Compromiso" 98–101.

27. "Lirio" is technically an "iris." However, Spaniards generally use the word to refer to a lily.

28. See also, Janés, "Prólogo" (in Atencia, *Señal* xx): "este mundo [de la casa] . . . es el que permite seguir a Atencia en la búsqueda de su identidad definitiva" ("this world [of the house] . . . is what permits Atencia to proceed with her search for her definitive identity"). Also, Zambrano ("Reposo" 11) notes the "interior revelation" encountered in Atencia's poems. For a detailed analysis of this poem's ekphrastic style, see Ugalde, "Time" 8.

29. Morales Zaragoza ("Poética" 9) distinguishes between the practical Martha and the contemplative Mary "for whom only love counts." Jordan and Cherry, in their comments on Velázquez's 1618 painting, *Kitchen Scene with Christ in the House of Martha and Mary,* in the National Gallery of London, observe that: "According to the exegetical writings of Saint Augustine, Martha's concern about her work in preparing a meal for the Lord establishes her as the 'type' of the active life, while Mary's wish to sit at the feet of the Lord and listen to his words establishes her as the 'type' of the contemplative life: two poles that were seen not as bad and good,

but rather as good and best. Thus this story became one of the key biblical texts in the Christian controversy over whether 'faith' or 'good works' is more efficacious in the salvation of the human soul" (*Spanish Still Life* 39). For the biblical episode of Mary and Martha, see Luke 10.38–42.

30. E.g., "Aniversario" (11), "Diego de Siloé" (134), "Les amours" (240), "Al sur" (283), "Hacia las tres" (322), "Mermelada inglesa" (334), and "Canastos" (346).

31. See also *Llama* 36.

32. See also Janés (*Señal* xxvi–xxviii).

33. Her father's umbrella was black.

34. A frail ("serete") is a small basket used for the display of such goods; it serves as another example of Atencia's linguistic precision.

35. *Puente* (24) and *Intrusa* (34, 46). See also "la niña que fuiste" ("the girl you were" [*Llama* 18]); "una joven, yo misma, niña" (a young woman, I myself, a girl [*Llama* 29]); and "niña yo en ti" (I as girl in you [*Llama* 36]).

36. See also "Inés" (84) and "Ahora que amanece" (14).

37. See Ciplijauskaité ("Recent" 156–57), Ugalde ("María Victoria Atencia" 60) and Metzler, "Images" for Atencia's selection of these figures to develop and explore her female self.

38. The allusion is to Pascal's "thinking reed."

39. In "Ocaso en los cristales" (*Llama* 55) she reflects on the diminution of passion, but the expression of sexual desire is not a concern of her work. Janés writes of Atencia's conviction "de no abandonarse a la pasión" (not to abandon herelf to passion [*Señal* xxv]). Nevertheless, on desire in Atencia, see Janés's "Una brisa, Un erotismo soterrado" (A breeze, a buried eroticism [*Señal* xxix–xxxii]).

40. Ugalde ("María Vicente Atencia" 57) observes that "Muñecas" (24) reveals Atencia's "poignant longing to stop time."

41. See also 51, 89, *Llama* 23.

42. *American Heritage Dictionary* 1071. The rhetorical thrust of my line of argument obliges me at this time toward this reading. In another context, I would argue that Swedish crystal is not particularly prized and that Atencia is reacting to the Spanish male's preoccupation with the Swedish women who began to invade the coasts of Spain in the 1970s. Moreover, Atencia's "Rosa de Jericó" should be contrasted with Rosalía's "Cuido una planta bella."

43. See Persin's "Yet Another Loose Can(n)on."

44. Compare Yeats's "Leda and the Swan": "A sudden blow: the great wings beating still / Above the staggering girl" (*Collected Poems* 211). Moreover, in "Cerco continuo" (141) she may be revising the myth of Icarus. See Pertusa, "Culturalismo" 23–25 for further pertinent comments on Hecuba and Icarus.

45. She is also a novelist and critic.

46. From the presentation Rosa Chacel made at Janés's first public reading (Ateneo of Madrid, Nov. 2, 1978).

47. *Las estrellas vencidas* (1964); *Límite humano* (1973); written in "Pamplona, 1963 — Madrid, 1965" (*Límite* 80).

48. The *Libro de alienaciones* is composed of two sections: *Isla del suicidio* and *Libro de alienaciones*. We know that they were written during the seventies because a selection of both books was included in *Antología personal (1959–1979)*, whose "Preliminar" the writer signed in February of 1979.

49. In "Poemas rumanos" she refers to Costanza as "la ciudad de mi infancia" (the city of my infancy [*En busca de Cordelia* 47]), and in a series of reflections on the sculptures of Brancusi — the Rumanian sculptor — finds emblems of her negative psychic state at that time ("la profunda soledad del alma humana" [the profound solitude of the human soul]) from which by reflection she emerges ("No todo es espanto. / Inesperadamente nos inunda la luz" [Not all is fright. Unexpectedly light inundates us (*En busca de Cordelia* 49 and 55 respectively)]).

50. The Spanish surrealist tradition flourished, in poetry, in Alberti's *Sobre los ángeles* (1929) and Lorca's *Poeta en Nueva York* (1929; published 1940); in painting, its brilliance is apparent in the 1930 canvases of Salvador Dalí; in the cinema, the films of Luis Buñuel develop surrealist imagery and montage. *Un chien andalou*, the film by Buñuel and Dalí, is a stunning example of Spanish surrealist art. Spanish surrealism did not follow the French model in pursuing automatic writing. However, its artists did select disarticulated images to express their dreams, and they did reveal a strong social conscience. In addition, they usually betrayed an antireligious bias, in reaction to the strict religious environment of their childhood. Such tendencies are also found in Andréu's work, as we shall see. Furthermore, in Spain in mid-century and beyond, "postismo" — a child of surrealism — flourished (see Debicki, *Spanish Poetry* 77–80).

51. Eugénie Lemoine-Luccioni, according to Jardine (*Gynesis* 169), believes that woman is fundamentally divided: "this division-in-herself marks woman's specificity [and] means that alienation is fundamental to her being-in-the-world (rather than merely fundamental to culture)."

52. In Ugalde's *Conversaciones* (41–42), Janés confirms some of my observations on *Cordelia* but contradicts others.

53. "A phrase coined by Keats to describe his conception of the receptivity necessary to the process of poetic creativity." Though its thrust is positive, it appears to have a negative side. Keats wrote in a letter: "*Negative Capability*, that is when man is capable of being in uncertainties, Mysteries, doubts, without any irritable reaching after fact and reason." See Drabble, *Oxford* 689.

54. Liz Yorke, in reference to Hélène Cixous and Catherine Clément, makes an interesting observation on the sorceress: "The history written by

women will not be a 'true' history but will be reconstituted, re-membered out of the exclusions and negations of patriarchy, and will be written by those who play out their lives 'between symbolic systems, in the interstices, 'offside.' " She adds: "the hysteric and the sorceress as producers of incommunicable, individual symbolism are particularly named as in danger from, and dangerous to, the symbolic order. They are seen as anomalous figures, but ones who are ultimately conservative in that they are incapable of disturbing the social formation. None the less, in pointing to the woman on the periphery who is situated at the margins of the symbolic system as especially placed to dramatize the repressed of culture, this post-Freudian, post-Lacanian perspective proves extraordinarily fertile to the analysis of women's poetry" (*Impertinent Voices* 81).

55. See, respectively, "Convite" 27–32, "Presencia" 33–37, "Lindareja" 37–48.

56. Ugalde, "Feminization" (175) develops Ostriker's (*Stealing* 178) idea by maintaining that Janés is encountering a "fluid" female identity "in which the self—not an ego committed to defending its own boundaries but an array of selves—feels equivalent to and interchangeable with the 'other.' "

57. See for example "Iris," "Chillida," "Burning Bright," "Albores de San Juan."

58. See "En vano en la tierra" (*Libro de alienaciones* 90).

59. These two texts should be side by side as they are in the book itself, for as Ugalde writes: "Es un formato que reconoce y aprecia tanto lo material como lo espiritual, subvirtiendo el tradicional orden vertical que metafísica y moralmente asigna al cuerpo y a la materia, una posición de inferioridad" (It's a format which recognizes and appreciates the material as much as the spiritual, subverting the traditional vertical order that metaphysically and morally assigns the body to matter, a position of inferiority ["Subjetividad" 521]).

60. It is possible that a subversive allusion to Pegasus is present here— an hierarchically masculine poetic inspiration.

61. Pasero ("Clara Janés" 237) shows that the erotic is also present in *Vivir* (1986); she observes too that *Creciente fértil* "is a metaphorical reference to the ancient Fertile Crescent as well as to the whole of the female body and more specifically to the womb" (238).

62. The words I use in this paragraph are basically those of Cixous's "Laugh of the Medusa" and Irigaray's "This Sex Which Is Not One."

7

Amparo Amorós, Ana Rossetti, Blanca Andréu

In the 1980s, spain threw open the doors of its presses to women poets. Amorós, Rossetti (b. 1950), and Andréu (b. 1959) are part of a new constellation of Spanish women poets who—in point of fact—began to appear on the poetic horizon in the late 1970s.[1] An anthology by Ramón Buenaventura published by Ediciones Hiperión at the end of 1985, *Las diosas blancas: Antología de la joven poesía española escrita por mujeres* (The white goddesses: An anthology of young Spanish poetry written by women), focuses attention on a group of twenty-two generally unknown women poets whose first poems were published after Franco's death and who were born between the late 1940s and 1966. Although Buenaventura's introduction to his anthology, and to one of his "white goddesses," is both polemical and condescending, it is provocatively useful. In addition, the book has raised critical hackles and resulted in more attention being paid to women poets in twentieth-century Spain.[2]

During the 1980s, the first books of poetry of many women were published. Sharon Keefe Ugalde, in her indispensable *Conversaciones y poemas* (Conversations and poems), has interviewed seventeen women poets. The three I have selected—Amorós, Rossetti, and Andréu—have attracted a great deal of attention, both on this side of the Atlantic and in Spain, as their work has appeared.[3] Each one has a different gynocentric vision: Amorós is an intellectual in the vein of the major French Symbolists; Rossetti is a baroque poet, and her style seems anachronistic in its preference for seventeenth-century conceits; Andréu is a surrealist and is preoccupied with the anomie of the so-called generation X. As their poetry, their styles, and their points of view are very different from each other, these poets indicate directions pursued by postmodern women poets in Spain.

They belong to a "Generation" that still has no official name. Some refer to it as the "novísimos" (the newest ones)—to whom the term "culturalismo" (culturalism) has been applied.[4] Others call them the "Generation of the '70s" (whose major work appeared in the later sixties and early seventies). The "novísimos" were followed by the "post-novísimos" (the post-newest ones), but it is not germane to their gynocentric visions to draw distinctions along such generational lines. I shall be speaking of the poets of the 1980s, and I agree with Debicki, who in his recent *Spanish Poetry* refers to them as postmoderns.

Coupled with the spate of poetry by women in the mid-1980s, there arose a genuine interest in their precursors, which has not abated in the 1990s. Clara Janés has edited an anthology called *Las primeras poetisas en lengua castellana* (The first poetesses in the Castilian language), containing poems written by women who were born between the fifteenth and seventeenth centuries. Luzmaría Jiménez Faro has compiled the *Panorama antológico de poetisas españolas* (Anthological panorama of Spanish poetesses), which runs from the fifteenth century to the present day. In addition, the journal *Litoral* issued a special number in 1986 entitled *Literatura escrita por mujeres en la España contemporánea* (Literature written by women in contemporary Spain), which covers 1920 to the present. Moreover, a campaign has begun to save women poets from oblivion. The poems of Carolina Coronado (1820–1911) have been recovered, edited by Torres Nebrera, and the complete works of Angela Figuera Aymerich (1902–84) and Elena Martín Vivaldi (who first published in the 1940s) have appeared. Attention has also finally been paid to the work of women whose poetic careers were interrupted by the Civil War. Rosa Chacel (1898–1994), better known for her novels, has published *Versos prohibidos* (Forbidden verses) in 1978 and reissued her sonnets, *A la orilla de un pozo* (On the edge of a well) from 1936; her complete poems were published in the 1990s. Ernestina de Champourcin's *Primer exilio* (First exile) was published in 1978 (and her complete poems also appeared in the 1990s); and in 1985 Carmen Saval Prados (b. 1929) published her poems, *Sonámbula obediencia* (Sonambulistic obedience).

This trend has meant that contemporary women poets receive a good deal of attention. In 1987 the Sunday color supplement of *El País* carried interviews with Ana Rossetti and two other members of the group "las diosas blancas," Almudena Guzmán and Luisa Castro.[5] It is too early to know how these poets—and the many others who also began publishing at this time—might develop, but their work has certainly caused a stir in Spanish literary circles.

✧

Amparo Amorós is a highly intellectual poet, the "bluestocking" of the 1980s, who is highly regarded in literary circles. She is also a critic and teaches literature at a prestigious "Instituto" (grammar school) in Madrid. She has published four volumes of poetry: *Ludia* (1983), *La honda travesía del águila* (The eagle's deep crossing [1986]), *Quevediana* (1988), and *Arboles en la música* (Trees in music [1995]).[6] Despite the fact that Amorós's work is not predominantly feminist, I will focus below on the gynocentric threads I detect in her (muted) postmodern, gynocritical esthetic.

Amorós's first book is titled *Ludia*. In Latin, "ludia" means "actress"; it is related to "ludus," which is a "game, recreation, entertainment." Moreover, *Ludia* itself is prefaced by an epigram that links *playing* with *struggling* with *clarity* and *lucidity*:[7]

Lo lúcido es lo lúdico
y lo lúdico es lo agónico.

Octavio Paz—José Lezama Lima
(*Ludia* 9)

(The lucid is the ludic / and the ludic is the agonic.)

This epigram implies that what the poet perceives on one level to be a game, on another level she articulates as an "agonic" struggle. In addition, to achieve lucidity, the poet accepts the role chance and luck play in the poet's struggle with the recalcitrant logic of the poetic word. Amorós's esthetic is *lucid-ludic-agonic*.

As a poet, she combines her mental acuity with emotional reserve in order to articulate and question the complex dissonances of the postmodern condition. In so doing, she is beginning to articulate a female poetics of the late twentieth century.[8]

Ludia's first poem seems to represent the crossing of a bay:

No la menor distancia.

Aquí se tiende la bahía
con su arco de arena que
impreciso
5   titubea intentando

su fusión
con el mar.

Rodear el atajo:
la continua propuesta
10   de esta ausencia de límites
que actualidad hostiga.

Nada cuenta alcanzar el otro margen:
sólo el trayecto azul bajo el acaso.

(*Ludia* 13)

(Not the least distance. / Here the bay spreads out / with its arc of
sand that / imprecisely / staggers attempting / its fusion / with the
sea. / To go by the shortcut: / the continuous proposal / of this
absence of limits / which plagues the present. / To reach the other
bank counts for nothing: / only the blue route subject to chance.)

The impersonal, emotionally controlled speaker of line 1 suggests that
she could choose to cross this bay by the shortest possible route. Line 8,
the beginning of the third stanza, suggests that she could choose to take
a shortcut. Yet, in the text's closure (ll. 12–13), the self-confident lyrical
voice rejects all easy routes: the journey itself is what is important, not
the final destination.[9]

What is this journey? The last line of the poem foregrounds a para-
dox: a "trayecto azul" which is subject to an element of "acaso." The
"trayecto azul" is an allusion to the late-nineteenth-century poetic
ideal of *l'azur*—a grand *proyecto* (project) rather than a mere *trayecto*.
This great Symbolist project, undertaken by Mallarmé, began in Hispanic poetry with Rubén Darío and was further developed by Juan
Ramón Jiménez. It represents a desire to achieve the ideals or goals
Western—Judeo-Christian and phallogocentric—culture has represented as True and Beautiful. Amorós is expressing here her reservations as a woman about the struggle to attain one of those androcentric,
Western grand illusions, one of those logical and preestablished goals
patriarchal poetic traditions have conditioned her to admire.

The Amorós text does not totally reject such transcendent idealism
but it allows—in "el acaso" (l. 13)—for the fact that luck plays a role in
any such project—be it *blue* or not. The French Symbolists, principally
Mallarmé and Rimbaud, and later the French surrealists, experimented
with the role that chance plays in the production of a text that articu-

lates modern dissonance.[10] Such experimentation did not take place in Spain until the 1920s. Amorós, by juxtaposing *azul* and *azar* (="acaso") indicates her similarity with and her difference from the two principal ideals of poetic Modernism. In particular, a "trayecto azul" that permits *azar* to influence the attainment of its goal differs from the traditional, high Modern, Hispanic esthetic ideal. When Amorós accepts the element of chance, she is recognizing that any ideal (Truth, Beauty) is a fortuitous find, a gratuitous invention, ingenious fabrication, or concoction—or, as Jean-François Lyotard puts it—a "metanarration."[11]

Amorós chooses to open her first book of poems with an allusion to the two principal esthetic ideals of Modern poetry. On the one hand, the high Modern, optimistic current, with its declared faith in the capacity of the poetic word to communicate, to represent the (androcentric) ideals of Western culture. On the other hand, the low Modern, the pessimistic even nihilistic current,[12] which doubts the autonomy of the poet and is skeptical of the capacity of *man*-made language (and therefore the poetic word) to effect objective communication between human beings. Amorós is situating herself between these two esthetic ideals: her "trayecto azul" allows that art and life may have meaning, that there may be transcendent Truths; her "acaso" allows for the possibility that such meaning may be fortuitous, such Truths, metanarrations. She entertains the possibility that crucial features of both art and life are confected out of chance, subject to sheer luck. Amorós is a postmodern intellectual woman poet who situates herself in neither of the two principal, and male-made, esthetic currents in Modern Hispanic poetry.[13] She does this—subconsciously, I suspect—because she is a woman uncomfortable with the androcentric Truths canonized poetic traditions might articulate.

A second distinctive feature of Amorós's postmodern poetics is her revisionary mythmaking. In another poem from *Ludia*, she confronts the "azur/azar"—"trayecto/proyecto" polarity with a different and suggestive image—"fuego" (fire), with its connotations of knowledge, against "negrura" (blackness), ignorance:

> Con las manos cogíamos el fuego:
> se derramaba como ardiente vino
> y sus lenguas de grito proponían
> treguas a la negrura.
>
> 5   Al trasluz nuestras sombras simulaban

rituales murciélagos nocturnos
en la sima de un vientre sigiloso.

(*Ludia* 50)

(With our hands we grasped the fire: / it overflowed like glowing
wine / and its cry of tongues outlined / breaks in the blackness. / In
the gloaming our bodies simulated / ritual, nocturnal bats / on the
abyss of a secret belly.)

By grasping fire (l. 1)—that is, committing herself to culture, to the
poetic word—Amorós envisions in line 4 a "tregua" (truce or break)
in the total "negrura" of our human condition. By committing her-
self/ourselves to the ritual (l. 6) of love—the images throughout hint
at copulation—she/we momentarily transcend her/our eternal blackness.[14]

In another poem, whose title is in fact "Ludia," such a struggle is
undertaken against the play of "negras transparencias." In this agonic
tryst, "el azar" contributes to the final outcome:

Y tú, Ludia, que hostigas la espesura
con tu paso de dardo,
revélame el secreto
de este juego de negras transparencias
5   que descienden dejando a nuestros pies
lo que nunca de forma estipulada
pudiera sernos dicho.
Y juntos inventemos
las imposibles reglas
10   de lo que sólo regirá el destino:
la asombrosa ecuación de la altura
de los árboles mismos
y su cima de fronda entrelazada
filtrando los reflejos
15   de la invisible luz.
Y que sea el azar quien determine
la flecha y el carcaj venturoso
de la hora más bella:
una lúcida muerte
20   que destelle en la sombra
su certera mirada

como estrella de sonoro diamante
en la desolación de esta noche total.

(*Ludia* 28–29)

(And you, Ludia, who lashes the thicket / with your dart-step, / reveal to me the secret / of this game of black transparencies / which descend leaving at our feet / what never in stipulated form / could have been told to us. / And together, let us invent / the impossible rules / for what only fate will govern: / the astonishing equation of the height / of the trees themselves /and their crown of entwined frond / filtering the reflections / of the invisible light. / And let chance determine / the arrow and fortunate quiver / of the most beautiful hour: / a lucid death / which flashes in the shadow / its well-aimed look / like a sonorous diamond star / in the desolation of this total night.)

This hazardous crossing achieves a momentary beauty, expressed in the overdetermined metaphor—which is redolent with connotations from prior Spanish poetry—"estrella de sonoro diamante" (l. 22). This fortuitous accomplishment (l. 16) compensates for the darkness that surrounds us: "la desolación de [nuestra] noche total" (l. 23).

Moreover, this text is in fact an apostrophe to a deity named "Ludia" (l. 1). Who is this goddess? As far as I know, Ludia does not figure in traditional mythology. In Amorós's text, Ludia is similar to Diana, in that Diana was the goddess of the hunt. Images of hunting are found at the beginning of the poem, such as "dardo" (l. 2), and toward the end, "la flecha y el carcaj" (l. 17), "certera" (l. 21). However, what is hunted here is beauty (l. 18), and the ephemeral satisfaction of having produced a certain meaning in the total darkness that encircles us (l. 23). The element of chance and play (l. 4) is also apparent in this crossing: the hazardous hunt or crossing is a gamble that might pay off.

I suggest that Ludia is the poet's invention: a feminine entity, a goddess, capable of plumbing the *azur* heights and black depths, and of benefiting from pure chance in her *trayecto*/hunt. She is not a "white goddess"—as the patriarchs Robert Graves and Ramón Buenaventura would have had it—but a new gynocritical configuration, a deity who represents the possibility of disentangling or disengaging herself from the cul-de-sac into which the Western, phallogocentric culture has led her and all (wo)men.[15]

In Amorós's poems, it is women who suggest different paths to be taken. For example, in another poem, "Escena de caza" (Hunting scene), Daphne, whom Apollo converted into laurel, in place of representing—for example—death, symbolizes a momentary beauty, a complete life.[16] The poem begins:

> Como la persecución de una liebre
> por un galgo en campo raso, espectacular y definitivo.
>
> Ovidio, Metamorfosis. Dafne

Lo primero que alcanza a percibir
el testigo ocasional,
antes de alzar la mano deteniendo
la imagen, con un gesto
del ágil antebrazo que sustenta
la señal enguantada,
es el bronco jadeo
de los mastines
que integran la jauría.

(Like the pursuit of a hare by a greyhound on a level field, spectacular and definitive. Ovid, *Metamorphoses*. Daphne. The first thing that / the chance witness manages to perceive, / before raising her hand to stop / the image, with a gesture / from the nimble forearm that holds up / the gloved signal, / is the wild panting / of the mastiffs / that form the pack of hounds.)

Having described the formal configuration of the scene she beholds, "el testigo ocasional" (l. 2) brings it to a closure thus:

(—No ofendió con torpeza nuestras frentes
describiendo también los personajes—)

No podemos detener la belleza
más que un único instante
—piensa. Desciende el arco
que su brazo tensara unos segundos
y devuelve el tapiz al movimiento
asumiendo el peligro de la huida.

(Ludia 62–63)

([Ovid] did not clumsily offend our brows / by also describing the characters. / We can only detain beauty / for a unique instant /—she thinks. The arc that her arm drew / for a few seconds descends / and returns the tapestry to movement / leaving to supposition the danger of the flight.)

In this poem, Amorós is subverting the traditional symbolism accorded to Daphne; the poet empties the Daphne myth of meaning and makes us see it from another perspective. In place of the phallic persecution of Daphne, which foregrounds the strengths and skills of Apollo and the powerlessness of the woman who is transformed into a tree, we are presented with a tension between the beauty of an "único instante" and the other events constituted by the "chase" and the "escape." [17]

Elsewhere, Amorós returns to the metaphor of the port or bay; she suggests that opting for the easy route, the shortcut, is counterproductive because reality in itself is always changing:

Las naves nos traían desde lejos
monedas, letras, signos de futuro.
El puerto era el umbral de aquella casa
abierta a las mareas desde antiguo.

(*Ludia* 51)

(The ships would bring us from afar / monies, writings, signs of the future. / The port was the threshold of that house / open to the tides since old times.)

The port never changes, but what enters into it with the tides (coins, letters, signs of the future), is always different. It is the poet who plays in the waters of such a port. Or, in another—very long—poem, "La casa sumergida" (The submerged house [*Ludia* 59-61]), it is the poet who descends—as did Rosalía de Castro in "Cómo llovía, suaviño"—into the subterranean depths of her past—family, tradition—who plumbs the aquatic depths of her own subconscious thoughts, to search for the instant of light.

The optimistic artist of "el trayecto azul" confronts the skeptic and nihilist—who is conscious of the inexorable passing of time, of the darkness and desolation of the total night—and by chance, occasionally, finds some momentary truth. Amorós never expresses faith in the *proyecto azul* of a Darío or of a Juan Ramón—the high Modern esthetic; hers is defined as "trayecto" and not project. Yet, she is not as desperate as the low Moderns—whose implicit nihilism negates the possibilities of linguistic communication. Amorós places herself between both impulses, as the "águila" (eagle) of her second book indicates: her eagle is surrounded by desolation, yet it flies "remontándose sola / hacia la luz" (soaring alone / toward the light [*La honda travesía* 20]). Amorós is proceeding to explore herself, and in opposition to radical desolation, the poet encounters "el acorde fugaz de lo perfecto" (the fleeting harmony of that which is perfect [*La honda travesía* 55]). In consonance with her bittersweet philosophy, she asserts in "Estela" (Wake):

Burlar la gravedad inútilmente
tal vez resulte el símbolo
más fiel de la existencia.

(*La honda travesía* 21)

(To uselessly outwit gravity / may perhaps turn out to be the most faithful / symbol for existence.)

Amorós's inscription of the female self is still ongoing.[18]

In *Quevediana*, a collection of sonnets, her third book, she reveals her gynocritical mask.[19] *Quevediana* is a series of carnivalesque satires and critiques of contemporary society in which, for example, a woman scornfully observes the socialization to which young women are still subjected:

Consejos de la revista Petunia
para ligarse un yuppie

Si quiere, señorita, en un momento
llevarse al huerto un fuerte ejecutivo
siga usted los consejos que aquí escribo
aplicándose al tajo con talento.

Sonría, escuche mucho y hable poco
y, cuando esté segura del terreno
que pisa, contraataque con un loco
elogio de cuanto haya en él de bueno.

Porque haciéndolo así yo le aseguro
—aunque el sujeto le parezca un duro—
que al halago sutil de un cobista
no hay varón en la tierra que resista
porque oyendo una tal parafernalia
el *ego* le has dejáo como una dalia.

(*Quevediana* 37)

(Pieces of advice from the magazine *Petunia* on how to get off with a yuppie. / If, Miss, you once / want to lead a strong executive up the garden path, / follow the pieces of advice I give here / and apply yourself to the job with talent. / Smile, listen a lot, and speak little / and when you're sure of the ground / you tread, counterattack with a wild / praise of all the good that might be in him. / Because by doing it like this, I assure you, / —although the guy might seem to you a hard case— / that faced with the subtle flattery of a smarmy type / there's no male on the earth who can resist / because hearing such a paraphernalia / you've left his ego like a dahlia.)

What follows is a translation more in the spirit of Quevedo and the poem: "Petunia Tells You How To Land That Big Exec. When, Miss, your mind's made up / and it's time to whisk your yuppie off to bed, / follow the advice that I pen here / and sedulously apply yourself to the task. / Smile, listen a lot, speak little. / Once you're sure of the ground on which you've set your feet, / feed him a load of cock and bull / — about his brains, and brawn, and balls. / The guy might seem a nut too hard to crack, / but no dude on earth, I vouch, resists the charms / of a *dònna* who's so sly and *mobile*. / Slip him your sure and soothing mickey: / you'll bag his millions and his mobile dickie."

Amorós is acutely aware of the varieties of the female self. Her acerbic irony, and the tone of scorn with which she distances herself from the advice her speaker gives, speak eloquently for her implicit gynocritical vision.

Despite the fat that Amparo Amorós's tone in *Quevediana* is satirical, in her most recent volume, *Arboles en la música* (Trees in music [1995]), her voice has the fully centered authority of a mystic of this earth, of a mature and autonomous woman who has meditated on her experience and who has chosen to sing of its plenitude.[20] True to her French Symbolist roots, Amorós informs us that each of these seventeen poems was inspired by specific pieces of music (*Arboles* 107–9). But they are also inspired, I would argue, by the spirit of Hestia, that unsung deity of the indwelling spirit. These poems are paeans to immanent transcendence; they tell of the sacred within the heightened experience of daily life; they reconcile the speaker and her readers with the earth.

The archetypal feminine tree becomes the unifying symbol of the collection. The poet sits under the branches of a tree of life and heaven ("La Promesa" [The promise] 87–88) and meditates into stanzas, brings into song—whose muse is Terpsichore (see n. 23)—the varieties of fulfillment to be encountered on this earth. The first poem is addressed to its readers and urges them to behold the trees:

Escúchalos crecer. Permite que el silencio
les vaya abriendo paso como a una profecía:

no temas, existimos y podemos alzarnos
de la tierra a la luz.

(Arboles 9).

(Listen to them grow. Let silence / make its way through them like a
prophecy: / don't be afraid, we exist and we can raise ourselves / up
from earth to the light.)

The experiences that in part permit the poet to attain this light are
varied: the mystery of the creative act ("El Don" [The gift] and
"La Herencia" [Inheritance]); the bittersweet pleasures of love ("La
Tregua" [Truce]); the process of aging ("La Respuesta" [Reply] and
"El Fraude" [The fraud]); childhood ("El Combate" [Combat]); the
fairy tale ("El Reto" [The challenge]); dreams in which the unfathomable depths of the self are plumbed ("La Noticia" [News]); the beauty
of nature ("La Deuda" [The debt]). The mystery and marvel of these
experiences have a "femenino" (feminine) element (75), which phoenix-
like comes back to life to nest in "that which is most vegetable, / feminine, in the world" (97). Such epiphanies "Son mi casa, mi hacienda, el
alimento / que teje su cosecha en mi telar" (Are my house, my estate,
the food / that weaves its harvest in my loom [37]).

These meditations impart a mood of serenity in which the poet
seems to want her readers to join themselves to those small wonders
that constitute life: "Hay una gloria humilde en las cosas que en ser / lo
que son se consumen" (There's a humble glory in things that in being /
what they are consume themselves [26]). It seems that the poet advises us to find peace where we can: "Déjate ir, no peses, / no respires,
quédate quieto, suspendido, / y vuela, sabe, sueña. / Siente y olvídate"
(Let yourself go, don't weigh [your options], / don't breathe, keep still,
suspended, / and fly, know, dream [74]); and she urges us to cradle in
our hands—like a bird—what moments of fulfillment come our way:
"Acógelo en tus manos, / hospédalo en tu frente, recibe su secreto / sin
preguntarte nada: el sabrá / su razón aunque no la declare" (Receive it
in your hands, / house it in your brow, receive its secret / without asking
yourself anything: it will know its reason although it will not declare
it [49-50]). To close the collection, she proffers: "the day is that child
you take by the hand," an experience in which everything "returns to
its being and sings" (104).

Clearly, Amorós is a poet whose vision evolves with each book she
publishes. With the increasing depth of her insights, she holds a unique

place in contemporary Spanish poetry. She commands a serious readership who will await her future work with patience.

⊷

Ana Rossetti (b. 1950) has to date published six books of poetry:
Los devaneos de Erato (The flirtations of Erato [1980]); *Dióscuros* (Dios-
curi [982]); *Indicios vehementes* (Vehement indications [1984]); *Devocionario* (Prayerbook [1986]); *Yesterday* (1988); and *Punto umbrío* (Bleak
point [1995]).[21] She has become one of the more celebrated figures in
Spanish poetic circles; her books are reviewed immediately in the cultural sections of the newspapers, which also publish interviews with
the poet.[22] From a gynocentric viewpoint, she is unique for her deployment of feminist desire to subvert traditional human and spiritual
modes of love.

Both hetero- and homosexual desire are inscribed in *Los devaneos de
Erato*.[23] Lesbian passion is observed by the lyrical persona with interest and intrigue. When lesbian passion is spontaneous, the tone of the
poetic voice is gleeful. In "Advertencias de abuela a Carlota y a Ana"
(Grandmother's warnings to Charlotte and Ann"), two young girls
begin to investigate each other's bodies for the first time in their lives:
"Y en el juego, la introducida mano, / desabrochando escotes, / indaga,
sin malicia, entre la lisa / axila fraternal / el cosquilleo" (And during
the game, the hand inserted, / unbuttoning the low necks, investi-
gates, without malice, / the tickle / around the fraternal, / flat-chested
armpit [*Indicios* 30-31]).[24] When lesbian passion is militant, when it is
charged with intent and is conscious of its actions—in "De cómo resistí
las seducciones de mi compañera de cuarto, no sé si para bien o para
mal" (About how I resisted my room-mate's seductions, I don't know
whether for good or bad [*Indicios* 39])—Rossetti playfully subverts her
reader's conventional attitudes toward gender categories.[25]

Homoerotic masculine desire—one of the dominant themes of Rossetti's first novel *Plumas de España* (Feathers of Spain)—is represented
in the first poems with fascination, for example, when the lyrical persona—in "A un joven con abanico (To a youth with a fan [*Indicios* 49])—
discovers the first signs of femininity in a young man. In the second
book, *Dióscuros*, the speaker witnesses an act of masturbation in which
her own brother profanes his father's chair:[26]

> 1   Una vela separa del candelabro Imperio
>   y la enciende, y la mesa recorre.

Sobre el adamascado del mantel
el brillo desigual de la cubertería
5   y de las tenues guirnaldas del Limoges.
Por entre los calados respaldos
Louis se acerca a los vientres tersísimos
de las copas y los hace sonar.
Introduce los dedos en el estuche blanco
10   de una cala y ensimismado hurga
y acaricia los bordes de la alargada flor.
La otra mano, agitada, sobre la servilleta
que su mitra distingue ante el sitial del padre
derrama, incontenible, ardiente esperma.
15   Anna mira un momento y enrojece.
Sube a su cuarto desasosegada.

("Uno," *Indicios* 68])[27]

(He removes a candle from the Imperial / candelabrum, lights it and passes his eye over the table. / The varying sparkle of the cutlery / and the fine Limoges garlands / on the damask of the tablecloth. / Between the openwork backs of the chairs, / Louis approaches the highly polished bellies / of the glasses and makes them ring. / He inserts his fingers into the white sheath / of a calla lily and, lost in himself, pokes / and caresses the edges of the elongated flower. / His other hand, agitatedly, / sheds, uncontrollably, burning sperm onto the napkin / whose miter stands resplendent in front of the father's seat of honor. / Anna looks for a moment and blushes. / She goes anxiously up to her room.)

Besides the shock and glee the reader probably experiences here, this poem is a good example of the early Rossettian technique: she selects an aspect—real or imaginary—of the reality experienced by her lyrical subject (ll. 15-16); she creates a scenic frame that combines archaic ("candelabro Imperio" [l. 1]) and traditional ("Limoges" [l. 5]) elements with postmodern poetic topics (masturbation [ll. 12-15]); she then dramatizes the thematic situation and complicates it with psychosocial resonances ("el sitial del padre" [l. 13]).[28] In the more successful texts, the result is an unexpected surprise that undermines our (androcentric) expectations and preconceived notions of what poetry is.

Toward the desire of older homosexuals, her viewpoint is more critical, her tone more mocking, as when—in "Un señor casi amante de mi marido, creo, se empeña en ser joven" (A gentleman, almost my husband's lover, I think, insists on being young [*Indicios* 28–29])—the lyrical persona represents the vanity of the old homosexual, or his well-planned seduction of a young, inexperienced man (in "Inconfesiones de Gilles de Raïs" [The nonconfessions of Gilles de Raïs (*Indicios* 32)]).

Heterosexual passion—of women toward men—is found in numerous texts. "Cuando mi hermana y yo, solteras, queríamos ser virtuosas y santas" (When my sister and I, as single girls, wanted to be virtuous and saintly [*Indicios* 50–51]) graphically describes the corruption of "mi tan amado y puro seminarista hermoso" (my dearly beloved, pure, and beautiful seminarian).[29] Elsewhere, the young female poetic voice expresses delight at the sexual awakening of her own body,[30] and describes with great pleasure the skill and cunning she is capable of displaying to incite a young man to desire her.[31] However, she describes with a touch of bitter irony men who lack sexual desire: virgins like Saint Sebastian ("A Sebastián, virgen" [*Indicios* 38]), or ideologues such as Saint John the Baptist, and Nietzsche. In the case of Nietzsche, the speaker evokes, in "Homenaje a Lindsay Kemp y a su tocado de plumas amarillas" (Homage to Lindsay Kemp and her headdress of yellow feathers [*Indicios* 47–48]), the frustration of Salome and Lou Andreas Salomé respectively. The poem "Escarceos de Lou Andreas Salomé a espaldas de Nietzsche, claro" (Lou Andreas Salomé's amorous posturings behind Nietzsche's back, obviously) exemplifies the manner in which Rossetti perceives the strange, bittersweet pleasure experienced by a woman confronted with such a man:

1   Despiadada belleza, me aniquilas.
La luz roza en tu carne mi desierto,
mi camino de sed, mi pasión incesante
de hermosura. A escondidas te admiro.

5   Aterrada contemplo el universo
que me excluye de ti.
Carente de ternura al caminar irradias
y no miras a quienes, de verte, se hermosean.
Imposible placer, implícito deseo.

10   Límites míos
en tu desconcertante armonía dilúyense.
De tu amor desvestida permanezco
en el páramo extraño a tu lluvia seminal,
ya que a ti mismo engendras y fecundas.

15   Aún incluso desdeñas al obediente espejo.
     Mas ¿qué es de tu poder sin el sumiso esclavo?

                                                (*Indicios* 45)

(Merciless beauty, you annihilate me. / The light on your flesh brushes
my desert, / my parched road, my incessant passion / for loveliness. I
admire you behind your back. / Appalled, I contemplate the universe /
that excludes me from you. / Devoid of tenderness, you radiate as you
walk / and you do not look on those who are made lovely by seeing
you. / Impossible pleasure, implicit desire. / These limits of mine /
dissolve in your disconcerting harmony. / Stripped of your love, I
remain / in the wasteland that's estranged from your seminal shower, /
for you engender and fertilize yourself. / What's more, you scorn the
obedient mirror. / But, without the submissive slave, what would
happen to this power of yours?)

Nietzsche is the prototypical, egocentric chauvinist, whose beauty is
"merciless" (l. 1), "devoid of tenderness" (l. 7), "disconcerting" (l. 11).
The power of such a man has made him frigid, self-sufficient. He is
a minor god, or potentate, who ignores or simply is not aware of the
subjects who venerate him (ll. 5–8). Nietzsche is an emblem of masculine coldness that kills, rejects, and excludes desire. On the other
hand, Lou Andreas Salomé is the ardent, passionate woman—"my incessant passion" (l. 3)—who desires warmth and tenderness. However,
her vehement desire enslaves her, reduces her to a state of burning dryness—"my desert" (l. 2), "my parched [thirsty] road" (l. 3)—converts
her into a dry and sterile ardor (ll. 12–13).

Rossetti offers here a vision of amorous incompatibility seen through
the eyes of a woman: she makes her readers feel what a woman suffers.
She does this from a feminist's point of view, not from the dominant,
androcentric perspective traditional in Hispanic poetry. Indeed, this
text could be read as a Rossettian revision of a famous masculine poem
on the incompatibility of love, Bécquer's "Rima" 41 (137):

Tú eres el huracán, y yo la alta
torre que desafía su poder:
¡Tenías que estrellarte o que abatirme!
¡No pudo ser!

(You're the hurricane, and I the tall / tower that defies its power: / you
need to dash yourself to pieces or raze me to the ground! / It could
not be!)

The phallocentrism of "Rima" 41 ("tall tower," "lofty rock," "haughty me") forms an essential part of the Bécquerian vision; what Rossetti offers us is different, simply because it obliges us to see the tyrannical effect of such behavior. Rossetti makes us see the phallocratic tradition from a feminist perspective as she undermines the androcentric customs and pleasures reified by our culture. As Ugalde has demonstrated in her excellent studies, Rossetti's texts self-confidently displace masculine concerns and foreground the emotions and points of view of the Spanish woman of the post-Franco period.

A dramatic example of Rossetti's technique and attitude is "Cibeles ante la ofrenda anual de tulipanes" (Cybele beholds the annual tulip tribute [*Indicios* 27]), in which the tulips that are found around the statue of Cybele every spring in Madrid become phallic symbols. The goddess (Cybele) kneels in front of the "capullo" (bud) of one of those tulips and says: "Como anillo se cierran en tu redor mis pechos, / los junto, te me encrustas, mis labios se entreabren / y una gota aparece en tu cúspide malva" (My breasts close around you like a ring, / I bring them together, you encrust yourself to me, my lips half-open / and a drop appears on your mauve cusp).[32] In the closure to this poem—and in many other poems of *Los devaneos de Erato*—a reader notes immediately that the poetic speaker is revising androcentric culture with her feminist lense.

Rossetti's most renowned erotic poem, at least on this side of the Atlantic, has become "Calvin Klein, Underdrawers," a poem that appeared as one of the "Dispersos" (Uncollected poems) in the otherwise anthological *Yesterday*. It is a text that has spawned its readers.[33] It also demonstrates Rossetti's ingenious displacement of desire from the body of the male model to the body of the female beholder:

Fuera yo como nevada arena
alrededor de un lirio,
hoja de acanto, de tu vientre horma,
o flor de algodonero que en su nube ocultara
el más severo mármol travertino.
Suave estuche de tela, moldura de caricias
fuera yo, y en tu joven turgencia
me tensara.
Fuera yo tu cintura,
fuera el abismo oscuro de tus ingles,

redondos capiteles para tus muslos fuera,
fuera yo, Calvin Klein.

(Yesterday 54)

(If only I were snow-white sand / around a lily, / acanthus leaf, molded
around your stomach, / or cotton-plant flower concealing inside its
cloud / the hardest travertine marble. / If only I were a smooth box of
cloth, molding of caresses, / and could tauten myself / around your
youthful turgidity. / If only I were your waist, / if only the dark abyss
of your groin, / if only I were round capitals for your thighs, / if only I
were, Calvin Klein.)

Instead of identifying with the beautiful male body of the Calvin
Klein advertisement, we focus on the woman: whose desire, eroti-
cally expressed, forces us to imagine her stripping the briefs from his
thighs and reducing that "travertine marble" god into a spent youth.
In "Calvin Klein," Rossetti makes the female power of seduction paramount, as she undermines traditional views of gender and foregrounds
a woman's desire.

In addition to subverting traditional perceptions and modes of
human love, Rossetti demystifies spiritual love.[34] In *Devocionario* (1986),
she is inspired by the religious education young girls received during
the Franco era, and she offers a feminist revision of one of the most
deeply rooted patriarchal traditions of modern Spanish society: the influence the Catholic Church exerts on the State, and in particular of the
manner in which sacred, ecclesiastical rites twist a young girl's mind.[35]

In *Devocionario*, the lyrical voice confronts ecclesiastical iconography
—with stinging irony: the rites and statutes, the illustrations, draw-
ings, and engravings of the Church's missals and prayer books.[36] In
"Del prestigio del demonio" (On the devil's prestige), the poet presents
her readers with a convent for young girls: "las asiduas aulas femeninas
/—etéreo gineceo del convento—" (the assiduous, female classrooms,
/—ethereal gynaeceum of the convent—).[37] On a page of their prayer
books, the young girls study an engraving of effeminate angels, and
copy it for their greater glory. They then turn the page, and the tone
changes:

1   Pero, a vuelta de página, EL se erguía,
    su capa henchida—del águila era vuelo—
    la firmeza viril de su torso arrogante
    circundaba. Membrana endeble y tensa
5   auguraban sus ropas la dura vecindad

de su cuerpo perfecto, y, turbador, el pie
—peligrosa hendidura—insistentes acosos
prometía.
    Atrayente y temible
10   sin duda era el demonio, del masculino enigma,
único vaticinio.
Y reverentemente los lápices guardábamos.
La carne estremecida: crispación dolorosa
de insoportable ansia en la cintura ardiéndonos.

                      (*Devocionario* 37–38)

(But, after turning the page, there was HE standing straight up, / his billowing cloak—his was the flight of an eagle—/ surrounding the virile solidity of his arrogant / torso. Taut, frail membrane, / his clothes portended the hard proximity / of his perfect body, and his foot—/ dangerous cleft—disturbingly promised / relentless pursuits. / Attractive and fearsome / was the devil, undoubtedly, the one and only prediction / of the masculine enigma. / And reverently we'd put away our pencils. / Our flesh trembling: a painful tension / of unbearable yearning burning into our waists.)

The engravings provided by the religious school are so intense and dramatic that they manage to create a three-dimensional vision of the devil's corporal and sexual beauty (ll. 3–6). He makes these studious young female pupils look forward with delight to "the enigma of masculinity" (l. 10) that awaits them in the near future, and their young bodies are aroused with expectation (ll. 13–14) as they put away their pencils (in subconscious recognition, perhaps, of the notion that they are defective males).

The text corrosively demystifies ecclesiastical rites, because *Devocionario*'s young poetic persona learns not fear or devotion from her religious education but sexual fantasy. Moreover, the demystification is achieved by means of a thoroughly feminist perspective: as postmodern readers, we forget the traditional androcentric vision (that of the angel) and concentrate totally on the sexual awakening of the young woman's body (l. 14).[38]

An analogous demystification is applied to Holy Communion, which is perceived as an act of erotic seduction: the young female speaker ingests the host and drinks the wine in a subversively perverse manner.[39] In "Reliquia" (Relic), Rossetti plays with the religious connotation of the noun "reliquia," with the notion that the virginity of the poetic speaker is already a "reliquia," and also with the notion that the young lover's sperm is a "reliquia" of a failed act of coitus (of premature ejaculation):

> "La más cierta belleza no resiste el esfuerzo de guardarla."
>
> Gerard Manley Hopkins

1   Apenas asomado el lívido destello
la enardecida flor, hostigada y pujante,
su violencia apresura.
Desplegados los frunces, tanto caudal cautivo,
5   desbórdase del cáliz la llama estremecida
y su cinta desprende e irisándose
por tu vientre resbala.
Nácar ardiente sobre el plumón del vello,
sobre el negro emparrado de las ingles, vertido.
10   Solícito el pañuelo
quisiera retener del pálido granizo
tan quemante diadema
y tiende su gardenia de batista.
. . . . [*sic*]
El eco de tu huida en mi puerta aún clavado
15   y la liviana tela es pájaro de yeso,
rígida cartulina o dura nieve
por la alfombra encrespando sus opacas estrellas.

(*Devocionario* 15)

(The surest beauty cannot stand the effort to keep it safe. G. M. Hopkins. / No sooner has the pale spark peaked out / than the inflamed flower, pushing and pestering, / quickens its assault. / Holding so much volume captive, the trembling flame / unfurls its shirrs, overflows its calyx / and sheds its ribbon, which slithers / in iridescent drops upon your belly. / Shining mother-of-pearl is shed on the hair's down, / on the groin's black vines. / The handkerchief solicitously / would like to retain so burning a diadem / of the pale hail / and spreads its cambric gardenia. / . . . / The echo of your flight still nailed to my door, / and the fickle cloth is a bird of gypsum, / rigid construction paper or hard snow / curling its opaque stars on the carpet.)

The speaker splits herself into two heteronymous selves to dialogue with herself (l. 7). She displaces the religious discourse by focusing on the male's sexual organs (ll. 2, 8, 11), and by ever more pejorative references to her lover's sperm (ll. 8, 11, 16). Then the erotic vision is displaced by a feminist perspective: one in which the young lover is described as the opposite of a Rudolph Valentino—impatient (l. 2), violent (l. 3), a premature ejaculator (l. 7), and even a coward (l. 14). The feminist poetic persona mocks the man, referring to him as if he were a crowned king (l. 12), and treating his sperm as if it were a precious religious relic to be conserved in a luxurious lace handkerchief (ll. 10-17).

Rossetti achieves her stylistic effects by exaggeration and deflation. With her mock heroics, she is a twentieth-century Alexander Pope. Her stock-in-trade are archaic syntax and diction: hyperbaton (e.g., ll. 4-8); hyperbole (l. 8); climax (l. 8) and anticlimax (ll. 15-18); parody (l. 14); sarcasm (l. 13); irony (l. 12); and alliteration (l. 4). Her lexicon is rarefied and is drawn from regal and religious, sartorial and celestial registers. Her poetry obliges postmodern readers to reflect upon the distorting force that phallogocentric rites exercise on women.

By comparison with Clara Janés, Rossetti's perspective at this time is one of rebellion. Her desire is *feminist*, one of protest and advocacy—as Showalter defined these terms—as opposed to *female*, one of self-discovery. Rossetti certainly gives voice to the feminine, and she undermines the perception of woman as other as defined by Beauvoir: but does she give voice to herself in her early books? It seems to me, to appropriate a witty phrase, that her fixation on such matters as the "Immaculate Conception" has diverted her attention from "self-conception" (La Belle, *Herself Beheld* 114).

With respect to Rossetti's inscription of a female identity within her early work, she is also a rebel, or at most an agonist. She is fighting the demons of the uninscribed self of her past experience of life and art.[40] Rossetti perceives her past experiences as a girl and young woman in negative terms. The lessons she learned about love as a girl warped her style as a woman.[41] The religious education she received threatens her psychic independence, her mental, emotional, and creative capacities as an adult.[42] In "Purifícame" (Purify me), the speaker addresses the child that she was and implies that the psychosocial complex "infancy—fatherland—young girl" is throttling the inspiration of the adult woman.[43]

Moreover, her past experience prevents Rossetti from a fuller inscription of the feminized self. Poetic inspiration is an attic full of memories that tyrannize her, that oblige her to write:

Es mi memoria cárcel, tú mi estigma, mi orgullo,
yo albacea, boca divulgadora

que a tu dictado vive,
infancia, patria mía, niña mía, recuerdo.

(Devocionario 57).

(My memory is a prison, you / —infancy, my homeland, my little girl,
memory—/ my stigma, my pride, / I executrix, divulging mouth / that
lives by your dictation.)

Elsewhere, poetic creation is transformed into a "dulce venganza" —
a "sweet revenge" on the literary-historical past: on those strong predecessors who have mesmerized her (*Indicios* 58). The authority of the
past is a bane for Rossetti, a fact that helps explain her preocupation
with the suicides of Romantic poets (whom she sees as having been
killed off by their devotion to the poetic word).[44]

"Invitatorio" (Invitatory), which is prefaced by a quote on death
from the French writer Marcel Schwob (1867-1905), can stand as an
example of the existential and esthetic dichotomies of Rossetti's female
self. The desolate speaker splits herself in two and addresses her "melancholy soul":[45]

> "No te contemples en la muerte;
> deja que tu imagen sea llevada por
> las aguas que corren".
>
> Marcel Schwob

No hay cortejo comparable para ti,
alma melancólica, a esta multitud
de ecos silenciados, galería monótona
que la quietud repite y obstinada refleja
5   sus trastornados ritmos.
Y la muerte está ahí, en el espejo
que divulga las voces de las aguas,
en esa luna inerte donde la menta asoma
tiritando, mientras que entre los dientes
10   las culebras son besos, y en la inmóvil tristeza,
el frío, de sus parques, traza la geometría.
Y el tinte de tu rostro se hace pálido y verde.
Pero si alguna vez quieres sobrepasar,
desgarrar la cruel lámina y clavar el gladiolo
15   en la caverna húmeda del espejo,
te arrastraré a la danza delirante

que en un instante alberga mil figuras distintas,
podré decirte cómo derrochar la belleza
en la noche magnífica, incendiándola,
20 a usar los diccionarios como libros de música,
orquesta fugitiva para esta insurrección,
esta brillante fiesta que en tu obsequio preparo.
Pues sentir es el prodigio único
que me alerta y preocupa, y la audacia,
25 como un tenaz diamante rasgando las ventanas,
la joya y homenaje que prefiero.
Llámame pues si rompes esa fronda sombría
del espejo, si has llegado al final
hasta el papel de plata, de repente arañado,
30 si tu rostro al cristal desampara
y con agudo estruendo se desprende.
No siempre hay que creer lo que el espejo dice.
Tu rostro verdadero puede ser cualquier máscara.

(Indicios 94–95)

(Don't contemplate yourself in death; let your image be carried by the flowing waters. M. Schwob. / For you, melancholy soul, / there's no entourage comparable to this crowd / of silenced echoes, monotonous gallery / that imitates stillness and obstinately reveals / its mad rhythms. / And death is there, in the mirror / that spreads the waters' voices, / in that inert moon out of which mint peers / shivering, while snakes are kisses / between its teeth, and in its still gloominess, / the cold marks out the geometry of its parks. / And the tint of your face becomes pale and green. / But if you once want to get out, / shatter the cruel plate and thrust the gladiolus / into the humid cavern of the mirror, / I'll drag you off to the delirious dance / that in a moment shelters a thousand different figures, / I'll be able to tell you how to squander beauty / in the magnificent night, setting it alight, / to use dictionaries as books of music, / the fugitive orchestra for this revolt, / this brilliant party I'm throwing for you. / For to feel is the only prodigy / that alerts and concerns me, and audacity, / like a tough diamond slashing the windows, / the jewel and homage I prefer. / So call me if you break the mirror's / somber frond, if you've finally reached / the silver paper, suddenly clawing, / if your face abandons the glass / and works itself loose with a sharp crash. / You don't always have to believe what the mirror says. / Your true face can be any old mask at all.)

In this poem, the gleeful *self* of *Los devaneos* addresses the tragic and depressed *other* of "Indicios vehementes." The lyrical subject splits herself into two heteronymous selves, which I shall call the "feminized" and the "unemancipated"; her meditative tone employs a mixture of hendecasyllables and alexandrines,[46] with only one heptasyllable (l. 5).[47] The lines have a funereal resonance, and they parody the Spanish baroque style in their use of puns, hyperbatons, oxymorons, epithets, and antitheses.[48] The poem itself is an apostrophe to sadness, on which the speaker meditates in six separate sections:

In lines 1–5, the feminized, speaking *self* addresses her unemancipated *other*, a melancholy soul which is in mourning ("cortejo"), and which needs to be courted to escape from its prison of lugubrious and dampened sounds. In lines 6–12, the feminized *self* looks at herself in the mirror and describes the state of her soul mate, her unemancipated *other*: she sees herself as a body slowly decaying (l. 12) in a decadent fin-de-siècle, *modernista* park; or perhaps an Ophelia floating down the river of death. In lines 13–22, the mirror—as a *mise-en-abîme*—is transformed into a humid cavern (l. 15); the feminized *self* describes for the melancholy unemancipated *other* all the pleasures she will offer it (ll. 16–22), if the sad soul decides to flee from its cave, if it will only burst through the crystal of its frame (in front of which there stands a single gladiolus, not a vase of them as would be normal). In lines 23–26, the feminized *self* explains that she prefers to live with intense emotion and strong pleasures. In lines 27–31, once again, the feminized *self* repeats the offer to lead the unemancipated *other* out into the crazy dance of life, if it ("rostro") will burst through its prisonlike confines and flee from its "gloomy fronds." In lines 32–33, in the closure, the feminized *self* invites her unemancipated *other* to flee from sadness—melancholy, mourning—and to put on a different mask, one that will suit her for the frenetic dance of life.

Clearly, Rossetti initiates a profound self-analysis in this poem, one that is being conducted on many levels and puts her in touch with her subconscious mind. One of those levels is poetic, as we have already implied by pointing to its parody of Baroque style. In fact an esthetic code is clearly evidenced in the metaphor "to use dictionaries as books of music" (l. 20). Additional esthetic allusions are more obscure, but nonetheless present—in such lexemes as "gallery" (l. 3), "inert moon" (l. 8), "snakes" (l. 10), "parks" (l. 11). Taken together these lexemes constitute a *modernista* intertext. They allude to early Peninsular *modernismo*: to Juan Ramón Jiménez's *Almas de violeta* (Souls of violet) and *Arias tristes* (Sad arias), and Antonio Machado's *Soledades* (Solitudes).[49]

These allusions to early Spanish *modernismo* are the esthetic mirrors, windows, or caves, which the female *ephebe* will have to "scratch" with her "tenacious diamond" (l. 25). The *modernista* intertext indicates that Rossetti has begun to reflect seriously on her own situation vis-à-vis Modern poetry (and perhaps hints that her future work might provide us with a revisionary reading of her male precursors).

The above text actualizes phallic and vulvular metaphors: in lines 14–15 the masculine "gladiolus" is opposed to "the humid cavern of the mirror." The gladiolus has been selected as a phallic symbol to signify masculine drive and autonomy which, once introduced into the "humid cave" of the dispirited, feminine *other*, will fuse anima with animus and create the emancipated self. As for the mirror or the mirroring which, as La Belle has noted, "for women . . . is not a stage but a continual, evershifting process of self-realization" (*Herself Beheld* 10): it keeps the feminized self apart from its *other*. Irigaray writes that "the mirror is entrusted by the (masculine) 'subject' with the task of reflecting and redoubling himself" ("This Sex" 104). The poet deems such a narcissistic task foreign to her self-realization. She would prefer that the *other* trapped behind the mirror—like an "enraged and rebellious prisoner"—seize the gladiolus and inseminate the self.[50] If the depressed and imprisoned *other* can break out—break through the "cruel plate" (l. 14) of mercury—there will be a mercurial fusion of self with other out of which the emancipated female self will emerge.

In poems such as these, Rossetti is struggling against an anxiety of literary authority and against the education and culture that indoctrinated her in her "infancia." She is struggling with the traumas of childhood and early youth in the hope that she can more forcefully articulate her contemporary female self, signs of whose liberation she has clearly shown in her work to date.

Hence, Rossetti's poems display *jouissance* in their deflation of an androcentric vision of reality, but they are still on the threshold of a *jouiscience*. Rossetti reflects the anguish of modern life, as well as the anxiety of literary authority. She is not merely an erotic poet, despite remarks by some of her (predominantly male) Spanish readers.[51] Eroticism is the technique she deploys to explore herself as well as a weapon she uses to confront reality and literary history. Indeed, in her most recent book, *Punto umbrío* (1995), she is engaged in self-exploration and analysis in order to reconnect with the general and diverse erotic impulse in life, with love in all its varied manifestations as opposed to its purely sexual expressions. In *Punto umbrío* Rossetti sees perfect happiness and all-engrossing love as experiences of her past life (11–13); she implies that what was once sexually attractive to her in the devil is now repulsive (17). Her desire now is to find a silent place apart from the grief of living (23) in order to reconnect both with her own heart, with which she has lost touch (37, 57), and with her own writing self (33). In her agonic meditations, she mothers her heart back into her life (35) and in one of the last poems in the volume experiences its reflowering (59). Hence, *Punto umbrío* reveals that subversion and religious discourse have ceased to be Ana Rossetti's principal sources of inspiration. She is now clearly focused on the depths of her multifaceted self, a poetic self that her enchanted readers encourage her to unfold.

↬

Blanca Andréu (b. 1959) created an immense stir in 1980 with her first book of poetry, *De una niña de provincias que se vino a vivir en un Chagall* (About a girl from the provinces who came to live in a Chagall).[52] Since then, when Andréu was a "niña" of twenty-one, she has been closely watched by observers of Spain's literary life. In 1982, she published her second book—mainly of poetic prose—*Báculo de Babel* (Babel's staff).[53] Her third book, *Elphistone* (Elphistone), was published in 1988. In 1992, her first two books were translated into French.[54] As this poet and her work now command such serious attention, they warrant the critical regard of a wider audience.

Andréu's poetic personae find decay wherever they look. On one level, her texts are alogical visions of impending catastrophe; on another, they tap the tortured subconscious mind of today's youth; on still another level, they depict the horror, the doom, and despair encountered by a young woman in today's society. These modern thematic elements are expressed in a style that is both surreal and primitive: landscape dominates and intimidates the speaker. Their surrealism is comparable to that of *Poeta en Nueva York* (Poet in New York).[55] As in the Douanier Rousseau's canvases, they compose a natural landscape in which the human figure seems alien.

Like Rossetti, Andréu is involved in a struggle with her uninscribed self. Her first collection sets up a polarity between a traditional convent-educated girl from the Spanish provinces and a wild Russian girl from the steppes who suddenly finds herself living in a Chagall landscape.[56] In "Para Olga" (For Olga),[57] the background of the provincial "niña" is made clear (in phrases I italicize below):

Niña de greyes delicadamente *doradas,*
niña obsesión de la cigüeña *virgen*

. . . .

Niña que obedeció al autillo *apóstol*

. . . .

niña de crueles *sonatinas* y malévolos *libros* de Tom Wolfe,
o de encajes . . .

. . . . .

Niña pluscuamperfecta, niña que nunca fuimos.

(*Niña* 62)

(Girl of delicately gilded flocks, / obsession with the virgin-stalk
girl / . . . / Girl who obeyed the apostle-tawny owl / . . . / girl of cruel
sonatinas and malevolent books by Tom Wolfe, / or of laces . . . / . . . /
Pluperfect girl, girl we never were.)

Despite that final dismissive "girl we never were," the above syntagmas
indicate that this "provincial girl" possesses special talents for music
and literature, and that she has been imbued with her country's traditional values. As a good convent girl, she has learned her Latin—
"pluscuamperfecta"—selected as a pun, to mean "superperfect" as well
as "over and done with." This provincial "niña" has been educated, by
her family, her church, her "colegio," to be "superperfect."

There is certainly sufficient evidence in the cultural codes of her
texts to hint at the existence of a traditional bourgeois "niña" raised
to love the home, garden, animals, and cathedral town where she grew
up.[58] This "niña" appreciates music and literature.[59] Also, she has extensive knowledge of animals, trees, flora, fauna, ferns, and grasses.[60]

However, the "niña" who sympathizes with traditional cultural
values clashes in Andréu's work with one who finds traditional codes
hollow. The "niña pluscuamperfecta" mask is displaced by one referred
to as "la niña rusa" (the Russian girl [Marc Chagall was born in Rus-
sia]).[61] The following is an example from "Vendrá sin las estrellas lác-
teas" (It'll come without any milky stars):

Colegio: *niña que bebía los pomelos*
directamente en los labios de la noche,
que juraba acostarse con el miedo en la cama de nadie,
que juraba que el miedo
5   *la había violado hasta doscientos hijos.*

Amor, la niña rusa
que comulgaba reno asado
y bebía liquen.
Amor, la niña rusa que leía a Tom Wolfe.

(*Niña* 16; italics in original)

(High School: *girl who drank her grapefruits / straight out of the lips of the night, / who swore to sleep with fear in nobody's bed, / who swore that fear / had raped her into having up to two hundred children.* / Love, the Russian girl / who communed on roast reindeer / and drank lichen. / Love, the Russian girl who read Tom Wolfe.)

These lines hint at a constant preoccupation of Andréu's texts: the subversion of the ideal, provincial persona, one who—unlike the "niña rusa" in line 1 above—would have eaten her grapefruit with due decorum. The "girl who came to live in a Chagall" subverts that "girl of the provinces" by describing her latent, dark impulses and drives: she finds her school to be a site of terror and a place where she chooses to study Tom Wolfe.[62] In a later poem, the school and the "Russian girl" are again juxtaposed:

Duermo, espíritu de pupitre,
alma de la avispa párvula,
pómulo de la niña rusa que intrépida habitaba entre pingüinos
    vivos y animales de luto,
que irónica bebía arañas boreales
5   en la cuartilla lirio de la estepa.

Duermo, así, la acuárea infancia, así, el perfil niño y los
    brocales,
mármol nocturno de los pozos,
así el cierzo infantil.

Pero duermo también las brechas en la frente,
10   duermo el ahogo y el liquen malo,
duermo la sábana de arsénico que envenena las camas de los
    colegios feos,
que es tóxica a los peces que volaban
en los mares de almohada.

Duermo en la misma sábana de arsénico,
15   la misma tela de hilo de cicuta
bordada con la trenza de una agujita antigua,

la misma tela que impidió los sueños
del alto incienso blanco,

la eternidad de tiza.

(Niña 35)

(I sleep, desk-spirit, / infant wasp-soul, / cheekbone of the Russian girl who intrepidly lives among live penguins and animals in mourning, / who ironically drinks northern spiders / in the lily-notepaper of the steppes. / I sleep, thus, the Aquarian infancy, thus, the profile boy and the curbs, / nocturnal marble of the wells, / thus the infant north wind. / But I also sleep breaches in the brow, / I sleep drowning and bad lichen, / I sleep the arsenic sheet which poisons the beds in awful high schools, / which is toxic to fish that flew / in pillow's seas. / I sleep in the same arsenic sheet, / the same hemlock-linen cloth / embroidered with the braid of a tiny, ancient needle, / the same cloth that prevented dreams / of high, white incense, / the eternity of chalk.)

The depersonalized, lyrical speaker of this text "sleeps" and dreams of herself in certain horrendous situations. In the first stanza (ll. 1–5), she sees herself as the "Russian girl" thriving, like a character from a fairy tale, under the most extreme conditions in the Russian steppes. In the second stanza (ll. 6–8), she imagines herself as a child in a well of water (reminiscent of the end of García Lorca's "Romance sonámbulo" [Sleepwalking ballad]). In the third stanza (ll. 9–13), she witnesses herself under pain of mutilation and torture, and also as being poisoned by alien forces. In the final stanza (ll. 14–19), she envisions herself as part of a Greek myth: like the "cloth" of a human being's life, the *niña*'s trousseau is cut by the Fates so as to poison, kill, and repress; this *niña*'s experience prevents happiness and dreams of perfection ("dreams of high white incense"). These are the sheets which Bernarda Alba's daughters (alluded to elsewhere in the collection [30]) were set to embroider.

The Russian girl lives in a frighteningly primitive Chagall landscape, is embittered from within, and everywhere senses dread and imminent disintegration. She experiences only things that do not connect one with the other: "trees like nerves set on edge . . . weeping scythes," just as Lorca saw the "árbol de muñones" (pollarded tree) at the outset of *Poeta en Nueva York*.[63] Hence, a distinctive feature of Andréu's first collection is that it presents a fragmented sense of the female self: the poet struggles with the uninscribed "niña"-self in an attempt to articulate the authentic self of a female adolescent of the late twentieth century.

A second distinctive feature of Andréu's work is that it draws inspiration from the belief that the poet, in order to create, must sacrifice, ravage, defile, and damn the self; or (as Rimbaud put it) pulverize all five senses until they are in a state of total disarray. Andréu senses the imminent end of things. Her nightmares and hallucinations intimate catastrophe. With their incantatory formulas, her lines are reminiscent of some of the books of the Old Testament prophets; they seem to envision another Great Flood. The following poem depicts the artist in Promethean terms. However, the vultures that eat out Andréu's bowels are her own nightmares:

> Así, en pretérito pluscuamperfecto y futuro absoluto
> voy hablando del trozo del universo que yo era,
> de subcutáneas estrellas de sangre
> cazadas por el ángel de la anemia
> en el cielo arterial,
> diciendo leucocitos del alba y río de linfa,
> o bien de lo que quise:
>   el ligero Mediterráneo,
> la prohibición de envejecer,
>   la gavilla del sueño barbitúrico,
> y sobre todo, sobre todas las cosas,
> Mozart anfetamínico preámbulo de pájaros,
> Mozart en ala y aeropuerto,
> arco de violín príncipe o piloto: Mozart el Músico.
>
>   (*Niña* 24)

(Thus, in preterite pluperfect and absolute future / I keep on talking of the bit of the universe that I was, / of subcutaneous stars of blood / hunted by the angel of anemia / in the arterial sky, / speaking of leukocytes of the dawn and river of lymph, / or rather of what I liked: / the light Mediterranean, / the prohibition against growing old, / the sheaf of the barbiturate dream, / and above all, above all things, / amphetamine addict Mozart preamble of birds, / Mozart in wing and airport, / violin bow prince or pilot: Mozart the Musician.)

This is a vision of horror and disintegration coupled with a hedonistic view of life (get high on drugs and music; live in an absolute present).[64] However, the poet also undermines with irony those analytical categories which her education taught her to apply to the understanding of time; she has no grand romantic schemes, nor does she wish to speak for the whole of humanity. Hers is the voice of a self that is sick and bereft—a *damned* self that allows the artist access and insight through drugs into the subconscious mind, the "linfa" (lymph glands) and "leucocitos" (white blood cells) that constitute the heaven-sky-sea of inner toil and trauma. Her vision is nontranscendental in extremis.

Andréu visualizes inspiration, or writing poetry, as an ingesting of poison. She presents herself as a vampiress who drinks more than just blood:

Extraño no decirlo y hablar hidras pensadas
o hacer poesía de cálculo,
extraño no contarte que el cianuro Cioran viene sobre las diez,
o viene Rilke el poeta
a contarme que sí, que de veras tú pasas a mi sangre
pero de qué nos sirve.

Veneno y sombra extraña, extraño no decirlo, de metales muy fríos
y faltos de latido:
amor, es eso, yo bebo violas rotas,
pienso cosas quebradas,
en verdad yo me bebo la infancia del coñac,
bebo las locas ramas virginales,
bebo mis venas que se adormecen para querer morir,
bebo lo que me resta cuando dejo mi cuello
bajo la luna de guillotina,
bebo la sábana de los sacrificios y bebo el amor que salpica sueño,
pero de qué nos sirve.

(*Niña* 33)

(Strange not to say it and to speak thought-up hydras / or to make calculated poetry, / strange not to tell you that cyanide Cioran comes around ten o'clock, / or Rilke the poet comes / to tell me yes, that you really do get into my blood / but what's its use to us. / Poison and strange shade, strange not to say it, of very cold metals / and lack of palpitations: / love, it's that, I drink shattered violas, / I think broken things, / in truth I drink my own cognac-childhood, / I drink wild, virginal branches, / I drink my veins which get drowsy so as to wish to die, / I drink what is left to me when I leave my neck / under the guillotine moon, / I drink the sheet of sacrifices and I drink love that peppers dream, / but what's its use to us.)

The metaphor suggests that inspiration springs from ingesting corruption, from having internalized what is broken: nature (*viola*, the flower), culture (*viola*, the musical instrument), the human body ("my veins," "my neck"). The poetic persona meditates on childhood experience, on virginity, on love and passion. She sees herself as a vampire drinking blood from its own veins ("venas" is a preferred noun in the lexicon). Such creative need is presented as a type of suicide, a Dracula perversion, or a Promethean self-immolation. Andréu perceives of creation as sacrifice, and seems intent on sacrificing herself in order to write.

Andréu does not perceive of her art as giving peace or rest: "que no me den la dulce serpiente umbilical / ni la sala glucosa del útero" (let them not give me the sweet umbilical snake / nor the glucose room of the womb [14]). She perceives her art as a "salto al vacío" (jump into the void [38]). To articulate her vision, Andréu is prepared to jump into the self-destructive abyss of self. Nevertheless, on some inchoate level, Andréu believes art is needed to help people survive; that it can tentatively hint at a few, albeit indistinct, connections. In "Escucha, escúchame" (Listen, listen to me) she writes:

> Escucha, dime, siempre fue de este modo,
> algo falta y hay que ponerle un nombre,
> creer en la poesía, y en la intolerancia de la poesía,
>   y decir *niña*
> o decir *nube, adelfa*
> *sufrimiento,*
> decir *desesperada vena sola*, cosas así, casi reliquias,
>   casi lejos.
>
>   (*Niña* 20; italics in original)

(Listen, tell me, it was always this way, / something's lacking and it must be given a name, / believe in poetry, and in the intolerance of poetry, / and say *girl* / or say *cloud, oleander,* / *suffering,* / say *desperately single vein*, things like this, almost relics, / almost distant.)

This *poeta maldita* believes in her art, even though she suspects that in today's world her art is akin to a "relic" ("casi reliquias") from a former, more civilized age.[65]

A third distinctive feature of Andréu's gynocritical vision is its revision of literary stereotypes and male precursors. Andréu converts the mystics' "dark night of the soul" motif into a metaphor for artistic creation.[66] She combines the "dark night" with the metonym "hands," a traditional icon in art for prayer—and which hold the pen/phallus to write—and envisages them as cut off from the body. They are seen as autonomous objects, dipping into memory and creation by themselves:

Dame la noche que no intercede, la noche migratoria con cifras
   de cigüeña,
con la grulla celeste y su alamar guerrero,
palafrén de la ola oscuridad.
Dame tu parentesco con una sombra de oro, dame el mármol
   y su perfil leve y ciervo,
como de estrofa antigua.

Dame mis manos degolladas por la noche que no intercede,
palafrén de las más altas mareas,
mis manos degolladas entre los altos cepos y las llamas lunares,
mis manos migratorias por el cielo de agosto.

Dame mis manos degolladas por el antiguo oficio de la infancia,
mis manos que sajaron el cuello de la noche,
el destello del sueño con metáforas verdes,
el vino blasonado que se quedó dormido.

(Niña 47)

(Give me night that does not intercede, the migratory night with
ciphers of stork, / with the celestial crane and its warlike frog, /
palfrey-wave of darkness. / Give me your kinship with a gold shade,
give me marble / and its slight, stag profile, / like an ancient stanza's. /
Give me my hands cut off by night that does not intercede, / palfrey of
the highest tides, / my hands cut off between the highest boughs and
the lunar flames, / my migratory hands in the August sky. / Give me
my hands cut off by the ancient office of infancy, / my hands that cut
the night's neck open, / the glimmer of the dream with green
metaphors, / the emblazoned wine that fell asleep.)

The selection of "noche" (night) suggests the negativity of the "dark
night of the soul," but as is hinted at in the coital imagery of the first
stanza, night for Andréu is the time for creation.[67] In this night, the
poet's hands are "severed" ("mis manos degolladas"), but wrestle in
darkness to encounter light ("the glimmer of the dream"). These severed hands dipping into darkness figure the poet's hands, which hold
the pen, touch the keys, in order to give form to the poem.[68] Hence,
Andréu appropriates the mystics' "dark night of the soul" and gives it
both a terrestrial and feminist twist.

    Andréu also revises an aspect of Juan Ramón Jiménez's decadent
persona. The imagery and rhythm of the following lines allude to those

early Jiménez poems in which an effete neurasthenic took great pleasure in imagining his own death and burial:[69]

> Así morirán mis manos oliendo a espliego falso
> y morirá mi cuello plástico de musgo,
> así morirá mi colonia de piano o rosa tinta.
> Así la luz rayada,
> la forma de mi forma,
> mis calcetines de hilo,
> así mi pelo que antes fue barba bárbara de babilonios
> decapitados por Semíramis.
> Por último mis senos gramaticalmente elípticos
> o las anchas caderas que tanto me hicieron llorar.
> Por último mis labios que demasiado feroces se volvieron,
> el griego hígado,
> el corazón medieval,
> la mente cabalgadura.
>
> Así morirá mi cuerpo de arco cuya clave es ninguna,
> es la música haciendo de tiempo,
> verde música sacra con el verde del oro.
>
> (Niña 22)

(And so will my hands die smelling of imitation lavender and / my plastic neck of moss will die, as will / my dyed rose or piano colony. / So will the lined light, / form of my form, / my linen socks, / and my hair which earlier was barbarous beard of Babylonians / decapitated by Semiramis. / And last, my grammatically elliptical breasts / or the wide hips that made me weep so much. / And last, my lips which became too ferocious, / the Greek liver, / the medieval heart, / the mount-mind. / And so my arc body will die whose key is none at all, / it's music making time, / green sacred-music with the green of gold.)

The speaker here is conversant with many pre- and post-Christian cultures and traditions (Babylonian, Greek, medieval). She presents a dehumanized lyrical persona who envisions each part of herself dying off in the service of those civilizations—for the greater glory of art. The last line—"green sacred-music with the green of gold," which again recalls the "Sleepwalking Ballad"—caps a stanza which implies that the artist's body dies—not to elicit sympathy from friends, as in Jiménez—but to bring "music" into "time." [70]

Andréu also selects the myths surrounding Ophelia for revision. In

"Y quisimos dormir el sueño bárbaro" (And we wanted to sleep the barbarous dream), Ophelia's drowning is alluded to:

> y cómo apoderarse de algas y catedrales y de la lencería
>   de lágrima y de luz y terciopelo de la virgen Virginia
>   que alienta los muertómetros,
> que ondea disfrazada de Ofelia por los lagos.
>
> *(Niña* 44)

(and how can one take possession of algae and cathedrals and linen / of tear and light and velvet of the virgin Virginia / which feeds the death meters, / which floats on the lakes disguised as Ophelia.)

In these lines the poet is protesting against the condition assigned Ophelia by culture. Andréu is aware that if she fulfills society's traditional expectations for the female of the species—cathedrals, linen, tears, velvet, virgin—she will end up as another drowned Ophelia. For her, the problem is how to strip the accretions of seaweed from off this image of woman.

Moreover, Andréu takes Ophelia and transforms her—as did Atencia—into an artist who creates before she drowns. The first stanza of her longest poem reads:

> Cinco poemas para abdicar,
> para que sean un destello terrestre en mi tránsito
> mientras el vaivén de mi cuerpo me dote de viejo sueño y
>   tenga un altar adornado,
> mientras mis ojos suspendan la aspersión del líquido más
>   breve,
> 5   abandonen su aire lacustre y la ligereza de la lágrima cóncava
>   en donde beben grullas
> y otras zancudas con pie de bailarina,
> mientras mis manos sean hangares en las salinas negras para
>   aviones de turbios vuelos,
> mientras el súcubo murciélago diga en mi oído espuma y
>   diga oscuridad
> en las marinas negras.
>
> *(Niña* 28)

(Five poems before abdicating, / that they may be a terrestrial flash in my transit / while my body's to-and-fro can endow me with old dream and I can have a throne adorned, / while my eyes can stop the sprinkling of the briefest liquid, / can forsake their marshy air and the shallowness of the concave tear in which cranes drink, / and other wading birds with the foot of a ballerina / while my hands can be hangars on the black salt flats for planes of turbulent flights, / while the succubus bat can speak into my foam ear and can tell darkness / on the black coasts.)

In these lines, the lyrical subject is disintegrating and imagines herself floating in water (the floating bride was also one of Chagall's motifs). In this long poem, the Ophelia figure is surrounded by cranes and other long-legged wading birds (e.g., flamingos). Her hands provide shelter for objects (e.g., dragonflies), while perverted bats spray foam into her ears.[71] Andréu's Ophelia is conscious of impending disaster, but before she drowns (l. 3), she wants to produce "five poems" which will be "a terrestrial flash in my transit." This Ophelia throws herself into the river of destruction—for love of art, not for love of man—but creates instead of succumbing to the waters of oblivion. Moreover, in one of the last poems of the collection, the Ophelia-persona floats at night in the life/death sea of creation, and again sinks her hands into its waters to create:

Hundiré mis manos en noche que no existe sobre un mar que
    no existe,
mi garganta entre anzuelos de la flora marítima,
en agua ebria y en buques como pájaros,
en aquello que no será posible,
en todo lo que se alza cuando la noche se alza,
cuando encalla su cornamenta de ciervo temible y solloza,
estrofa antílope o estrella en metro antiguo,
y andará la locura como un óleo escarlata,

. . . .

Hundiré mis manos en este lugar leve donde duermen secretas
    las marinas flamígeras,
y hablaremos de las direcciones y de las cosas de la muerte,
y de las rutas, y de sus atrios abrasados.

                                                    (*Niña* 57-58)

(I shall sink my hands into night that does not exist on a sea that does not exist, / my throat among fishhooks of marine flora, / into intoxicated water and into ships like birds, / into that which will not be possible, / into all that rears itself up when the night rears itself up, / when it runs aground its dreadful stags' antlers and sobs, / antelope stanza or star in ancient meter, / and madness will walk about like a scarlet oil

painting, / . . . / I shall sink my hands into this slight spot where
flamboyant ships sleep secretly, / and we shall speak of directions and
of the things of death, / of routes, and of their burnt atriums.)

In this hallucinatory episode, Andréu reveals that "negative capability"
which we have already observed in Francisca Aguirre and Clara Janés:
a capacity for passively experiencing circumambient nature, a nature
that may be real, or one that is imagined in dreams. For Andréu, there
is a terrible violence, a horror, and a lack of connectedness, in her culture—but she will wrest from its motifs what she can to survive.

Andréu's revisionary mythmaking is the major characteristic of
Elphistone, her last book of poetry to date, in which the Galician Andréu
reveals another facet of her poetic persona: her fascination for myths
and legends of a seafaring nature.[72] She constructs a personal legend
around a figure called Elphistone, whom she had mentioned in a 1986
interview as: "el pálido fantasma del capitán Elphistone, que me ronda
y me cuenta naufragios" ("pale Captain Elphistone who haunts me and
tells me about shipwrecks" [Saval and García Gallego, *Litoral* 92]).

Her Captain Elphistone is a dark and enigmatic masculine figure
from the past, from a past that haunts the poet. He hints at the tyrannical, malevolent, and self-engrossed males of Western culture, but
Andréu's tone and perspective preclude such a suspicious reading. The
poems do actualize—intermittently—a sociopolitical code and hint,
perhaps, at the phallocratic institutions and culture from which Spain
has suffered, particularly from 1939 to 1975, but the text itself encourages no such interpretation. For my present purposes it would be con-
venient if Elphistone were a frigid and selfish patriarchal figure (like
Rossetti's Nietzsche). But he/it is not. Any allusions to such realities
are displaced by thoughts of a symbolic, psychological, and esthetic
nature. Captain Elphistone may be the masculine that haunts the poet
and which she wishes to confront, to exorcize, in order to develop as an
artist. He/it could represent, in Jungian terms, her animus which she
is impelled to explore.[73]

In the penultimate poem, "La partida" (The departure), the speaker
refers directly to Elphistone: "Como un rey de este mundo perdido en
la leyenda" (*Elphistone* 63). In fact, "Elphistone" recalls other mythical
kings and captains of art and poetry: W. B. Yeats's Celtic kings, Cuchu-
lain and Fergus; the Flying Dutchman, the ghost ship of Wagner; and
Coleridge's Ancient Mariner. "Final" (The end), the final poem of the
collection, identifies him as a pirate:[74]

Nada escucha Elphistone—Je suis de mon coeur le vampire—
cuando evalúa significados, pecios de viejos libros, de otros navíos,
vendavales o la repentina conciencia que elimina
una firme navegación.—Húmeda luna que recuerdas
el frío norte de la sangre, quién está haciendo la cuenta,
quién dirige las reputaciones más podridas que las tablas del barco,
    calafateadas
con muerte, quién—bajo los ángeles rapaces y herméticos—
ordena la inmortalidad, examina las pérdidas, rescata los prejuicios
    y aseveraciones
que nunca, en nigún lugar, por más que o a pesar de.
Y los apremios y las victorias—cinco presas—y la elegancia
en la piratería, oscuro capitán Elphistone, cuando la luna mira
    tu dignidad
ardiendo sobre la avaricia del cielo.

(Elphistone 67)

(Elphistone listens to nothing—"the vampire I am of my own heart"—
/ when he assesses meanings, the flotsam of old books, of other ships, /
storms or the unexpected awareness that revokes / a resolute course.—
Oh, humid moon who recalls / the cold north of the blood, who is
keeping tabs, / who controls reputations more rotten than a ship's
planks caulked / with death, who—under the predatory, hermetic
angels—/ ordains immortality, examines the losses, redeems prejudices
and assertions / which never, in no place, no matter how much or in
spite of. / And the judgments and the victories—five booties—and the
elegance / in piracy, obscure Captain Elphistone, when the moon
beholds your dignity / blazing above the avarice of the sky.)

This loved-and-hated, absent, godlike Elphistone represents the gestation of a polyfacetic legend:[75] "Con sus grandes botas pisotea la tierra /
con la sombra que divide" (with his huge boots he stomps the earth /
with the shadow that divides [*Elphistone* 19]); he has a "mueca defini-
tivamente fría como un hueso" (grimace as definitively cold as a bone
[*Elphistone* 20]). Death surrounds his ship (*Elphistone* 21); and "El viento
del norte como un cadáver . . . golpea en la popa" (the wind from the
north lashes against the poop like a corpse [*Elphistone* 43]). Moreover,
it appears that nothing exists beyond "allí donde no alcanza / el silbato
del capitán Elphistone" (there where Captain Elphistone's whistle does
not reach [*Elphistone* 43]).
    Moreover, Elphistone is identified with a force whose figure in the

texts is a horse—one that reminds us of Picasso's "Guernica": "un caballo que en la bodega relincha" (a horse who neighs in the hold [*Elphistone* 43]). However, toward the end of the book, the horse/Elphistone is
associated with truth and beauty, to which no one pays attention today.
Two passages from the long, revisionary folkloric poem, "Fábula de la
fuente y el caballo" (Fable of the fount and the horse), read:

> Era un caballo ateniense. En sus ojos brillaba el fuego
> de la verdad y la belleza,
> pero nadie lo conoció.
> Ese caballo que ahora viene vigilante hasta este poema
> con los ojos agrandados por el insomnio de la muerte,
> con la mirada de mi hermano y la sonrisa de fábula
> a veces miraba a los hombres,
> pero los hombres no sabían prestar atención a un caballo.
> Ni el sabio ni el indiferente se preocuparon de indagar.
>
> (*Elphistone* 49)

> En el interior de un verso sueco descansa la soledad
> y ahora ha llegado a este poema antes del amanecer
> con grandes ojos semejantes a los de un antiguo profeta,
> con ojos que no se preguntan si fue dios quien hizo la
> muerte,
> con grandes ojos elevados
> a la categoría de potencias.
>
> (*Elphistone* 50)

> (It was an Athenian horse. In its eyes burned the fire / of truth and
> beauty, / but nobody recognized it. / That horse, which now comes
> watchful to this poem / with eyes dilated by the insomnia of death, /
> with the look of my brother and a fable's smile, / looks at men at
> times, / but men don't know how to attend a horse. / Neither the wise
> nor the aloof bothered to inquire. . . . In the interior of a line of verse
> that plays dumb solitude rests / and now it's arrived at this poem
> before dawn / with large eyes similar to those of an ancient prophet, /
> with eyes that do not ask if it was god who made / death, / with large
> eyes elevated / to the category of powers.)

In *Elphistone*, Blanca Andréu is conscious of certain fragile truths that
have disappeared from our modern world, truths that she would like to
foreground in the form of a modern *celtic-andréu* myth. The fact that
she selects a male figure may well indicate her desire to appropriate the

androcentric past so as to deploy it in her own self-discovery. Hence, it may be that Elphistone represents the black shadow of the androcentric poetic tradition that has inspired Andréu to date. He represents the "anxiety of authority" which she is working through. That she is engaged on that process is hinted at by her silence during the last few years: in retreat, searching perhaps for Hestia—that unsung goddess of nontranscendent vision.[76]

As the reader will have noted, Andréu's gynocentric style draws on a woman-centered lexicon. Indeed, in her second book, *Báculo de Babel*, in which there are signs of hope ("pero hay claraboyas nuevas en la lírica muerte" [but there are new skylights in the death lyric (*Báculo* 13)])—she selects the metaphor of blood as a sign of potential rebirth and regeneration.

Rebirth is figured in two of the leitmotifs of the volume: the month of May (i.e, the spring solstice with its associations of sacrifice and renewal) and the angel (which in the Old Testament is also associated with slaughter). The lyrical voice speaks of "el fondo oscuro de mayo mi lengua morada micénica" (the dark depth of May in my purple, Mycenic tongue [*Báculo* 25]). "Morada" hints at blood, and Mycenae is related to epic poetry.[77] The poetic persona of *Báculo* is in empathetic touch with an epic, poetic past; she exclaims: "condúceme con mi corazón desconocido a la puerta de las tiendas todas donde venden altísimas gravitaciones ángeles infinitamente confusos" (lead me with my unknown heart to the door of all those shops where infinitely confused angels sell the highest gravitations [*Báculo* 27]). Elsewhere she maintains that: "sangro luz . . . arrastro mi sueño . . . originado por el ángel que divulga la sangre" (I bleed light . . . haul my dream . . . initiated by the angel that disseminates blood [*Báculo* 35]); at the end of this poem, she says: "emerjo . . . arrastrando y dejando ángulos letras que penden de los cielos de la sangre la sed" (I emerge . . . dragging and leaving angles-letters that hang from the skies of blood thirst [*Báculo* 35]). That Old Testament angel who decreed death has been given new life by Andréu.

Blood is an apposite symbol in that by shedding blood a woman's body renews itself. Whereas, for a man, to shed blood is to die—the worst possible shedding of blood being castration. Maybe for that reason, the ancient patriarchs wrote out of the discourses that have come down to us all reference to the blood of the primal mother, all allusions to the notion that her menstrual blood coagulates to give life. Andréu may be recuperating the prepatriarchal symbolic connotations for that holy blood of life.

In conclusion, although no one can predict how this poet's stunning, regenerative imagination will develop, and although at this time it is difficult to describe with real clarity her poetic imagination,[78] I trust that readers can sense that Blanca Andréu is unique in the way she perceives and presents her hallucinatory visions; she has evolved from her early desire to shock and is now beginning to inscribe a personal, female vision within her work. Blanca Andréu's poetic talent is diverse but powerful. Her work bears the historical weight of both Hispanic and European poetic traditions. The Galician Andréu's great-great-grandmother is Rosalía de Castro, and although I detect no struggle with Rosalía, Andréu herself will be aware of the weight of the Rosalía tradition on Hispanic poetry and on herself as a Galician. I cannot help but view the impact of Blanca Andréu's first book as comparable to that of Jiménez's *Ninfeas* and *Almas de violeta* at the beginning of this century, books whose style we now suspect and whose content we tend to discount but which heralded the emergence of a poetic genius in Hispanic poetry. In addition, it is clear to me that Andréu has confronted head-on the potentially stultifying tradition of Lorca's *Poeta en Nueva York* and that her struggle to appropriate and rework its originality is not in vain. As she springs from such strong and fertile traditions in Hispanic poetry, I await with intrigue her future visions (in the belief that her silence is temporary). For the above reasons and more, Blanca Andréu has attracted an important following—and numerous imitators—in Spain today. She is someone whom we—"en el otro costado" (on the other side)—need to watch.

Amorós, Rossetti, and Andréu are paradigmatic of recent developments in Spanish poetry. They find their initial literary inspiration in very different traditions—French Symbolism, Baroque culture, surrealism—and articulate distinct gynocentric visions. While there is protest in Rossetti, each of these poets is involved with female self-discovery and with the inscription of authentic—and audaciously new—female selves within Spanish poetry.

Notes

1. The year of Amorós's birth is never given. However, in her most recent book it was revealed that she was born on February 4 (*Arboles 115*). José Olivio Jiménez, in his astute commentary on *La honda travesía del águila*, states: "que Amparo Amorós vela tercamente la fecha de su nacimiento como aspirando a que se la considere intemporalmente 'transgene-

racional'" ([she] obdurately veils her date of birth as if she were aspiring to be considered intemporally 'transgenerational'" ["Ausencia" 183]).

2. *Las diosas blancas* went immediately into a second, revised, edition. I refer to the first edition. For Buenaventura's account of the four major attacks on the anthology and details of his defense, see Saval and García Gallego, *Litoral* 238–43. Editorial Hiperión regularly publishes poetry by women (in excellent editions), especially by the "white goddess" group. Two important anthologies appeared, one from *Litoral* and the other by Luzmaría Jiménez Faro. And publishing houses (e.g., Torremozas) dedicated to producing only poetry by women have arisen in the last few years.

3. Rossetti started off the eighties with *Los devaneos de Erato* (1980); her most recent book is *Punto umbrío* (1995). Amorós's first publication is *Ludia* (1983) and her most recent is *Arboles en la música* (1995). Andréu published *De una niña de provincias que se vino a vivir en un Chagall* in 1980, *Báculo de Babel* in 1982, and *Elphistone* in 1988.

4. They have been called *culturalistas* (culturalists) and the *escuela veneciana* (Venetian school) because of their frequent intertextual references to Western culture (especially to Grecian and to fin-de-siècle themes and movements). They use literature, cinema, music, art, architecture, history, etc. in the exploration of their poetic personae.

5. For Coronado, see Torres Nebrera. For interviews see Fernández-Rubio, "Ana Rossetti"; Armada, "Luisa Castro"; and Cruz Ruiz, "Almudena Guzmán."

6. Moreover, her complete poems to 1992, *Visión y destino: Poesía 1982–1992* (Vision and destiny: Poetry) have already appeared; they contain some unpublished material, a thirty-page introduction, and a complete bibliography. Her second volume was immediately translated into French and her most recent is to be published soon in a bilingual edition.

7. For the poet's observations on *Ludia*, see Ugalde, *Conversaciones* 85.

8. Amorós herself objects to such an idea, see Ugalde, *Conversaciones* 78, 81, 82.

9. With respect to Amorós's poem "No la menor distancia," the reader might wish to compare it with a Cavafy poem, employed by Martín Gaite in her recent *La reina de las nieves* (311): "Cuando el viaje emprendas hacia Itaca / haz votos por que sea larga la jornada. / Llegar allí es tu vocación. / No debes, sin embargo, forzar la travesía."

10. In Ugalde's *Conversaciones*, Amorós—like the French Symbolists—emphasizes the importance of music in her esthetics.

11. Lyotard writes: "I will use the term *modern* to designate any science that legitimates itself with reference to a metadiscourse . . . making an explicit appeal to some grand narrative, such as the dialectics of Spirit, . . . the emancipation of the rational or working subject, or the creation of wealth"

(*Postmodern* xxiii). "I define *postmodern* as incredulity toward metanarratives" (xxiv).

12. For Amorós's discussion of the nihilist temptation, see Ugalde, *Conversaciones* 86.

13. See her "Novísimos" (esp. 66) for where she situates herself. In this article she also discusses "la poética del silencio" (poetics of silence).

14. Ugalde, *Conversaciones* (xiii) writes of the feminist erotic relationship: "El «yo», sujeto masculino, y el «tú», objeto femenino, en la tradición petrarquesca, renacen como un «nosotros» que se comparte con igualdad" (The "I," masculine subject, and the "you," feminine object, in the Petrarchan tradition, are reborn as an "us" that is shared equally). For Amorós's discussion of an erotic pre-text for parts of *Ludia*, see Ugalde, *Conversaciones* 89. And for her belief that "luz" not "oscuridad" predominates in her work, see Ugalde, *Conversaciones* 90.

15. Breysse, in his introduction to the French version of *La honda travesía del águila* alludes to a certain feminism in Amorós's intentions (Amorós, *Profonde traversée* 10–11). He also discusses the intellectual poetic trend to which she belongs (8–9).

16. For the female hero's quest for a lost "green world" of matrilineal roots, consult Sherno ("Gloria Fuertes' Room"), who discusses Daphne (87) and explains Annis Pratt's and Carol Christ's concepts of female development.

17. For a very different reading of this poem—more objective than mine —see Debicki, "Life as Art" 34–36.

18. See for example, "La cita" (*Visión y destino* 194–96), a volume that also contains some unpublished poems in which Amorós is developing her thoughts on poetics.

19. For Amorós's comments on the sonnet, see her "Los novísimos" (67).

20. The reader can consult Debicki, "Life as Art" (44–47), for an extensive discussion. Debicki had been provided with a prepublication photocopy of the text.

21. *Indicios* also includes all her previously published poetry. *Yesterday* is principally an anthology. Since the late 1980s, Rossetti has devoted herself to drama and the novel. However, her fifth book, *Punto umbrío*, appeared as this book went to press.

22. *Devaneos* received the II Premio Gules de Poesía, for which one of the judges was Francisco Brines. *Devocionario* received the III Premio Internacional de Poesía Rey Juan Carlos I. For interviews, see for example *El País (suplemento)*, March 8, 1987, 32–33. Her novel, *Plumas de España*, was not well received, but it was reviewed immediately: see Angel Basanta's review, *ABC (Literario)*, April 9, 1988, 4; and Leopoldo Azancot's in *El País (III Libros)*, March 20, 1988, 17

23. "Erato" was the muse of amorous or erotic poetry and, according to an American critic (De Mott, "Yarnsmith" 3), she had an intense sexual drive. Rossetti herself alludes to Erato and in her interview with Jesús Fernández Palacios, reprinted as a prologue to *Indicios vehementes*, Rossetti affirms: "Yo no evoco por añoranza, pero utilizo el pasado como fuente de conocimiento, como única experiencia. Además, ¿tengo yo la culpa de que las musas sean hijas de Mnemosine?" (I do not evoke out of longing, but I use the past as a source of knowledge, as unique experience. Besides, am I to blame that the Muses are daughters of Mnemosine? [14]). The nine daughters of Mnemosine and Jupiter/Zeus, who are the nine poetic muses, are: Calliope, muse of epic poetry; Clio, of history; Euterpe, of lyric poetry; Melpomene, of the Tragedy; Terpsichore, of song and chorus; Erato, of love poetry; Polimnia or Polihimnia, of sacred poetry; Urania, of astronomy; Talia, of comedy. See Gayley, *Classic Myths* 37. I must emphasize that there is no unanimous consensus on the names and functions of the muses: see the *Oxford Classical Dictionary* (704).

24. Like Rossetti's first books, *Los devaneos de Erato* and *Dióscuros*, are unobtainable today. I cite only from *Indicios vehementes*.

25. See also, "Cierta secta feminista se da consejos prematrimoniales" (A certain feminist sect gives premarital advice [*Indicios* 36–37]).

26. Rossetti says these poems were inspired by the "ambientes de casa de mi abuela" (atmosphere and surroundings of my grandmother's house [Ugalde, *Conversaciones* 155])

27. See also, "Onán" (*Indicios* 52).

28. For Rossetti's "estructura[s] cuidadosa[s]" (careful structures) see Ugalde, *Conversaciones* 169.

29. See also, "Nikeratos renuncia al disimulo," "Una enemiga mía sueña con el diablo," "Diotima a su muy aplicado discípulo," "Murmullos en la habitación de al lado," and "Anatomía del beso" (*Indicios* 23, 26, 40, 41, and 44 respectively).

30. See also in *Los devaneos:* "El gladiolo blanco de mi primera comunión se vuelve púrpura" (*Indicios* 25); and in *Dióscuros:* "Dos," "Cuatro," "Cinco," "Siete," (*Indicios* 69, 71, 72, and 74 respectively).

31. See also, "El jardín de tus delicias" and "A un traje de pana verde que por ahí anda perturbando a los muchachos" (*Indicios* 22 and 43 respectively).

32. For Rossetti's own comments on this poem, see Ugalde, *Conversaciones* 156.

33. See Ferradans, "Revelación"; Makris, "Mass Media" 241–46; and Rosas and Cramsie, "Apropriación" 5–6.

34. For the Rabelaisian carnival of desire in Rossetti, the truly postmodern reader might wish to consult Servodidio's implosive "Ana Rossetti."

35. Therefore, Rossetti's muse has become Polimnia, or Polihimnia—the muse of sacred poetry. Rossetti began to focus on girls' religious educa-

tion in *Dióscuros*. For a more extensive analysis of *Devocionario*, see Ugalde, "Erotismo" and "Subversión"; and Wilcox, "Observaciones."

36. For a detailed account of the profound impression religious books and church rites made on her young mind, see Ugalde, *Conversaciones* 151–52.

37. Greene and Kahn quote Barthes on the gynaeceum: "the feminine world of *Elle*, a world without men, but entirely constituted by the gaze of the man, is very exactly that of the gynaeceum" (*Making* 4).

38. Compare the first chapter of Esther Tusquets's *El mismo mar de todos los veranos*.

39. In "Festividad del dulcísimo nombre" (Festivity of the sweetest name), upon receiving the host, the body of Christ, the young speaker says: "enamorada yo / entreabría mi boca, mientras mi cuerpo todo / tu cuerpo recibía" (enamored, I would open my mouth, while my whole body / received yours in its entirety [*Devocionario* 13]). Later, upon drinking the wine, Christ's blood, in "Exaltación de la preciosa sangre" (Exaltation of the precious blood), she concludes: "Labios míos temblando, del precioso regalo / de tu mano, tiñéndose. Tu sabor penetrando / mi inviolada saliva, comulgándose, / y el fervor confundido en delirio de besos" (Lips of mine, trembling, becoming stained / by the precious gift / from your hand. Your taste penetrating / my inviolate saliva, receiving communion, / and the ardor mingled with a delirium of kisses [*Devocionario* 14]).

40. For example, Rossetti was fixated on the idea that religious language was the ideal register for the expression of profound feelings and emotions. And she was overwhelmed by the past: "No me pidáis que vuelva, / pues la inocencia es irrecuperable" (Don't ask me to go back / for innocence is irretrievable [*Indicios* 54]). She told Coco: "Las primeras noticias de las palabras de amor, yo las tuve a través del devocionario, porque en todas las plegarias de antes y después de la comunión, en todos los himnos, yo adivinaba un amor superior a cualquier otro de cualquier literatura. Yo no he visto decir a ningún amante, ni a ningún novio, palabras tan encendidas, tan ardientes como las que se pueden decir a Jesús" (My first knowledge of words of love came through the prayerbook, because in the prayers spoken before and after communion, in all hymns, I detected a love that was superior to any other in any literature. I have never seen words as inflamed, as ardent as those spoken to Jesus, addressed to any lover or boyfriend ["Verdadera" 53]).

41. In "Custodio Mío" (*Devocionario* 40–41), love is seen as an executioner, whom the poetic persona hates, and at whom she screams "apártate de mí" (get thee from me)—in a deliberate subversive parody of Christ's words to the devil (see Matthew 4.1–11). See also "Just Call Me the Angel of the Morning" (*Devocionario* 46–47), where her experience as an adolescent is seen to have harmed her capacity to love.

42. For Rossetti's doubt and distrust, see Ugalde (*Conversaciones* 160), where she also implies that her attitudes began to change when her friends began to die of AIDS. Suicide is a constant theme of *Indicios vehementes*. Rossetti has confessed, in an interview with Emilio Coco, that "El durmiente" (The Sleeper [*Indicios* 87–88]): "salió de un amigo mío que se suicidó tomándose unas pastillas" (was inspired by a friend of mine who committed suicide by taking pills ["Verdadera" 52]). Another poem presents the interior monologue of a person who is on the verge of committing suicide ("Ahora" [*Indicios* 83–84]); another reflects on the suicide—in 1949— of an American politician, James Forrestal (1892–1949 [81–82]).

43. "Purifícame" is based on a line from the well-known prayer of Saint Ignatius of Loyola—"Agua del costado de Cristo, purifícame."

44. *Indicios* reveals Rossetti's fascination with the deaths of the young English Romantics: Chatterton (1752–70 [90–91]), Keats (1795–1821 [89]), and Shelley (1792–1822 [85–86]); and another deals with the drowning of the German poet, Carolina von Günderode (1780–1806 [92–93]); and see n. 42 above.

45. As she did in "Introito," where the speaker splits herself in two heteronymous selves and describes herself to herself through her *other*— "desconocido mío" (my unknown self)—as engulfed in "la tristeza" and "de la soledad . . . soberana" (sadness . . . sovereign of solitude [79–80]).

46. Twelve, not fourteen, syllables in Spanish.

47. Lines 15 and 23 are scanned as hendecasyllables only if the use of syneresis ("caverna húmeda") and diaeresis ("pues") is accepted.

48. For Rossetti's preference for the style of seventeenth-century Spanish poetry, see Ugalde, *Conversaciones* 162.

49. For Jiménez, see "Elegíaca" in *Almas de violeta* (*Primeros libros* 1537), and "Los gusanos de la muerte / harán su nido en mi pecho, / donde el corazón un día / alzó fragancia de ensueños" (The worms of death / will make their nest in my chest, / where my heart once / raised its fragrance of dreams [from *Arias tristes* (*Primeros libros* 291–92)]). For Machado, see "Fue una clara tarde triste y soñolienta / tarde de verano. La hiedra asomaba / al muro del parque, negra y polvorienta" (It was a clear, sad, and dreamy / evening, summer evening. Black and dusty ivy peeked / over the wall of the park [91]), and "Me dijo un alba de la primavera" (A spring dawn told me [108]).

50. These are Sandra Gilbert's words, in relation to Mary Elizabeth Coleridge, in "Literary Paternity" (493).

51. For example, José Infante has written in his introduction to her *Devocionario* that Ana Rossetti's religion is "la . . . del cuerpo" and that "el erotismo no sólo está en su boca. . . . Está en la cosmovisión de su pensamiento" (the body's . . . eroticism is not only in her mouth . . . it's in her entire mental outlook [7 and 8]).

52. Andréu, *De una niña*, 3d rev. ed., with a prologue by Francisco Umbral (Madrid: Hiperión, 1983). For her present rejection of Umbral and his "insolence," see her interview with Mora ("Memoria"). For the origin of this title—chosen by a friend—and for the solecism it contains, see Ugalde, *Conversaciones* 254-55; and Sherno, "Between Water and Fire" (534). The book received the Premio Adonais.

53. Andréu, *Báculo*, 2d ed. (Madrid: Hiperión, 1986). It received the "Premio Mundial de Poesía mística Fernando Rielo." A poet does not necessarily have to be a "mystic" (i.e., a San Juan or a Santa Teresa) to receive this prize. I translate literally from their 1987 English flyer: "There is a sign which justifies this initiative [a prize for mystical poetry]: the growing sensitivity to the celestial transcendence of the human spirit in the face of the physicalistic materialism which powerfully conditions the contemporary dialectic. The mystical model holding primacy over this prize is oriented toward a mastery of elevated spirituality in the context of authentic literary creation; its moral substance involves a poet's expressing a state of 'being in love' with God. The stringency of this model should, however, be tempered by human understanding and openness which will permit the prize's being awarded to poets who, though distinguished more for their literary creativity than their mystical wealth, contribute a sensibility worthy of respect. This prize is also grounded in a mystical premise: a response to the need besetting true poets who, though not classifiable as mystics in terms of a typical definition, nevertheless dream buried in a datum essential to art the mystery of suffering is the poet's companion."

54. And in 1995, Hiperión issued all three of these books in one volume. In addition, Andréu figures rather prominently in the 1995 La Pléiade anthology of ten centuries of Spanish poetry in *Anthologie bilingue de la poésie espagnole*.

55. She discusses her surrealism with Ugalde, *Conversaciones* 252-53. Sherno's recent "Between Water and Fire" contains very illuminating comments on Andréu's surrealism (533-37).

56. On Chagall and Andréu, see Newton ("Reflexión" 195-96). She also provides detailed readings of several poems from *De una niña*.

57. It is one of two with a title in the *augmented* collection of twenty-nine poems. The other title is in Italian, "Maggio."

58. I adapt the term "cultural code" from Roland Barthes, who in *S/Z* analyzed the manner in which codes constitute a literary text. With respect to home and garden, the poet selects, for example: "la casa . . . y el álamo . . . o jardín feo" (the house . . . and the poplar . . . or ugly garden [29]), "piano" (piano [21]), "salones" and "balcones" (rooms, balconies [29-30, 44]), "los ventanales empapados" (large windows soaked [59]), "alfileres y horquillas de una niña de nácar que te besa los pies y los guarda en vitrinas" (brooches and hairpins of a mother-of-pearl girl who kisses

your feet and keeps them in display cabinets [45]). In addition, Andréu writes "para mi caballo" (for my horse [32]), of "mis antiguas láminas de mica" (my old mica engravings [44]), and of a "colegio" ("la lengua llena de espuma de colegio" [tongue full of foam of grammar school (43)]). Other images depend on familiarity with a large church (probably inspired by Orihuela, see Ugalde, *Conversaciones* 251): "la catedral" and "el claustro" (cathedral, cloister [14]), "ojos litúrgicos agrandados de antorchas" (liturgical eyes enlarged by torches [39]).

Architectural terms are not uncommon: "ojiva," "arbotante," "manuelino," "peraltada" (pointed arch, flying buttress, Manueline, cambered). (Manueline is the Portuguese style of architecture of the fifteenth and sixteenth centuries.)

59. Shakespeare, the Arthurian legend, and Byzantine history are alluded to; numerous writers and musicians are mentioned by name: Rilke, Rimbaud, Baudelaire, Saint-John Perse, Cioran, Pavese, Garcilaso, Quevedo, Lorca, Juan Ramón Jiménez, Virgil, Mozart, Bach. Such allusions reflect the "culturalismo" of the time (see n. 4 above). On this, see also her interview with Ugalde. In my opinion, Andréu is ill at ease with both high culture—Alejandría, Rilke—and with the *culturalista* style of the time.

60. In their dream sequences the texts refer to beasts of the air ("pájaro, paloma, tórtola, cigüeña, perdiz, búho, autillo, alondra, corneja, urraca, tordo, mirlo, arrendajo, libélula, luciérnaga, murciélago, avispa, araña" [bird, dove, turtledove, stork, partridge, owl, tawny owl, lark, crow, magpie, thrush, blackbird, jay, dragonfly, glowworm, wasp, spider]); they also refer to water animals ("pato, oca, ánade, ánsar, albatros, gaviota, grulla, peces, pulpo, pingüino, hipocampo, rana, sapo" [duck, goose, duck [or goose], [wild or tule] goose, albatross, seagull, crane, fishes, squid, penguin, sea horse, frog, toad]); and they allude to animals on land ("caballo, palafrén, potro, yegua, reno, corzo, ciervo, chacal, jabalí, antílope, búfalo, gato, saurio, tiranosaurio, dinosaurio, pterodáctilo, topo, serpiente, lombriz, escorpión, cucaracha" [horse, palfrey, colt, mare, reindeer, roe deer, stag, jackal, wild boar, antelope, buffalo, cat, saurian, tyrannosaur, dinosaur, pterodactyl, mole, serpent, worm, scorpion, cockroach]). The poems also refer to trees ("cipreses, álamo, cerezo, abedules, roble, encina, castaño" [cypresses, poplar, cherry, birch, oak, holm oak, chestnut]); to fruits ("zarza, zarzamora, mora, pomelo" [blackberry, blackberry bush, mulberry, grapefruit]); to spices ("espliego, romero, laurel" [lavender, rosemary, laurel]); to ferns, grasses, weeds ("liquen, yedra, musgo, cicuta, tojo, ortiga, helecho, lianas" [lichen, ivy, moss, hemlock, gorse, nettle, fern, liana]); to shrubs ("adelfa, magnolia, hortensia" [oleander, magnolia, hydrangea]) and to flowers ("jazmín, ciclamen, anémona, lirio, lila, jacinto, pasionaria, vinca, amaranta" [jasmine, cyclamen, anemone, lily,

lilac, hyacinth, passionflower, vinca, amaranth]). Some symbols are traditional ("cigüeña" associated with babies), while others are idiosyncratic ("zarzas" associated with the womb). For this aspect of Andréu's style, see Sherno, "Between Water and Fire" 536–37.

61. The *Encyclopaedia Britannica*'s brief entry on Chagall may help us understand the title of Andréu's book. It notes that Marc Chagall is "famous for his dreamlike paintings based on personal experience or spontaneously created images of symbolic meaning that are combined with formal aesthetic elements by virtue of their inner force, rather than by rules of logic. Preceding Surrealism, his early works, such as 'I and my Village' were among the first expressions of psychic reality in Modern art. . . . His style changed little over the years; among his recurring motifs are rooftop violinists and floating brides" (*Macropaedia* 2:707). See also Sherno, "Between Water and Fire" 534, 539.

62. See Ugalde, *Conversaciones* 247—where the author of *The Bonfire of the Vanities* is discussed.

63. There are numerous manifestations of Andréu's sense of imminent doom. She sees herself enveloped by devastation (*Niña* 15). Her "antiguas láminas de mica" (old mica engravings [44]) become become transformed into "la maleza mica . . . que irradia angustia, espejos" (the mica thicket . . . that radiates anguish, mirrors [41]). Another poem cites a challenge to youth from Saint-John Perse: "Corónate, juventud, de una hoja más aguda" (Crown yourself, youth, with a sharper leaf). However, it depicts youths who are bored with sex and with life, who are homosexual or hermaphroditic, who are addicted to drugs, and whose fathers bring them nothing but death: "y de una niña triste con la vena extendida, / de una aguja levantada por nieve increíble" (and about a sad girl with her swollen vein, / about a needle raised for incredible snow [*Niña* 18]). The poetic voice concludes by speaking for today's youth; she declares that they have not found, "no encontramos," Saint-John Perse's "hoja más aguda" (*Niña* 17–19).

64. For pertinent observations on the drug culture and its link with surrealism and the "poète maudit," see Sherno's "Between Water and Fire" 535ff.

65. But see Sherno's recent essay, "Blanca Andréu," in which she argues that Andréu's faith is language is a distinctive feature of her first two books but absent in her third. She argues that Andréu is intent on fusing sign and signified. Her study illuminates many areas of Andréu's (inchoate) vision. Andréu's quest for language may be analogous to that delineated in Gilbert and Gubar's "Ceremonies," where they find in contemporary poets an alphabet of the "womb." They conclude: "Thus, the complex process of reinventing, relearning, or reviewing the alphabet becomes for these writers a crucial act of both self-definition and self-assertion" (43).

66. As noted above (n. 53), she was awarded a prize for "mystical" poetry. Sherno sees her as a mystic. In Andréu's recent interview with Mora, she says she is reading theology.

67. She confirms this in her interview with Ugalde. Elsewhere in the book, she says to herself: "es tu hora es la noche . . . tu obra nocturna rara / es la que muestra sonrisa y griterío" (it's your hour it's the night . . . your rare, nocturnal opus is what displays a smile and clamor [21]). She also exclaims: "Duermo . . . y la poesía huye de mí como una frase acabada" (I sleep . . . and poetry flees from me like a finished phrase [25]).

68. This section lends itself to a Freudian-feminist reading (pen/phallus).

69. For example, from *Arias tristes:* "Yo me moriré... Mi cuerpo estará amarillo" (I will die... My body will be yellow [Jiménez, *Primeros libros* 257]).

70. This poem may well be totally ironical. Its intention may be to imply that the only function civilization/art has is to die off in order to give birth to younger ("verde" [green]) cultures.

71. Andréu's depiction of Ophelia is reminiscent of Holman Hunt's pre-Raphaelite painting of Ophelia's drowning. For acute analysis of the revision of the Ophelia figure, see Ugalde, "Feminization" 176–79.

72. *Elphistone* is dedicated to Juan Benet, her husband, who died in 1993.

73. For Juan Benet's influence on this book, see the interview Mora conducted with Andréu ("Memoria"). For Andréu's own observations on Elphistone, see Ugalde, *Conversaciones* 255–57. Also see Sherno ("Gloria Fuertes' Room") for pertinent comments on Jung's belief that a mature personality transcends gender. Sherno (97–98 n. 1) is citing Pratt.

74. "Final" indicates the stylistic change that occurred between the 1983 *De un niña de provincias* and the 1988 *Elphistone*.

75. One of whose facets is literary: "cinco presas" ("five captives") is a clear allusion to Espronceda's "Canción del pirata" (The pirate's song). Juan Marsé, in his recent novel *El embrujo de Shanghai*, has a comparable figure, Capitán Blay, who entrances the protagonist, Daniel. When Captain Blay dies, and the folder of facts both of them had been collecting is lost, Daniel says: "Pero algo no se perdió. Porque de algún modo, después de tanto callejear juntos por el barrio y de aguantar sus monsergas, y a pesar de . . . [mis] ganas de dejarle plantado y escapar corriendo a la torre, al ámbito de la ensoñación, el viejo pirado había conseguido contagiarme una brizna de aquel virus que le sorbía el entendimineto" (157–58). Both Marsé and Andréu select old seafarers to symbolize their ambivalence toward the past, and to suggest their mesmerization by this masculinized past.

76. For Hestia, see my introduction. On Andréu's silence since 1988 and her disinclination to write more poetry, see Mora's interview with her ("Memoria").

77. This was the city of Agamemnon in the *Iliad*, in ruins today.

78. For instance, the present reader is never sure when she is *deathly* serious, and when she is ironical (and see above n. 70). Such incongruities may recede as her voice matures (or as readers become used to her style).

Conclusion

AN IRREFUTABLE BODY of work by Spain's women poets has been ignored by literary historians: *eppure, si muove!* I have explored only the tip of the iceberg in these essays, but I trust that future students and teachers will reassess the work of the poets studied here, and that they will recuperate the work of others whom for reasons of space and time I could not include.

Let me mention a few pertinent names. For the 1920s, the poetry of Rosa Chacel and Josefina de la Torre must be reassessed. For the period stretching from 1939 to 1975, there are numerous unstudied poets whose work calls for a gynopoetic reading. Some of these are: María Beneyto, María Elvira Lacaci, Susana March, and Elena Martín Vivaldi; as well as Elena Andrés, Pureza Canelo, Ana María Fagundo, and Julia Uceda. For the 1980s and 1990s, there are many poets worthy of study, for example: Juana Castro, Luisa Castro, Almudena Guzmán, Andrea Luca, María del Carmen Pallarés, Rosa Romojaro, Fanny Rubio, and María Sanz. The poets I mention here have already caught the attention of sharp critics; future studies will bring them the wider audience they deserve.

The *great*-great-grandmother of the poets of the 1980s is Rosalía de Castro, in whose poetry young poets and readers alike can encounter a feminist vision, one that adds to her originality as well as to her status as a unique poet of Modern Spanish literature. Their great-grandmothers are the poets of the 1920s, whose gynocentric visions offer an alternative to the dominant and canonized style of the decade and should be heeded in future reassessments of that "Generation" of poets. Their grandmothers are Carmen Conde, Concha Zardoya, Angela Figuera, and Gloria Fuertes. Both Conde and Zardoya have extensive bodies of work, a part of which is gynocentric; their different visions need to be considered in future judgments on what actually constituted that "first post-Civil War generation" of Spanish poets.

In the work of Figuera and Fuertes gynocentric and gynocritical Spanish poetry takes root. Figuera's poetry offers her granddaughters today both positive actions (subvert and demystify) as well as a cautionary tale (loss of confidence). Fuertes confronts the discourse on the marginalization of the woman poet and subverts it; she also initiates the discourse of confidence in self (and other) and thereby provides a salutary example for future poets. Gynopoetics grows wings and flies in the work of the mothers of the poets of the 1980s: Francisca Aguirre, María Victoria Atencia, and Clara Janés, in whose work the female voyage-in of self-discovery is yielding astounding visions. The poets of the 1980s themselves, Amorós, Rossetti, and Andréu, are developing completely different styles and visions, and draw their inspiration from totally different sources; they will no doubt in due course confront the large body of their sister precursors' work.

Throughout these essays I have tried to link my analysis to four broad, gynopoetic concepts: negative gynocentric vision (marginalization, anxiety of authority, anger); positive gynocentric vision (self-revelation, emancipation, descent into the cave of mind/body, intimacy, interpersonal relationships, connectedness); gynocritical vision (revision of cultural and literary myths, foregrounding of the matriarchal Goddesses, nontranscendentalism); and gynocentric style (vulvular imagery, metaphors of entrapment, weaving, blood, the mirror and the sea, the text as palimpsest, the exoskeletal text, the text as the fluid movement of the female body). I would now like to summarize in very general terms the similarities and differences I encountered between 1863 and 1990. Rosalía de Castro was marginalized as a poet by political and social forces operative during the Restoration period, and in her poetry she reflects on the additional marginalization women suffer through marriage and motherhood: they are "doves" with "blood on their wings," as she put it in "Sin nido." Champourcin and Méndez articulate the marginalized vision of older women: abused by marriage, abandoned by their husbands or lovers, reduced to a state of widowhood, barren, scarred for life by the fact of infant mortality. Conde produces a powerful set of meditations on both infant mortality and the effects of sterility. Conde also meditates on the marginalization experienced by a "bluestocking," as did Zardoya apparently—she knew she did not belong to "the other world, the world of men." Moreover, Conde reflects on geriatric marginalization—the loss of physical beauty and the obligation to live as a widow—as did both Champourcin and Méndez. Figuera also refers to loss of beauty, but in her work marginalization is manifested in her loss of self-confidence and in her despair of her talent as a poet.

Anger is expressed by both Figuera and Rosalía: it is expressed by Rosalía to condemn the injustice to women and the ravages to her country, and by Figuera to condemn the oligarchy of Church, State, and Armed Forces.

For Fuertes, marginalization is experienced because she as a woman dares to be herself in a man's world: live alone, be an unconventional poet, irreverently debunk male myths. In Aguirre, marginalization takes on masochistic proportions and may have contributed to her silence as a poet since 1978. Although marginalization was a concern of the young Clara Janés, it has ceased to inform her vision. In fact the four poets just mentioned—but notably Fuertes and Janés—develop strategies to counteract or compensate for the marginalization they experience. In the work of Atencia, Amorós, Rossetti, and Andréu marginalization is not a concern. In the course of their conversations with Ugalde, these and other poets recognize the effects of gender marginalization in contemporary Spanish society, but they dismiss it as a factor in their poetic lives. We can therefore conclude that by late 1970s, the discourse on marginalization was no longer considered a source of inspiration.

Marginalization is the negative pole of the gynocentric vision I have been studying in these poets; its positive pole is self-determination. Rosalía's struggle for autonomy is manifested in the fact that in her struggle with Antonio de Trueba she forged a vision that unmasks him for the sop that he is. Also, she foregrounds numerous strong and diverse female personae; she is involved in a search for her own matrilineal heritage, and she promotes a nontranscendental vision (e.g., her poems illuminate a partial aspect of reality, not its totality). Champourcin and Méndez initiate the inscription of dynamic female personae who express a woman's sensual and sexual desire. They also articulate a life-embracing vision (in their nontranscendental perspectives on reality). Conde sustains the discourse on desire; Zardoya develops aspects of the nontranscendentalism of her predecessors by her meditation on life's small pleasures. Méndez promotes a nontranscendental vision of life in her embrace of living; Champourcin and Fuertes manifest it in their treatment of God and the Virgin. In Aguirre, there is a concern for intimacy and interpersonal engagement, conjoined with a minimalist vision of life. Atencia transforms the room into a space of freedom, and she is in the process of discovering her authentic self through an array of historical, literary, and cultural female personae. Janés—like her precursors of the 1920s and the Franco era—appreciates life's small pleasures, but her full self-realization springs from her exploration of female desire, in which area she has no peers. The erotic discourse Janés has perfected is a poetic gem. Amorós, Rossetti, and Andréu are also involved in an exploration of the female self. Rossetti is in the process of discovering her authentic self via her meditations on eroticism, and via her tentative confrontations with her literary forebears. Amorós and Andréu devote their energies to the articulation of a female poetics. The discourse on mothering requires special comment: in Rosalía and Aguirre it is presented as a negative experience that leads to a woman's entrapment; but in Champourcin, Méndez, Conde, Zardoya, and Atencia, it is a source of inspiration and is a factor in their voyage toward autonomy. With Figuera, this discourse of motherhood and mothering is corrosively demystified. The positive bonds between mothers and daughters are treated intermittently. They appear in Champourcin, are developed by Méndez and Zardoya, and are most fully articulated by Conde. Later Aguirre alludes to them and Atencia foregrounds them.

The gynocritical vision—of revisionary mythmaking, of subversion of phallogocentric goals and phallocratic ideals—is manifested in many ways. A subversion or critique of androcentric dicta occurs in Rosalía, Champourcin, Méndez, Conde, Zardoya, Figuera, Fuertes, Aguirre, Atencia, and Rossetti: to undermine a host of ego-bound, pragmatic, goal-oriented male ideals. Linked to this are the various impulses to demystify the hegemonic power structure (Figuera's subversion of Fascist Spain, Rossetti's treatment of the Church). Even Méndez's appropriation of the masculine hegemony over land, sea, and sky can in retrospect be viewed as an early manifestation of this strategy. Revision of male esthetics and subversion of the male poetic canon occur in Méndez, Figuera, Fuertes, Aguirre, and Andréu, where such poets as Bécquer, Machado, Jiménez, Guillén, Lorca, and Celaya are rebutted. The subversion of folktales—Cinderella, Little Red Riding Hood, Sleeping Beauty—and their reinscription into a feminized discourse is found in Méndez and Fuertes. Revisionary mythmaking is present in Rosalía (Penelope); it is initiated by Conde's *Mujer sin Edén*, and becomes a strategy of the post-Franco era in Aguirre, Atencia, Amorós, and Andréu, who reappropriate such figures as Penelope, Ophelia, and such topoi as the "dark night of the soul." Linked to this is the rejection of the traditional Judeo-Christian God (Figuera, Fuertes) and the embracing of matriarchal goddesses (hinted at in Méndez and Fuertes, developed in Janés).

A fourth aspect to the gynopoetics discussed in these essays is the gynocentric style. Figuera develops the strategy of exoskeletal poetics, which I see as her strategy for survival as a poet and self-realization as an artist. But the exoskeletal style also appears in Rosalía, Atencia, and Janés. Fuertes evolves a "symbiotic" poetics in her self-realization as an artist; she is unique in her articulation of self-reliance, as well as in her textualization of her life and her body. Indeed, her work initiates these discourses in Spanish poetry. In Janés, we noted the nonlinearity or fluidity of style recommended by French feminists; this is also a feature of Andréu's work. I have observed it as a strategy deployed by some recent poets, and Ciplijauskaité found its origins in Rosalía. Corporality, the expression of the body urged by the French feminists, is present in the work of Fuertes and Janés. The palimpsestic text is noted in Rosalía and Méndez, since which time poets have become less reserved; however, Atencia's "Rosa de Jericó" and Janés's lapidary poems are also palimpsests. I have also been able to point out examples of lexicon, image, symbol, and metaphor whose impetus is gynocentric and whose deployment constitutes a broadening of Spanish poetic discourse. The female figure is a standard metaphor (Rosalía, Figuera, Fuertes, Aguirre, Atencia, Andréu); it occurs in reference to body parts and vulvular imagery (Champourcin, Fuertes); it is also manifested in empathy for or identification with the witch in Rosalía ("meigas"), Fuertes, and Janés. Blood is a preferred metaphor (in Méndez, Conde, Andréu); weaving is another (in Zardoya, Aguirre); the sea is a constant preoccupation (Rosalía, Méndez, Conde, Fuertes, Aguirre, Atencia, Amorós, Andréu); the mirror is a recurrent metaphor (Champourcin, Rossetti). Also, there is a tendency toward feminization (Rosalía, de la Torre, Zardoya).

In selecting and reading such an extensive body of work as that produced between 1863 and 1990, I have not been able to pay as much attention as I would have liked to a close analysis of all of these distinctive gynopoetic features. However, I trust that these essays demonstrate that the work of these poets warrants such an undertaking, as well as further analysis and specification of these gynocentric visions. I am confident that others will take up the challenge; I urge them to do so and encourage them in their endeavor.

Works Cited

Abel, Elizabeth. "Introduction." In *The Voyage In: Fictions in Female Development*, ed. Abel, Marianne Hirsch, and Elizabeth Langland. Hanover, N.H.: University Press of New England, 1983. 3-19.

Actas de las cuartas jornadas de investigación interdisciplinaria: Literatura y vida cotidiana. Zaragoza: Seminario de Estudios de la Mujer de la Universidad Autónoma de Madrid, 1987.

Actas del X Congreso de la Asociación de Hispanistas, Barcelona. Ed. A. Vilanova et al. Vol. 3. Barcelona: Promociones y Publicaciones Universitarias, 1992.

Actas do Congreso internacional de estudios sobre Rosalía de Castro e o seu tempo. 3 vols. Santiago de Compostela: Servicio de Publicacións da Universidade, 1986.

Aguirre, Angel Manuel. "La influencia de Rosalía de Castro en Juan Ramón Jiménez." *Cuadernos de Zenobia y Juan Ramón Jiménez* 6 (1991): 40-51.

Aguirre, Francisca. *Itaca*. Madrid: Ediciones Cultura Hispánica, 1972.

———. *La otra música*. Madrid: Ediciones Cultura Hispánica, 1978.

———. *Los trescientos escalones*. San Sebastián: Caja de Ahorros Provincial de Guipúzcoa, 1977.

Albert Robatto, Matilde. *Rosalía de Castro y la condición femenina*. Madrid: Partenón, 1981.

Alberti, Rafael. *La arboleda perdida. Memorias*. Vols. 1 and 2. Barcelona: Seix Barral, 1979.

Aleixandre, Vicente. *Obras completas*. Vol. 1: *Poesía (1924-1967)*. 2d ed. Madrid: Aguilar, 1977.

———. "Unas palabras." In Atencia, *Ex libris*: 7-8.

Alonso, Dámaso. *Poesía de la edad media y poesía de tipo tradicional*. Buenos Aires: Losada, 1942.

Alonso, Dámaso, and José M. Blecua. *Antología de la poesía española. Poesía de tipo tradicional*. Introduction by José M. Blecua. Madrid: Gredos, 1956.

Alonso Montero, Xesús. *Rosalía de Castro*. Madrid: Júcar, 1972.

Alvarez, Carlos. "Prólogo." In Angela Figuera, *Belleza cruel*. Barcelona: Editorial Lumen. Colección El Bardo, 1978.

Amorós, Amparo. *Arboles en la música*. Palma de Mallorca: Calima Ediciones, 1995.

———. *La honda travesía del águila*. Barcelona: Edicions del Mall, 1986.

———. *Ludia*. Madrid: Rialp, 1983.

———. "¡Los novísimos y cierra España! Reflexión crítica sobre algunos fenómenos estéticos que configuran la poesía de los años ochenta." *Insula* 512-13 (1989): 63-67.

———. *La profonde traversée de l'aigle*. Ed. and trans. Laurence Breysse. N.p. (printed in Mayenne, France): Librairie José Corti, 1989.

———. *Quevediana*. Valencia: Consorci d'Editors Valencians (Mestral Libros), 1988.

———. *Visión y destino: Poesía 1982-1992*. Madrid: Ediciones La Palma, 1992.

Andréu, Blanca. *Báculo de Babel*. 2d ed. Madrid: Hiperión, 1986.

———. *Elphistone*. Madrid: Visor, 1988.

———. *De una niña de provincias que se vino a vivir en un Chagall*. 3d rev. ed. Prologue by Francisco Umbral. Madrid: Hiperión, 1983.

———. *El sueño oscuro (Poesía reunida 1980-1989)*. Madrid: Hiperión, 1994.

Anthologie bilingue de la poésie espagnole. Ed. Nadie Ly. Paris: Gallimard, 1995.

Armada, Alfonso. "Luisa Castro." *El País*, 20 Dec. 1987: 36, 39-40.

Ascunce [Arrieta], José Angel. "Prólogo." In Champourcin, *Poesía a través del tiempo*.

Ascunce Arrieta, José Angel. "Ernestina de Champourcin a través de sus palabras." *Insula* 557 (1993): 22-24.

———. "La poesía de Ernestina de Champourcin: entre lo lúdico y lo sagrado." *Insula* 557 (1993): 19-23.

Atencia, María Victoria. *Antología poética*. Ed. José Luis García Martín. Madrid: Castalia, 1990.

———. *Ex libris*. Madrid: Visor, 1984.

———. *La intrusa*. Seville: Renacimiento, 1992.

———. *De la llama en que arde*. Madrid: Visor, 1988.

———. *Marta & María*. Madrid: Caballo griego para la poesía, 1984.

———. *Obras completas*. Diskette, ed. M. V. Atencia. Málaga, 1995.

———. *La pared contigua*. Madrid: Hiperión, 1989.

———. *El puente*. Valencia: Pre-Textos, 1992.

———. *La señal. Poesía 1961-1989*. Málaga: Excmo. Ayuntamiento de Málaga, 1990.

———. *Trances de Nuestra Señora*. Intro. by Rosa Chacel. Madrid: Hiperión, 1986.

Azorín [José Martínez Ruiz]. *Clásicos y modernos*. Madrid: Renacimiento, 1913.

———. *El paisaje de España visto por les españoles*. Madrid: Renacimiento, 1917.

———. *Leyendo a los poetas*. Zaragoza: Librería General, 1929.

Barja, Juan. See Castro, *Follas*.

Barnstone, Akiki, and Willis Barnstone. *A Book of Women Poets from Antiquity to Now*. New York: Schocken Books, 1980.

Barnstone, Willis, ed. *Spanish Poetry: From Its Beginnings through the Nineteenth Century: An Anthology*. New York: Oxford University Press, 1970.

Barthes, Roland. *S/Z*. New York: Hill & Wang, 1974.

Bécquer, Gustavo Adolfo. *Rimas*. Ed. José Carlos de Torres. Madrid: Castalia, 1986.

Bellver, Catherine G. "Exile and the Female Experience in the Poetry of Concha Méndez." *Anales de la literatura española contemporánea* 18.1 (1993): 27–42.

———. "Gloria Fuertes: Poet of Social Consciousness." *Letras femeninas* 4.1 (1978): 29–38.

———. "*El personaje presentido:* A Surrealist Play by Concha Méndez." *Estreno* 16.1 (1990): 23–27.

Blanco García, C. "A problemática da escritora na obra de Rosalía de Castro." In *Actas do Congreso* 1:293–98.

Blecua, José M., ed. *Poesía de la edad de oro*. Vol. 1: *Renacimiento*. 3d ed. Madrid: Castalia, 1986.

Bosch, Rafael. "La poesía de Angela Figuera y el tema de la maternidad." *Insula* 186 (1962): 5–6.

Briesemeister, D. "Rosalía de Castro dentro da poesía feminina do seu tempo: motivos e constantes." In *Actas do Congreso* 1:239–50.

Brooks, Cleanth. *The Well Wrought Urn*. New York: Harcourt, Brace, 1947.

Buenaventura, Ramón, ed. *Las diosas blancas: Antología de la joven poesía española escrita por mujeres*. Madrid: Editorial Hiperión, 1985, 1986.

Cabello, Susan U. "Carmen Conde: On Being a Woman and a Poet." *Letras femeninas* 10.1 (1984): 27–32.

Cano, José Luis. *Poesía española del siglo XX: De Unamuno a Blas de Otero*. Madrid: Guadarrama, 1960.

Cano Ballesta, Juan. *La poesía española entre pureza y revolución (1930–36)*. Madrid: Gredos, 1972.

Cansinos-Assens, Rafael. "Crítica literaria. *Canciones de mar y tierra* (versos) por Concha Méndez Cuesta." *La Libertad* (Madrid). N.d. [1930?].

Cappuccio, Brenda Logan. "Gloria Fuertes frente a la crítica." *Anales de la literatura española contemporánea* 18.1 (1993): 89-112.

Cardwell, R. A. "Rosalía de Castro, ¿precursora de 'los modernos'?" In *Actas do Congreso* 2:439-53.

Carter, Angela. *Wise Children.* New York: Farrar, Straus & Giroux, 1992.

Castro, Luisa. *Baleas e baleas.* Ferrol: Esquio, 1988.

———. *Ballenas—Baleas e baleas.* Madrid: Hiperión, 1992.

———. *Los hábitos del artillero.* Madrid: Visor, 1990.

———. *Odisea definitiva. Libro póstumo.* 2d ed. Madrid: Arnao, 1986.

———. *Los versos del eunuco.* Madrid: Hiperión, 1986.

Castro, Rosalía de. *Cantares gallegos.* Trans. Juan Barja de Quiroga. Madrid: Akal, 1985.

———. *Cantares gallegos.* Ed. Ricardo Carballo Calero. 7th ed. Madrid: Cátedra, 1984.

———. *En las orillas del Sar* Ed. Xesús Alonso Montero. Madrid: Cátedra, 1985.

———. *Follas novas.* Trans. Juan Barja. Madrid: Akal, 1985.

———. *Obras completas.* Vol. 1: *Obras en verso.* Ed. Victoriano García Martí. 1944. 9th rev. ed. Madrid: Aguilar, 1982.

———. *Obras completas.* Vol. 2: *Obras en prosa.* Ed. Arturo del Hoyo. 1944. 7th rev. ed. Madrid: Aguilar, 1982.

———. *Poesía.* Trans. and ed. Mauro Armiño. 3d ed. Madrid: Alianza, 1984.

Chacel, Rosa. "Dos palabras." In Janés, *Kampa* 98-101.

———. *Versos prohibidos.* Madrid: Caballo Griego para la Poesía, 1978.

———. *Poesía (1931-1991).* Ed. Antoni Marí. Barcelona: Tusquets, 1992.

Champourcin, Ernestina de. *Ahora.* Madrid: Librería León Sánchez Cuesta, 1928.

———. *Antología poética.* Ed. Luzmaría Jiménez Faro. Madrid: Torremozas, 1988.

———. *La ardilla y la rosa. (Juan Ramón en mi memoria).* Madrid: Los Libros de Fausto, 1981.

———. *Cartas cerradas.* Mexico: Finisterre, 1968.

———. *Cántico inútil.* Madrid: Aguilar, 1936.

———. *Cárcel de los sentidos.* Mexico: Finisterre, 1964.

———. *En silencio.* Madrid: Espasa Calpe, 1926.

———. *Hai-Kais espirituales.* Mexico: Finisterre, 1967.

———. *El nombre que me diste.* Mexico: Finisterre, 1960.

———. *La pared transparente.* Madrid: Los libros de Fausto, 1984.

———. *Poemas del ser y del estar.* Madrid: Alfaguara, 1974.

———. *Poesía a través del tiempo.* Barcelona: Anthropos, 1991.

———. *Presencia a oscuras.* Madrid: Rialp, 1952.

———. *Primer exilio.* Madrid: Rialp, 1978.

———. *La voz en el viento.* Madrid: Compañía General de Artes Gráficas, 1931.

Chodorow, Nancy. *The Reproduction of Mothering.* Berkeley: University of California Press, 1978.

El Ciervo: Revista Mensual de Pensamiento y Cultura 520-21 (1994): 21.

Ciplijauskaité, Biruté. "La cárcel estrecha y sus modulaciones." In *Actas do Congreso II:* 321-30.

———. "El compromiso alado de María Victoria Atencia." In *La cultura española en el posfranquismo. Diez años de cine, cultura y literatura en España (1975-1985),* ed. Samuel Amell and Salvador García Castañeda. Madrid: Editorial Playor, 1988. 95-102.

———. "Los diferentes lenguajes del amor," *Monographic Review/Revista monográfica* 6 (1990): 113-27.

———. "Escribir entre dos exilios: Las voces femeninas de la generación del 27." In *Homenaje al Profesor Antonio Vilanova,* ed. Adolfo Sotelo Vázquez and María Cristina Carbonell. Barcelona: Promociones y Publicaciones Universitarias, Universidad de Barcelona, 1989. 2:119-26.

———. "Hacia una nueva esencialidad. *Lapidario* de Clara Janés." *El ciervo* (May 1989): 40.

———. *La novela femenina contemporánea (1970-1985). Hacia una tipología de la narración en primera persona.* Barcelona: Anthropos, 1988.

———. "Recent Spanish Poetry and the Essential Word." *Studies in Twentieth Century Literature* 16.1 (Winter, 1992): 149-63.

———. "La serena plenitud de María Victoria Atencia." *Alaluz* 22 (1990): 7-12.

———. "El *yo* invisible de Ernestina de Champourcin y las poéticas de la vanguardia." *Bazar* (Málaga) 1 (1994): 8-13.

———, ed. *Novísimos, postnovísimos, clásicos: Poesía de los años 80 en España.* Madrid: Editorial Orígenes, 1991.

Cixous, Hélène. "From 'Sorties' in La jeune née." In *New French Feminisms,* ed. Marks and Courtivron 90-98.

———. "The Laugh of the Medusa." In *New French Feminisms,* ed. Marks and Courtivron 245-64.

Coco, Emilio. "La verdadera Ana Rossetti: Entrevista con la autora de *Devocionario.*" *Zarza Rosa: Revista de poesía* (Valencia), Oct.-Nov. 1986: 49-73.

Conde, Carmen. *Al aire.* Málaga: Librería Anticuaria El Guadalhorce, 1987.

———. *Cita con la vida.* Madrid: Biblioteca Nueva, 1976.

———. *Corrosión.* Madrid: Biblioteca Nueva, 1975.

———. *Desde nunca.* Barcelona: Libros Río Nuevo, 1982.

———. *Derramen su sangre las sombras.* Madrid: Torremozas, 1983.

————. *A este lado de la eternidad.* Madrid: Biblioteca Nueva, 1970.

————. *Hermosos días en China.* Madrid: Torremozas, 1985.

————. "Introducción." In *Poesía femenina española viviente,* ed. Carmen Conde. Madrid: Ediciones Arquero, 1954.

————. *La noche oscura del cuerpo.* Madrid: Biblioteca Nueva, 1980.

————. *Obra poética: 1929–1966.* 2d ed. Madrid: Biblioteca Nueva, 1979.

————. *Del obligado dolor.* Madrid: Almarabu, 1984.

————. *El tiempo es un río lentísimo de fuego.* Barcelona: Libros Río Nuevo, 1978.

Coronado, Carolina. *Poesías.* Madrid: Castalia, 1991.

Cruz Ruiz, Juan. "Almudena Guzmán." *El País,* 20 Dec. 1987: 37, 42, 44, 46.

Crystal, David. *An Encyclopedic Dictionary of Language and Languages.* Oxford: Blackwell, 1992.

Darío, Rubén. *Poesías completas.* Ed. Ernesto Mejía Sánchez. Mexico: Fondo de Cultura Económica, 1952.

Davies, Catherine. "Rosalía de Castro's Later Poetry and Anti-Regionalism in Spain." *Modern Language Review* 79.3 (1984): 609–19.

————, ed. *Women Writers in Twentieth-Century Spain and Spanish America.* Lewiston, N.Y.: Edward Mellen Press, 1993.

Daydí-Tolson, Santiago. *The Post–Civil War Spanish Social Poets.* Boston: Twayne, 1983.

Debicki, Andrew P. "Una dimensión olvidada de la poesía española de los '20 y '30: la lírica visionaria de Ernestina de Champourcín." *Ojáncano* 1.1 (1988): 48–60.

————. "Life as Art, Art as Life: The Poetry of Amparo Amorós." In *Essays in Honor of Frank Dauster,* ed. Kirsten F. Nigro and Sandra M. Cypess. Newark, Del.: Juan de la Cuesta, 1995.

————. *Poetry of Discovery: The Spanish Generation of 1956–71.* Lexington: University Press of Kentucky, 1982.

————. *Spanish Poetry of the Twentieth Century: Modernity and Beyond.* Lexington: University of Kentucky Press, 1994.

De la Cruz, Sor Juana Inés. *Lírica.* Ed. Raquel Asún. Barcelona: Ediciones B, 1988.

De la Torre, Josefina. *Marzo incompleto.* Las Palmas de Gran Canaria: El Museo Canaria, 1968.

————. *Poemas de la isla.* Las Palmas de Gran Canaria: Compañía Ibero-Americana de Publicaciones, 1930.

————. *Versos y estampas.* Prologue by Pedro Salinas. 8th supplement of *Litoral.* Málaga: Imprenta "Sur," 1927.

De Mott, Benjamin. "The Yarnsmith in Search of Himself." Review of John Fowles, *Mantissa, New York Times Book Review,* 29 Aug. 1982: 3.

Dexter, Miriam Robbins. *Whence the Goddesses: A Source Book.* New York: Pergamon Press, 1990.

Deyermond, Alan. "Spain's First Women Writers." In *Women in Hispanic Literature: Icons and Fallen Idols,* ed. Beth Miller. Berkeley and Los Angeles: University of California Press, 1983. 28–52.

Diego, Gerardo. *Poesía española contemporánea (1901–1934).* 4th ed. Madrid: Taurus, 1968.

Dijkstra, Bram. *Idols of Perversity: Fantasies of Feminine Evil in Fin-de-siècle Culture.* New York: Oxford University Press, 1986.

Drabble, Margaret, ed. *The Oxford Companion to English Literature.* 5th ed. Oxford: Oxford University Press, 1985.

Eliot, T. S. *Selected Essays.* 3d ed. 1932. Rpt. London: Faber & Faber, 1969.

Espejo-Saavedra, Rafael. "Sentimiento amoroso y creación poética en Ernestina de Champourcín." *Revista/Review Interamericana* 12.1 (1982): 133–39.

Evans, Jo. "Carmen Conde's *Mujer sin Edén:* Conventional Notions of 'Sin.'" In Davies, *Women Writers* 71–83.

Feal Deibe, C. "Sobre el feminismo de *Cantares gallegos.*" In *Actas do Congreso* 1:307–16.

Fernández-Rubio, Andrés. "Ana Rossetti: El mundo por montera." *El País,* 8 Mar. 1987: 32–33.

Ferradans, Carmela. "La revelación del significante: erótica textual y retórica barroca en 'Calvin Klein, Underdrawers' de Ana Rossetti." *Monographic Review/Revista Monográfica* 6 (1990): 183–91.

Figuera Aymerich, Angela. *Obras completas.* Introduction and bibliography by Roberta Quance, preliminary note by Julio Figuera Andú. Madrid: Ediciones Hiperión, 1986.

Flores, Angel, and Kate Flores, eds. *The Defiant Muse: Hispanic Feminist Poems from the Middle Ages to the Present: A Bilingual Anthology.* New York: City University of New York, Feminist Press, 1986.

Foster, Francis Smith. "Neither Auction Block nor Pedestal: 'The Life and Religious Experience of Jarena Lee, A Coloured Lady.'" In Stanton, *Female* 126–51.

Fuertes, Gloria. *Antología poética (1950–1969).* Ed. Francisco Ynduráin. Barcelona: Plaza Janés, 1979.

———. *Historia de Gloria (Amor, humor y desamor).* 3d ed. Ed. Pablo González Rodas. Madrid: Cátedra, 1981.

———. *Mujer de verso en pecho.* Madrid: Cátedra, 1995.

———. *Obras incompletas.* 9th ed. Madrid: Cátedra, 1984.

———. *Poeta de guardia.* Intro. by José Battló. Barcelona: Lumen, 1979.

Furman, Nelly. "The Politics of Language: Beyond the Gender Principle." In Greene and Kahn, *Making* 59–79.

Galerstein, Carolyn L., ed. *Women Writers of Spain: An Annotated Bio-Bibliographical Sourcebook*. New York: Greenwood Press, 1986.

García Gómez, Emilio. *Las jarchas romances de la serie árabe en su marco*. 2d ed. Madrid: Alianza, 1990.

García Lorca, Federico. *Obras completas*. Vol 1. Ed. Arturo del Hoyo. 20th ed. Madrid: Aguilar, 1978.

García Martín, José Luis. "Introducción." In Atencia, *Antología:* 7–48.

———. *La segunda generación poética de la posguerra*. Badajoz: Depto. de Publicaciones de la Excma. Diputación, 1986.

Gardiner, Judith Kegan. "Mind Mother: Psychoanalysis and Feminism." In Greene and Kahn, *Making* 113–45.

Gayley, Charles Mills. *The Classic Myths in English Literature and in Art*. Boston, 1911.

Gilbert, Sandra. "Literary Paternity." In Hazard Adams and Leroy Searle, eds., *Critical Theory since 1965*. Tallahassee: Florida State University Press, 1986. 486–96.

Gilbert, Sandra M., and Susan Gubar. *The Madwoman in the Attic: The Woman Writer and the Nineteenth-Century Literary Imagination*. New Haven: Yale University Press, 1979.

———. "Tradition and the Female Talent." In Nancy Miller, *Poetics* 183–207.

Gilbert, Sandra Caruso Mortola, and Susan Dreyfuss David Gubar. "Ceremonies of the Alphabet: Female Grandmatologies and the Female Authorgraph." In Stanton, *Female* 21–48.

Gilligan, Carol. *In A Different Voice: Psychological Theory and Women's Development* Cambridge: Harvard University Press, 1982.

Gimbutas, Marija. *The Language of the Goddess*. New York: Harper & Row, 1989.

González del Valle, Luis. *El Canon. Reflexiones sobre la recepción literaria-teatral (Pérez de Ayala ante Benavente)*. Madrid: Huerga y Fierro, 1993.

González Muela, Joaquín. *La nueva poesía española*. Madrid: Alcalá, 1973.

Greene, Gayle, and Coppélia Kahn. "Feminist Scholarship and the Social Construction of Woman." In Greene and Kahn, *Making* 1–36.

———, eds. *Making a Difference: Feminist Literary Criticism*. London: Methuen, 1985.

Guillén, Jorge. *Aire nuestro I: Cántico*. Barcelona: Barral, 1977.

———. *Aire Nuestro. Final*. Barcelona: Barral Editores, 1981.

Gullón, Ricardo. *Direcciones del modernismo*. Madrid: Gredos, 1963.

Guzmán, Almudena. *La playa del olvido*. Asturias: Altair, 1984.

———. *Poemas de lida sal*. Madrid: Libros Dante, 1981.

———. *Usted*. Madrid: Hiperión, 1986.

Ilie, Paul. "Autophagous Spain and the European Other." *Hispania* 67.1 (1984): 28–35.

Irigaray, Luce. "This Sex Which Is Not One." In *New French Feminisms*, ed. Marks and Courtivron 99–106.

Jaffe, Catherine. "Gender, Intersubjectivity, and the Author/Reader Exchange in the Poetry of María Victoria Atencia." *Letras Peninsulares* 5.2 (1992): 291–302.

Janés, Clara. *Antología personal (1959–1979)*. Madrid: Rialp, 1979.

———. *En busca de Cordelia y Poemas rumanos*. Salamanca: Alamo, 1975.

———. *Creciente fértil*. Madrid: Hiperión, 1989.

———. *Eros*. Madrid: Hiperión, 1981.

———. *Las estrellas vencidas*. Madrid: Agora, 1964.

———. *Kampa*. Madrid: Hiperión, 1986.

———. *Lapidario*. Madrid: Hiperión, 1988.

———. *Libro de alienaciones*. Madrid: Ayuso, 1980.

———. *Límite humano*. Madrid: Oriens, 1973.

———. "Prólogo." In Atencia, *La señal*.

———. *Ver el fuego*. Zaragoza: Olifante-Ibercaja, 1993.

———. *Vivir*. Madrid: Hiperión, 1983.

———, ed. *Las primeras poetisas en lengua castellana*. Madrid: Editorial Ayuso, 1986.

Jardine, Alice A. *Gynesis: Configurations of Woman and Modernity*. Ithaca: Cornell University Press, 1985.

———. "Opaque Texts and Transparent Contexts: The Political Difference of Julia Kristeva." In Nancy Miller, *Poetics* 96–116.

Jiménez, José Olivio. "De la ausencia a la presencia: Una aventura del pensamiento y la imaginación." *Los cuadernos de la actualidad*. Año 8, 45–46 (Nov.–Dec. 1987): 182–83.

Jiménez, Juan Ramón. *Españoles de tres mundos*. Ed. Ricardo Gullón. Madrid: Alianza, 1987.

———. *Libros de poesía*. 3d ed. Ed. Agustín Caballero. Madrid: Aguilar, 1967.

———. *El modernismo: Notas de un curso (1953)*. Ed. Ricardo Gullón and Eugenio Fernández Méndez. Mexico: Aguilar, 1963.

———. *Primeros libros de poesía*. 3d ed. Ed. Francisco Garfias. Madrid: Aguilar, 1967.

———. *Tercera antolojía poética*. Madrid: Biblioteca Nueva, 1957.

Jiménez-Fajardo, Salvador, and John C. Wilcox, eds. *After the War: Essays on Recent Spanish Poetry*. Boulder, Colo.: Society of Spanish and Spanish-American Studies, 1988.

Jiménez-Faro, Luzmaría, ed. *Panorama antológico de poetisas españolas (Siglos XV al XX)*. Madrid: Editorial Torremozas, 1987.

The Johns Hopkins Guide to Literary Theory and Criticism. Ed. Michael Groden and Martin Kreiswirth. Baltimore: The Johns Hopkins University Press, 1994.

Jones, Ann Rosalind. "Inscribing Femininity: French Theories of the Feminine." In Greene and Kahn, *Making* 80–112.

Jordan, William B., and Peter Cherry. *Spanish Still Life from Velázquez to Goya*. London: National Gallery Publications, 1995.

Juhasz, Suzanne. *Naked and Fiery Forms: Modern American Poetry by Women: A New Tradition*. New York: Farrar, Straus & Giroux, 1976.

Kaplan, Cora. *Salt and Bitter and Good: Three Centuries of English and American Women Poets*. New York: Paddington Press, 1975.

Kaplan, Sydney Janet. "Varieties of Feminist Criticism." In Greene and Kahn, *Making* 37–58.

Kessler, Carol Farley. "Matriarchy." In *The Oxford Companion to Women's Writing in the United States*, ed. Cathy N. Davidson and Linda Wagner-Martin. New York: Oxford University Press, 1995. 553–54.

Kirkpatrick, Susan. *Las Románticas: Women Writers and Subjectivity in Spain, 1835–1850*. Berkeley and Los Angeles: University of California Press, 1989.

Kristeva, Julia. *Desire in Language: A Semiotic Approach to Literature and Art*. Ed. Leon S. Roudiez. New York: Columbia University Press, 1980.

Kulp-Hill, Kathleen. *Manner and Mood in Rosalía de Castro: A Study of Themes and Style*. Madrid: José Porrúa Turanzas, 1968.

La Belle, Jenijoy. *Herself Beheld: The Literature of the Looking Glass*. Ithaca: Cornell University Press, 1988.

Landeira, Joy Buckles. "Ernestina de Champourcín." In Galerstein, *Women Writers* 88–91.

———. "Ernestina de Champourcin." In Levine et al., *Spanish Women* 141–47.

Lechner, Johannes. *El compromiso en la poesía española del siglo XX*. 2 vols. Leiden: Universitaire Pers, 1975.

Levine, Linda, and Ellen Marson. "Introduction: View from a Tightrope: Six Centuries of Spanish Women Writers." In Levine et al., *Spanish Women* xv–xxxiv.

Levine, Linda Gould, Ellen Engelson Marson, and Gloria Feiman Waldman, eds. *Spanish Women Writers: A Bio-Bibliographical Sourcebook*. Westport, Conn.: Greenwood Press, 1993.

Lyotard, Jean-François. *The Postmodern Condition: A Report on Knowledge*. Trans. G. Bennington and B. Massumi. Minneapolis: University of Minnesota Press, 1984.

Machado, Antonio. *Poesías completas*. Ed. Manuel Alvar. Madrid: Austral, 1988.

Makris, Mary. "Mass Media and the 'New' Ekphrasis: Ana Rossetti's 'Chico Wrangler' and 'Calvin Klein, Underdrawers.'" *Journal of Interdisciplinary Literary Studies* 5.2 (1993): 237–49.

Mandlove, Nancy. "Oral Texts: The Play of Orality and Literacy in the Poetry of Gloria Fuertes." *Siglo XX* 5.1–2 (1987–88): 11–16.

———. "*Historia* and *Intra-Historia*: Two Spanish Women Poets in Dialogue with History." *Third Woman* 2.2 (1984): 84–93.

———. "The Letter Poems of Gloria Fuertes." *Letras femeninas* 10.1 (1974–84): 33–38.

———. "Used Poetry: The Trans-parent Language of Gloria Fuertes and Angel González." *Revista Canadiense de Estudios Hispánicos* 7.2 (1983): 297–309.

Mantero, Manuel. "Angela Figuera y la maternidad a la redonda." In *Poesía española contemporánea: Estudio y antología (1939–65)*. ed. Mantero. Barcelona: Plaza & Janés, 1966. 83–86.

March, K. N. "Rosalía de Castro como punto de referencia ideolóxico-literario nas escritoras galegas." In *Actas do Congreso* 1:283–92.

Marks, Elaine, and Isabelle de Courtivron. "Introduction III: Contexts of the New French Feminisms." In *New French Feminisms*, ed. Marks and Courtivron. 28–38.

———, eds. *New French Feminisms: An Anthology*. Amherst: University of Massachusetts Press, 1980.

Marsé, Juan. *El embrujo de Shanghai*. 2d ed. Barcelona: Plaza & Janés, 1993.

Marson, Ellen Engelson. "Gloria Fuertes." In Levine et al., *Spanish Women* 194–210.

Martín Gaite, Carmen. *La reina de las nieves*. Barcelona: Anagrama, 1994.

Martín Vivaldi, Elena. *Tiempo a la orilla (1942–1984)*. Granada: Excmo. Ayuntamiento, 1986.

Mayoral, Marina. *La poesía de Rosalía de Castro*. Madrid: Gredos, 1974.

Méndez, Concha. *Antología poética*. Mexico D.F.: Joaquín Mortiz, 1976.

———. *Canciones de mar y tierra*. Prologue by Consuelo Berges. Buenos Aires: Talleres Gráficos Argentinos, 1930.

———. *Entre el soñar y el vivir*. Mexico: Universidad Nacional Autónoma, 1981.

———. *Inquietudes*. Madrid: Juan Pueyo, 1926.

———. *Lluvias enlazadas*. La Verónica: La Habana, 1939.

———. *Memorias habladas, memorias armadas*. Madrid: Mondadori, 1990

———. *Poemas: 1926–1986*. Introduced and selected by James Valender. Madrid: Hiperión, 1995.

———. *Poemas. Sombras y sueños*. Mexico: Rueca, 1944.

———. *Surtidor*. Madrid, 1928.

———. *Vida a Vida y Vida o Río*. Intro. Emilio Miró. Madrid: Caballo Griego para la Poesía, 1979.

———. *Villancicos*. 2d enlarged ed. 1967.

Menéndez Pidal, Ramón. "Cantos románicos andalusíes." *Boletín de la Real Academia Española* 31 (May–Aug. 1951): 187–270.

————. *Flor nueva de romances viejos.* 16th ed. Buenos Aires: Espasa Calpe, 1967.

Metzler, Linda. "Images of the Body in the Poetry of María Victoria Atencia." *Anales de la literatura española contemporánea* 18.1–2 (1993): 173–81.

Miller, M. LaFollette. "Rosalía de Castro: Su autoconcepto como poeta y como mujer." In *Actas do Congreso* 1:65–72.

Miller, Nancy K., ed. *The Poetics of Gender.* New York: Columbia University Press, 1986.

————. *Subject to Change: Reading Feminist Writing.* New York: Columbia University Press, 1988.

Minogue, Sally. *Problems for Feminist Criticism.* London: Routledge, 1990.

Miró, Emilio. "Poetisas del '27." *Insula* 557 (1993): 3–5.

————. "Preliminar." In Méndez, *Vida a vida* 11–34.

Moi, Toril. *Sexual/Textual Politics: Feminist Literary Theory.* 1985. Rpt. Routledge: New York, 1988.

Mora, Rosa. "La memoria crece con el tiempo." Interview with Blanca Andréu. *El País,* 1 Sept. 1994: 14.

Morales Zaragoza, María Luisa. "La poética de dos polaridades de lo femenino." In Atencia, *Marta & María* 9–14.

Murguía, Manuel de. *Los precursores.* Coruña: Biblioteca Gallega, 1885.

Newton, Candelas. "El discurso heroico de Carmen Conde." *Monographic Review/Revista monográfica* 6 (1990): 61–70.

————. "La reflexión sobre el signo en la poesía de Blanca Andréu." *Letras Peninsulares* 2.2 (1989): 193–209.

Noia Campos, M. C. "Elementos literarios feminos na poesía de Rosalía de Castro." In *Actas do Congreso* 1:265–82.

Onís, Federico de. *Antología de la poesía española e hispanoamericana (1882–1932).* Facs. ed. New York: Las Americas, 1961.

Ortner, Sherry . "Is Female to Male as Nature Is to Culture?" In *Woman, Culture and Society,* ed. Michelle Zimbalist Rosaldo and Louise Lamphere. Stanford: Stanford University Press, 1974. 57–87.

Ostriker, Alicia Suskin. *Stealing the Language: The Emergence of Women's Poetry in America.* Boston: Beacon Press, 1986.

Palau de Nemes, G. "Visión del modernismo hispanoamericano en un poema de Rosalía de Castro." In *Actas do Congreso* 2:337–46.

Pasero, Anne M. "Clara Janés." In Levine et al., *Spanish Women* 230–41.

Pérez, Janet. *Contemporary Women Writers of Spain.* Boston: Twayne, 1988.

Pérez Priego, Miguel Angel, ed. *Poesía femenina en los Cancioneros.* Madrid: Castalia, 1989.

Persin, Margaret H. "Gloria Fuertes and (Her) Feminist Reader." *Revista/Review Interamericana* 12.1 (1982): 125–32.

————. "El humor como semiosis en la poesía de Gloria Fuertes." In *Poesía como proceso: Poesía española de los años 50 y 60.* Madrid: Ediciones José Porrúa Turanzas, 1986.

———. "La imagen del / en el texto: el ékfrasis, lo postmoderno y la poesía española del siglo XX." In Ciplijauskaité, *Novísimos* 43-63.

———. "Yet Another Loose Can(n)on: The Place and Space of Women's Poetry in Twentieth-Century Spain." *Siglo XX/Twentieth Century* 12.1-2 (1994): 195-206.

Pertusa, Inmaculada. "El culturalismo particular de María Victoria Atencia." *Ariel* (1993): 17-32.

Poullain, Claude Henri. *Rosalía Castro de Murguía y su obra literaria (1836-1885).* Madrid: Editora Nacional, 1974.

Quance, Roberta. "Angela Figuera: Poesía social y segundo sexo." *Cuadernos Interdisciplinarios de Estudios Literarios* 4.1 (1993): 199-206.

———. "Entre líneas: posturas críticas ante la poesía escrita por mujeres." *La Balsa de la Maedusa* 4 (1989): 73-96.

———. "La mujer, el barro y la biblia." *Zurgai: Revista de Poesía* (Bilbao) Dec. 1987: 10-16.

Rabuzzi, Kathryn Allen. *The Sacred and the Feminine: Toward a Theology of Housework.* New York: Seabury Press, 1982.

Ramos, Alicia. *Literatura y confesión.* Madrid: Editorial Arame, 1982.

Register, Cheri. "American Feminist Literary Criticism: A Bibliographical Introduction." In *Feminist Literary Criticism: Explorations in Theory,* ed. Josephine Donovan. 2d ed. Lexington: University Press of Kentucky, 1989. 1-28.

———. "Review Essay: Literary Criticism." *Signs* 6.2 (1980): 268-82.

Richards, Judith C. "The Word without End: Mythic and Linguistic Revision in Carmen Conde Abellán's *Mujer sin Edén.*" *Monographic Review/Revista monográfica* 6 (1990): 71-80.

Rodríguez Pequeño, Mercedes. *La poesia de Concha Zardoya. Estudio temático y estilístico.* Valladolid: Universidad de Valladolid, 1987.

Rogers, Timothy J. "The Comic Spirit in the Poetry of Gloria Fuertes." *Perspectives in Contemporary Literature* 7 (1981): 88-97.

Rosas, Yolanda, and Hilda Cramsie. "La apropriación del lenguaje y la desmitificación de los códigos sexuales de la cultura en la poesía de Ana Rossetti." *Explicación de textos literarios* 20.1 (1991-92): 1-12.

Rossetti, Ana. *Los devaneos de Erato.* Valencia: Prometeo, 1980.

———. *Devocionario.* Intro. José Infante. Madrid: Visor, 1986.

———. *Dióscuros.* Málaga: Jarazmín, 1982.

———. *Indicios vehementes: Poesía: 1979-1984.* Prologue by Jesús Fernández Palacios. Madrid: Hiperión, 1985.

———. *Plumas de España.* Barcelona: Seix Barral, 1988.

———. *Punto umbrío.* Madrid: Hiperión, 1995.

———. *Yesterday*. Prologue by Pablo García Baena. Madrid: Torremo-zas, 1988.

Rubiera Mata, María Jesús, ed. *Poesía femenina hispano-árabe*. Madrid: Cas-talia, 1989.

Rubio, Fanny. "A la busca del cuerpo (femenino) perdido (esbozo)." In *Actas de las cuartas jornadas* 67–87.

Ruether, Rosemary Radford. *Liberation Theology: Human Hope Confronts Christian History and American Power*. New York: Paulist Press, 1972.

Sánchez-Barbudo, Antonio. *La segunda época de Juan Ramón Jiménez (1916–1953)*. Vol. 1. Madrid: Gredos, 1962.

Sánchez Mora, E. "Rosalía de Castro ¿bachillera o ángel del hogar?" In *Actas do Congreso* 1:251–58.

Sánchez Romeralo, Antonio. "Rosalía de Castro en Juan Ramón Jiménez." In *Actas do Congreso* 3:213–22.

Sappho: A Garland: The Poems and Fragments of Sappho. Trans. Jim Powell. New York: Farrar, Straus & Giroux, 1993.

Saval, Lorenzo, and J. García Gallego, eds. *Litoral: Femenino. Literatura es-crita por mujeres en la España Contemporánea*. Málaga: Editorial Lito-ral (Revista de la Poesía y el Pensamiento), 1986.

Saval Prados, Carmen. *Sonámbula obediencia*. Supplement of *Litoral*. Málaga: Imprenta Sur, 1982.

Schulman, Ivan. "Reflexiones en torno a la definición del modernismo." In *Estudios críticos sobre el modernismo*, ed. Homero Castillo. Madrid: Gredos, 1968. 325–57.

Servodidio, Mirella. "Ana Rossetti's Double-Voiced Discourse of Desire." *Revista hispánica moderna* 45 (1992): 318–27.

Sherno, Sylvia R. "Between Water and Fire: Blanca Andréu's Dream Land-scapes." *Revista hispánica moderna* 47.2 (1994): 533–42.

———. "Blanca Andréu: Recovering the Lost Language." *Hispania* 77.3 (1994): 384–93.

———. "Carnival: Death and Renewal in the Poetry of Gloria Fuertes." *Modern Language Notes (Hispanic)* 104.2 (1989): 370–92.

———. "Gloria Fuertes and the Poetics of Solitude." *Anales de la literatura española contemporánea* 12 (1987): 311–26.

———. "Gloria Fuertes' Room of Her Own." *Letras femeninas* 16.1–2 (1990): 85–99.

———. "The Poetry of Gloria Fuertes: Textuality and Sexuality," *Siglo XX/20th Century* 7.1–2 (1989–90): 19–23.

———. "Weaving the World: The Poetry of Gloria Fuertes." *Hispania* 72.2 (1989): 247–55.

Showalter, Elaine. "Feminism and Literature." In *Literary Theory Today*, ed. Peter Collier and Helga Geyer-Ryan. Ithaca: Cornell University Press, 1990. 179–202.

———— *A Literature of Their Own: British Women Novelists from Bronte to Lessing.* Princeton, N.J.: Princeton University Press, 1977.

————. "Piecing and Writing." In Nancy Miller, *Poetics:* 222–47.

————. "Toward a Feminist Poetics." In Showalter, *New Feminst Criticism* 125–43.

————, ed. *The New Feminist Criticism: Essays on Women, Literature, and Theory.* New York: Random House, 1985.

Smith-Rosenberg, Carroll. "The Female World of Love and Ritual." *Signs* 1 (1975): 1–30.

Snow, Joseph. "The Spanish Love Poet: Florencia Pinar." In *Medieval Women Writers,* ed. Katherina M. Wilson. Athens: University of Georgia Press, 1984. 320–32.

Spivak, Gayatri Chakravorty. "In a Word: Interview with Ellen Rooney." *differences* 1.2 (1989): 124–56.

Stanton, Domna C. "Autogynography: Is the Subject Different?" In Stanton, *Female* 3–20.

————. "Difference on Trial: A Critique of the Maternal Metaphor in Cixous, Irigaray, and Kristeva." In Nancy Miller, *Poetics* 157–82.

————, ed. *The Female Autograph: Theory and Practice of Autobiography from the Tenth to the Twentieth Century.* Chicago: University of Chicago Press, 1987.

Stern, Samuel Milos. *Hispano-Arabic Strophic Poetry.* Ed. L. P. Harvey. Oxford: Clarendon Press, 1974.

Stevens, Shelley. "La apología feminista de Rosalía de Castro." In *Actas do Congreso* 1:259–64.

————. *Rosalía de Castro and the Galician Revival.* London: Tamesis Books, 1986.

Stimpson, Catharine. "Ad/d Feminam: Women, Literature, and Society." In *Selected Papers from the English Institute: Literature and Society,* ed. Edward Said. Baltimore: The Johns Hopkins University Press, 1978.

Tornsey, Cheryl B. "The Critical Quilt: Alternative Authority in Feminist Criticism." In *Contemporary Literary Theory,* ed. G. Douglas Atkins and Laura Morrow. Amherst: University of Massachusetts Press, 1989. 180–99.

Torres Nebrera, Gregorio, ed. *Carolina Coronado: Treinta y nueve poemas y una prosa (Antología poética: 1840–1904).* Extremadura: Editora Regional, 1986.

Torrente Ballester, Gonzalo. *Panorama de la literatura española contemporánea.* Vol. 1. 2d ed. Madrid: Ediciones Guadarrama, 1961.

Trueba, Antonio de. *El libro de los cantares.* Leipzig: F. A. Brockhaus, 1868.

Ugalde, Sharon Keefe. *Conversaciones y poemas. La nueva poesía femenina española en castellano.* Madrid: Siglo XXI, 1991.

———. "Erotismo y revisionismo en la poesía de Ana Rossetti." *Siglo XX/20th Century*, 7.1–2 (1989–90): 24–29.

———. "The Feminization of Female Figures in Spanish Women's Poetry of the 1980s." *Studies in Twentieth Century Literature* 16.1 (Winter, 1992): 165–84.

———. "Huellas de mujer en la poesía de Clara Janés." *Anales de la literatura española contemporánea* 18.1–2 (1993): 193–209.

———. "María Victoria Atencia." In Levine et al., *Spanish Women* 54–65.

———. "La poesía subversiva de Concha García." Unpublished paper.

———. "La subjetividad desde 'lo otro' en la poesía de María Sanz, María Victoria Atencia, y Clara Janés." In *Actas del X Congreso* 307–15.

———. "Subversión y revisionsimo en la poesía de Ana Rossetti, Concha García, Juana Castro y Andrea Luca." In Ciplijauskaité, *Novísimos* 117–39.

———. "Time and Ekphrasis in the Poetry of María Victoria Atencia." *Confluencia* 3.1 (1987): 7–12.

Ulacia Altolaguirre, Paloma. *Concha Méndez: Memorias habladas, memorias armadas*. Madrid: Mondadori, 1990.

Umpierre, Luz María. "Inversión de valores y efectos en el lector en 'Oración' de Gloria Fuertes." *Plaza* 5–6 (1981–82): 132–44.

Unamuno y Jugo, Miguel. *Andanzas y visiones españolas*. In *Obras completas*, ed. Manuel García Blanco. Vol. 1. Madrid: Escelier, 1966.

Valender, James. "Introducción." In Méndez, *Poemas* 9–41.

Valdivieso, Teresa L. "Significación del discurso poético: Un poema de Gloria Fuertes." *Letras femeninas* 2.2 (1976): 15–22.

Valis, Noel. "Introducción." In Coronado, *Poesías* 7–43.

Varela, José Luis. *Poesía y restauración cultural de Galicia en el siglo XIX*. Madrid: Gredos, 1958.

Villar, Arturo del. "La vida con las palabras de Ernestina de Champourcin." *Alaluz* 18.2 (1986): 5–9.

Walker, Barbara G. *The Woman's Encyclopedia of Myths and Secrets* San Francisco: Harper & Row, 1983.

Walker, Cheryl. *The Nightingale's Burden: Women Poets and American Culture before 1900*. Bloomington: Indiana University Press, 1982.

Welter, Barbara. "The Cult of True Womanhood: 1820–1860." *American Quarterly* 28 (Summer 1966): 152.

Wilcox, John C. "Impresiones juanramonianas en los primeros libros de poesía de Angela Figuera Aymerich." In *Estudios juanramonianos ofrecidos a Francisco H.-Pinzón en su LXXV cumpleaños*, ed. Arturo del Villar. Madrid: Los Libros de Fausto, 1993. 107–15.

———. "Observaciones sobre el *Devocionario* de Ana Rossetti." In *La Chispa '89: Selected Proceedings*, ed. Gilbert Paolini. New Orleans: Tulane University Press, 1989. 335–44.

———. *Self and Image in Juan Ramón Jiménez (Modern and Post-Modern Readings)*. Urbana: University of Illinois Press, 1987.

———. "Self-Referentiality in Antonio Machado's *Poema de un día: Meditaciones rurales* (CXXVIII)." In *A Ricardo Gullón: Sus discípulos*, ed. Adelaida López de Martínez. Erie, Pa.: ALDEEU, Spanish Professionals in America, 1995. 243–60.

———. "Spanish Poetry from the Mid 1930s to the Mid 1980s: An Introduction." In Jiménez-Fajardo and Wilcox, *After the War* 15–28.

Yeats, William Butler. *The Collected Poems of W. B. Yeats*. New York: Macmillan, 1956.

Ynduráin, Francisco. "Prólogo." In Fuertes, *Antología* 9–45.

Yorke, Liz. *Impertinent Voices: Subversive Strategies in Contemporary Women's Poetry*. London: Routledge, 1991.

Zambrano, María. "El reposo de la luz." In Atencia, *Trances* 9–12.

Zardoya, Concha. *Altamor*. Madrid: Ayuso, 1986.

———. *La casa deshabitada*. Madrid: Insula, 1959.

———. *El corazón y la sombra*. Madrid: Insula, 1977.

———. *Corral de vivos y muertos (Poemas para españoles)*. Buenos Aires: Losada, 1965.

———. *Debajo de la luz*. Barcelona: Instituto de Estudios Hispánicos, 1959.

———. *El desterrado ensueño*. New York: Hispanic Institute, 1955.

———. *Un dios que nos domina*. Madrid: Endymión, 1992.

———. *Diotima y sus edades (Autobiografía en cuatro tiempos)*. Barcelona: Ambito literario, 1981.

———. *Dominio del llanto*. Madrid: Adonais, 1947.

———. *El don de la simiente*. Madrid: Torremozas, 1993)

———. *Donde el tiempo resbala (Romancero de Bélgica)*. Montevideo: Cuadernos Julio Herrera y Reissig, 1966.

———. *Elegías. Lírica hispana*. Caracas, 1961.

———. *Los engaños de Tremont*. Madrid: Agora/Alfaguara, 1971.

———. *La estación del silencio: Elegías*. Madrid: Endymión, 1989.

———. *Forma de esperanza*. Granada: Genil-Excma. Diputación Provincial, 1985.

———. *Gradiva y un extraño héroe*. Madrid: Torremozas, 1987.

———. *La hermosura sencilla*. New York: Hispanic Institute, 1953.

———. *Las hiedras del tiempo*. Madrid: Biblioteca Nueva, 1972.

———. *Hondo sur*. Madrid: El Bardo, 1968.

———. *Manhattan y otras latitudes*. El Ferrol: Colección Esquío de Poesía/ Sociedad de Cultura Valle-Inclán, 1983.

———. *Marginalia*. Madrid: Endymion, 1994.

———. *Mirar al cielo es tu condena: Homenaje a Miguel Angel*. Madrid: Insula, 1957.

———. *No llega a ser ceniza lo que arde*. Madrid: Corcel, 1985.

———. *Pájaros del Nuevo Mundo.* Madrid: Adonais, 1946.

———. *Patrimonio de ciegos.* Madrid: Devenir, 1992.

———. *Los perplejos hallazgos.* Madrid: Orígenes, 1986.

———. *Poemas a Joan Miró.* Madrid: Los Libros de Fausto, 1984.

———. *Retorno a Magerit.* Madrid: Comunidad de Madrid, 1983.

———. *Los ríos caudales (Apología del 27).* Madrid: Corcel, 1982.

———. *Ritos, cifras y evasiones.* Madrid: Ayuso, 1985.

———. *Los signos.* Alicante: Ifach, 1954.

Index

Figuera, Angela (*continued*)
  "Me explico ante Dios," 195n.13; "Miedo,"
  186; "Morena," 183, 187, 188; "Mujer,"
  186-87, 188; *Mujer de barro*, 138, 173,
  178, 192; "Mujeres del mercado," 182-
  84; "Mundo concluso," 176-77; "Poeta,"
  192; "Poeta puro," 192; "Posguerra," 179-
  80, 195n.11; "Puentes," 185; "Rebelión,"
  189; "Regreso," 195n.11; "Río," 175; "Sangre, La," 180; *Soria pura*, 173, 174, 192;
  "Tierra," 187; *Toco la tierra: letanías*, 174,
  193-94; "Tus manos frías," 176; *Vencida
  por el ángel*, 173, 185, 195n.12; "Vencida por
  el ángel," 185; *Víspera de la vida*, 173
Finch, Anne, 25, 29
Finisterre, Alejandro, 130n.47
"First generation" of post-Civil War Span-
  ish poets. *See* Generations
Flapper, 90, 114
"Flor del agua, La" (C. Coronado), 38n.31
Flores, Angel, and Kate Flores, 18, 22,
  35-36n.22, 37n.25, 38nn.28 and 33
Flowers. *See* Imagery
"Fonte frida" (*romance*), 36n.22
Forrestal, James, 318n.42
Foster, Francis Smith, 32n.5
Franco, Francisco, xv, xvii, 2, 6, 137, 164, 177,
  185, 194n.2, 233, 267, 273, 290, 328
Frauenlieder, 15
Free-indirect style. *See* Style
Freud, Sigmund, 7, 11, 13, 33-34n.14, 81n.57,
  169n.17
"Fue una clara tarde triste y soñolienta" (A.
  Machado), 318n.49
Fuertes, Gloria, xv, xvii, 19, 30, 40n.49,
  106, 137, 138, 159, 259, 325-29; imagery,
  220-23; inscription of self, 223-26; marginalization, 198-205; nontranscendentalism, 212-13; religious impulse, 218-20;
  self-sufficiency, 205-8; subversion of
  androcentrism, 213-17; subversion of male
  poets, 208-13
—Works: "A buenas horas," 228n.26; "A
  la muerte," 219-20; "A no ser en tus
  manos," 221; "Adobado con ternura,"
  230n.43; "Ahora habla Dios," 229n.30;
  "Algo dentro de mí me quiere mucho,"
  207-8; "Algo es algo," 204-5; "Anginas
  justicieras," 218; *Antología y poemas del
  suburbio*, 227n.7; "Autobio" ("Comprendo
  que los poetas"), 197-98; "Autobio"
  ("Nunca vi claro lo del clero"), 217, 223;

"Autobiografía," 223; "Aviso" ("Está seco,
  sus ramas sin hojas"), 214-15; "Aviso"
  ("Los dinosaurios"), 228n.25; "Bomba,"
  228n.26; "Cabra sola," 201; "Cada uno
  copula como pueda," 222; "Camello, El,"
  229n.30; "Canción de las locas," 206;
  "Carta a mí misma," 206; "Cena fría,"
  226; "Clase, La," 229n.32; "Con pluma no
  con plomo," 228n.23; "Contra la atómica,"
  228n.26; "Cosas, Las," 211-12; "Cuando
  me sonrieron los chavales de las chabo-
  las," 223-24; "Cuarto oscuro," 227n.10;
  "Cuestiones fúnebres," 228n.22; "Curada
  de espanto," 219; "Dictador particular,"
  218; "Difícil, por ahora, ser demente,"
  225-26; "Domesticar al destino," 210-11;
  "En Estados Unidos," 198; "En retaguardia," 225; "Esquirla, La," 209; "Está
  claro," 216; "Estaba un pajarito," 200;
  "Estás prisionero," 200; "Gracias, amor,"
  208; "Hace tiempo que la felicidad," 206;
  "Hago versos, señores," 225; "Hay frases,"
  228n.26; "Hay tantas . . . ," 229n.28;
  "Hervida realidad, La," 210-11; *Historia
  de Gloria*, 198, 227n.2, 229n.40; *Isla ignorada*, 198, 227n.3; "Jueves Santo," 229n.30;
  "Linda tapada, La," 202; "Lo confieso,"
  205; "Maja de Solana, La," 221; "Mal
  humor," 213; "Maletilla," 201; "Me pedían
  unos versos para el concurso de floricultura," 227n.13; "Me sigue persiguiendo la
  poesía," 230n.43; "Miradme aquí," 205;
  "Mística terrenal," 219; "Monstruo, El,"
  215; *Mujer de verso en pecho*, 198, 227n.2,
  229n.33; "Multinacionales—El Presidente," 228n.27; "Nací en una buhardilla,"
  199; "Nací para poeta o para muerto,"
  201; "No dejan escribir," 198-99; "No
  es lo mismo," 226; "No reíros de nada,"
  218; "No sé de dónde soy," 224; "No
  sé porque me quejo," 201; "Nota a mí
  misma," 224; "Nota biográfica," 223;
  Obras incompletas, 198, 227n.2; "Ojalá
  sea mentira," 228n.19; "Oración," 216;
  "Oración para ir tirando," 216; "Otra
  versión," 217; "Paliduchas," 221; "Poema
  para niños adúlteros," 229n.28; "Poema
  para un desconocido," 222; "Poética,"
  212; "Por fin," 209-10; "Problemas, Los,"
  230n.43; "Prologuillo," 203; "¿Qué sería
  de Dios sin nosotros?" 228n.22; "Quién
  coserá mis senos," 230n.44; "Rapto," 210;

JOHN C. WILCOX is professor of Spanish at the University of Illinois at Urbana-Champaign. He began to write this book when his students complained that there was nothing, or very little, written in either Spanish or English that would enable them to confront Spanish women's poetry for themselves. He is a specialist in twentieth-century Spanish Peninsular poetry, a field in which he is the author of numerous scholarly articles and reviews. His passion for Spanish poetry began with a dissertation, directed by Ricardo Gullón, entitled "W. B. Yeats and Juan Ramón Jiménez" (Austin, 1976). In 1987 he published *Self and Image in Juan Ramón Jiménez: Modern and Post-Modern Readings* (Urbana: University of Illinois Press). With Salvador J. Fajardo he edited *At Home and Beyond: New Essays on Spanish Poets of the Twenties* (1983), *After the War: Essays on Recent Spanish Poetry* (1988), as well as two issues on poetry for the journal *Anales de la literatura española contemporánea* (1991 and 1993).